**WITHDRAWN
NDSU**

Resources
for
American Literary Study

EDITORS
Jackson R. Bryer, *University of Maryland*
Richard Kopley, *The Pennsylvania State University, DuBois*

EDITORS EMERITI
Martha E. Cook, *Longwood College*
Maurice Duke, *Virginia Commonwealth University*
M. Thomas Inge, *Randolph-Macon College*
George C. Longest, *Virginia Commonwealth University*
Carla Mulford, *The Pennsylvania State University, University Park*
Robert Secor, *The Pennsylvania State University, University Park*

ASSOCIATE EDITOR
Gib Prettyman, *The Pennsylvania State University, Fayette–The Eberly Campus*

REVIEW EDITOR
MaryEllen Higgins, *The Pennsylvania State University, Greater Allegheny*

EDITORIAL ADVISORY BOARD
Ralph Bauer, *University of Maryland*
Bernard W. Bell, *The Pennsylvania State University, University Park*
Alfred Bendixen, *Texas A & M University*
Lawrence I. Buell, *Harvard University*
Phyllis Cole, *The Pennsylvania State University, Brandywine*
Jerome Klinkowitz, *University of Northern Iowa*
Joel Myerson, *University of South Carolina*
James Nagel, *University of Georgia*
Jeanne Campbell Reesman, *University of Texas at San Antonio*
David S. Reynolds, *Baruch College, CUNY*
Gary F. Scharnhorst, *University of New Mexico*
Robert Secor, *The Pennsylvania State University, University Park*
David S. Shields, *The Citadel*
G. Thomas Tanselle, *New York, NY*
Linda Wagner-Martin, *University of North Carolina, Chapel Hill*

EDITORIAL ASSISTANT
Donna Brantlinger Black

RESOURCES
for
AMERICAN LITERARY STUDY

Volume 34

Editors
Jackson R. Bryer
and
Richard Kopley

Associate Editor
Gib Prettyman

Review Editor
MaryEllen Higgins

AMS Press, Inc.
New York

Resources
for
American Literary Study

Volume 34

Copyright © 2011 by AMS Press, Inc.
All rights reserved

ISSN: 0048-7384
Set ISBN-13: 978-0-404-64625-7
Volume 34 - ISBN-10: 0-404-64634-4
Volume 34 - ISBN-13: 978-0-404-64634-9

All AMS books are printed on acid-free paper that meets the guidelines for performance and durability of the Committee on Production Guidelines for Book Longevity of the Council on Library Resources.

AMS Press, Inc.
Brooklyn Navy Yard, 63 Flushing Ave – Unit #221
Brooklyn, NY 11205-1073, USA
www.amspressinc.com

Manufactured in the United States of America

RESOURCES FOR AMERICAN LITERARY STUDY

CONTENTS
VOLUME 34   2009

Editors' Note   ix

Prospects 18
Prospects for the Study of Stephen Crane   1
   PATRICK K. DOOLEY

Articles
Aprons and Pearls: Images of Phillis Wheatley   33
   JENNIFER HARRIS

Poe, Scott's Fiction, and the Holt Source Collection: The Example of *Ivanhoe* and "The Fall of the House of Usher"   47
   ALEXANDER HAMMOND

W. D. Howells's Unpublished Letters to J. Harvey Greene   73
   DONNA CAMPBELL

Young Edith Jones: Sources and Texts of Early Poems by Edith Wharton   95
   IRENE C. GOLDMAN-PRICE

New Information on Hemingway's "3 very fine weeks" in Constantinople in 1922   107
   DAVID ROESSEL

"To Weave the Whole Thing Together": Thomas Wolfe's Revisions of *From Death to Morning*   129
   PARK BUCKER

The Magic Tower: An Unpublished One-Act Play by Tennessee Williams   185
   NICHOLAS MOSCHOVAKIS AND DAVID ROESSEL

Review-Essays
Breaking Fresh Ground: New Releases from the Willa Cather Edition   215
   JAMES A. JAAP

Art as "An Everyday Affair": William Carlos Williams's Correspondence with His Brother   223
   NATALIE GERBER

Reconsidering Allen Ginsberg at the End of an Epistolary Era   231
   TONY TRIGILIO

Reviews

Greil Marcus and Werner Sollors, eds., *A New Literary History of America* — 239
HILARY K. JUSTICE

Sheila L. Skemp, *First Lady of Letters: Judith Sargent Murray and the Struggle for Female Independence* — 242
LISA M. LOGAN

Karen Lentz Madison and R. D. Madison, eds., *Ned Myers; or, A Life before the Mast*, by James Fenimore Cooper, with a historical introduction by William S. Dudley and Hugh Egan — 245
JASON BERGER

Anne E. Boyd, ed., *Wielding the Pen: Writings on Authorship by American Women of the Nineteenth Century* — 248
MELISSA J. HOMESTEAD

Glen M. Johnson and Joel Myerson, eds., *Collected Works of Ralph Waldo Emerson, Volume VIII: Letters and Social Aims*, by Ralph Waldo Emerson, with a historical introduction by Ronald A. Bosco — 251
WESLEY T. MOTT

Peter West, *The Arbiters of Reality: Hawthorne, Melville, and the Rise of Mass Information Culture* — 255
SARAH WADSWORTH

Katherine Wolff, *Culture Club: The Curious History of the Boston Athenaeum* — 258
JOEL MYERSON

Nancy Craig Simmons and Ron Thomas, eds., *Journal. Volume 7: 1853–1854*, by Henry D. Thoreau — 260
KRISTEN CASE

Ted Genoways, *Walt Whitman and the Civil War: America's Poet during the Lost Years of 1860–1862* — 263
GREGORY EISELEIN

James E. Caron, *Mark Twain: Unsanctified Newspaper Reporter* — 266
MICHAEL J. KISKIS

Carolyn L. Karcher, ed., *Bricks Without Straw: A Novel*, by Albion Tourgée — 269
PETER SCHMIDT

Pierre A. Walker and Greg W. Zacharias, eds., *The Complete Letters of Henry James, 1872–1876. Vol. 1* — 272
LELAND S. PERSON

Denise D. Knight and Jennifer S. Tuttle, eds., *The Selected Letters of Charlotte Perkins Gilman* 276
  LISA LONG

Susan Goodman and Carl Dawson, *Mary Austin and the American West* 279
  BEVERLY A. HUME

Thomas P. Riggio, ed., *Letters to Women. New Letters, Volume II*, by Theodore Dreiser 282
  CLARE EBY

Scott Donaldson, *Fitzgerald and Hemingway: Works and Days* 285
  JAMES M. HUTCHISSON

David M. Earle, *All Man!: Hemingway, 1950s Men's Magazines, and the Masculine Persona* 288
  THOMAS STRYCHACZ

Arlyn Bruccoli and Matthew J. Bruccoli, eds., *The Four Lost Men: The Previously Unpublished Long Version*, by Thomas Wolfe 290
  SHAWN HOLLIDAY

Christopher Bigsby, *Arthur Miller 1915–1962* 293
  KATHERINE EGERTON

James L. W. West III, ed., *Letters to My Father*, by William Styron 296
  JEAN W. CASH

Carol Sklenicka, *Raymond Carver: A Writer's Life* 299
  ROBERT MILTNER

Index
Index to Volume 34 303

Submission Guidelines 313

Grateful acknowledgment is made for permission to print and/or reprint the following:

Bernard Lemercier's lithograph of Phillis Wheatley, which appeared in the January 1837 issue of *Revue des Colonies*, by permission of and courtesy of the Photographs and Prints Division, Schomburg Center for Research in Black Culture, The New York Public Library, Astor, Lenox and Tilden Foundations.

"Phillis Wheatley, Negro Servant to Mr. John Wheatley, of Boston," the frontispiece to Phillis Wheatley's *Poems on Various Subjects, Religious and Moral* (1773), by permission of and courtesy of the Manuscripts, Archives and Rare Books Division, Schomburg Center for Research in Black Culture, The New York Public Library, Astor, Lenox and Tilden Foundations.

Material from the Palmer C. Holt Poe Collection by permission of Manuscript, Archives, and Special Collections (MASC), Holland and Terrell Libraries, Washington State University, Pullman, WA.

T. Y. Crowell's Aug. 12, 1887, letter to W. D. Howells by permission of and courtesy of John T. Narrin and William Griffing.

W. D. Howells's letters to J. Harvey Greene, dated between 1854 and 1887, by permission of and courtesy of John T. Narrin and William Griffing.

James Redpath's May 1, [1856], letter to J. H. Greene by permission of and courtesy of John T. Narrin and William Griffing.

Edith Jones Wharton's letters to Anna Catherine Bahlmann, from The Anna Catherine Bahlmann Papers Relating to Edith Wharton in the Yale Collection of American Literature, Beinecke Rare Book and Manuscript Library, by permission of the estate of Edith Wharton and the Watkins/Loomis Agency.

Photographs from the scrapbooks of Admiral Thomas Kinkaid courtesy of the U.S. Naval Historical Center, Washington Naval Yard, Washington, DC, and Gerald L. Vincent.

Tennessee Williams's *The Magic Tower*, from the Tennessee Williams Collection at the Harry Ransom Humanities Research Center, The University of Texas at Austin, by generous permission of The University of the South, represented by Georges Borchardt, Inc., New York; copyright © 2011 by The University of the South.

Editors' Note

We continue to be delighted to see excellent new archival work on American literature; publishing such work is the mission of this journal. We present here not only a discussion of previously unpublished letters by W. D. Howells, a consideration of previously unpublished letters by Edith Wharton, and a previously unpublished play by Tennessee Williams but also a study of the image of Phillis Wheatley, a major new source for Edgar Allan Poe's "The Fall of the House of Usher," a manuscript resource for Ernest Hemingway biography, and the revisions for Thomas Wolfe's *From Death to Morning*. Supplementing these works are a consideration of the future of the study of Stephen Crane, three review-essays, and twenty-one reviews.

We welcome the return of David Roessel and Nicholas Moschovakis and the introduction to our pages of Patrick K. Dooley, Jennifer Harris, Alexander Hammond, Donna Campbell, Irene C. Goldman-Price, and Park Bucker. We renew our invitation to all scholars of American literature to submit to *Resources for American Literary Study* your latest discoveries.

To prepare this yearly volume, we rely—with much gratitude—on the fine work of many others. We wish to recognize Associate Editor Gib Prettyman, Review Editor MaryEllen Higgins, Editorial Assistant Donna Brantlinger Black, and the distinguished members of our Editorial Advisory Board. We are very sorry to report the passing of one of these distinguished members, John C. Broderick—who served ably on the Board since the founding of *RALS* in 1971. We continue to appreciate the steady hands of AMS Press Director Gabe Hornstein and AMS Press Executive Editor David Ramm. And even as we warmly recognize once again the critical support of Kent Cartwright, Chair of the Department of English at the University of Maryland, College Park, we warmly recognize anew the critical support of Madlyn L. Hanes, Vice President for Commonwealth Campuses of the Penn State University.

Prospects for the Study of Stephen Crane

PATRICK K. DOOLEY
St. Bonaventure University

In a survey of nearly nineteen hundred books, essays, book chapters, and reviews for *Stephen Crane: An Annotated Bibliography of Secondary Scholarship*, I located (so far as possible), annotated, and sorted by category everything written in English from 1901 (the year after Crane died) until 1991. In the first ninety years of commentary, scholars were particularly keen on three activities: (1) getting a handle on the life of Crane (1871–1900)—a formidable genius who blossomed early in his twenties only to flame out like a meteor, succumbing to tuberculosis five months short of his twenty-ninth birthday; (2) commenting on his works—especially his best seller on both sides of the Atlantic, *The Red Badge of Courage* (1895), written by a twenty-two-year-old novelist/journalist who had never witnessed combat; and (3) taking sides on textual controversies concerning which of the four versions of *Red Badge* and which of the three versions of *Maggie: A Girl of the Streets* (1893) should be considered authoritative.

Since 1992, this bibliography has been updated by six essays published between 1999 and 2010, thereby adding nearly three hundred additional articles and almost two dozen books to the corpus of Crane commentary. Between 1992 and 2010, while now less exercised about textual controversies, Crane scholars continue to be intrigued about his life and the historical contexts that inform his writings, and they remain intensely engaged in disclosing the magic of his style and in unpacking the layers of meaning and the literary techniques employed in his best works.

"Crane is loud, now," was how the inestimable Louis J. Budd—Twain scholar, former editor of *American Literature*, and the James P. Duke Emeritus Professor of English at Duke University—described the situation several years ago (personal communication). There are no signs that the volume of Crane scholarship is diminishing; in fact, a number of controversies refuse to go away, and several new interpretive tacks are emerging. In what follows, the areas that have been of most interest to Crane commentators are surveyed with an eye to numerous intriguing research opportunities. After longer sections on the texts of Crane's works, his biography, and the persistent interest paid to *The Red Badge of Courage*, attention is given to his poetry, war journalism, western tales, social commentary pieces, and late potboilers. The last section provides details about major archival holdings of Crane's manuscripts and memorabilia and gives information on the bibliographies devoted to him and his works.

Texts and Contexts

Today's Crane scholars have the luxury of easy access to Crane's texts and correspondence, as well as a detailed and reliable chronology of his life and travels. Such was not always the case. The first revival of interest in Crane was triggered by the issue of *The Work of Stephen Crane*, a twelve-volume edition edited by Wilson Follett (1887–1963) and published by Knopf between 1925 and 1927. Follett recruited distinguished writers—notably Willa Cather (1873–1947), Sherwood Anderson (1876–1941), Thomas Beer (1889–1940), Carl Van Doren (1885–1950), and H. L. Mencken (1880–1956)—to write short introductions to these volumes. With the Follett edition, the scope and sweep of Crane's oeuvre were made widely available, even if some of the texts reprinted were not completely reliable and not all of Crane's writings were included. As a matter of fact, identifying and locating missing, unknown, and unattributed Crane pieces were the overriding features of Crane scholarship from 1930 to the 1960s. The excitement, competition, rivalry, and jealousy among Crane scholars, with Robert W. Stallman at the eye of the storm, were wonders to behold. Hoping to rise above the fray, Thomas A. Gullason produced *The Complete Short Stories and Sketches of Stephen Crane* and *The Complete Novels of Stephen Crane*, and Olov W. Fryckstedt compiled *Stephen Crane: Uncollected Writings*.

By the mid-1960s, believing the time to be ripe for a truly "complete" and accurate collection of Crane's works, a team of textual scholars at the University of Virginia (under the leadership of Fredson Bowers) launched a project to provide a critical edition of "every known piece of his [Crane's] creative work and journalism, but excluding his letters and memoranda" (Bowers vii). (Inevitably, some Crane pieces have been discovered since the Virginia edition. See, for example, the essay by Michael Robertson, David Holmes, and Roxanna Paez, who argue that seventeen additional unattributed articles in the *New-York Tribune* should be included in Crane's newspaper contributions; on the basis of a stylometric statistical analysis, including an investigation of the presence of Crane's signature traits of scorching irony and witty hyperbole, they make a convincing case that these unattributed pieces deserve additional scholarly examination.) The ten volumes of the Virginia edition appeared between 1969 and 1976. Unlike Follett before him, Bowers enlisted experienced Crane scholars—James Colvert, Edwin Cady, and J. C. Levenson—to introduce and comment upon each volume. Though Bowers's careful textual work was initially admired and praised, controversy arose, and condemnation was eventually pronounced on his "critical" texts for *Maggie* and *The Red Badge of Courage*.

With regard to perhaps the two most significant of Crane's works, a brief account of their complicated textual and publishing history may be helpful. In 1893 Crane published *Maggie*, and it was ignored. Two years later, *Red Badge* was on top of the best-seller lists in America and England and making Crane an overnight celebrity. Seeking to capitalize on his fame, his publisher, Appleton, brought out a shortened and bowdlerized version of *Maggie* in 1896. A final complication occurred in 1969, when Bowers produced an edition of *Maggie* that was a hybrid of Crane's earlier versions, a version now totally ignored.

As for *Red Badge*, it was first published by the Bacheller Syndicate in a truncated and serialized newspaper version in 1894 (see Joseph Katz's *Facsimile Reproduction*); the "standard" and best-selling Appleton version appeared in 1895. Bowers again enters the picture: comparing the manuscript of the *Red Badge* with the Appleton version, Bowers believed he could discern which changes had been made at the behest of Appleton's somewhat overbearing editor, Ripley Hitchcock, and which emendations Crane had made on his own. As a result, Bowers produced another hybrid text of Crane's writings. Finally, and further complicating the situation, in 1982 Harry Binder published "*The Red Badge of Courage* Nobody Knows: Expanded Version." The Binder version "restored" the allegedly forced Hitchcock deletions and added a whole chapter (and many paragraph-length passages) that appears in the *Red Badge* manuscript. Of course, round after round of point and counterpoint claims about the merits/demerits of the Bowers and Binder textual variants litter the landscape of Crane scholarship.

In 1984, scholarly work on Crane was made easier with the Library of America's *Stephen Crane: Prose and Poetry*. J. C. Levenson reprinted what he regarded as the best of the University of Virginia edition (amounting to less than half of the published works, but none of Crane's unpublished works or discarded drafts). Levenson also declined to reprint either of Bowers's problematic editions; instead, he reprinted the 1893 *Maggie* and the 1895 Appleton version of *Red Badge*.

The ready accessibility of Crane texts has spoiled some scholars and has also fostered some glaring omissions, which now, happily, provide the current cohort of commentators with interesting research projects and exegetical topics. Several areas of study are especially promising.

To begin with, the Follett introductions ought to be revisited. Here lie rich resources and angles of vision that have been ignored for decades. Beyond the introductions by the literary notables cited above, the comments by Robert H. Davis (1869–1942) on Crane's war tales, Amy Lowell

(1874–1925) on his poetry, Charles Michelson (1869–1948) on "The Open Boat" (1897), William Lyon Phelps (1865–1943) on the Whilomville stories, and Follett himself on *The Monster* (1898) are gems. For that matter, the lengthy introductions and comprehensive textual essays in the University of Virginia edition should also be reexamined. Further, as already noted, Levenson did not reprint a number of Crane sketches and stories in the Library of America edition. Unfairly ignored, for instance, are Crane's mini-masterpieces, "The Snake" (1896), "A Lovely Jag in a Crowded Car" (1895), and "Three Miraculous Soldiers" (1897). These, as well as a number of other Crane pieces that are routinely ignored, deserve better. Along this line, Edwin Cady begins his introduction to the 768 pages of text and more than 400 pages of notes in volume 8, *Tales, Sketches, and Reports*, by observing, "Although there is nothing of Stephen Crane's finest artistic quality in this volume, its publication is an event of decided importance" (xvi). Cady's deprecating comment is far wide of the mark—dozens of early, middle, and late Crane essays contained therein deserve attention. In a word, Crane scholars are encouraged to take a close look at the abundance of Crane pieces in volume 8 of the Virginia edition (as well as other volumes) and also to track down the pieces that Levenson declined to include in his Library of America reprint. Some tales and stories in volume 8 are forgettable, but a great many are decidedly not. In any case, it has been more than twenty-five years since Cady and Levenson gave us *their* sorting of the wheat from the chaff; now it is time for a new generation to take up the scholarly winnow.

While the Bowers edition (and the Levenson reprinting) provides scholars with reliable texts, it also prunes away the context for Crane's texts. Locating the original appearances of Crane's pieces in newspapers or magazines recaptures the rich cultural, historical, and literary settings. Charles Johanningsmeier's recent tour-de-force essay on the syndicated newspaper appearances of *Red Badge* examines "the kind of 'cultural work' the novel performed in the mid-1890s" (228). Johanningsmeier argues that since even Crane himself was convinced that this truncated and simplified version of his classic was both inferior to and different from the 1895 Appleton version, scholars have summarily dismissed the syndicated version. This was the version, though, that introduced Crane to hundreds of thousands of readers and rescued him from poverty, introduced him to important backers, gave him an entrée to influential editors and their magazines, and brought him the publicity that launched his career. Hence, the newspaper version of *Red Badge* was insignificant neither to Crane nor to the public that read it. With reference to the latter, Johanningsmeier examines the newspapers in which serialized installments appeared, considering, for example, the advertisements that surrounded Crane's text. It is interesting that these ads were evenly balanced between masculine "coded" merchandise—such as whisky, leather boots, and guns—and products aimed at women—such as soaps, children's dresses, and furs. Some advertisements were aimed at both genders, including proto Viagra-like remedies for "Lost Manhood" and "Loss of Power of the Generative Organs in Either Sex." Perhaps nothing is new after all! Newspaper versions were accompanied by a variety of pen-and-ink drawings, complete with captions—neither of which can be found in the book versions. Johanningsmeier's skillful account of the differences of text, tone, emphasis, and ending between the newspaper and book versions challenges Craneans to explore further the cultural work that first publication of *Red Badge* performed for its first readers. Since several other newspapers took advantage of the Bacheller Syndicate's offering of *Red Badge*, numerous other newspaper appearances await scrutiny by patient and dogged scholars.

Continuing in this vein, Michael Robertson's well-regarded book, *Stephen Crane, Journalism, and the Making of Modern American Literature*, examines the initial appearance of a number of Crane sketches. Crane published the short story "Not Much of a Hero" (1892; which Levenson does not reprint) about "an Indian fighter," in the *New-York Tribune* on the heels of more than two years of extensive coverage of The Battle of Wounded Knee. Furthermore, his impressionistic sketch, "The Fire" (1894), branded a hoax when Robert W. Stallman and E. R. Hagemann reprinted it in *The New York City Sketches of Stephen Crane and Related Pieces*, had originally appeared under the title "When Every One is Panic Stricken" in a newspaper on November 25, 1894. Robertson explains,

> The sketch appeared in one of the Sunday *Press*'s supplementary sections, which contained a miscellaneous assortment of news, fiction and feature articles. One subhead line reads, "A Realistic Pen Picture of a Fire in a Tenement"—a signal that the *Press* offered the article as an artistic representation of a typical urban event rather than a factual report. The evidence suggests that Crane, his editors and readers understood the articles to be part of the fact-fiction discourse for the 1890s journalism. (87)

Seeing Crane's sketches in their original placement reveals the shifting, permeable membrane between journalism and works of creative imagination. It also makes us reflect on the relative standing of these two genres. Both involve a selective attention to a few details (with a corresponding neglect or at least a conscious bracketing of the rest) and the absence of necessity for a strict chronological sequence of events. Accordingly, a systematic comparison via a close textual study of "Stephen Crane's Own Story" (1897) and "The Open Boat" offers even the most seasoned and astute scholar a challenging research project.

The nature of perception itself warrants investigation in Crane. His poignant meditation "London Impressions" (1897) shows how little of the richness of reality is made available to sentient beings. Beyond that, it reveals the ways in which awareness is conditioned by sensory equipment and limited by attention spans. And, in the case of human observers, it further shows how our "realities" are prepackaged by language and conditioned by cultural heritage. As Crane phrases it in "London Impressions," each of us sits "in his own little cylinder of vision, so to speak" (*Stephen Crane: Prose and Poetry* 971).[1] Milne Holton was so captivated with Crane's insight into the processes of world-making that Crane's formula, "cylinder of vision," provided him with both the thesis and the title of a provocative study of Crane's fiction and journalistic writing. I also explicate Crane's "cylinder of vision" image, using William James's metaphor of the stream of consciousness and his concept of selective attention as frameworks in "Metaphysics and Epistemology: Exploring the Epiphanies of Experience," the second chapter of *The Pluralistic Philosophy of Stephen Crane* (26–49). I there examine the epistemological subtlety embedded in "Crane at Velestino" (1897), "Stephen Crane Tells of War's Horrors" (1897), and a number of Crane's other journalistic postings from the Greco-Turkish War. Given Crane's lifelong fascination with combat, scores of his early, middle, and late war tales and his journalistic dispatches need to be scrutinized, not only for their vivid dramatizations of humans under stress, but also for their philosophical sophistication.

With regard to the fiction/journalism divide, Nancy Huston Banks begins her review of *Maggie* and *Red Badge* in the November 1895 *Bookman* by observing that "the question whether journalism helps or hinders a writer to create literature has recently been discussed by the local press with fresh interest, and [its] discussion is likely to continue for a long time" (rpt. in Weatherford 96). Arriving more than a century after Banks's prediction, Robertson's fine 1997 account of the relationship between journalism and novels greatly advances the discussion, but there is much more to be learned from exploring these mutually catalytic and symbiotic genres. Recovering Crane's historical situation via the literary and cultural context of his stories should pay important heuristic dividends and yield insights on the intellectual agenda that engaged him and his turn-of-the-last-century colleagues: artists, journalists, scientists, clergy, philosophers, and novelists. For example, seeing who and what was published alongside his works opens up the possibility of tracking the vectors of influence both *to* and *from* Crane.

Upon reading *Maggie* in 1891, William Dean Howells (1837–1920) famously remarked, "This man has sprung into life full-armed" (qtd. by Elbert Hubbard, rpt. in Weatherford 76). More than thirty years later, in his essay "Stephen Crane and the Genius Myth," Floyd Dell, in an attempt to dispel the lurid gossip and nasty rumors about Crane, asserted that no more needs be claimed beyond that "he was a genius and he was unconventional" (637). Neither the "full-armed" nor the genius account still has currency, but even the most patient and skilled Crane biographers have had difficulty tracking down which authors and works Crane read and which ones influenced him in one way or another. Here are some promising places to search for influences: the 1892 *New-York Tribune* (which ran his Sullivan County Sketches), the 1894 *New York Press* (which published "An Experiment in Misery" [1894], "An Experiment in Luxury" [1894], and "When a Man Falls" [1894]), the 1894 *Arena* (which offered "Men in the Storm"), and the 1898 *New York World* (which carried his Spanish-American War dispatches). With reference to the last newspaper, see the informative essay by John Patrick Leary, which not only treats the impact of Crane's reports but also includes the added bonus of a reproduced illustration of a "pirate" sitting at a bar listening to the *World*'s famous news correspondent tell a war story. Scholars should look, too, at the newspaper spaces that Crane shared with some other authors also under contract with the Bacheller and McClure syndicates.

It is now time to look further, temporally and geographically, for the impact of Crane on both British and American authors. The task at hand is to discern the extent to which Crane's images, techniques, and themes resonate in the works of his fellow writers. In some cases, smoking-gun examples of direct influence will be found. More likely, but nonetheless illuminating and helpful, will be instances of indirect "conversations" between Crane and other authors. For example, we may recall Crane's Greco-Prussian War tale, "Death and the Child" (1898), wherein the child, left at home by his fleeing and panicked parents, changes his modeling game so that his sticks and stones no longer represent the usual ponies, sheep, and shepherds but instead stand for troop movements in the battle being waged far below at the base of the mountain. Crane writes, "He paused frequently to get a cue of the manner from the soldiers fighting on the plain. He reproduced, to a degree, any movements which he accounted rational to his theory of sheep-herding, the business of men, the traditional and exalted living of his father" (*Stephen Crane: Prose and Poetry* 950–51). Then we may note the uncanny similarity between Crane's passage and the opening scene in William Faulkner's (1897–1962) *The Unvanquished* (1938), in which twelve-year-old Ringo and Bayard construct out of twigs, chips, and mud a miniature "living map" of the siege of Vicksburg. If and when Faulknerians ascertain how much of Crane Faulkner read, they will be positioned to assess Crane's influence upon him. But even until then, our appreciation of both authors is deepened by noting these structural parallels and thematic consonances.

Crane's Biography

Capturing Crane's life has proved to be a fascinating but maddeningly elusive quest. Crane scholarship has been challenged not only by Crane's own posing and dissembling but also by Thomas Beer's unreliable 1923 *Stephen Crane: A Study in American Letters*. The problem is that events, letters, drafts, and bons mots that Beer fabricated continue to be attributed to Crane. The trio of Paul Sorrentino ("The Legacy of Thomas Beer") and Stanley Wertheim ("Thomas Beer," with Sorrentino) and John Clendenning ("Thomas Beer's *Stephen Crane*" and "Stephen Crane and His Biographers") has convincingly documented Beer's forgeries.[2] Incidentally, when reading standard reference book entries on Crane, use the "Beer test": if the author repeats an anecdote such as "[Leo Tolstoy's (1828–1910)] *War and Peace* [1865–69] goes on and on like Texas" or says that Harold Frederic (1856–98) once described Henry James (1843–1916) as "an effeminate old donkey who lives with a herd of other donkeys around him and insists on being treated as if he were the Pope," one can be sure that Beer's "biography" has been uncritically accepted. More generally, with regard to reference book sources, a reliable litmus test is spotting commentators who orate that Crane died at twenty-nine—clearly these "experts" did not check the date and month of his death before they did the math. Another handy fact-check is to see how they describe Crane's ordeal in "The Open Boat"—it lasted thirty hours, but some reference books have him languishing at sea for several days.

John Berryman's psychoanalytic biography, *Stephen Crane*, published in 1950, further muddied the waters. In 1968, Robert Stallman set out to correct Beer's fabrications and to contest Berryman's Freudian interpretations. However, in much of his volume, *Stephen Crane: A Biography*, Stallman himself, instead of Crane, is the focus. More recently, reliable accounts supported with evidence and based on documented events characterize the landmark ur-biographies compiled by Wertheim and Sorrentino: *The Correspondence of Stephen Crane* and *The Crane Log: A Documentary Life of Stephen Crane, 1871–1900*. Invaluable, too, is Wertheim's 1997 *A Stephen Crane Encyclopedia*. An exhaustive knowledge of Crane's life and works and the literature and culture of fin de siècle America (and England) enables Wertheim to provide countless illuminating connections among characters, themes, symbols, and images within the several genres of Crane's oeuvre.

In his Whilomville story "The Angel-Child" (1899), Crane writes, " 'How do you pronounce the name of that barber up there on Bridge Street hill?' And, then, before anyone could prevent it, the best minds of the town were splintering their lances against William Neeltje's signboard" (*Stephen Crane: Prose and Poetry* 1127). Likewise, to date, would-be Crane biographers continue to splinter their lances on the life of Crane. The recent biographies of Crane by Christopher Benfey, George Monteiro (*Stephen Crane's Blue Badge of Courage*), and Linda Davis (*Badge of Courage: The Life of Stephen Crane*) have attracted both effusive praise and sharp criticism.[3]

The current state of affairs in Crane biography is a puzzling one. The careful detective work and patient scholarship of Wertheim, Sorrentino, and others have steadily accumulated and sorted out the raw material for biographers. Then, too, biographers now have access to Crane's works through the critical edition of Crane works by the University of Virginia. Still, the elusiveness of Crane's ever-fascinating life has had the effect of throwing down a gauntlet to biographers. As a result, many of the obsessed-with-Crane's-life cohort have produced fictional/nonfictional accounts. Some of these part historical fiction/part biography volumes are impressively discerning; many, ironically, have a ring-of-truth quality about them. Several of these studies have opened up new and insightful angles of vision for readers (often new ones) of his works.

Will a definitive biography, *the* life of Stephen Crane ever be written? Can it be? What vexing and intriguing questions! Those who embark on the task will be faced with exhilarating, frustrating, and daunting work. It is hoped that eventually Craneans will have their biographer, probably in the person of Paul Sorrentino, whose long-awaited biography is now under contract with Harvard University Press.

Meanwhile, Sorrentino, also editor of *Stephen Crane Studies*, has been busy. His 2006 *Stephen Crane Remembered* presents more than sixty biographical documents, including reminiscences by Crane family members, friends, and acquaintances, as well as comments from contemporaries and early reviews. Two other indispensable resources for would-be biographers are the reliable and useful chronology compiled by Wertheim and Sorrentino for *The Correspondence of Stephen Crane* and the somewhat more detailed one that Levenson includes in his Library of America *Stephen Crane: Prose and Poetry*. And of course, scholars ought to restudy the treasure trove of information contained in the firsthand reports of two of young Crane's friends, Frederic M. Lawrence (dates unknown) and Corwin Knapp Linson (1864–1959). Lawrence's manuscript was written about 1930 and was brought into print as *The Real Stephen Crane* in 1980 by Joseph Katz. Lawrence was a close friend of Crane (he was "Pudge" in the Sullivan County stories), and his warm rapport and familiarity with Crane are obvious. Linson's longer and more impressionistic memoir, *My Stephen Crane*, dates from the mid-1920s, was edited by Edwin Cady and published in 1958. Linson was one of the artist friends with whom Crane "enjoyed" poverty at various New York City slumming locations. Three of Linson's eyewitness accounts of living with Crane are especially vivid, illuminating, and important: first, Crane's initial inspiration for *Red Badge* while he scanned several of the *Century Magazine*'s series "Battles and Leaders of the Civil War"; second, the trip that Crane and Linson shared "In the Depths of a Coal Mine" (1894) and thereafter in the Scranton, Pennsylvania, hotel room where Crane worked on his draft of his newspaper report and Linson finished his drawings (seven of which are reproduced in my "Openness to Experience in Stephen Crane's 'In the Depths of a Coal Mine' "); and third, Linson's account of Crane's showing him, in early 1894, several poems. Though Crane dubbed his poems "pills," Linson thought they were better described as "pictures."

Full-scale biographies aside, competent and careful scholars of Crane need to continue to examine aspects, periods, and developments in Crane's life. Already a number of illuminating essays have appeared that have reexamined the early testimonials and memoirs of Crane's friends, family members, and contemporaries. Many of these reminiscences were triggered by the appearance of Beer's *Stephen Crane* in 1923 and the release of the Knopf edition, *The Work of Stephen Crane*, in 1925 through 1927. Knopf editor Wilson Follett reflects on Crane's life and work in "The Second Twenty-Eight Years: A Note on Stephen Crane, 1871–1900"; this is one of the earliest and best essays on him (see also H. E. Bates). Already noted, Sorrentino's *Stephen Crane Remembered* has helped scholars by collecting many of the reminiscences of Crane's contemporaries. Not contained in Sorrentino's volume, roughly sorted by periods and events in Crane's life, the following remembrances and commentaries are noteworthy enough to merit examination. Concerning his early childhood, see Frank W. Noxon, Mrs. George Crane, Post Wheeler and Hallie Ermine Rives, and Edna Crane Sidbury; on the Crane family, see Gullason ("The Fiction of the Reverend Crane" and "Stephen Crane's Sister") and Robert K. Crane ("Family Matters" and "Stephen Crane's Family Heritage"); on his attendance at Pennington Seminary, where his father had earlier been principal, see Gullason ("The Cranes"); regarding his boarding school days at Claverack College and Hudson River Institute, see Katz ("Stephen Crane at Claverack College"), Thomas F. O'Donnell, Vincent Starrett, Gullason ("Stephen Crane at Claverack"), Wertheim ("Why Stephen Crane Left Claverack"), and Harvey Wickham; for his experiences at Lafayette College, see Robertson (*Stephen Crane at Lafayette*), David E. E. Sloane, Ralph Chamberlin, and Gullason ("Stephen Crane at Lafayette College"); and for his one semester at Syracuse University, see Mansfield J. French, George Chandler, Claude E. Jones, Thomas E. Martin, John Mayfield, Clarence Loomis Peaslee, Gullason ("Stephen Crane at Syracuse University"), and Lester G. Wells. For an overall assessment of the reach of Crane's formal education, see Lyndon Upson Pratt and Sorrentino ("New Evidence"). For details on his early newspaper days and his days at the Needham building (having been recently abandoned by the Art Students'

League) and various New York City tenements, see R. G. Vosburg, Curtis Brown, Hamlin Garland, Bernard Weinstein, Sorrentino ("Nelson Green's Reminiscences"), and Willis Fletcher Johnson. For his dealings with agents and publishers, see Frederic Lewis Allen and Irving Bacheller. For his connections with Elbert Hubbard (1856–1915) and the *Philistine,* see Claude Bragdon, Sorrentino ("The Philistine Society's Banquet"), and Bruce A. White. For his final days in England, see Helen R. Crane, Edwin Pugh, Ford Madox Ford, Joseph Conrad, Jesse Conrad, Eric Solomon, and Katz ("The Estate of Stephen Crane"). Readers may notice that a number of these reminiscences and short articles appeared in the *Stephen Crane Newsletter,* edited by Katz and published first at Ohio State University and then at the University of South Carolina. Katz oversaw five years of quarterly volumes from 1966 to 1970. Perhaps, in part, because copies of the *Newsletter* are somewhat difficult to locate, it has been largely forgotten. However, since this is a Crane resource that contains groundbreaking and valuable material, scholars ought to revisit and reexamine it. Another important resource, requiring an extended visit to Syracuse University, is Melvin Schoberlin's unfinished biography of Crane, "A Flagon of Despair."[4]

Finally, returning to a suggestion made earlier with regard to influence upon Crane by his fellow journalists, more attention has recently been paid to Crane's friendships with other authors. See David Traxel's examination of Crane and Richard Harding Davis (1864–1916) and Sorrentino's essay on the Crane–William Dean Howells relationship ("A Re-examination"). Traxel concedes that a Crane-Davis friendship was unlikely; indeed, one can scarcely imagine more diametrically opposed demeanors and temperaments. Yet Traxel argues that Crane and Davis actually shared fairly common backgrounds. In fact, their differences had to do with the nineteenth century's "code of gentility" and the city. Davis adhered to the code and thereby gained great financial success and popular esteem; he thought the city a picturesque place to visit. Crane flouted the code of gentility, a response that gained him artistic freedom and notoriety; he thought the city a dangerous and thereby interesting combat zone.

Sorrentino's examination of Crane and Howells counters the commonly accepted view that Howells was the mentor and Crane the acolyte. Sorrentino shows how both struggled with self-doubt about their choice of professions: "[T]hey encouraged each other to remain committed to their literary goals and inspired each other to write about social problems in New York City, at times almost thinking as of one mind as they made similar verbal and thematic choices" (49). Any discussion of the Howells–Crane friendship will naturally begin with Crane's account, "Howells Discussed at Avon-by-the-Sea" (1891; *Stephen Crane: Prose and Poetry* 457), and his interview of the Dean, "Howells Feels the Realists Must Wait" (1894; *Stephen Crane: Prose and Poetry* 615–18). His relationship with Frederic (see

Robert M. Myers's *Reluctant Expatriate* for an overview) likewise needs attention; Crane's review-essay "Harold Frederic" (1898; *Stephen Crane: Prose and Poetry* 984–87) is an excellent starting point.

More generally, then, Crane's relationships on both personal and literary levels with a host of other authors should be pursued. The two volumes of *The Correspondence of Stephen Crane* edited by Wertheim and Sorrentino have regularly been scrutinized for information about Crane's life and travels, but they have been underused as a resource to recreate Crane's artistic network and his dealings with and reaction to his American and British counterparts. *The Correspondence* volumes reprint four letters to Crane from Hamlin Garland (1860–1940) and four from Crane in return. (Any discussion of the Garland and Crane relationship should start with Wertheim's 1967 essay "Crane and Garland: The Education of an Impressionist" and needs to include Donald Pizer's pioneering essay, "The Garland-Crane Relationship," and Keith Newlin's recent full-length biography, *Hamlin Garland: A Life.*) *The Correspondence* also contains other important letters: eight from Howells, with seven Crane replies; eleven from Joseph Conrad (1857–1924); and a dozen and a half more to Cora Crane (1865/ 6–1910), with several replies from Crane. Also to be found are several exchanges between Crane and such writers as Ford Madox Ford (1873–1939), H. G. Wells (1866–1946), Elbert Hubbard, and Henry James.

Then, too, not to be missed is the "General Index" of *The Correspondence*, which reveals dozens of other mentions and third-party judgments regarding Crane and the above-named authors, as well as comments by a number of other Crane contemporaries. Two last comments are necessary regarding *The Correspondence* as a research tool. First, Crane's letters reveal a young man more socially adept and more open to guidance and advice from others than is the customary view of him. And second, with reference to the issue of Crane's savvy about magazines, their editors, and his fellow contributors, readers may wish to note his November 5, 1895, letter to *The Youth's Companion*. Seeking to capitalize on the publicity burst from *Red Badge*'s inclusion on the best-seller list, the magazine had approached Crane about providing some of his stories. He was pleased with the request, but before he submitted any of his tales, he explained, "I would be very glad to write for the Companion.... I might perchance do a story that you would like. Such possible stories I would send you, if I was informed of *your literary platform* and I would be happy to hear from you concerning it" (1:133, emphasis added). Leaving Crane's fascinating biography, we may now turn to scholarship opportunities regarding his works.

The Red Badge of Courage

Since the publication of *The Red Badge of Courage* (it has never gone out of print), countless Crane scholars have found ample complexity and ambiguity—much of it fueled by the various versions of the novel—to inspire and energize generations of commentators. What remains to be examined by current and future scholars? Much, after all, has been learned. It is now indisputable that Chancellorsville was the historical source for the novel. Building on earlier hints and short pieces—the best of the lot are by Roy Morris, Charles LaRocca, and Cecil D. Eby—LaRocca produced in 1995 an annotated historical edition of the novel, and in 2006 Perry Lentz brought forward a fact-filled and tightly argued volume, *Private Fleming at Chancellorsville: "The Red Badge of Courage" and the Civil War*. Offering reliable information about all aspects of the Civil War, including details about uniforms, tactics, strategy, maps, photographs, muskets, sharpshooters, artillery, cavalry, battlefield hospitals, and medical care, Lentz contends that "the more readers know about the American Civil War, the more they can appreciate Crane's depiction of 'An Episode' within it" (2). Whether and how such comprehensive background knowledge enhances our appreciation of Crane's fictional narrative is not obvious.

Regarding the benefit of information on the historical antecedents of *Red Badge*, see the fine essay by Pizer, "What Unit Did Henry Belong to at Chancellorsville, and Does it Matter?" Pizer explores the places wherein historical facts fit *Red Badge* and the places where the search for an exact historical source is a distraction. He concludes that Crane "was not interested in rendering the battle and its participants in a manner consistent with full historical accuracy . . . [rather,] he shaped a narrative closer to the pattern in his (Crane's) head" (11). And so though Lentz's study is replete with interesting information about the life and times of soldiers during the Civil War, Pizer wonders how important it is to establish, for example, to which regiment the *fictional* Henry Fleming belonged.

And even if researchers have arguably come to the end of the line regarding the historical antecedents of the novel, many interesting issues remain unresolved. Two perennial favorites are the religious symbolism in the work and Fleming's growth or regression during the course of the novel's three days of combat.

As to the former, Alfred North Whitehead (1861–1947) famously remarked that the history of western philosophy is best understood as a series of footnotes to the thought of Plato. With regard to religious readings of *Red Badge*, Stallman stands in as Plato. In his 1951 introduction to the Modern Library edition of *Red Badge*, Stallman proposes that Christian symbols are the key to the novel. Focusing upon Jim Conklin as Jesus Christ, Stallman argues that the novel's central theme is redemption and asserts, in support of his reading, that the iconic sentence at the end of chapter 9—"the red sun was pasted in the sky as a wafer" (*Stephen Crane: Prose and Poetry* 137)—refers to the communion wafer of the Holy Eucharist. Thereafter, for more than six decades—most recently in Monteiro's "Crane's 'Red Wafer' Again"—debate has raged about whether attention to religious symbolism informs or detracts from the reader's appreciation of Henry's story. Stallman's challenging readings continue to provide fruitful points of departure for scholars.

As for the second topic, the degree of self-insight and maturity that Fleming does (or does not) acquire is not only a seminal scholarly issue but also a surefire starter for classroom discussion.[5] Beyond questions about the pace, direction, and outcome of Henry's struggles, there is the added question of the degree of his self-insight. Becoming clear about the extent of Fleming's self-insight is complicated by deciding which edition of *Red Badge* should be regarded as authoritative. The Binder edition drastically skews the controversy, presenting readers with a cocky, even pompous and self-deluded adolescent, whereas the Appleton version better supports the orthodox reading that Fleming matures. Still, regardless of which edition is selected, lively disagreement remains concerning the existence and extent of his maturation and which factors have been the catalysts of his (supposed?) growth. And so, even if there has been closure on locating the historical sources of *Red Badge*, debate regarding Fleming's growth is far from over. In other words, journal editors will continue to welcome commentaries and arguments about Fleming's maturation/regression/stagnation.

Other research opportunities dealing with race, class, and gender have lately attracted increased attention. On these matters, consult a variety of strong studies: Verner D. Mitchell's thoughtful examination of race in *Red Badge* (he correctly observes that "signs of 'gender' and 'race' in Crane's fiction have gone largely uninterrogated" [62]); Andrew Lawson's discussion of *Red Badge* in terms of class, especially tensions between the recruits and their officers; Myers's elaboration (" 'The Subtle Battle Brotherhood' ") of a similar sort of tension among the democratically conditioned recruits who chafe at their order-giving superiors; and Scott Derrick's consideration of "homosexual interests or anxieties" (172) in Crane's biography, which might find their ways into *Red Badge*.

Then too, there is always a need to explore further the influence of other authors and their works on *Red Badge*. See the "Literary Resources" section of my 2010 bibliographical essay on *Red Badge* for a survey of recent, and some unfairly neglected older (pre-1980s) scholarship in this area. Some source-hunting essays are convincing and invite further investigation; many are, as Mark Twain (1835–1910) put it, "stretchers." Crane's elusive biography is also an important factor contributing to the speculation about what and who influenced him. However, in the final analysis, the point of identifying possible authorial and/or literary antecedents is their ability to deepen our understanding of Crane's narrative. In a word, while a survey of the scholarly literature on *Red Badge* may be daunting, the next generation of scholars need not fear that it will be unable to discover any new or transforming readings of this great American classic.

The Monster

After Crane's signature novel, *Red Badge*, *The Monster*, the last novel completed in his lifetime, is increasingly garnering impressive amounts of insightful and provocative commentary, especially in the last decade and a half. As noted earlier, Crane's oeuvre is today seen as significant for the "critical work" that it performed for his contemporaries. In addition, perhaps more than any other of his works, *The Monster* offers twenty-first-century readers a unique glance at the nineteenth-century America that Crane dramatized and critiqued. Accordingly, we may fruitfully ask probing questions about this small masterpiece. For example, how does Crane handle the matter of race in this novella, and how does he describe the ways in which a largely rural and agrarian America faced the moral, legal, and technological demands involved in becoming urbanized and modernized? Such critical questions present Crane scholars with a challenging research opportunity.

A special roundtable discussion, "Teaching Crane's *The Monster*," was held at the 2008 American Literature Association meeting in San Francisco. The session, organized by me and sponsored by the Crane Society, assembled an all-star panel—Bert Bender, Donna Campbell, John Dudley, James Nagel, and Jeanne Reesman—to address several questions: (1) Is *The Monster* Crane's most sophisticated literary work? (2) Does it dramatize his most carefully considered reflections on morality? and (3) How significant is race in *The Monster*, not only for Crane and his contemporaries, but also for readers more than a century later?

At the session, *The Monster* was situated in its original context by way of a consideration of Peter Newell's (1862–1924) drawings, which accompanied the work's initial appearance in *Harper's New Monthly Magazine* in August 1898. Copies of Newell's twelve illustrations were distributed, and it was noted that only four depict white characters while eight depict blacks. The panel members were asked whether the two-thirds preponderance of the drawings of blacks indicated that, for the editors of *Harper's*, as well as for Newell and Crane, race was a central issue. As a discussion-starter, the range of prior scholarship on the issue was summarized: race is insignificant (Wertheim, "Crane's *The Monster*"); race is essential (Molly Hiro, Lee Clark Mitchell, and Adam Zachary Newton); and Crane is ambivalent (Price McMurray and John Cleman). From the spirited discussion by the panel and vigorous comments from the audience, we could readily see that race is an important matter for Crane scholars—one that needs careful research and clear rethinking. Of related interest and also needing examination are Crane's casual and offhanded comments about pickaninny children and his blackface/vaudevillian-like characterization of the adult blacks of Watermelon Alley in the Whilomville Tales "The Knife" (1899) and "The City Urchin and the Chaste Villagers" (1899).

Also, *The Monster* is replete with observations that involve morality, law, and the transforming impact of technology upon late nineteenth-century American culture. On the first matter, my chapter "Ethics: Tolerance, Compassion and Duty" in *The Pluralistic Philosophy of Stephen Crane* surveys Crane's attention to the whole gamut of moral responses: premoral duties to animals, paradigmatic moral obligations to humans in need, and optional extramoral heroic responses in emergency and crisis situations. Against this background, Henry Johnson's duty to rescue Jimmie; Dr. Trescott's obligation to provide medical care to Johnson after the fire; and his extraordinary and long-term care for Henry, at the expense of his medical practice and his family's social life, are examined. On these matters, see also William M. Morgan's helpful treatment of the muscular heroism of Johnson and the moral courage of Trescott and John Dudley's excellent discussion of the stages of Trescott's moral journey.

Nan Goodman's expertly informed examination, "The Law of the Good Samaritan: Cross-Racial Rescue in Stephen Crane and Charles Chesnutt," not only explores race and morality in *The Monster* but also deals with legal issues having to do with a "duty" to rescue and the standing of the "law" of the Good Samaritan in Crane's day and in ours. Goodman opens the way for multiple research opportunities.

And there have been excellent studies recovering the autobiographical triggers that inspired Crane's *The Monster* and clarifying the setting and culture of fin de siècle American life. On the first point, Elaine Marshall conjectures about Crane's familiarity with the 1892 lynching of the black man Robert Lewis in Port Jervis, which may have been the germ of his story. For a more recent discussion of the lynching and its supposed impact on Crane, see Jean M. Lutes. On the second point, Jonathan Tadashi Naito explores Crane's fascination with electric streetlights as a measure of his awareness of advancing technology. We may recall, for instance, Crane's description in chapter 3 of *The Monster*: "The shimmering blue of the electric arc-lamps was strong in the main street of the town. At numerous points it was conquered by the orange gale of the outnumbering gas-lights in the windows of the shops." The narrator then continues his comments by describing "the shrill electric street car" (*Stephen Crane: Prose and Poetry* 395), which is, of course, in sharp contrast to Dr. Trescott's choice of horse-drawn transportation. Then, too, after the fire breaks out in the Trescott home, the fire companies use human power and ropes to bring the pumps and fire hoses to the scene of the tragedy. Citizens, even in a small upstate New York village, must face advancing technology. (For related essays on Crane's depiction of late nineteenth-century American society in flux, see Robert A. Morace's examination of games, play, and entertainments, as well as the sections of Bill Brown's book that deal with material and popular culture, including references to photography in *The Monster*.)

Clearly, Crane uses *The Monster* to pose important questions regarding race, morality, law, and technology in turn-of-the-last-century America. Furthermore, it is a novella of astonishing stylistic and literary sophistication. Here, then, is a work that is finally being rightly placed in the select company of Crane's best works. As such, it commands the close attention of Crane commentators.

Poetry

A full-length analysis of Crane's poetry waited until Daniel Hoffman's *The Poetry of Stephen Crane* was published in 1957; his monograph was so comprehensive and convincing that there seemed to be little left to do beyond filling in minor lacunae and registering quibbles with some of his Freudian interpretations of the impact that the Crane family's religious predilections had had upon him. Volume 10 of Bowers's Virginia edition, *Poems and Literary Remains*, appearing in 1975, became the standard resource along with Andrew T. Crosland's compilation, *A Concordance of the Complete Poetry of Stephen Crane*, which is keyed to the Virginia edition. Crosland's volume provides scholars with useful word counts and frequency lists.

The long shadow cast by Hoffman's insightful analyses has remained a fixture of the Crane literary landscape. That is not to say that nothing more has been said or that there is nothing more that deserves scholarly attention in Crane's verses. It should be added that a dozen and a half of Crane's poems, including "A flagon of despair," were not reprinted by Levenson and have thereby been generally ignored. Moreover, in the five decades since Hoffman's study appeared, several different critical strategies have emerged that may be profitably applied to Crane's poetry by the current cohort of scholars who will bring their own responses and insights to bear.

For those so inclined, good places to begin a project are Colvert's fine introduction to *Poems and Literary Remains* and Judith P. Saunders's helpful examination of the general themes Crane explored and the artistic strategies that he employed. Hoffman's essay "Many Red Devils upon the Page: The Poetry of Stephen Crane," wherein he skillfully reprises his *The Poetry of Stephen Crane* volume, should not be missed. Then, too, those interested will have easy access to the best commentaries on Crane's poetry, collected in volume 80 of Thomson Gale's *Poetry Criticism*, published in 2008. Project editor Michelle Lee compiled seventy-eight pages of criticism, both essays and book chapters, published between 1943 (David H.

Dickason's "Stephen Crane and *The Philistine*") and 1997 (Keith Gandal's "A Spiritual Autopsy of Stephen Crane").

Lee chose eleven representative and influential essays. Beyond examining the breakthrough style, unusual themes, and novel poetics of Crane's verse, two of the essays she reprints also explore the ways in which Crane's poetry sheds light on key biographical elements, especially his rebellious lifestyle and Bohemianism (John Blair and Gandal) and his philosophical outlook. As noted earlier, Crane was fond of calling his poems "pills." In light of this, I ("[Stephen Crane] Philosopher-Poet") examine Crane's stanzas as mini-syllogisms of argumentation in his explication of most of the poems from *War is Kind* (1899) and *The Black Riders* (1895), plus a number of his uncollected poems, notably "Blue Battalions" (1898) and "A man adrift on a slim spar" (1929).

Scholars may revisit Crane's poetry on its own terms, but there are also interesting lines of influence to be traced: from Edgar Allan Poe (1809–49); Samuel Taylor Coleridge (1772–1834); Alfred, Lord Tennyson (1809–92); and John Bunyan (1628–88) to Crane and from Crane to Robinson Jeffers (1887–1962) and perhaps Kenneth Rexroth (1905–82).

War Journalism and Stories

Red Badge looms so large that the critical commentary on it long ago surpassed the cottage-industry state. As a result, most of Crane's remaining war-related works have been pretty much shunted aside. Scholars interested in these lacunae are encouraged to begin with William Crisman's wonderfully comprehensive survey of Crane's war journalism/fiction. Crisman explores the self-reflexive and self-referential paradoxes involved in Crane's journalism: "Journalists or journalism becomes the objects of fiction . . . the craft of reporting itself, rendering the event into language, gains center attention" (207). Moving through his analysis, Crisman places Crane's journalism in wider and wider contexts—the wars themselves, the political agendas, and the social milieu of the day—and eventually, for Crane, the most fundamental context, the meaning of human life and the nature of language. Also essential is Robertson's 1999 essay, "Stephen Crane's *Other* War Masterpiece," in which he convincingly argues that Crane wrote *two* war masterpieces, "War Memories" (1899) and *Red Badge*. The former resists easy categorization because of its novella-like length, its straddling journalistic reportage and fiction, and its innovative stylistic experiments. Robertson's "War Memories" essay provides scholars with strategies to reexamine Crane's Greco-Turkish War stories/dispatches, "Crane at Velestino" and "Death and the Child," and his Spanish-American War stories, "The Price of the Harness" (1900) and "The Clan of No-Name" (1899). Of Crane's Civil War stories, "Three Miraculous Soldiers"

(1897) and "The Little Regiment" have been especially neglected. Among his Spanish-American War dispatches, "Stephen Crane at the Front for the *World*" (1898), "Stephen Crane's Vivid Story of the Battle of San Juan" (1898), and "Regulars Get No Glory" (1898) have been little noticed. And except for his very late gem "The Upturned Face" (1900), his other significant Spitsbergen tales—"The Kicking Twelfth" (1900), "The Shrapnel of Their Friends" (1900), and "And If He Will, We Must Die" (1900)—have been passed over. Also, given Crane's lifelong fascination with courage and cowardice, there is much interesting work to be done in tracking these themes throughout all of his tales, journalism, and poetry.

Sibling Rivalries: Bowery Tales and Western Stories

Maggie: A Girl of the Streets has benefited from a good deal of close examination and expert scrutiny while attention to *George's Mother* (1896) has languished. Monteiro's insightful biography, *Stephen Crane: Blue Badge of Courage*, with its notable insights into the temperance writings of Crane's father (especially his *Arts of Intoxication* [1890]), Francis Willard's *Women and Temperance* (1883), and the Woman's Christian Temperance Union (WCTU) activities of Crane's mother, has done much to underscore the view that the interpretive key to *George's Mother* is to be found in Crane's original title, "Woman Without Weapons." Beyond clarifying Crane's second-best Bowery Tales, his comments (in "The Drunkard's Progress") offer helpful interpretive leads to a number of Crane's New York City sketches published between 1892 and 1894, including a dozen pieces (from volume 8 of the Virginia edition, *Tales, Sketches, and Reports*) that are not reprinted in Levenson's Library of America volume, notably "A Lovely Jag in a Crowded Car" and three of Crane's Tenderloin sketches.

Similarly, while "The Blue Hotel" (1896) has received the lion's share of scholars' attention, Crane's other great western tale, "The Bride Comes to Yellow Sky" (1898), has been relegated to also-ran status, although there have been some interesting examinations of the parodic humor embedded in the elaborate social rituals adhered to by Jack Potter, his bride, and Scratchy Wilson. And, Crane's awareness of advancing technology is eloquently expressed in the stage-setting opening paragraph of "The Bride Comes to Yellow Sky": "The great Pullman was whirling onward with such dignity of motion that a glance from the window seemed to prove that the plains of Texas were pouring east-ward" (*Stephen Crane: Prose and Poetry* 787). Then too, Crane's first few sentences neatly reprise the closing of the frontier and the effort in the dime-novel western, at least imaginatively and nostalgically, to keep it open. These themes may help scholars to explicate "A Man and Some Others" (1897) and "Moonlight on the Snow" (1900). In a word, there are attractive scholarly projects not only in *George's Mother* and "The Bride Comes to Yellow Sky" but also in a number of Crane's New York City tales and several of his western stories (including nine tales from volume 8 of the Virginia edition that were not reprinted by Levenson).

Crane's Social Commentary Pieces

To appreciate the cultural work of Crane's novels and stories, we must include his artful and powerful pieces of social criticism. "An Experiment in Misery" and "An Experiment in Luxury," when examined in tandem, reveal interesting twists in Crane's outlook; likewise, his pair of urban vignettes, "The Broken-Down Van" (1892) and "When a Man Falls" (1894), should be examined together. Though Crane faithfully adhered to his maxim "preaching is fatal to art," his skill at social commentary and dexterity at condemnation by indirection are unmatched. His exposés of the impact of the injustice and greed that the haves visit upon the have-nots and the indifference of nature vis-à-vis both groups provide narrative momentum for "Nebraska's Bitter Fight for Life" (1895), "In the Depths of a Coal Mine," and my "The Mexican Lower Classes" (1895). Crane has a half-dozen other Mexican travel pieces that are generally skipped over—see my "Crane's Sociological Savvy: An Examination of His Mexican Travel Dispatches" for a useful avenue of exegesis of Crane's Mexican tales.

Cultural Work in Crane's Potboilers

Only a handful of enthusiasts celebrate the virtues of *The Third Violet* (1896) and *Active Service* (1899); see especially Lillian Gilkes and Gullason ("The Jamesian Motif"). Fewer yet are fans of *The O'Ruddy* (see Gilkes and Joan H. Baum). Yet all three of his less-than-successful experimental narratives may be mined for the social and cultural information embedded in them. So even as they had to put aside their reservations about the artistic merits of *Active Service*, Robertson ("Cultural Work") explores Crane's awareness of the decline of the genteel Victorian tradition, D. A. Boxwell stresses Crane's awareness of stereotypes fueled by mass culture, and Andrew J. Furer connects Crane's commentary on the strenuous life with the fitness regimens championed by William James (1842–1910) and Theodore Roosevelt (1858–1919).

Deserving special mention is Charlotte Rich's fine explication of Crane's wrestle with the new woman in *Active Service*. Rich's fine essay breaks new ground on the topic of women in Crane and should lead the way to a consideration of the other women in Crane's fiction: Mrs. Kelsey as an example of the old woman in *George's Mother*; Mrs. Scully as a traditional wife and mother in "The Blue Hotel"; and Maggie as a defeated new woman, especially in contrast to Nell, "a woman of brilliance and audacity" (*Stephen Crane: Prose and Poetry* 59). Farther afield among the women characters depicted in Crane's early and middle New York City tales, the daughter caregiver in his poignant 1900 story, "A Desertion," merits scrutiny from the perspective of feminist theory. As for *The Third Violet*, the takeoff essays are by Campbell, who argues that Crane's attempt at a novel of manners is replete with turn-of-the-last-century social and cultural information, and Sorrentino ("Stephen Crane's Struggle"), who sees the work as a critique of the popular fiction of many of Crane's contemporaries.

Similarly, the child-centered *Tales of Whilomville* (1899–1900; that is, those tales beyond *The Monster* and the three Watermelon Alley tales noted earlier) has not been given much attention, yet it offers a clear (even if romanticized) glimpse of the worlds of children and village life in small-town America. Levenson suggests in his introduction to *The Tales of Whilomville* that the value of these sometime-saccharine stories can be traced beyond the cultural insight that these stories offer to Crane's unique realism, which does not aim at a direct rendering of observed objects, but instead offers a penetrating entrée into another's world, especially the lived experiences of young people. Incidentally, in his Library of America volume, Levenson bypassed three stories, "Making an Orator" (1899), "The Stove" (1900), and "The Little Pilgrim" (1900), which, in terms of the lived experience of children, are as valuable as the eleven he included in his reprinting.

More generally, there are especially exciting and challenging opportunities throughout Crane's works to gain insights with respect to literature and painting. Nagel, in his well-received and influential study, *Stephen Crane and Literary Impressionism*, argues that impressionistic art provides access to crucial and overlooked elements in Crane's fictive world. Nagel explains that "the characters in Impressionistic fiction are constantly in a state of having to interpret the world around them and to distinguish the 'real' from their own views of it ... [because of] the ineluctable flux in human perceptions of even the most stable object ... reality is a matter of perception; it is unstable, ever changing, elusive and inscrutable" (12, 13, 22). A half-dozen years later, inspired, one supposes, by Nagel, Michael Fried ventured into the same painting/literature interface with his examination of consonances between Crane and Thomas Eakins (1844–1916). And in 2009, John Fagg's *On the Cusp: Stephen Crane, George Bellows, and Modernism*, offers Crane scholars an informative, full-length, and detailed comparison of Crane's narrative art and the pictorial worlds of American realist George Bellows (1882–1925) and to a lesser extent those of John Sloan (1871–1951) and Edward Hopper (1882–1967). Fagg's investigation of the impact of modernity reveals that Crane and Bellows shared many formal artistic characteristics, notably Crane's fondness for episodes and

Bellows's partiality for small, human-interest vignettes. Fagg's convincing diagrams illustrate how both artists frame and structure their sketches. Fagg is explicit about the premise of his study when he explains that his "interdisciplinary approach is not designed to draw out direct comparisons of oppositions between writing and painting, but works instead to show similar shifts in perspective and formal practice occurring across different disciplines, and thus, by implication, across the wider culture" (4–5). Fagg's monograph, then, provides multiple insightful analyses that can lead to promising research programs for twenty-first-century scholars.

It is striking that while Nagel extols the benefits of seeing Crane through an impressionistic lens, Fried and Fagg see Crane responding to the artistic tendencies of realism and naturalism. The important point for future scholars to notice, however, is that careful attention to painterly themes and techniques may disclose unnoticed contours on both sides of the word/pigment artistic divide. Undoubtedly, there is much to be gained in the conversation between Crane and his fellow American painters.

Special Collections and Library Holdings

The most important resources for Crane study are at Syracuse University, Columbia University, and the University of Virginia. As already mentioned, the unfinished Schoberlin biography of Crane, as well as the Schoberlin Collection, is at Syracuse. Furthermore, Edward Lyon's essay "The Stephen Crane Collection at Syracuse University" describes the letters (the majority of which were published in *Stephen Crane's Love Letters to Nellie Crouse*, edited by Cady and Wells), manuscripts, inscriptions and annotations, photographs, and books from Crane's library. In addition to these Crane items, the Syracuse holdings include items and reminiscences by Crane's class and baseball teammate, Mansfield French (1872–1953); Corwin Linson's memoir, *My Stephen Crane*; and important items from his great uncle, Methodist Episcopal Bishop Jesse Truesdale Peck (1811–83); his uncle George Myers Peck (1820–97); and some of the writings of Crane's father, Jonathan Townley Crane (1819–80).

Columbia University has numerous Crane holographs and typed manuscripts and related memorabilia. See Baum, *Stephen Crane (1871–1900): An Exhibition of His Writings Held in the Columbia University Libraries, September 17–November 30, 1956*, along with Roland Baughman and Lewis Leary. Herbert Cahoon's *A Brief Account of the Clifton Waller Barrett Library* describes the University of Virginia rare book archives, housing Linson's wonderful oil portrait of Crane and "the largest group of his notebooks, scrapbooks and letters ever brought together," not to mention the whole holograph manuscript of *Red Badge*, "with the discarded version of the novel on the verso of the pages on which the final version was written"

(1). Virginia also holds *The Notebooks of Stephen Crane*, edited by Donald J. and Ellen B. Greiner.

Noteworthy items may also be found in Dartmouth College's George Mather Adams collection (see *A Stephen Crane Collection* by Herbert Faulkner West) and at the University of South Carolina in its Matthew Bruccoli Collection (see Bruccoli). For an account of Crane items in the New York Public Library's Berg Collection, see John D. Gordan.

Finally, a smattering of heretofore-undiscovered Crane letters and manuscripts continue to surface. The letters are generally described and published in *Stephen Crane Studies*. When manuscripts are found that were not included in the Virginia critical edition, the usual routine is to call upon Sorrentino to prepare a history and analysis of the newly located text. His subsequent essays feature the full-dress critical apparatus that records all substantive and accidental variants and also all editorial emendations, which are recorded in the "Copy-Text and Historical Collations" section of his articles. These rediscovered manuscripts are usually published in *Studies in Bibliography* (see Sorrentino, " 'This Majestic Lie,' " " 'An Episode of War,' " and " 'The Devil's Acre' ").

Bibliographies

In 1972, Stallman released a nearly 700-page and purportedly definitive volume, *Stephen Crane: A Critical Bibliography*. Unfortunately, but predictably, he resisted few opportunities to celebrate his own discovery of unattributed Crane pieces and regularly privileged his literary interpretations (and he often denigrated the commentary of other scholars). As a result, this potentially valuable book was infected by an edgy polemic that stirred up nasty commentary, generating as much heat as light and leading to feuds instead of helpful conversation among the cohort of Crane commentators. My 1992 *Stephen Crane: An Annotated Bibliography of Secondary Scholarship* has been updated in articles in the 1999 special issue of *War, Literature and the Arts* and in essays in *Stephen Crane Studies*. Most recently, a bibliography confined to *Red Badge*, for *EBSCOhost*, was edited by Eric Carl Link and published by Salem Press (*"Red Badge": Critical Insights*).

In conclusion, despite—indeed, because of—the rich body of secondary commentary on Stephen Crane, multiple intriguing research projects await attentive readers of the astounding prose, poetry, and journalism of this penetrating thinker, perceptive observer, and precocious stylist. While casual, first-time readers continue to be startled by the power of *Red Badge*, Crane aficionados have always been aware of so much to be appreciated in his works. Crane never was a one-hit wonder, but now the whole corpus of his works is increasingly scrutinized, especially *The Monster*, his *two* Bowery novels, and his New York City and western tales and sketches. Above all, perhaps, the synergy that results from a tandem reading of his journalism and his fiction will launch the next wave of intense interest in Crane. Multiple opportunities await; it will be fascinating to see the insights on Crane, and on American literature and culture generally, that will emerge.

NOTES

1. Quotations from Crane's works will be taken from J. C. Levenson's Library of America reprinting, *Stephen Crane: Prose and Poetry*, with page numbers cited in parentheses.

2. It is striking that these late twentieth-century debunkers of Beer are, in effect, underscoring (and making more emphatic) many of the contentions of an essay that Ernest Boyd published just one year after Beer's *Stephen Crane* appeared. Boyd argues that Beer fabricated key items in his narrative, and he shows how Beer's own personality is indelibly stamped on his portrait of Crane.

Readers should note that after Clendenning rehearses the extent to which Beer's biography has been thoroughly discredited, he concedes, "to his credit Beer should be remembered as the first to move Crane from the periphery into the center of American literature ... [Beer] in effect, rescued Crane—saved him from neglect, scandal, and misunderstanding" ("Stephen Crane and His Biographers" 29). Perhaps Clendenning's suggestion should be extended, though such a recommendation may well be regarded as heretical by many mainline Craneans. Beer's biographical inventions notwithstanding, his grasp of the nuances, techniques, and subtleties of Crane's innovative and unrepeatable style and his skillful articulation of the general themes and problematics of Crane's artistic project remain invaluable. A reconsideration of Beer's understanding and appreciation of Crane's *writings* is long overdue; hence, Craneans need to revisit his *Stephen Crane: A Study in American Letters* and his impressionistic cultural history, *The Mauve Decade: American Life at the End of the Nineteenth-Century*, as well as his introduction to the Follett edition of *The O'Ruddy* (first published in 1903), his "Fire Feathers" (which has the best critical commentary on the Follett edition project), "Mrs. Stephen Crane," and "Stephen, Henry and the Hat." Additionally, Beer investigators will want to survey the Beer Family Papers in the Yale University Archives.

3. The biographies by Benfey, Monteiro, and Davis propose tantalizing, if thesis-driven, explications of Crane's life and works. The first two used the wealth of findings in the Wertheim-Sorrentino ur-biographies, and they have maintained high standards of historical research; Davis's interesting and informative book falls somewhat short on both counts.

The thesis of Benfey's fascinating and seminal biography, *The Double Life of Stephen Crane*, is that the secret to understanding Crane is to notice that he first imagined events and then lived in search of verification or correction of his hypotheses: " . . . the shape of Crane's career has a peculiar fascination for the biographer. If most writers tend to write about their experience, however disguised, Crane did the reverse; he tried to live what he'd already written. . . . For Crane lived his life backwards, or rather he wrote it forwards" (10). Monteiro's *Stephen Crane's Blue Badge of Courage* offers a familiar pair of familial imperatives—the social outreach impulses of his father's sermons and the rhetoric of his mother's temperance movement speeches—as the mooring anchors of Crane's life and work.

In her 1995 *American Scholar* article "The Red Room: Stephen Crane and Me," Davis explains that her lifelong obsession with Crane may be traced to events in her own life and her reading Crane's *The Monster*. In 1998, her *Badge of Courage: The Life of Stephen Crane*, aimed at a general audience, was published.

Scholars who intend to use any of these Crane biographies as jumping-off points for critical and exegetical commentary need to keep in mind the wide range of audiences and the considerable variance of standards in Crane biographies. As a case in point, James Hynes praises Davis's book in his review for the *American Scholar*: "[T]his brisk and authoritative biography of Crane . . . gives us not only a complete and engaging account of Crane's brief life, but also a compelling invitation to reread his works" (146). Overall, however, respected Crane scholars have been less enthusiastic. James Nagel's review of her book for *Stephen Crane Studies* is generally condemnatory. He charges that, "as a work of serious scholarship, *Badge of Courage* is guilty of the most egregious and elementary of errors of judgment: Davis continually makes assertions that are not substantiated by the evidence and, often, cannot be known" (22). In Nagel's view, Davis's biography belongs among the other discredited volumes on Crane's life, and so it should be shelved alongside Beer's "biography."

Pace Nagel, to what extent should we consider Beer's *Stephen Crane: A Study in American Letters* and Davis's *Badge of Courage: The Life of Stephen Crane* "biographies"? Both authors (Beer much more so) have a somewhat elastic regard for scholarly standards of evidence and necessary documentation, and both (again Beer much more so) are sometimes cavalier about basic facts. Still, it must be acknowledged that both of these "biographies" made a substantial impact upon Crane scholarship insofar as they vividly captured important elements of Crane's life (and persona) and piqued new interest in his works.

4. Schoberlin worked for over a dozen years (with a hiatus of three years while he was on active duty in the Navy at the Pacific front during World War II) on a biography of Crane. His working title was "Flagon of Despair," and he expected that it would become his doctoral dissertation at Johns Hopkins University. Clendenning notes that " 'Flagon of Despair' is an odd mixture of valuable information, blunders, fictitious romantic extravagance, and wild speculation" ("Stephen Crane and His Biographers" 42). Schoberlin was also an avid collector of Crane manuscripts, editions, pictures, and letters, and he interviewed many people connected with Crane. Schoberlin abandoned the project about 1950; Bowers, then at work on the Crane Virginia edition in the mid-1960s and 1970s, encouraged him to finish his biography. He never did—his collection and the nearly 200,000-word manuscript of "Flagon" are in Syracuse University's George Arents Research Library for Special Collections. When Colvert was working on his biography (*Stephen Crane*), he made a careful study of the Schoberlin material collection. See his 1986 essay, "Searching for Stephen Crane: The Schoberlin Collection." The collection is so extensive and important that any scholar interested in systematically and patiently investigating this archival trove will have ample material for a master's thesis, perhaps even for a PhD dissertation.

5. Beyond the persistent pedagogical interest in *Red Badge*, recently more attention has been paid to the teaching of Crane's other works, especially his short fiction. Consult the special fall 2007 issue of *Eureka Studies in Teaching Short Fiction*, which devotes five essays to teaching Crane: "The Open Boat" (Hal Blythe and Charlie Sweet), "The Pace of Youth" (1895; Charles W. Mayer), "The Bride Comes to Yellow Sky" (1898; Stephen B. Tietz and John J. Stinson), "The Blue Hotel" (1896; Meredith Farmer), and *The Monster* (Jacqueline Wilson-Jordan). This special issue also contains Gerald Stacy's survey of the patterns of style in Crane's short stories. Stacy's essay and Nagel's 1999 analysis of Crane's place in the American short-story cycle tradition ("The American Short-Story Cycle") offer valuable approaches and innovative pedagogical strategies regarding his works.

WORKS CITED

Allen, Frederic Lewis. "The Agent and an Author: Stephen Crane." *Paul Revere Reynolds*. New York: Privately printed, 1944. 48–60. Print.

Bacheller, Irving. "The High-Brow Decade." *Coming Up the Road*. Indianapolis: Bobbs-Merrill, 1928. 267–316. Print.

Banks, Nancy Huston. "The Novels of Two Journalists." *The Bookman* Nov. 1985: 217–20. Rpt. in Weatherford 96–98. Print.

Bates, H. E. "Stephen Crane: A Neglected Genius." *The Bookman* Oct. 1931: 10–11. Print.

Baughman, Roland. *Manuscript Collection in the Columbia University Library.* New York: Columbia UP, 1959. Print.
Baum, Joan H. *Stephen Crane (1891–1900): An Exhibition of His Writings Held in the Columbia University Libraries, September 17–November 30, 1956.* New York: Columbia UP, 1956. Print.
Beer Family Papers. Manuscripts and Archives, Yale U Lib., New Haven.
Beer, Thomas. "Fire Feathers." *Saturday Review of Literature* Dec. 19, 1925: 425–27. Print.
———. Introduction. *The O'Ruddy.* Vols. 7 and 8 of *The Work of Stephen Crane.* Ed. Wilson Follett. New York: Knopf, 1926. 7: ix–xv. Print.
———. *The Mauve Decade: American Life at the End of the Nineteenth-Century.* New York: Knopf, 1926. Print.
———. "Mrs. Stephen Crane." *American Mercury* Mar. 1934: 289–95. Print.
———. *Stephen Crane: A Study in American Letters.* New York: Knopf, 1923. Print.
———. "Stephen, Henry and the Hat." *Vanity Fair* Aug. 1922: 63, 88. Print.
Benfey, Christopher. *The Double Life of Stephen Crane.* New York: Knopf, 1992. Print.
Berryman, John. *Stephen Crane.* New York: Sloane, 1950. Print.
Binder, Henry, ed. *The Red Badge of Courage: An Episode of the Civil War.* New York: Norton, 1982. Print.
———. "*The Red Badge of Courage* Nobody Knows: Expanded Version." *"The Red Badge of Courage" by Stephen Crane.* Ed. Henry Binder. New York: Norton, 1982. 111–58. Print.
Blair, John. "The Posture of the Bohemian in the Poetry of Stephen Crane." *American Literature* 61.2 (1989): 215–29. Print.
Blythe, Hal, and Charlie Sweet. "Understanding the Method of Narration in 'The Open Boat.'" *Eureka Studies in Teaching Short Fiction* 8.1 (2007): 6–14. Print.
Bowers, Fredson. "Foreword." *Bowery Tales.* Vol. 1 of *The Works of Stephen Crane.* Ed. Fredson Bowers. Charlottesville: UP of Virginia, 1969. vii–ix. Print.
Boxwell, D. A. "'Whipping the Turks': Stephen Crane's Orientalism." *American Literary Realism* 31.1 (1998): 1–11. Print.
Boyd, Ernest. "Thomas Beer." *Portraits: Real and Imaginary.* New York: Doran, 1924. 208–16. Print.
Bragdon, Claude. "The Purple Cow Period." *Merely Players.* New York: Knopf, 1905. 61–70. Print.
Brown, Bill. *The Material Unconscious: American Amusement, Stephen Crane, and the Economies of Play.* Cambridge, MA: Harvard UP, 1997. Print.
Brown, Curtis. "Some Old Press Men." *Contacts.* New York: Harper, 1935. 254–80. Print.
Bruccoli, Matthew J. "Stephen Crane, 1871–1971: An Exhibition from the Collection of Matthew J. Broccoli." *Bibliographical Series of the University of South Carolina* 6 (1971): 1–19. Print.
Budd, Louis J. Personal communication. July 1999.
Cady, Edwin. Introduction. *Tales, Sketches and Reports.* Vol. 8 of *The Works of Stephen Crane.* Ed. Fredson Bowers. Charlottesville: UP of Virginia, 1973. xxi–xli. Print.
Cahoon, Herbert. *A Brief Account of the Clifton Waller Barrett Library.* Charlottesville: UP of Virginia, 1960. Print.
Campbell, Donna M. "More than a Family Resemblance? Agnes Crane's 'Victorious Defeat' and Stephen Crane's *The Third Violet.*" *Stephen Crane Studies* 16.1 (2007): 14–24. Print.
Chamberlin, Ralph. "Lafayette's Most Notorious Flunk-Out." *Lafayette Alumnus* Feb. 1961: 16–17, 27. Print.
Chandler, George. "I Knew Stephen Crane at Syracuse." *Syracuse University Library Associates Courier* 3.1 (1963): 12–13. Print.
Cleman, John. "Blunders of Virtue: The Problem of Race in Stephen Crane's 'The Monster.'" *American Literary Realism* 34.2 (2002): 119–34. Print.

Clendenning, John. "Stephen Crane and His Biographers: Beer, Berryman, Schoberlin and Stallman." *American Literary Realism* 28.1 (1995): 23–57. Print.

———. "Thomas Beer's *Stephen Crane:* The Eye of His Imagination." *Prose Studies* 14.1 (1991): 68–80. Print.

Colvert, James. Introduction. *Poems and Literary Remains.* Vol. 10 of *The Works of Stephen Crane.* Ed. Fredson Bowers. Charlottesville: UP of Virginia, 1975. xvii–xxix. Print.

———. "Searching for Stephen Crane: The Schoberlin Collection." *Syracuse University Library Associates Courier* 21.1 (1986): 5–34. Print.

———. *Stephen Crane.* New York: Harcourt, 1984. Print.

Conrad, Jesse. "Recollections of Stephen Crane." *The Bookman* Apr. 1926: 134–37. Print.

Conrad, Joseph. Introduction. Beer, *Stephen Crane* 1–33. Print.

Crane, Mrs. George. [Crane's sister-in-law]. "Stephen Crane's Boyhood." *New York World* June 10, 1900: E3. Print.

Crane, Helen R. "My Uncle, Stephen Crane." *American Mercury* Jan. 1934: 24–29. Print.

Crane, Rev. J. T. [Crane's father]. *Arts of Intoxication: The Aim, and the Results.* New York: Carlton & Lanahan, 1890. Print.

Crane, Robert K. "Family Matters: Stephen Crane's Brother Wilbur." *Stephen Crane Studies* 3.2 (1994): 13–18. Print.

———. "Stephen Crane's Family Heritage." *Stephen Crane Studies* 4.1 (1995): 1–47. Print.

Crane, Stephen. *The Complete Novels of Stephen Crane.* Ed. Thomas A. Gullason. Garden City: Doubleday, 1967. Print.

———. *The Complete Short Stories and Sketches of Stephen Crane.* Ed. Thomas A. Gullason. Garden City: Doubleday, 1963. Print.

———. *The Correspondence of Stephen Crane.* Ed. Stanley Wertheim and Paul Sorrentino. 2 vols. New York: Columbia UP, 1988. Print.

———. *The New York City Sketches of Stephen Crane and Related Pieces.* Ed. Robert W. Stallman and E. R. Hagemann. New York: New York UP, 1966. Print.

———. *The Notebooks of Stephen Crane.* Ed. Donald J. Greiner and Ellen B. Greiner. Charlottesville: Bibliographical Soc. of the U of Virginia, 1967. Print.

———. *The Red Badge of Courage; an Episode of the American Civil War.* New York: Appleton, 1895. Print.

———. *Stephen Crane: Prose and Poetry.* Ed. J. C. Levenson. New York: Lib. of America, 1984. Print.

———. *Stephen Crane's Love Letters to Nellie Crouse.* Ed. Edwin H. Cady and Lester G. Wells. Syracuse: Syracuse UP, 1954. Print.

———. *Stephen Crane's Novel of the Civil War: "The Red Badge of Courage": A Historically Annotated Edition.* Ed. Charles LaRocca. Fleischmanns, NY: Purple Mountain, 1995. Print.

———. *Stephen Crane: Uncollected Writings.* Ed. Olov W. Fryckstedt. Uppsala, Sweden: Studia Anglistica Upsaliensia, 1963. Print.

———. *The Work of Stephen Crane.* Ed. Wilson Follett. 12 vols. New York: Knopf, 1925–27. Print.

———. *The Works of Stephen Crane.* Ed. Fredson Bowers. 10 vols. Charlottesville: UP of Virginia, 1969–76. Print.

Crisman, William. " 'Distributing the News': War Journalism as Metaphor for Language in Stephen Crane's Fiction." *Studies in American Fiction* 30.2 (2002): 207–27. Print.

Crosland, Andrew T. *A Concordance to the Complete Poetry of Stephen Crane.* Detroit: Gale, 1975. Print.

Davis, Linda. *Badge of Courage: The Life of Stephen Crane.* Boston: Houghton, 1998. Print.

———. "The Red Room: Stephen Crane and Me." *American Scholar* 64.2 (1995): 207–20. Print.

Dell, Floyd. "Stephen Crane and the Genius Myth." *The Nation* Dec. 10, 1924: 637–38. Print.

Derrick, Scott. "Behind the Lines: Homoerotic Anxiety and the Heroic in Stephen Crane's *The Red Badge of Courage*." *Monumental Anxieties: Homoerotic Desire and Feminine Influence in Nineteenth-Century U.S. Literature*. New Brunswick: Rutgers UP, 1997. 170–90. Print.

Dickason, David H. "Stephen Crane and *The Philistine*." *American Literature* 15.3 (1943): 279–87. Print.

Dooley, Patrick K. "Crane's Sociological Savvy: An Examination of His Mexican Travel Dispatches." *Stephen Crane Studies* 11.2 (2002): 2–10. Print.

———. "Openness to Experience in Stephen Crane's 'In the Depths of a Coal Mine.'" *Caverns of Night: Coal Mines in Art, Literature, and Film*. Ed. William B. Thesing. Columbia: U of South Carolina P, 2000. 186–98. Print.

———. *The Pluralistic Philosophy of Stephen Crane*. Urbana: U of Illinois P, 1993. Print.

———. "*The Red Badge of Courage*: Criticism and Commentary." Link 39–73. Print.

———. *Stephen Crane: An Annotated Bibliography of Secondary Scholarship*. New York: Hall, 1992. Print.

———. "Stephen Crane: An Annotated Bibliography of Secondary Scholarship: An Update." "Stephen Crane in War and Peace." Spec. issue of *War, Literature and the Arts* (1999): 250–98. Print.

———. "Stephen Crane: An Annotated Bibliography of Secondary Scholarship: Book Chapters through 1997 [Updates]." *Stephen Crane Studies* 8.2 (1999): 13–27; 10.2 (2001): 12–34; 12.2 (2003): 2–19; 14.2 (2005): 10–23; 18.1 (2009): 10–29. Print.

———. "[Stephen Crane] Philosopher-Poet." Lee 71–93. Print.

Dudley, John. "'Subtle Brotherhood' in Stephen Crane's *Tales of Adventure*: Alienation, Anxiety, and the Rites of Manhood." *American Literary Realism* 34.2 (2002): 95–118. Print.

Eby, Cecil D. "The Source of Crane's Metaphor, 'Red Badge of Courage.'" *American Literature* 32.2 (1960): 204–7. Print.

Fagg, John. *On the Cusp: Stephen Crane, George Bellows, and Modernism*. Tuscaloosa: U of Alabama P, 2009. Print.

Farmer, Meredith. "'This Registers the Amount of Your Purchase': The Price of Expectation, the Force of Context." *Eureka Studies in Teaching Short Fiction* 8.1 (2007): 69–80. Print.

Faulkner, William. *The Unvanquished*. New York: Random, 1938. Print.

Follett, Wilson. "The Second Twenty-Eight Years: A Note on Stephen Crane, 1871–1900." *The Bookman* Jan. 1929: 532–37. Print.

Ford, Ford Madox. "Stephen Crane." *American Mercury* Jan. 1936: 36–45. Print.

French, Mansfield J. "Stephen Crane, Ball Player." *Syracuse University Alumni News* 15.4 (1934): 3–4. Print.

Fried, Michael. *Realism, Writing, Disfiguration: On Thomas Eakins and Stephen Crane*. Chicago: U of Chicago P, 1987. Print.

Furer, Andrew J. "'I fear the war business is getting rather tuckered': The Uses of War in Stephen Crane's *Active Service*." *American Literary Realism* 33.1 (2000): 21–32. Print.

Gandal, Keith. "A Spiritual Autopsy of Stephen Crane." *Nineteenth-Century Literature* 51.4 (1997): 500–530. Print.

Garland, Hamlin. "Stephen Crane As I Knew Him." *Yale Review* 3.3 (1914): 494–506. Print.

Gilkes, Lillian. "*The Third Violet, Active Service* and *The O'Ruddy*: Stephen Crane's Potboilers." *Stephen Crane in Transition: Centenary Essays*. Ed. Joseph Katz. DeKalb: Northern Illinois UP, 1972. 106–26. Print.

Gilkes, Lillian, and Joan H. Baum. "Stephen Crane's Last Novel: *The O'Ruddy*." *Columbia Library Columns* 6.2 (1957): 41–48. Print.

Goodman, Nan. "The Law of the Good Samaritan: Cross-Racial Rescue in Stephen Crane and Charles Chesnutt." *Shifting the Blame: Literature, Law, and the Theory of Accidents in Nineteenth-Century America*. Princeton: Princeton UP, 1998. 98–132. Print.

Gordan, John D. "Novels in Manuscript: An Exhibition from the Berg Collection." *Bulletin of the New York Public Library* 69.6 (1965): 317–29, 396–413. Print.
Gullason, Thomas A. "The Cranes at Pennington Seminary." *American Literature* 36.4 (1968): 530–41. Print.
———. "The Fiction of the Reverend Jonathan Townley Crane, D. D." *American Literature* 43.2 (1971): 263–73. Print.
———. "The Jamesian Motif in Stephen Crane's Last Novels." *The Personalist* 42.1 (1961): 77–84. Print.
———. "Stephen Crane at Claverack: A New Reading." *Syracuse University Library Associates Courier* 27.2 (1992): 33–46. Print.
———. "Stephen Crane at Lafayette College: New Perspectives." *Stephen Crane Studies* 3.2 (1994): 2–12. Print.
———. "Stephen Crane at Syracuse University: New Findings." *Syracuse University Library Associates Courier* 29 (1994): 127–40. Print.
———. "Stephen Crane's Sister: New Biographical Facts." *American Literature* 49.2 (1977): 234–38. Print.
Hiro, Molly. "How it Feels to Be without a Face: Race and Reorientation of Sympathy in the 1890s." *Novel* 39.2 (2006): 179–203. Print.
Hoffman, Daniel. "Many Red Devils upon the Page: The Poetry of Stephen Crane." *Sewanee Review* 102.4 (1994): 588–603. Print.
———. *The Poetry of Stephen Crane.* New York: Columbia UP, 1957.
Holton, Milne. *Cylinder of Vision: The Fiction and Journalistic Writings of Stephen Crane.* Baton Rouge: Louisiana State UP, 1972. Print.
Hubbard, Elbert. "Crane as a Genius." *Roycroft Quarterly* May 1, 1896: 16–26. Rpt. in Weatherford 75–80. Print.
Hynes, James. "A Most Alive Person." Rev. of *Badge of Courage: The Life of Stephen Crane*, by Linda Davis. *American Scholar* 67.4 (1998): 146–48. Print.
Johanningsmeier, Charles. "The 1894 Syndicated Newspaper Appearances of *The Red Badge of Courage*." *American Literary Realism* 40.3 (2008): 226–47. Print.
Johnson, Willis Fletcher. "The Launching of Stephen Crane." *Literary Digest International Book Review* Apr. 1926: 288–90. Print.
Jones, Claude E. "Stephen Crane at Syracuse." *American Literature* 7.1 (1935): 82–84. Print.
Katz, Joseph. "The Estate of Stephen Crane." *Studies in American Fiction* 10.2 (1982): 135–50. Print.
———, ed. *"The Red Badge of Courage" by Stephen Crane: A Facsimile Reproduction of the New York Press Appearance of December 9, 1894.* Gainesville: Scholars' Facsimiles and Reprints, 1967. 9–42. Print.
———. "Stephen Crane at Claverack College and Hudson River Institute." *Stephen Crane Newsletter* 2.4 (1968): 1–5. Print.
LaRocca, Charles. "Stephen Crane's Inspiration." *American Heritage* 42.3 (1991): 108–9. Print.
Lawrence, Frederic M. *The Real Stephen Crane.* Ed. Joseph Katz. Newark: Newark Public Lib., 1980. Print.
Lawson, Andrew. "The Red Badge of Class: Stephen Crane and the Industrial Army." *Literature and History* 14.2 (2005): 53–68. Print.
Leary, John Patrick. "America's Other Half: Slum Journalism and the War of 1898." *Journal of Transactional Studies* 1.1 (2009): 1–33. Print.
Leary, Lewis. Foreword. *Stephen Crane: An Exhibition.* New York: Columbia UP, 1956. 3–10. Print.
Lee, Michelle, ed. *Poetry Criticism: Excerpts from Criticism of the Works of the Most Significant and Widely Studied Poets of World Literature.* Vol. 80. Detroit: Gale, 2008. Print.

Lentz, Perry. *Private Fleming at Chancellorsville: "The Red Badge of Courage" and the Civil War.* Columbia: U of Missouri P, 2006. Print.

Levenson, J. C. Chronology. Stephen Crane, *Stephen Crane: Prose and Poetry.* 1353–58. Print.

———. Introduction. *Tales of Whilomville.* Vol. 7 of *The Works of Stephen Crane.* Ed. Fredson Bowers. Charlottesville: UP of Virginia, 1969. ix–lx. Print.

Link, Eric Carl, ed. *"The Red Badge of Courage": Critical Insights.* Pasadena: Salem, 2010. Print.

Linson, Corwin Knapp. *My Stephen Crane.* Ed. Edwin Cady. Syracuse: Syracuse UP, 1958. Print.

Lutes, Jean M. "Lynching Coverage and the American Reporter-Novelist." *American Literary History* 19.2 (2007): 456–81. Print.

Lyon, Edward. "The Stephen Crane Collection at Syracuse University." *Syracuse University Library Associates Courier* 21.1 (1986): 135–46. Print.

Marshall, Elaine. "Crane's 'The Monster' Seen in Light of Robert Lewis's Lynching." *Nineteenth-Century Literature* 51.2 (1996): 205–24. Print.

Martin, Thomas E. "Stephen Crane: Athlete and Author." *The Argot* (Syracuse U) 3.5 (1935): 1–2. Print.

Mayer, Charles W. " 'The Pace of Youth': Prelude to 'The Bride Comes to Yellow Sky.' " *Eureka Studies in Teaching Short Fiction* 8.1 (2007): 15–26. Print.

Mayfield, John. "S. C. at S. U." *Syracuse University Library Associates Courier* no. 29 (1968): 8. Print.

McMurray, Price. "Disabling Fictions: Race, History and Ideology in Crane's 'The Monster.' " *Studies in American Fiction* 26.1 (1998): 51–72. Print.

Mitchell, Lee Clark. "Face, Race, and Disfiguration in Stephen Crane's *The Monster.*" *Critical Inquiry* 17.1 (1990): 174–92. Print.

Mitchell, Verner D. "Reading 'Race' and 'Gender' in Crane's *The Red Badge of Courage.*" *CLA Journal* 40.1 (1996): 60–71. Print.

Monteiro, George. "Crane's 'Red Wafer' Again." *Stephen Crane Studies* 17.1 (2007): 13–15. Print.

———. "The Drunkard's Progress: Bowery Plot, Social Paradigm in Stephen Crane's *George's Mother.*" *Dionysos: The Journal of Literature and Addiction* 9.1 (1999): 5–16. Print.

———. *Stephen Crane's Blue Badge of Courage.* Baton Rouge: Louisiana State UP, 2000. Print.

Morace, Robert A. "Games, Play, and Entertainments in Stephen Crane's *The Monster.*" *Studies in American Fiction* 9.1 (1981): 65–81. Print.

Morgan, William M. "Between Conquest and Care: Masculinity and Community in Stephen Crane's *The Monster.*" *Arizona Quarterly* 56.3 (2000): 63–92. Print.

Morris, Roy. "On Whose Responsibility?: Historical Underpinnings of *The Red Badge of Courage.*" *Memory and Myth: The Civil War in Fiction and Film.* Ed. David Sachsman. Lafayette: Purdue UP, 2007. 137–50. Print.

Myers, Robert M. *Reluctant Expatriate: The Life of Harold Frederic.* Westport: Greenwood, 1995. Print.

———. " 'The Subtle Battle Brotherhood,' The Construction of Military Discipline in *The Red Badge of Courage.*" "Stephen Crane in War and Peace." Spec. issue of *War, Literature and the Arts* (1999): 128–41. Print.

Nagel, James. "The American Short-Story Cycle and Stephen Crane's *Tales of Whilomville.*" *American Literary Realism* 32.1 (1999): 35–42. Print.

———. Rev. of *Badge of Courage: The Life of Stephen Crane,* by Linda Davis. *Stephen Crane Studies* 13.1 (2004): 22–24. Print.

———. *Stephen Crane and Literary Impressionism.* University Park: Pennsylvania State UP, 1980. Print.

Naito, Jonathan Tadashi. "Cruel and Unusual Light: Electricity and Effacement in Stephen Crane's *The Monster.*" *Arizona Quarterly* 62.1 (2006): 35–63. Print.

Newlin, Keith. *Hamlin Garland: A Life.* Lincoln: U of Nebraska P, 2009. Print.

Newton, Adam Zachary. "Creating the Uncreated Features of His Face: Monstration in Crane, Melville, and Wright." *Narrative Ethics.* Cambridge, MA: Harvard UP, 1995. 175–239. Print.

Noxon, Frank W. "The Real Stephen Crane." *Step Ladder* 14.1 (1928): 4–9. Print.

O'Donnell, Thomas F. "John B. Van Patten: Stephen Crane's History Teacher." *American Literature* 27.2 (1955): 196–202. Print.

Peaslee, Clarence Loomis. "Stephen Crane's College Days." *Monthly Illustrator and Home and Country* Aug. 1896: 27–30. Print.

Pizer, Donald. "The Garland-Crane Relationship." *Huntington Library Quarterly* 24.1 (1960): 75–82. Print.

———. "What Unit Did Henry Belong to at Chancellorsville, and Does it Matter?" *Stephen Crane Studies* 16.1 (2007): 2–13. Print.

Pratt, Lyndon Upson. "The Formal Education of Stephen Crane." *American Literature* 10.4 (1939): 460–71. Print.

Pugh, Edwin. "Stephen Crane." *The Bookman* Dec. 1924: 162–64. Print.

Rich, Charlotte. "Nora Black and the New Woman in *Active Service.*" "Stephen Crane in War and Peace." Spec. issue of *War, Literature and the Arts* (1999): 223–35. Print.

Robertson, Michael. "The Cultural Work of *Active Service.*" *American Literary Realism* 28.2 (1996): 1–10. Print.

———. *Stephen Crane at Lafayette.* Easton, PA: Friends of the Skillman Lib. of Lafayette College, 1990. Print.

———. *Stephen Crane, Journalism, and the Making of Modern American Literature.* New York: Columbia UP, 1997. Print.

———. "Stephen Crane's *Other* War Masterpiece." "Stephen Crane in War and Peace." Spec. issue of *War, Literature and the Arts* (1999): 160–71. Print.

Robertson, Michael, David Holmes, and Roxanna Paez. "An Ironist at the Seashore: Possible Additions to the Crane Canon." *Stephen Crane Studies* 9.2 (2000): 1–33. Print.

Saunders, Judith P. "Stephen Crane: American Poetry at a Crossroads." *Teaching Nineteenth-Century American Poetry.* Ed. Paula Bernat Bennett, Karen L. Kilcup, and Philipp Schwieghauser. New York: MLA, 2007. 186–99. Print.

Schoberlin, Melvin. "A Flagon of Despair." MS. Unpublished biography of Stephen Crane. George Arents Research Lib. for Special Collections, Syracuse U, Syracuse.

Sidbury, Edna Crane. [Daughter of Crane's Brother William Howe Crane]. "My Uncle, Stephen Crane, as I Knew Him." *Literary Digest International Book Review* Mar. 1926: 248–50. Print.

Sloane, David E. E. "Stephen Crane at Lafayette." *Resources for American Literary Study* 2.1 (1972): 102–5. Print.

Solomon, Eric. "A Note on the Ford Madox Ford–Stephen Crane Connection." *Stephen Crane Studies* 16.1 (2007): 25–26. Print.

Sorrentino, Paul. "The Legacy of Thomas Beer in the Study of Stephen Crane and American Literary History." *American Literary Realism* 35.3 (2003): 187–211. Print.

———. "Nelson Green's Reminiscences of Stephen Crane." *Resources for American Literary Study* 24.1 (1998): 49–83. Print.

———. "New Evidence on Stephen Crane at Syracuse." *Resources for American Literary Study* 15.2 (1985): 179–85. Print.

———. "The Philistine Society's Banquet for Stephen Crane." *American Literary Realism* 15.2 (1982): 232–38. Print.

———. "A Re-examination of the Relationship Between Stephen Crane and W. D. Howells." *American Literary Realism* 34.1 (2001): 47–65. Print.

———. *Stephen Crane Remembered.* Tuscaloosa: U of Alabama P, 2006. Print.

———. "Stephen Crane's Manuscript of 'The Devil's Acre.'" *PBSA* 94.3 (2000): 427–32. Print.

——. "Stephen Crane's Manuscript of 'This Majestic Lie.'" *Studies in Bibliography* 36 (1983): 221–29. Print.

——. "Stephen Crane's Sale of 'An Episode of War' to *The Youth's Companion*." *Studies in Bibliography* 37 (1984): 243–48. Print.

——. "Stephen Crane's Struggle with Romance in *The Third Violet*." *American Literature* 70.2 (1998): 265–91. Print.

Stacy, Gerald. "Patterns of Style in Stephen Crane's Short Stories." *Eureka Studies in Teaching Short Fiction* 8.1 (2007): 62–68. Print.

Stallman, Robert. Introduction. "*The Red Badge of Courage*" *by Stephen Crane*. New York: Modern Lib., 1951. v–xxxiii. Print.

——. *Stephen Crane: A Biography*. New York: Braziller, 1968. Print.

——. *Stephen Crane: A Critical Bibliography*. Ames: Iowa State UP, 1972. Print.

Starrett, Vincent. "Stephen Crane at Claverack." *Stephen Crane Newsletter* 2.1 (1976): 4. Print.

Stinson, John J. "Getting Engaged with 'The Bride': Student Writing and Crane's Story." *Eureka Studies in Teaching Short Fiction* 8.1 (2007): 34–47. Print.

Tietz, Stephen B. "Teachable Fiction Comes to Yellow Sky." *Eureka Studies in Teaching Short Fiction* 8.1 (2007): 27–33. Print.

Traxel, David. "Stephen Crane and Richard Harding Davis—An Unlikely Friendship." "Stephen Crane in War and Peace." Spec. issue of *War, Literature and the Arts* (1999): 11–22. Print.

Vosburg, R. G. "The Darkest Hour in the Life of Stephen Crane." *Criterion* Feb. 1901: 26–27. Print.

Weatherford, Richard M., ed. *Stephen Crane: The Critical Heritage*. London: Routledge, 1973. Print.

Weinstein, Bernard. "Stephen Crane and New Jersey." *William Carlos Williams, Stephen Crane, Philip Freneau: Papers and Poems Celebrating New Jersey's Literary Heritage*. Ed. W. John Bauer. Trenton: New Jersey Hist. Commission, 1989. 55–73. Print.

Wells, Lester G. "The Syracuse Days of Stephen Crane." *Syracuse* 10.2 (1959): 12–14, 40–42. Print.

Wertheim, Stanley. "Crane and Garland: The Education of an Impressionist." *North Dakota Quarterly* 35.1 (1967): 23–28. Print.

——. *A Stephen Crane Encyclopedia*. Westport: Greenwood, 1997. Print.

——. "Stephen Crane's *The Monster* as Fiction and Film." *William Carlos Williams, Stephen Crane, Philip Freneau: Papers Celebrating New Jersey's Literary Heritage*. Ed. W. John Bauer. Trenton: New Jersey Hist. Commission, 1989. 97–105. Print.

——. "Why Stephen Crane Left Claverack." *Stephen Crane Newsletter* 2.1 (1967): 5. Print.

Wertheim, Stanley, and Paul Sorrentino. *The Crane Log: A Documentary Life of Stephen Crane, 1871–1900*. New York: Hall, 1994. Print.

——. "Thomas Beer: The Clay Feet of Stephen Crane Biography." *American Literary Realism* 22.3 (1990): 2–16. Print.

West, Herbert Faulkner. *A Stephen Crane Collection*. Hanover, NH: Dartmouth College Lib., 1948. Print.

Wheeler, Post, and Hallie Ermine Rives. "Rebels in Embryo: Sign O'Lanthorn." *Dome of Many-Colored Glass*. New York: Doubleday, 1955. 19–22, 98–104. Print.

White, Bruce A. "Stephen Crane and the 'Philistine.'" *Elbert Hubbard's "The Philistine: A Periodical of Protest': A Major American "Little Magazine."* Lanham, NY: UP of America, 1989. 52–87. Print.

Wickham, Harvey. "Stephen Crane at College." *American Mercury* Mar. 1926: 291–97. Print.

Willard, Frances E. *Women and Temperance: or The Work of the Woman's Christian Temperance Union*. Hartford: Park, 1883. Print.

Wilson-Jordan, Jacqueline. "Teaching a Dangerous Story: Darwinism and Race in Stephen Crane's 'The Monster.'" *Eureka Studies in Teaching Short Fiction* 8.1 (2007): 62–69. Print.

Aprons and Pearls: Images of Phillis Wheatley

JENNIFER HARRIS
Mount Allison University

This essay begins with an anecdote. In 2005, at the annual conference of the Society for the History of Authorship, Reading, and Publishing, a scholar observed how few images were available of pre–Civil War African diasporic authors. I responded by noting an etching of Quobna Ottobah Cugoano (c. 1757–c. 1791) by Richard Cosway (1742–1821), as well as a lithograph of Phillis Wheatley (c. 1753–1784) in formal attire, which I had stumbled across on a PBS Web site.[1] While the etching of Cugoano elicited little interest—probably due to his status as an African-British subject in combination with his less dramatic life story—the idea of a previously unknown portrait of Wheatley was met with some excitement. Another scholar asked me to forward the link. Her reply to my e-mail was quite telling. Without firm evidence that the lithograph was actually of Wheatley, interest dissipated, evident in the scholar's implicit dismissal of the image.

I found it an intriguing response from a scholar of print culture. Whether or not the portrait is actually of Phillis Wheatley, it has been circulated as such. Five years later, this image is no longer rare; indeed, it is featured on several Web sites about Wheatley and her poetry, and, most notably, in Gwendolyn DuBois Shaw's *Portraits of a People: Picturing African Americans in the Nineteenth Century*.[2] Most curious to me is that, in the intervening period, no one appears to have undertaken any investigation of its origins: just as one scholar dismissed it out of hand due to the impossibility of its actually being a portrait for which Wheatley sat, others have presented it at face value without considering its anachronisms. The lack of investigation is evident in that the accompanying text and credit rarely changes from Web site to Web site: "a rare portrait of Phillis Wheatley shows her facing forward, wearing an evening dress and jewelry. The portrait appeared in *Revue des Colonies* in Paris between 1834 and 1842. Image Credit: Schomburg Center" ("Historical Documents").

While a "new" uninvestigated image purporting to be of Wheatley may initially seem trivial in comparison to a recovered Wheatley letter or poem, I would argue that the popularity of this image suggests otherwise, especially given the power of images to shape interpretations.[3] Moreover, the circulation of any such image of Wheatley—particularly in a culture in which her writings, as well as the bodies of black women, have historically been overdetermined—deserves scrutiny. As I will demonstrate later in this essay, Wheatley, it seems, has been used by many to represent much: she has alternately been held up as exceptional, dismissed as derivative (most famously by Thomas Jefferson [1743–1826; see Jefferson 178]), celebrated as an example of black achievement despite adversity, castigated as insufficiently radical, and redeemed for potential subversiveness. In short, the politics of time and place has irrevocably shaped Wheatley's reception and representation, as well as the uses to which she has been put. Straw horse or heroine, at some point Wheatley has become less a "who" than a "what"—a treatment not equally meted out to her male peers.

Moreover, the fact that a nineteenth-century French representation has found a following in the cyberspace of twenty-first-century North America is neither incidental nor innocuous. This "new" Wheatley appears more secular—less confined by the dictates and mores of late eighteenth-century Boston society, if not actually rebelling against them—and thus more in keeping with the attitudes of our own society. However, to indulge such a reading uncritically is to efface the complexity of Wheatley's history, her reception, and her uses by previous generations. In particular, it is to ignore the desiring nature of Wheatley's audience—a desiring my students participate in when stating a preference for the *Revue* portrait. Taking into account the history of such an image enables us to consider the ways in which portraits of Wheatley have never been stable entities; rather, they have been repeatedly recontextualized and reinterpreted as a means of advancing a variety of political and national purposes.

The *Revue des Colonies* lithograph of Wheatley (see fig. 1) may be described as follows: an African woman is standing and facing the viewer directly. She is adorned with a pearl necklace and drop earrings, a choice of jewelry that symbolizes purity and restraint, but also wealth and self-possession. The pearl necklace sits loosely around her neck, definitely not a choker, which might invoke the image of shackles. Her bosom is exposed in an off-the-shoulder, high-waisted white gown, which is inspired by styles of ancient Greece and reflects fashions introduced during Napoleon's regime, over a decade after her death (Ribeiro 124–29). Her hair also reflects post-Revolutionary trends to dress women's hair more naturally, including shorter hair (Ribeiro 132). In this case, however, there are additional consequences: Wheatley's hair is not simply short; it is cropped, waved, and asserts her African heritage.

By contrast, the portrait of Wheatley most familiar to scholars (see fig. 2) shows a demure and contemplative seated woman, her hair and bosom covered by conservative colonial American garb. She does not make eye contact with the viewer, but instead gazes upward. The presence of a pen

Fig. 1. "Phillis Wheatley, Imp. De Lemercier, Benard et C[ie]." Lithograph. *Revue des Colonies* Jan. 1837: 286.
Courtesy of and by permission of the Photographs and Prints Division, Schomburg Center for Research in Black Culture, The New York Public Library, Astor, Lenox and Tilden Foundations

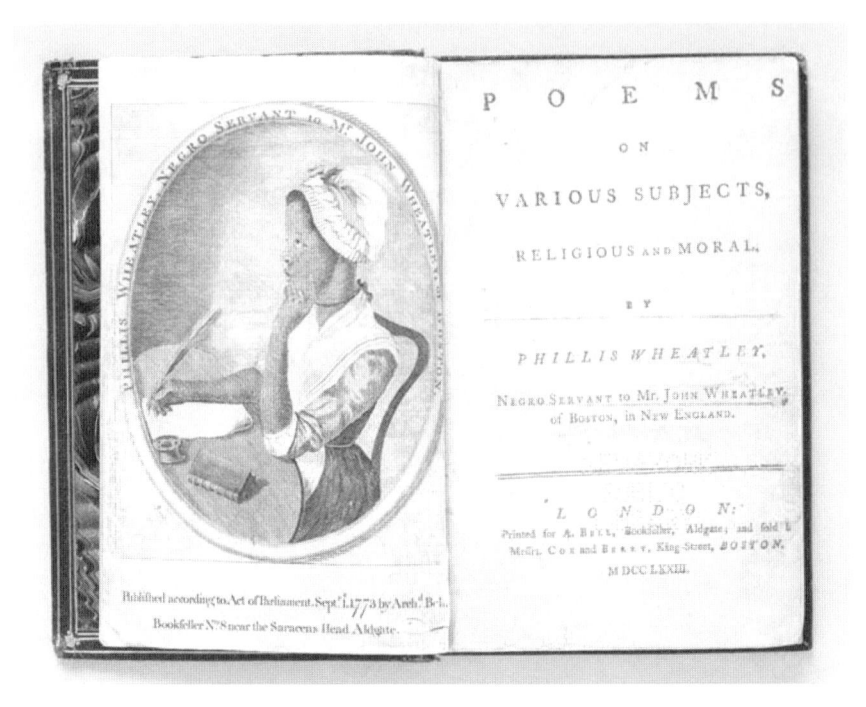

Fig. 2. "Phillis Wheatley, Negro Servant to Mr. John Wheatley, of Boston." Woodcut. Frontispiece of Phillis Wheatley, *Poems on Various Subjects, Religious and Moral* (London: printed for A. Bell, 1773).
Courtesy of and by permission of the Manuscripts, Archives and Rare Books Division, Schomburg Center for Research in Black Culture, The New York Public Library, Astor, Lenox and Tilden Foundations

in one hand and the book before her attests to her literacy and authorship, a vexed issue for the real-life poet who would have to prove each before a panel of "the most respectable characters in Boston."[4] The surrounding frame circumscribes her, literally and figuratively, because the words within—"Phillis Wheatley, Negro Servant to Mr. John Wheatley, of Boston" —ensure that we view her through the lens of her enslaved status. Although she is ostensibly lost in thought, if we follow the trajectory of Wheatley's eyes, we encounter the word "Negro" in the frame. Her social position is again reinforced by her clothing, which indicates that she is a servant, though not a minor one, as evidenced by the pleating on her cap.[5] Appearing as the frontispiece of her 1773 volume, *Poems on Various Subjects, Religious and Moral*, this woodcut was more in keeping with Wheatley's public persona in the Americas. Certainly it was reported that her mistress thought it a good and worthy likeness and thus displayed it on her mantel (Robinson 18).

The two portraits invite different readings. For today's reader it is impossible to view the 1773 portrait without considering Wheatley as a woman who tried to maneuver within a society in which her options were limited, never voicing overtly rebellious sentiments, apparently deferring to those in power, yet including in her poems subtly nuanced critiques of the power structure itself. By contrast, the Parisian Wheatley does not convey deference and does not need to prove ownership of her work. There are not even any indicators that she is enslaved; rather, she is adorned in a way that implies her freedom. When juxtaposed with the earlier representation, the Parisian Wheatley appears almost defiant, her very dress and pose challenging a racially based class and caste system, which declared that she could not be a "lady." Most notably, in contrast to the 1773 woodcut, the Parisian Wheatley features clothing, jewelry, and a hairstyle that, in combination with her pose, deliberately signal her attractiveness as a woman. This is not to say that the earlier version features an unattractive figure; she appears to embody what commentators of the time referred to as a "well-turned arm" and "trim waist." But the *Revue* portrait draws attention to her softness, her breasts, and—in the full version, which does not appear online—invites contemplation of the folds of her gown and the womanly curves beneath it. Certainly anyone familiar with the lines of neoclassical French fashion of the late eighteenth century would be able to anticipate a gown that revealed even more curves—though the image leaves these to the imagination. In comparing the two Wheatleys, we infer obviously different conclusions: one woman does domestic work; the other appears to have domestics.

The Parisian Wheatley might be seen as a refutation of and rebuttal to the image originally published in the 1773 volume, which would have no doubt been available to the publishers of the *Revue des Colonies*.[6] It seems clear that the Parisian Wheatley appealed and continues to appeal more to certain desires of Wheatley's audience—whether romantic or revolutionary—than its earlier counterpart. This might be a gendered romanticization of Wheatley, but it is one with a certain allure. The much discussed 1960s critique of Wheatley as insufficiently radical and a de facto apologist for slavery is not overtly challenged by the 1773 portrait; indeed, for the 1960s critic who called her "an early Boston Aunt Jemima" and a "colonial handkerchief head," whose life and work are "utterly irrelevant to the identification and liberation of the Black man," the 1960s critique might be affirmed by the earlier image (qtd. in Robinson 26–28).[7]

The irony, of course, is that the 1773 woodcut is generally believed (without firm evidence) to be based on a drawing by Wheatley's friend Scipio Moorehead (dates unknown), a fellow slave in Boston, to whom she also dedicated a poem (Carretta, "Introduction," Wheatley, *Complete Writings* xviii). This raises the possibility of Wheatley's own artistic input into Morehead's drawing. Thus the 1773 portrait stands as a possible moment of Wheatley's controlling or at least influencing her representation, in contradistinction to the ways in which she was and continues to be reworked and reinterpreted in support of a variety of political positions.

Certainly Cyrille Charles Auguste Bissette (1795–1858), editor of the *Revue des Colonies*, deployed Wheatley to advance his own political goals. The *Revue*, published in Paris from 1834 to 1842, took as its mandate the need to effect change in the status of black members of the French colonial world, change even beyond the abolition of slavery, though obviously that was key (Bongie 266–70). To that end, a series of short biographical essays on historical figures of the black diaspora appeared in the *Revue* beginning in mid-1835. As Kelly Duke Bryant has observed, these profiles served to inculcate racial pride in black readers while also providing potential role models. At the same time, the achievements of such figures contradicted the suppositions that blacks were incapable of reason or artistic production and thus could be excluded from Enlightenment notions of humanity (273–74). Individuals profiled include a doctor (Jacques Derham [aka Jacques Durham; 1762–date unknown]), a leader of the Haitian Revolution (Henri Christophe [1767–1820]), an Abbot (Arsène Fridoil [1815–52]), an educator and ethnologist (David Boilat [1814–1901]), and several writers. The only other woman featured is Anne Florence (d. 1836), the musical and religious protégé of a well-known nun.[8] This series is the original context in which the Parisian Wheatley image, currently circulating online, appeared.

The *Revue*'s January 1837 piece on Wheatley is, in many ways, unexceptional. There is the portrait, a reprint of a short biographical essay by French abolitionist Henri Grégoire (1750–1831) highlighting her achievements, and his translations of selections from her poetry. Where Wheatley's entry differs from the other entries is in the selection of image: the *Revue*'s biographies of literary figures such as Ignatius Sancho (c. 1729–1780), Olaudah Equiano (c. 1745–1797), and others reproduce the most commonly available images of them, but Bissette varied his practice for Wheatley. Notably, Bissette approached the lithographic workshop of Lemercier, Benard & Co. to produce an image to represent the poet. Founded in Paris in 1837, Joseph Lemercier's (1803–84) operation was decidedly commercial, its oeuvre encompassing "magazine advertisements, calendar illustrations, bulletins, flyers, product packaging, bureaucratic forms, and popular prints" (Rosen, "Lemercier et Compagnie" 8–9). Bissette either commissioned a new portrait of Wheatley or drew from Lemercier's collection of stock images. Certainly Lemercier's collection was substantial; although he regularly discarded lithographic stones no longer of value, he kept a total of fifty thousand others in his warehouse for consultation. Presumably some of these were preserved because of the identity of the artists while others were maintained because the images were profitable and might be re-used (Rosen, "Lemercier et Compagnie" 6–8). Because Lemercier's commissions were quite broad, it is not surprising that a number feature colonized subjects. That said, it seems unlikely that this lithograph was drawn from a colonial context—images from this context tended to be scenes that highlighted the exotic. In such scenes, black men and women were dressed in non-European garb, or versions modified to suit more tropical climes. Unfortunately, Lemercier's stones disappeared over one hundred years ago, preventing any review of his archive (Rosen, "Lemercier et Compagnie" 7).

What is open for us to explore, however, is the possible creator of the image of Wheatley that was published in the *Revue*. Lemercier provided employment for a number of artists of the period. As Fernand Hue writes, due to Lemercier's mastery of his form, "[t]he important editors, the renowned artists wanted to have their works printed by him" (qtd. in Rosen, "Lemercier et Compagnie" 38–39; translation mine). A signature in the lower right-hand corner of the Wheatley lithograph, cropped from the image reproduced online, provides a tantalizing clue. When presented with the image, Lemercier expert Jeffrey Howard Rosen responded:

> I would think that the artist who composed the lithograph was either Achille Devéria [1800–1857] or Carle Vernet [1758–1836]. The scribbled signature in the lower right-hand side actually resembles BOTH of the artist's signatures, if you can believe it. . . . And not incidentally, their visual or graphic styles very much resembled each other too, largely because of the prevailing aesthetic of the time. ("Re: Lemercier")

How we interpret this lithograph might depend on who crafted it. Just as the possibility that Scipio Moorehead, an enslaved African American, composed the 1773 image influences how we read it, so does a Devéria or a Vernet make a difference, despite all their stylistic similarities. Achille Devéria was a French painter, known for his portraits of writers and other figures of the world of arts, who would become *conservateur en chef* at the Bibliothèque Nationale in 1855 (Morel 7). He is best recognized today for his "libertine" prints—in other words, explicitly pornographic, though very pretty, pieces. By contrast, Carle Vernet is remembered for his detailed, witty, and satirical observations of daily life (Fisher et al. 346). Certainly irony was not absent from Vernet's life: while Napoleon rewarded him for his art, Vernet also lost a sister to the guillotine (Ruutz-Rees 4).

To consider the implications of each: in the context of Devéria's work, the details that the Parisian Wheatley is dressed as a lady and that her attractiveness is foregrounded become meaningless—the dress appears more risqué, the loose pearls more sensual, the gaze potentially seductive, as per his 1850 representation of a *Young Woman with a Rose*. His libertine works, after all, appear to have exclusively featured the wealthy. However, if the engraver is the witty Vernet, accustomed to the whims of power, do we then interpret Wheatley's gaze as more knowledgeable, potentially mocking viewers for their expectations? Just as interpretations of Wheatley's 1773 image have shifted over time according to the political orientation of the spectator, so must we consider the ways in which the spectator's interpretation might vary according to the politics of the composer.

That said, the difference between a reading vis-à-vis Devéria versus Vernet—or any other potential artist, for that matter—depends upon the reader of the *Revue* being able to decipher the signature, a less-likely possibility (though we cannot deny that some might try and succeed). Thus, in attempting to recapture the meaning of this image as it was originally circulated, we must consider that Bissette's framing has the power to supplant the artist's inclination. Therefore, I would suggest that we contemplate Wheatley's representation in the context of the portraits that accompany the biographies in other issues of the *Revue*. While the religious leaders—and the devout Anne Florence, who died at seventeen—are represented in the appropriate religious apparel, the male secular figures are portrayed in more formal attire and the poses of statesmen. (The ubiquitous image of Olaudah Equiano exemplifies the visual renderings of men.) In this context, the 1773 woodcut of Wheatley appears decidedly modest, not simply in terms of dress, but also in terms of pose. What such a comparison highlights is the point that this new lithograph resituates Wheatley in relation to the visual stature of her male peers. Allowing for gender differences, she is dressed as they are dressed and framed as they are framed. Her gown may be anachronistic, given that her death predated such a fashion, but to dress her in the style of a *lady* of pre-1784 would be to render her politically suspect to a postrevolutionary reader—and this is not what seems to be Bissette's intent. Instead, Wheatley appears the picture of revolutionary elegance, the political implications of which are palpable. That is, this image is of a post–French Revolution Wheatley who appears to embody the ideals of the new nation—namely, *liberté* and *égalité*—and she does so unapologetically.

For Bissette, then, it appears to be less a matter of who Phillis Wheatley was and more a matter of whom he would have Phillis Wheatley be for his contemporary black reader, and what effect or action this desired identity might inspire. Bissette isn't simply crafting a more palatable Wheatley; rather, he is rendering her visually on a par with the male figures he features, embodying principles of equality and visible advancement beyond slavery or dependency. In this way, she becomes a contemporary icon intended to inspire action in his diasporic readers, not a relic or reminder of an enslaved past. Bissette's reinvention is in keeping with what Chris Bongie observes as the *Revue*'s "literary and cultural agenda that has much in common with the project of postcolonial revisionism"—contesting "Eurocentric representations of colonial history" and creating "an alternative canon" of literary figures (270).

For those who might argue that, to a greater degree than the 1773 woodcut, the lithograph glosses over the lived reality of Wheatley's enslavement, as well as the impoverishment she faced in freedom, I would counter that it does so only when removed from this context. As Anna Brickhouse has argued, the abolitionist *Revue* situates Wheatley's writing in such a way as to highlight its antislavery themes, juxtaposing it with documentary articles that critique colonial practices (101–12). The result is to highlight any embedded critique while concomitantly raising the question of how a lady who is adorned in fashions signifying freedom might also be subject to the injustices of slavery documented within.

The importance of depicting Wheatley as a lady cannot be underestimated. While some might bemoan the tendency to use the bodies and appearances of female authors as ciphers through which the validity of their perspective or work is judged, in Wheatley's case the importance of images is great—something she would have no doubt understood. Following the racialized beliefs of the dominant culture of the time, enslaved women were often represented as insufficiently feminine, a lack that was also key to the stereotype of hypersexuality often imposed upon enslaved women to justify white male licentiousness and concomitant abuses of power. Thus, the supposed privileges of genteel women—such as male protection and respect—did not need to be extended to black women. In early nineteenth-century France, the exhibition of a nearly nude Saartjie Baartman (1789–1815), an enslaved Khoisan woman—an exhibition that continued in a more extreme form for 159 years after her death—exemplified such a stereotype (Crais and Scully).[9]

Subject to this stereotype, the bodies of black women were both overdetermined and undifferentiated in the white imaginary, the legacy of which still permeates our culture. Even as the abolitionist emblem featured an enslaved woman with the caption "Am I Not a Woman and a Sister?" her physical composition varies little from her male counterpart's, kneeling in supplication, hands clasped in prayer, with the exception that the curve of her breasts is evident. While, as Jean Fagan Yellin observes, the female slave appears physically weak by comparison (9), her weakness and breasts serve to signal her gender, not a femininity associated with cultivation or gentility. Thus, although such an image might serve to humanize the figure for its white viewer, this does not necessarily translate to equalizing the subject.

When compared with the abolitionist image, the two portraits of Wheatley, no matter how different, reveal a shared purpose: to individualize the subject and to present her as a lady, albeit according to the values associated with the culture in which each image was produced. In the United States, this was a Puritan culture, which imagined itself in opposition to European decadence, privileging restraint over excess. Accordingly, the tradition of representing black women as ladies in the antebellum United States, at least in literature, is to represent them as embodying the attributes of the cult of true womanhood, which Barbara Welter famously identified as "piety, purity, submissiveness, and domesticity" (152). No one can deny that the 1773 portrait of Wheatley presents a woman who appears to embody these virtues; indeed, if Wheatley did have any say in this representation, it would have been to her advantage to insist upon such a rendering, which contradicts the stereotype of sexual licentiousness while also suggesting the worth of her writings.

By contrast, the image of Wheatley in the *Revue* boasts a décolletage that would undermine any attribution of purity—not to mention submissiveness—by her more conservative Boston contemporaries. Domesticity is entirely absent as a concern. However, Bissette's compatriots, as members of a more permissive French culture, would not have been alarmed by the nature of her dress or as preoccupied with the need to represent black women in opposition to sexualized stereotypes. In part, this is due to the fact that Bissette's France was not plagued to the same degree by white anxieties about miscegenation. This is no doubt a result of the proportionately smaller percentage of black residents—Sue Peabody estimates that blacks composed no more than .025 percent of the population in France in the late eighteenth century (4). Granted, this was a factor of laws passed to minimize black immigration from the colonies, namely, the Déclaration pour la police des Noirs. However, such laws proved unenforceable, were often ignored (as in the case of Thomas Jefferson and the Hemings family[10]), and even met with active resistance in some cases. Laws intended to minimize miscegenation suffered a similar fate (Peabody 125–31). This is not to say France was exempt from racism—the laws cited above clearly indicate otherwise. Rather, it is to say that while a portrait of a black woman in a cleavage-baring dress might not be read in exactly the same way as that of a white woman similarly dressed—something dependent on the reader and context, of course—it certainly did not invite the same reading as it would have in the United States. As this portrait is framed by poems that attest to the author's piety, in a journal dedicated to black advancement and thus guaranteeing sympathetic readers, Wheatley's status as a "lady" is not threatened by an exposed bosom. Bissette has thus re-visioned Wheatley in a way that validates her reputation while also rendering her more appealing to his own audience and their desire that she embody and/or reaffirm their politics. Whether they are aware of it or not, those contemporary Web site designers who prefer his rendering of Wheatley affirm a similar set of desires for a more revolutionary author.

The tendency to reimagine Wheatley's visual representation did not end with Bissette. Henry Louis Gates Jr.'s 2003 book on the poet likewise subjects the 1773 woodcut to subtle yet meaningful revisions. The portrait appears on the cover; notably the textual frame signifying her enslavement is removed, a retroactive visual liberation of Wheatley. That the black-and-white image is tinted so that her gown is rendered an undeniable pink and her bonnet trimmed in the same way serves to enhance further her femininity, an enforcement of gender emphasized by the photograph of Gates towering over her. The irony is evident: Wheatley, a slave for most of her life, so often censored in life and reinterpreted after death, continues to be deployed to meet the needs and desires of others, from French editors to 1960s Black Power activists to twenty-first-century academics and publishers. The fact that the images of black male authors of a similar period (such as Equiano and Ignatius Sancho) have not been subject to the same treatment is telling—perhaps because those images for the most part do not challenge how we want to perceive the author.[11]

In the absence of any context, the image of Wheatley in the *Revue* could indeed appear imagined, as the unnamed scholar I began with suggested. Whether its many current online incarnations romanticize or simplify her life, or sanitize her slavery, is beyond the scope of this essay. So, too, is the issue of whether treating the image as factual might alter perceptions of her poetry. But the fact that it has found a new audience cannot be denied; in just over two years, more than three thousand users have downloaded it from one site alone, LuciaM's "Phillis Wheatley: Slave, Poet, American." Independent of her own words or intent, the *Revue* image has become one more way to reframe Phillis Wheatley to meet the desires of others.

NOTES

1. See the 1784 etching "Mr. and Mrs. Cosway," in which Cugoano serves as a set piece, demonstrating the Cosways' wealth and fashionable status (Carretta, "Introduction," *Thoughts* xv).

2. Shaw addresses both of the images discussed here, as well as a third portrait that is said to be of Wheatley, but the attribution of that portrait strains credulity (58–61).

3. Certainly this has been my experience: when introduced to the French image of Wheatley, my students report a shift in their perceptions of her and her poetry.

4. See the publisher's note, which prefaces the panel's signed letter (Wheatley, *Complete Writings* 8). This woodcut image of Wheatley (fig. 2), image number "485600, title page and frontispiece, *Poems on Various Subjects, Religious and Moral*, by Phillis Wheatley (ca. 1753–1784), September 1, 1773," is reprinted by permission of and courtesy of the Manuscripts, Archives and Rare Books Division, Schomburg Center for Research in Black Culture, The New York Public Library, Astor, Lenox and Tilden Foundations.

Lemercier's lithograph of Wheatley (fig. 1), item "ps_scg_038, Bernard Lemercier Imprimerie Lithographs and Co., Paris, Phyllis Wheatley, *Revue des Colonies*, 1834–1842, lithograph," is reprinted by permission of and courtesy of the Photographs and Prints Division, Schomburg Center for Research in Black Culture, The New York Public Library, Astor, Lenox and Tilden Foundations.

5. Shaw interprets this image as conveying less deference and more agency, an example of "revolutionary and defiant visual rhetoric" (29). While I find her reading compelling, I differ in that I read the frame as crucial to the composition and the cap, though fashionable, in this context as suited to a superior servant. In reading Wheatley's garb in this way, I follow Carretta and others ("Introduction," Wheatley, *Complete Writings* xviii).

6. Wheatley's work was much circulated and commented upon in England. Copies of such abolitionist writing clearly made their way to interested individuals in France, as evidenced by the practices of the *Revue*.

7. Little thought is given to the reality that, as William H. Robinson observes, "if Phillis Wheatley had been of a fiery militant persuasion, the colonial press would not have welcomed her written charges" (39). Less thought is given to the fact that the kinds of poems the commentator apparently wished she wrote would be anachronistic.

8. Anne Florence was the prodigy of Blessed Anne-Marie Javouhey (1779–1851), founder of the Sisters of Saint Joseph Cluny.

9. Baartman was exhibited in a state of partial undress in both England and France. Following her death, various body parts—including her genitals—were preserved and exhibited in France's Musée de l'Homme, where they remained on display until the mid-1970s.

10. See Annette Gordon-Reed for a discussion of Jefferson's failure to register either Sally or James Hemings, as well as a discussion of the ways in which such a failure was part of a common practice of ignoring the laws (174–75).

11. The only significant reworking I have seen of such portraits has been the image composed for Angelina Osborne's *Equiano's Daughter: The Life and Times of Joanna Vassa*. However, the revision is not so much in the actual portrait of Equiano but in the addition of an imagined image of his daughter, thus contextualizing him differently. Interestingly, The Royal Albert Memorial Museum, Exeter, possesses a portrait whose subject is often identified as Equiano. While this identification has been disputed, the painting nonetheless serves as the cover of Carretta's 2005 biography of the subject (see John Madin for further discussion). Neither image contradicts or substantially revises the frontispiece image of Equiano, excepting the insertion of a second person.

WORKS CITED

Bongie, Chris. *Islands and Exiles: The Creole Identities of Post/Colonial Literature*. Stanford: Stanford UP, 1998. Print.

Brickhouse, Anna. *TransAmerican Literary Relations and the Nineteenth-Century Public Sphere*. Cambridge, UK: Cambridge UP, 2004. Print.

Bryant, Kelly Duke. "Black But Not African: Francophone Black Diaspora and the *Revue des Colonies*, 1834–1842." *International Journal of African Historical Studies* 40.2 (2007): 251–82. Print.

Carretta, Vincent. *Equiano, the African: Biography of a Self-Made Man*. New York: Penguin, 2005. Print.

———. "Introduction." *Thoughts and Sentiments on the Evil of Slavery and Other Writings*. By Quobna Ottobah Cugoano. Ed. Carretta. New York: Penguin, 1999. ix–xxviii. Print.

———. "Introduction." Wheatley, *Complete Writings* xiii–xli. Print.

Crais, Clifton, and Pamela Scully. *Sara Baartman and the Hottentot Venus: A Ghost Story and a Biography*. Princeton: Princeton UP, 2008. Print.

Devéria, Achille-Jacques-Jean-Marie. *Young Woman with a Rose.* 1850. Oil on canvas. Norton Simon Museum, Pasadena, CA.
Fisher, Jay McKean, et al. *The Essence of Line: French Drawings from Ingres to Degas.* University Park: Pennsylvania State UP, 2005. Print.
Gates, Henry Louis, Jr. *The Trials of Phillis Wheatley: America's First Black Poet and Her Encounters with the Founding Fathers.* New York: Basic Civitas, 2003. Print.
Gordon-Reed, Annette. *The Hemingses of Monticello: An American Family.* New York: Norton, 2008. Print.
Grégoire, Henri. "Literature des Noirs: Phillis Wheatley." *Revue des Colonies* Jan. 1837: 286–91. Print.
"Historical Documents: Portrait of Phillis Wheatley c.1834." *Africans in America: Resource Bank.* PBS.org; WGBH Educational Foundation, 1998, 1999. Web. Jan. 18, 2011. <http://www.pbs.org/wgbh/aia/part2/2h77.html>.
Jefferson, Thomas. *Notes on the State of Virginia: With Related Documents.* Ed. David Waldstreicher. New York: Bedford/St. Martin's, 2002. Print.
LuciaM. "Phillis Wheatley: Slave, Poet, American." *Google Earth.* Google Earth Community, Forums, Earth-Moderator Selected, History Illustrated (Moderated). Mar. 31, 2008. Web. Jan. 19, 2011. <http://bbs.keyhole.com/ubb/ubbthreads.php?ubb=showthreaded&Number=688713&site_id=1#import>.
Madin, John. "The Lost African: Slavery and Portraiture in the Age of Enlightenment." *Apollo: The International Magazine of Art and Antique* Aug. 2006: 34–39. Print.
Morel, Dominique. *Achille Devéria, témoin du romantisme parisien, 1800–1857.* Catalog, Musée Renan-Scheffer, June 18–Sept. 29, 1985. Paris: Musées de la ville de Paris, 1985. Print.
Osborne, Angelina. *Equiano's Daughter: The Life and Times of Joanna Vassa.* London: Untold Stories Project/Krik Krak, 2007. Print.
Peabody, Sue. *"There Are No Slaves in France": The Political Culture of Race and Slavery in the Ancien Régime.* New York: Oxford UP, 2002. Print.
Ribeiro, Aileen. *Fashion in the French Revolution.* New York: Holmes, 1988. Print.
Robinson, William H. *Phillis Wheatley in the Black American Beginnings.* Detroit: Broadside, 1975. Print.
Rosen, Jeffrey Howard. "Lemercier et Compagnie: Photolithography and the Industrialization of Print Production in France, 1837–1859." Diss. Northwestern U, 1988. Print.
———. "Re: Lemercier query." Message to the author. Jan. 28, 2009. E-mail.
Ruutz-Rees, Janet Emily. *Horace Vernet.* New York: Scribner, 1880. Print.
Shaw, Gwendolyn DuBois. *Portraits of a People: Picturing African Americans in the Nineteenth Century.* Seattle: U of Washington P, 2006. Print.
Welter, Barbara. "The Cult of True Womanhood: 1820–1860." *American Quarterly* 18.2 (1966): 151–74. Print.
Wheatley, Phillis. *Complete Writings.* Ed. Vincent Carretta. New York: Penguin, 2001. Print.
———. *Poems on Various Subjects, Religious and Moral.* London: printed for A. Bell, 1773. Print.
Yellin, Jean Fagan. *Women and Sisters: The Antislavery Feminists in American Culture.* New Haven: Yale UP, 1989. Print.

Poe, Scott's Fiction, and the Holt Source Collection: The Example of *Ivanhoe* and "The Fall of the House of Usher"

ALEXANDER HAMMOND
Washington State University

This essay has a four-part purpose: first, to review Edgar Allan Poe's (1809–49) knowledge of Sir Walter Scott (1771–1832) and the scholarship on Scott's importance for Poe's critical thinking about fiction (sections 1–3); second, to introduce the resources of the Palmer C. Holt Poe Collection at Washington State University for studying the sources of Poe's creative work (section 4); third, to illustrate the promise of this little-used archive by examining Holt's unpublished findings on Poe's borrowings from Scott's fiction, especially from *Ivanhoe* (1819), relative to published source scholarship (sections 5–6);[1] and, fourth, to interpret Holt's annotations of *Ivanhoe* as a source for "The Fall of the House of Usher" (1839; sections 7–8). As will be seen, Holt remains the only scholar to recognize that "The Mad Trist" of Sir Launcelot Canning—from which Poe's narrator reads to calm down an agitated Roderick Usher in the climactic scene of that tale (*Collected Works* 2: 413–14)—mirrors the well-known episode in *Ivanhoe* in which the Black Knight (a disguised Richard the Lionheart [1157–99]) assaults the door of a hermit. To clarify the significance of Holt's source finding, I review the widespread circulation of *Ivanhoe* and other Scott works in Poe's era; suggest that readers would have seen "The Mad Trist" in "The Fall of the House of Usher" as a crude, recognizable imitation of *Ivanhoe* and of the historical romance generally; and argue that Poe uses this story within a story to locate himself and his intricate, self-referential Gothic tale in a literary marketplace that consumed, as Emily B. Todd and James D. Hart have observed, thousands of posthumous reprints of Scott's fiction, as well as newly published historical romances written by his many living imitators (E. B. Todd 495–501; Hart 73).

1. On Poe's Reading of Scott

In his 1985 edition of Poe's *Brevities*, Burton R. Pollin observed that "Poe greatly respected Sir Walter Scott as a historical novelist, not as a poet, but there is no general survey of Poe and Scott" (*Collected Writings* 2: 518). Even though no general survey exists, Poe scholars and editors have provided ample means for documenting the author's knowledge of Scott both before and after the older writer's death in 1832. One of Poe's classmates at the University of Virginia recalled that he and Poe "were familiar with English poetry from Chaucer to Scott" (Stovall 6). In 1925, Killis Campbell summed up the author's knowledge of Scott as follows:

> [Poe] was deeply interested in [Scott], but primarily on account of his novels. He quotes from Scott's poems only twice, very briefly in each instance, and he refers to his poems less than half a dozen times.... [Poe] was far more attracted to [Scott's] novels than to his poetry. From references and comments in one or another of his critical papers, we may reasonably infer that he had read *Waverley, Ivanhoe, Rob Roy, The Pirate, The Bride of Lammermoor,* and *Anne of Geierstein*; and allusions less specific in nature make it probable that he had also read *Kenilworth, Guy Mannering,* and *The Antiquary*. He alludes to Scott or to his writings some twenty-two times. (173, 180)

Campbell based his generalizations primarily on James A. Harrison's 1902 edition of the *Complete Works of Edgar Allan Poe*, albeit without specific citations. Pollin made the Scott references in this edition accessible through his *Dictionary of Names and Titles in Poe's Collected Works* (1968), which repaired the inadequate index to the *Complete Works* and excluded non-Poe items (vii–x, xiii–xiv). Harrison's extensive but imperfect gathering of Poe's criticism and essays can be supplemented and cross-checked with the indexed selections in G. R. Thompson's 1984 edition of Poe's *Essays and Reviews* and with the annotated texts of "brief essay notes" that Poe gathered in series such as "Pinakidia" (1836) and "Marginalia" (1844–49), as well as his nonfiction prose in the *Saturday Literary Messenger* and the *Broadway Journal*, in volumes 2–5 of Pollin's edition of *Collected Writings of Edgar Allan Poe* (1985–97). These various volumes reveal a Poe who read Scott early and referred to him confidently, especially when making comparative literary judgments.

2. Poe's Use of Scott in Reviews

Beginning with his earliest reviews in 1835, Poe cited Scott's historical romances as a standard against which to measure the work of authors such as Robert Montgomery Bird (1806–54), Edward Bulwer-Lytton (1803–73), William Gilmore Simms (1806–70), and G. P. R. James (1799–1860; cf. *Complete Works* 8: 63–64, 73, 223; 9: 168–69; 10: 53, 132; 12: 190–92, 224; 16: 157; *Essays and Reviews* 160, 167, 171, 173, 174, 473, 485, 851, 1090,

1378, 1452). Poe's 1835 critique of Bird's *The Hawks of Hawk-Hollow* (1835), suggests that it should bear the subtitle "*A Romance by the author of Waverley*" and elaborates the conceit for "the sake of certain pleasantly mirthful, or pleasantly mournful recollections connected with *Ivanhoe*, with the *Antiquary*, with *Kenilworth*, and above all with that most pure, perfect, and radiant gem of fictitious literature the *Bride of Lammermuir* [*sic*]."[2] Using this measure, Poe found *Hawks* to be a "positive failure" not unlike such lesser Scott works as "the Redgauntlets, the Monasteries, the Pirates, and the Saint Ronan's Wells"; argued that Bird's heroine Harriet Falconer is "a copy ... of Di[ana] Vernon" from *Rob Roy* (1817); and concluded that *Hawks* "is, in many respects, a bad imitation of Sir Walter Scott" (*Complete Works* 8: 63–64, 67–68, 73). In the same year Poe sneered at Morris Mattson's *Paul Ulric* (1835) for stupidly borrowing "the proceedings of the *Secret Tribunal*" from Scott's *Anne of Geierstein* (1829) in ignorance "that the Great Unknown's account of these proceedings was principally based on fact" (8: 197).

In his reviews of 1836, Poe continued to cite Scott in evaluating current fiction, including fulsome praise of *Ivanhoe* and *The Bride of Lammermoor* (1819), which features the proud, tragic, love-thwarted hero Edgar Ravenswood with whom Poe seemed to identify. Thus in a review of Bulwer's *Rienzi: The Last of the Tribunes* (1835), Poe judged the author to be "unsurpassed by any writer living or dead" even though "Scott has excelled [Bulwer] in *many* points, and 'The Bride of Lammermuir' [*sic*] is a better book than any individual work by the author of Pelham—'Ivanhoe' is, perhaps, equal to any" (*Complete Works* 8: 223). Poe's enthusiasm for Henry Chorley's (1808–72) *Conti the Discarded* (1835) occasioned the following Scott comparison: "[I]t bears no little resemblance to that purest, and most enthralling of fictions, the Bride of Lammermuir [*sic*]; and we have once before expressed our opinion of this, the master novel of Scott. It is not too much to say that no modern composition, and perhaps no composition whatever, with the single exception of Cervantes' Destruction of Numantia, approaches so nearly to the proper character of the dramas of [Æ]schylus, as the magic tale of which [Edgar] Ravenswood is the hero" (8: 233–34). In other reviews from 1836, Poe lectured James French (1807–88) on poor management of "mannerisms" borrowed from Scott for dealing with multiple story lines (9: 123–24); implied Scott's status to be "the first to blend history, ... successfully, with fiction" while dismissing G. P. R. James as "an indifferent imitator of the Scotch novelist" (9: 169); and emphasized the account of the real-life original of Scott's "Di[ana] Vernon" in *Rob Roy* in a notice of Captain Basil Hall's (1788–1844) memoirs (9: 171–74).

In later reviews and "Marginalia" entries, Poe continued to presume references to Scott would be familiar to his readers. In his 1839 review of

William Gilmore Simms's *Damsel of Darien* (1839), Poe illustrated its derivative nature by labeling the character of Felipe Davila a "humble" imitation of "the old Jew in 'Ivanhoe' " (*Complete Works* 10: 53). When he qualified his normally high praise for Bulwer in an 1841 notice of *Night and Morning* (1841), Poe concluded that even though the author would "never write a bad book" compared to the "drivellers around him," Bulwer was "altogether inferior" to Scott except in unimpressive "philosophical discussions" that "the Caledonian had the discretion to avoid" in fiction (10: 131, 132). Less harshly, in 1845 Poe observed that one "charm" for the reader of Scott and Bulwer (and Benjamin Disraeli [1804–81] and William Godwin [1756–1836] and Charles Brockden Brown [1771–1810]) is their skillful use of "autorial comment" (12: 224).

In an extended review of "The Drama" in 1845, Poe demonstrated his "remembrance of that most passionate and romantic of novels" *The Bride of Lammermoor* (now with the title correctly spelled) by comparing it to an operatic version (presumably Gaetano Donizetti's [1797–1848] *Lucia di Lammermoor* [1835]) with Mrs. Anna Cora Mowatt in the role of Scott's Lucy Ashton (*Complete Works* 12: 190–92). In his 1845 "Marginalia," which as was his custom heavily borrowed from his reviews, Poe again found Bulwer-Lytton as a "novelist" to be "generally inferior" to Scott (16: 157). And in the "Supplementary Marginalia"—Poe's late-in-life selections first printed posthumously by Rufus W. Griswold (1815–57) in 1850—the author's familiar comparisons to Scott are repeated: G. P. R. James is "an indifferent imitator of the Scotch novelist"; "Scott has excelled [Bulwer] in *many* points, and 'The Bride of Lammermoor' is a better book than any individual work by the author of Pelham—'Ivanhoe' is, perhaps, equal to any" (see *Collected Writings* 2: xxix–xxxiii, 520, 517).

3. Scott's Influence on Poe's Critical Thinking

Poe's references to Scott in reviews inform an early line of scholarship on the two writers: analysis of Scott's influence on Poe's formulations about fiction, genre, and audience in his criticism. Scott's "On the Supernatural in Fictitious Composition: and Particularly in the Works of Ernest Theodore William Hoffmann" (1827) in the *Foreign Quarterly Review* has long been considered Poe's source of the terms "grotesque" and "arabesque" (see 335; 348–49). Poe's knowledge of Scott's essay seems certain because of its synopsis of Hoffman's "*Der Majorat*—the Entail" (336–48), the obvious source for the name "Roderick," the fissure in the mansion, and the motif of reading a text within a text with mirrored sound effects in "The Fall of the House of Usher." Early discussions of Poe's use of this 1827 essay include Palmer Cobb's 1908 study of Hoffmann's influence on Poe (23), Margaret Alterton's 1925 *Origins of Poe's Critical Theory* (13, 16,

25–26), and Arthur Hobson Quinn's 1941 *Edgar Allan Poe: A Critical Biography* (289), all credited in notes to Poe's tales in Thomas Ollive Mabbott's 1978 edition (*Collected Works* 2: 394, 474n1).

Broader assessments of the importance of Scott for Poe's critical thinking include Robert D. Jacobs's *Poe: Journalist and Critic* (1969), which notes the importance of Scott's 1827 essay for the title and preface of Poe's 1840 *Tales of the Grotesque and Arabesque* (165n13), as well as the impact of Scott's definition of romance on Poe's distinctions between poetry and prose beginning with the 1831 "Letter to Mr. _____ _____," which prefaces *Poems, Second Edition* (Jacobs 38; 223–24). Michael L. Allen found Scott's practice in fiction important for Poe's view of audience, and for his sense of the roles of the "few" and the "many" in literary commerce, in the 1969 *Poe and the British Magazine Tradition* (20–21, 82, 133–34). And while Pollin argued that Victor Hugo may be the source for Poe's term "grotesque" in his 1970 *Discoveries in Poe* (3–4), Paul A. Newlin continued the majority analysis in "Scott's Influence on Poe's Grotesque," which affirms the priority of Scott's 1827 essay and traces its role in Poe's "defense of the artistry he has given to the commercial form" (11). Subsequent development of the importance of Scott's *Foreign Quarterly Review* essay for Poe's thinking about the "grotesque and arabesque" and Germanism may be found in G. R. Thompson's 1973 *Poe's Fiction: Romantic Irony in the Gothic Tales* (see 110–15; 219n28, 227–29nn2–9), as well as in Thomas S. Hansen and Pollin's 1995 *The German Face of Edgar Allan Poe: A Study of Literary References in His Works* (60–66, 86, 100, 103).

In 1980, Michael Davitt Bell broadened the claim for the importance of Scott's practice of romance for Poe in a study that included Brown, Washington Irving (1783–1859), Nathaniel Hawthorne (1804–64), and Herman Melville (1819–91) in *The Development of American Romance: The Sacrifice of Relation* (4, 15–16, 87–125, 161). In 1987, George Dekker followed with close comparative readings of Scott's historical romances against a wide range of fiction in that mode by U.S. writers (albeit with only brief attention to Poe) in *The American Historical Romance* (see esp. 18, 20, 43, 270–79, 321–24, 346n21). More recently, Thompson and Eric Carl Link offered an extended analysis of the influence of Scott's 1824 *Britannica* supplement on "Romance," and his romance/novel distinctions, on Poe and other nineteenth-century American writers in *Neutral Ground: New Traditionalism and the American Romance Controversy* (73–79, 82–84, 122–27).

4. The Palmer C. Holt Poe Collection

Depending on its date, scholarship on specific borrowings from Scott in Poe's creative work presupposes the data summarized above, as does the unpublished and undated work on Poe and Scott by Palmer C. Holt (1914–2000) in the archives at Washington State University. Holt was a private collector and Poe scholar whose contributions to our understanding of Poe's use of Scott, and of many other writers of the nineteenth century and earlier, are accessible largely only through the holdings of Manuscripts, Archives, and Special Collections at Washington State University's Holland and Terrell Libraries. While still a graduate student at the University of Chicago, Holt began tracing Poe's use of sources, and over the years he assembled a large library of the works that Poe read or reviewed during his lifetime (albeit often in later editions than Poe could have used), kept current with relevant Poe scholarship as it appeared, and created as a research tool a handwritten concordance of all the poetry and fiction in Harrison's seventeen-volume edition of Poe's *Complete Works*. Holt's concordance partly overlaps with Bradford A. Booth and Claude E. Jones's *Concordance of the Poetical Works of Edgar Allan Poe* (1941), which Holt's notes do not suggest he employed, perhaps because it is based on Campbell's *The Poems of Edgar Allan Poe* (1917) rather than on Harrison's 1902 edition. In 1968, Holt's concordance would be usefully complemented by Pollin's *Dictionary of Names and Titles in Poe's Collected Works*, which is, of course, keyed to the Harrison edition. Taking detailed notes on Pollin's *Dictionary* ("[Pollin notes]"), Holt evidently continued to use his own concordance for research, to all indications even after the tool was superseded by Pollin's *Word Index to Poe's Fiction* (1982) and Elizabeth Wiley's *Concordance to the Poetry of Edgar Allan Poe* (1989)—perhaps because these computer-generated guides include little context for the word occurrences indexed and are based not on Harrison but on later scholarly editions of Poe's poems and fiction edited by Mabbott and Pollin.

In the course of Holt's largely private labors, he would publish only two articles on Poe's sources, "Notes on Poe's 'To Science,' 'To Helen,' and 'Ulalume' " in 1959 and "Poe and H. N. Coleridge's Greek Classical Poets: 'Pinakidia,' 'Politian,' and 'Morella' Sources" in 1962. Clearly the extensive source annotations in Mabbott's editions of Poe's *Poems* (1969) and *Tales and Sketches* (1978), as well as those in Pollin's edition of Poe's long fiction in *The Imaginary Voyages* (1981, vol. 1 of *Collected Writings*), must have overlapped many of Holt's yet-to-be-published findings. (By contrast, Stuart Levine and Susan Levine's annotated edition of *The Short Fiction of Edgar Allan Poe* [1976] devotes little attention to Poe's sources.) The private scholar nevertheless persisted, took particularly detailed notes on Mabbott's annotations in the process,[3] and planned to devote his retirement from a long teaching career to work on a comprehensive book on Poe's use of sources. In the draft of an unfinished essay titled "Amenities of Seeking Poe Sources," Holt poignantly wonders what drives individuals to "a pursuit which tends to absorb the hours and years of a lifetime." It was the massive scale of his primary research, I suspect, that prevented Holt from completing more than fragments of his projected study before illness rendered him unable to continue.

In the late fall of 1995, Holt's family generously donated his papers and the working core of his extensive library to Washington State University. To facilitate the donation, Pollin selected approximately four hundred books, periodicals, and reference works that Holt had annotated as source materials for Poe's writings, a gift supplemented in 2003 with thirty-two more annotated texts and additional manuscript materials. In his annotations, Holt underscored words and passages and made very brief marginal notes in pencil—each of them bookmarked with tiny paper slips—in order to identify direct or indirect sources and analogues for Poe's poetry, fiction, and occasionally criticism. Clearly drawing on his concordance, Holt confined most of his identifications of Poe sources to cross-references by volume and page number in Harrison's edition of Poe's *Complete Works* or, when tracing a more general influence, with a Poe title or brief allusion, sometimes qualified with a question mark.

5. Holt, Scott, and Poe Source Scholarship

My concern here is with only a small segment of Holt's collection at Washington State University, his annotated volumes of Sir Walter Scott's fiction. The relevant texts make up, with numerous duplications, a total of forty-three separate volumes (an additional six annotated books, which involve Scott's poetry, and one volume of his posthumously published journal are reserved for separate attention when they can be examined together with Holt's discursive manuscript notes on individual Poe poems).[4] It is clear from the physical distribution of his annotations that Holt read and reread the entire corpus of Scott's fiction and, pencil in hand, marked the material he considered sources for or influences on Poe's creative work. At times, Holt's annotations of Poe's borrowings are merely notations of archaic words or unusual language common to both writers, at times they constitute still-undeveloped findings, and at still other times they have clearly been superseded by published scholarship. In the following survey of relevant source scholarship—most but not all recorded in the volumes of Mabbott's scholarly edition of Poe's poetry and short fiction (*Collected Works*)[5]—published work on Poe's borrowings from Scott's fiction provides the context for an overview of Holt's most important annotations, both when his findings overlap known sources and when they suggest avenues for further exploration.

Studies of Poe's earliest fiction suggest that he experimented with tongue-in-cheek imitation of Scott's historical romances in at least one of his Folio Club tales. In 1931, James Southall Wilson argued that "the stout gentleman who admires Sir Walter Scott" in Poe's planned but never-published Folio Club collection would have contributed "King Pest," which "opens in the most familiar Scott manner, with two men, at first unnamed, in an ale-house" (218). Mabbott cited Wilson's article, granted that the Folio Club member who "admired Scott presumably told ... a historical story," but perfunctorily rejected Wilson's claim that it would have been "King Pest" in favor of "Epimanes" (*Collected Works* 2: 201, 206–7n2, 239). In 1972, I analyzed reasons for accepting Wilson's selection for the stout gentleman; elaborated on the Scott manner at the beginning of "King Pest"; and connected the identity of the Folio Club member to Irving's 1822 "The Stout Gentleman," a comic tale in which Geoffrey Crayon reports a nervous gentleman's glimpse of the broad backside of the still-anonymous "Author of Waverley" ("Reconstruction" 30–31). I subsequently pointed out that Scott acknowledged his "portly person," as well as the sighting of him in "The Stout Gentleman," in Dr. Dryasdust's "Prefatory Letter" to *Peveril of the Peak* (1822; "Further Notes" 39–40). Holt marked the latter reference to "The Stout Gentleman" when annotating the Scott romance, albeit without making explicit the link to Poe's Folio Club character ([HC.4, vol. 14], vii; cf. [EW.14], 6).[6]

Others of Holt's source attributions, especially when they do not directly overlap published scholarship, stand in need of more development than brief annotations allow. In Scott's *Quentin Durward* (1823), Holt marked a pairing of Heraclitus and Democritus as laughing and weeping philosophers as a source for Poe's identical linkage in his juvenile poem "Oh Tempora! O, Mores!" (1868; Scott [HC.4, vol. 15], vol. 1, chap. 6, 100–101; cf. [EW.15] chap. [6], 76; cf. *Collected Works* 1: 9–10; 12nn13–16). Holt found in Scott's *The Antiquary* (1816; [HC.4, vol. 3], vol. 1, chap. 17, 179; vol. 2, chap. 18, 177; cf. [EW.3] chap. [17], 134; chap. [39], 308) possible sources for the comic Dutch names in Poe's "The Devil in the Belfry" (1839; *Collected Works* 2: 366) and for the phrase "leg-bail" in "Epimanes" (1836; 2: 128). Holt claimed that the ballad "Cumnor Hall" (1784), which Scott quoted in his 1831 "magnum opus" introduction to *Kenilworth: A Romance* (1821), functioned as a source for Poe's "The Haunted Palace" (1839; [HC.4, vol. 11], vol. 1, x; cf. [EW.11] chap. [41], 392, and "Essay on the Text" 395–96; cf. [EW.25A&B] n. pag.; cf. *The Prefaces* 171). In the romance, Holt designated Kenilworth castle, its decor and setting, and the court royalty it hosted as sources for the same allegorical poem ([HC.4, vol. 11], vol. 2, chap. 5, 74; chap. 12, 123–24, 127; chap. 18, 201; cf. [EW.11] chap. [13], 252–55; chap. [25], 254; chap. [31], 291–92, 294). In Scott's *The Pirate* (1822; [HC.4, vol. 12], vol. 1, chap. 19, 243; vol. 2, chap. 18, 222; cf. [EW.12] chap. [19], 179–81; chap. [38], 357–58), Holt found a source that links the epigraph and the whirlpool in "The Descent into the Maelström" (1841; *Collected Works* 2: 577, 594–95n). And in Scott's *Peveril of the Peak* (1822; [HC.4, vol. 14], vol. 2, chap. 20, 263; cf. [EW.14] chap. [43], 442), Holt found a character using the phrase "the twin stars of Leda" to praise a woman's eyes, a metaphor that appears in both "Ligeia" (1838) and "A Valentine" (1846). While Mabbott suggested an alternative source for the metaphor—the image of "Ledaean stars" from a Cowley poem quoted in Isaac Disraeli's *Curiosities of Literature* (1791–1823; *Collected Works* 1: 388, 390n2; 2: 313, 332n11)—Holt's precedent is clearly less oblique.

Some Holt annotations simply duplicate published scholarship. Where Holt linked Poe's "MS Found in a Bottle" to Scott's prose note on the "Demon Frigate" in *Rokeby* (canto 2, stanza 11; [HC.3] 728n18; cf. *Poetical Works* 389n18), Mabbott quoted the same note as a thematic source for Poe's tale (*Collected Works* 2: 132). And where Poe indicated that lines quoted in "Al Aaraaf" (1829) were "imitated from Sir W. Scott," Holt traced the lines to the song "Mary" in Scott's *The Pirate* ([HC.4, vol. 12], vol. 1, chap. 12, 162–63; cf. [EW.12] chap. [12], 119–20), precisely the same information offered by Mabbott (*Collected Works* 1: 110–11, 124n141). Other Holt annotations extend published findings. Where Mabbott footnoted the term "levin" in Poe's "Israfel" (1831) as "an obsolete word for lightning, revived by Scott" (1: 174, 178n12), Holt marked specific instances of "levin" in Scott's *Guy Mannering* (1815; [HC.1] chap. 27, 207; cf. [EW.2] chap. [27], 144), as well as in his poetry.[7] Where Mabbott speculated that Poe in "Romance" (1829) was recalling a childhood trip to Scotland when he had his narrator refer to a "painted paroquet," that is, a popinjay (*Collected Works* 1: 128–29n5), Holt suggested that Poe borrowed the image from Scott's detailed description of this ritual Scottish archery target in *Old Mortality* (1816; [HC.4, vol. 5], vol. 1, chap. 2, 180; cf. [EW.4B] chap. [2], 16).

Similarly, where Pollin argued that the probable source for the name and character of Ermengarde in Poe's "Eleonora" (1841) is Scott's *The Betrothed* (1825; "Poe's Use" 332–33; see also *Collected Works* 2: 645), Holt not only made the same linkage when he annotated *The Betrothed* (Scott [HC.4, vol. 18], vol. 1, chap. 13, 145, and passim; cf. [EW.18A] chap. [13], 107 and passim), but also found the name Ermengarde in Scott's "Harold the Dauntless" (1817; [HC.3] canto 1, stanza 14, 373; canto 3, stanza 5, 382; cf. *Poetical Works* 522, 532). Although no Holt annotations support Mabbott's linking of "Hop-Frog" (1849) to Scott's *The Black Dwarf* (1816; *Collected Works* 3: 1335n6), where Mabbott traced Poe's use of "Runic rhyme" in "The Bells" (1849) to Thomas Gray's "Descent of Odin" (1768; *Collected Works* 1: 435ff., 439n10), Holt showed that Scott similarly used the term in "Harold the Dauntless" and explained it in reference to Gray's poetry in *The Pirate* ([HC.3] canto 3, stanza 5, 382; cf. *Poetical Works* 532; [HC.4, vol. 12], vol. 1, chap. 15, 185; vol. 2, chap. 1, 4 and passim; cf. [EW.12] chap. [15], 137; chap. [19], 176–77 and passim).

In his *Edgar Allan Poe: A Critical Biography*, Quinn suggested that the name "Dubourg" (both a Parisian street and a French laundress) in "Murders in the Rue Morgue" (1841) reflects a memory of "the Misses Dubourg who kept the school in London [Poe] attended as a boy" (311). Again Holt identified an alternative source in Scott, who used the name "Dubourg" for a French business agent in *Rob Roy* ([HC.4, vol. 4], vol. 1, chap. 1, 9; chap. 13, 150; cf. [EW.5] chap. [1], 8; chap. [13], 110, 405). In 1936, John Robert Moore suggested that the latter novel, in which the character of Diana Vernon sneers at her cousins as "Ouran-Outangs," may be one source for Poe's murderous "Ourang-Outang" in "The Murders in the Rue Morgue" (Moore, "Poe, Scott" 56). More persuasively, Moore argued that the main source for Poe's primate and his behavior is a literal, murderous orangutan named Sylvan in Scott's *Count Robert of Paris* (1832; 56–57; for Mabbott's agreement, see *Collected Works* 2: 523–24). In his annotations of *Rob Roy* and *Count Robert*, Holt not only supported Moore's case by identifying these specific antecedents for the ape in the "Rue Morgue" (Scott [HC.4, vol. 4], vol. 1, chap. 9, 109; cf. [EW.5] chap. [9], 81; [HC.4, vol. 23], vol. 2, chap. 2, 15–19; cf. [EW.23A] chap. [26], 271–72) but also linked the use in *Count Robert* of the name "Astarte" to Poe's "Eulalie" (1845), "Ulalume" (1847), and "Duc de L'Omelette" (1832; Scott [HC.4, vol. 23], vol. 2, chap. 3, 75; cf. [EW.23A] chap. [3], 38; cf. *Collected Works* 1: 349, 417; 2: 35), as well as the reference to "Chian wine" in the same romance to Poe's "Shadow" (1835; Scott [HC.4, vol. 23], vol. 1, chap. 13, 215; cf. [EW.23A] chap. [13], 139; cf. *Collected Works* 2: 189).

In 1951, Moore returned to Scott to discuss Poe's mining of *Anne of Geierstein* for material for both "The Raven" (1845) and "The Domain of Arnheim" (1847), including the name "Arnheim" itself ("Poe's Reading" 493–96). In 1981, Donald A. Ringe found in the same historical romance convincing parallels between the setting in "The Pit and the Pendulum" (1842) and the dungeon into which Scott's protagonist Arthur Pilipson is thrown. While Holt noted these published parallels (Scott [HC.4, vol. 22], vol. 1, chap. 10, 158; chap. 11, 165–67; chap. 15, 223–25; vol. 2, chap. 3, 45–46; cf. [EW.22] chap. [10], 106; chap. [11], 115–16ff.; chap. [15], 153–54; chap. [21], 235–36), he also found in *Anne of Geierstein* a possible source for "The Gold-Bug" (1843) that Moore and Ringe overlooked. Near the end of Scott's romance, the protagonist carries a coded letter that is accidently exposed to a charcoal fire, at which point a secret message emerges that reads, "The bearer may *not* be trusted" ([HC.4, vol. 22], vol. 2, chap. 12, 192; cf. [EW.22] chap. [31], 343–44). Accidental exposure of a parchment to heat is, of course, the means by which Legrand becomes aware of Captain Kidd's cipher in Poe's tale (*Collected Works* 3: 832–35).

In addition, Holt also found that *Anne of Geierstein* explains an oblique illustration of the diddler's "Audacity" in Poe's "Diddling Considered as

One of the Exact Sciences" ("Raising the Wind"; 1843): "The diddler would not fear the daggers of the Frey Herren" (*Collected Works* 3: 870). In 1976, the Levines conjectured that this may be Poe's version of "Fray Gerundio," the title character in a comic eighteenth-century Spanish history (*Short Fiction* 554n7). In notes to "Diddling" in his 1978 edition, Mabbott, puzzled by the reference, translated it as "The Free Gentlemen" while acknowledging that he had found no source to explain why Poe associates the term with "desperadoes" (*Collected Works* 3: 882n12). In 1995, Hansen and Pollin argued that Poe, lacking German, confusedly cited from memory the aristocratic title "Freiherr" used by the author of a book on assassins (56). By contrast, Holt much more convincingly suggested in his annotations that "Frey Herren" is Poe's German translation of Scott's "Free Companions," the members of secret societies in Germany whose menacing daggers are mentioned repeatedly in *Anne of Geierstein* ([HC.4, vol. 21], vol. 1, chap. 4, 71; chap. 17, 269, and passim; cf. [EW.22] chap. [4], 43; chap. [17], 187, and passim; cf. *Complete Works* 8: 197).

6. Holt on *Ivanhoe* and "The Fall of the House of Usher"

As this survey shows, even though published scholarship on Poe's use of Scott has eclipsed many of Holt's findings, his annotations still offer promising leads for future research and criticism. To illustrate the promise, I end with a more extended analysis of one of Holt's unique findings: Poe's borrowings from Scott's *Ivanhoe* to construct "The Mad Trist" in "The Fall of the House of Usher." Before doing so, I should recall the complexity of Poe's attitudes toward literary borrowing, which he constantly attacked in his reviews. A telling example is Poe's accusing Henry B. Hirst of stealing the image of death by "slanderous tongues" from the author's own "Lenore" (misdated 1830 by Poe, who cited the long-line version of 1844–49). Never admitting that he himself lifted the phrase from Shakespeare (see *Collected Works* 1: 337, 338n11–12), Poe offered Hirst sardonic advice about appropriating others' literary property: " 'Steal . . . the more you put in your book that is not your own, why the better your book will be:—but be cautious and steal *with an air*' " (*Complete Works* 13: 213). As scholars such as Meredith McGill and Jonathan Elmer have suggested, when Poe stole, he was often playing an ironic game (McGill, "Poe, Literary Nationalism" 289–301; Elmer 32–72). When Poe borrowed from *Ivanhoe* to create "The Mad Trist," I think he did so with an air.

Holt's marginal notes to *Ivanhoe*, which he marked in several different editions,[8] inevitably overlap familiar scholarship on two of Poe's well-known borrowings from this famous romance: the name "Rowena" and the dark-lady/light-lady counterpoint for "Ligeia" (see *Collected Works* 2: 306, 333n24, and Scott [HC.2] chap. 2, 57, 59; chap. 4, 81–82; chap. 7, 133–34;

cf. [EW.8] chap. [2], 30, 31; chap. [4], 43–44; chap. [7], 71–72). The thorough Holt also found additional parallels in *Ivanhoe* for Poe's use of "Frey Herren" ("Free Companions") and "Chian wine" (see part 5, above, and Scott [HC.4, vol. 8], vol. 1, chap. 2, 37; chap. 15, 179; vol. 2, chap. 5, 67; chap. 7, 83, 89; cf. [EW.8] chap. [2], 30; chap. [15], 135; chap. [21], 172). More significantly, Holt discovered unrecognized source material in Scott's romance for Poe's "The Raven." In the eighth stanza of that poem, the narrator turgidly says of the raven "from the Nightly shore" that enters his chamber though a "window lattice," " 'Though thy crest be shorn and shaven, thou,' I said, 'art sure no craven' " (*Collected Works* 1: 366). Mabbott tried to redeem this line by arguing that "Nightly" is a chivalric pun and observing that "sometimes cowardly knights had their heads shaved" (1: 372n45). Holt marked concrete sources for Poe's association of knights, ravens, shorn crests, and cowardice in *Ivanhoe*. Specifically, Scott's villainous Knight Templar, the Norman Brian de Bois-Guilbert, carries a shield that displays "a raven in full flight, holding in its claws a skull, and bearing the motto, *Gare le Corbeau*" ([HC.2] chap. 8, 154; cf. [EW.8] chap. [8], 83). Rebecca resists Bois-Guilbert's advances by calling him "Craven knight!—Forsworn priest" and by threatening to cast herself out of a "latticed window" ([HC.2] chap. 24, 361; cf. [EW.8] chap. [24], 199). And the "gay plumage" of knights bloodied in tournaments and battles in *Ivanhoe* is "shorn from . . . crests" or, like Bois-Guilbert's, "partly shorn away, partly burnt" ([HC.2] chap. 12, 206–7; chap. 31, 478; cf. [EW.8] chap. [12], 112; chap. [31], 265).

In scholarship other than Holt's, connections of "The Fall of the House of Usher" with Scott have been rare. Jeffrey Savoye suggested that the description of the ruins of the Hermitage castle in Scott's 1814 *Border Antiquities of England & Scotland* inspires the creation of Usher's house (70–72). And Moore suggested that *The Bride of Lammermoor* must have been an important general source for the tale given Scott's "melancholy young hero, last of his doomed family, dwelling almost alone in a crumbling house, the rooms of which are draped in black; the hero's burial of his nearest relative with his own hands in a family vault inside the house; . . . and the nearby body of water which swallows up the last survivor of his race" ("Poe, Scott" 55–56). Holt, however, found no specific borrowings by Poe for "Usher" or his other creative work in *Lammermoor* ([HC.4], vol. 7; cf. [EW.7A]).

There is only one published effort to link Scott's *Ivanhoe* specifically with "The Fall of the House of Usher": Mabbott's odd footnote to the description in "The Mad Trist" of its hero Ethelred as being "by nature of a doughty heart" and under the influence of "the wine he had drunken" (*Collected Works* 2: 413). Mabbott stated in his note: "Ethelred may get his name from a character in *Ivanhoe*, who is doughty indeed" (2: 422n31).

Because there is no character named "Ethelred" in Scott's romance, Savoye suspected that Mabbott got carried away in this instance by pursuing "ephemeral influences" (73n4). Because Mabbott's edition was posthumously edited, this note may incorrectly represent his actual source finding. Holt recognized that Poe's Ethelred is almost certainly modeled on (not named for) a "doughty" equivalent in *Ivanhoe*, the hard-drinking, sluggish Saxon knight Athelstane of Coningsburgh.

Athelstane is the "ally and kinsman" of Lady Rowena's guardian (and Ivanhoe's father) Cedric the Saxon, the latter of whom intends that his beautiful ward marry Athelstane in order to reestablish the Saxon monarchy to which the Saxon knight is heir. Scott's description of the knight suggests that Cedric's plans are less than wise:

> Athelstane . . . , on account of his descent from the last Saxon monarchs of England, was held in the highest respect by all the Saxon natives of the north of England. . . . He was comely in countenance, bulky and strong in person, and in the flower of his age—yet inanimate in expression, dull-eyed, heavy-browed, inactive and sluggish in all his motions, and so slow in resolution that the soubriquet of one of his ancestors was conferred upon him, and he was very generally called Athelstane the Unready. . . . [H]is hereditary vice of drunkenness had obscured his faculties, never of a very acute order, . . . [over] a long course of brutal debauchery. (Scott [HC.2] chap. 7, 136; cf. [EW.8] chap. [7], 73)

Rowena, in love with Ivanhoe, resists marrying this dim-witted knight in spite of his Saxon bloodlines, even though when not sodden with drink Athelstane can display rather comic stout-heartedness. He does so, as Holt recognized, in the Ashby tournament when he joins forces against an incognito Ivanhoe only to be knocked unconscious with his own battle-ax by the Black Knight (Scott [HC.2] chap. 12, 212; cf. [EW.8] chap. [12], 114–15). He again shows himself "not cowardly" and earns the epithet "doughty" from the jester Wamba when he attempts to rescue a woman he thinks is Rowena from the always-dangerous Bois-Guilbert. Predictably, the latter delivers a mighty blow to the helmet, a blow that Athelstane cannot parry with his mace, one that again renders him senseless ([EW.8] chap. [31], 268; not annotated by Holt). Indeed the knight, presumed dead, is prepared for burial by monks who eventually discover their error but do not want to waste their labors by admitting the fact.

Holt also recognized that Athelstane's response to this treatment in *Ivanhoe* is a source for the equally undead Madeline Usher's return from the grave to interrupt the reading of "The Mad Trist" (*Collected Works* 2: 416). After Athelstane's ostensible death, Cedric finally agrees, in the presence of King Richard and near the bier of Athelstane, to be reconciled with his son Ivanhoe and allow the latter to marry his ward Rowena, but with the following condition:

> "The Lady Rowena must [first] complete two years' mourning, as for a betrothed husband.... The ghost of Athelstane himself would [otherwise] burst his bloody cerements, and stand before us to forbid such dishonor to his memory."
>
> It seemed as if Cedric's words had raised a specter; for scarce had he uttered them ere the door flew open, and Athelstane, arrayed in the garments of the grave, stood before them, pale, haggard, and like something arisen from the dead. (Scott [HC.2] chap. 42, 671; cf. [EW.8] chap. [42], 376)

In "The Fall of the House of Usher," of course, Usher calls the narrator a "*Madman*" and insists that the house's duplication of the sounds in "The Mad Trist" means that his prematurely entombed sister has escaped her coffin and "*stands without the door*"; then, "[a]s if in the superhuman energy of his utterance there had been found the potency of a spell," the "antique" panels of the door slowly draw back and reveal the "enshrouded figure of the lady Madeline of Usher" with "blood upon her white robes" (*Collected Works* 2: 416). While I suspect few contemporary readers recognized Poe's borrowing here, those who did must have contrasted the original with the richly problematic status of Poe's reanimated Madeline. To modern readers, of course, this Madeline has been variously understood as Usher's incestuously close twin sister "emaciated" after a "bitter" but literal struggle to escape premature entombment (2: 416); as a vampire newly emerged from her coffin; as a guilty hallucination shared by the brother and his friend who bury her; and, symbolically, as Usher's double, indeed, even as his feminine side—all possibilities sharply different from the comic, literal materiality of Athelstane's return in *Ivanhoe*. The latter event, for example, elicited this writerly joke from Scott in his notes to the 1830 magnum opus edition: "The resuscitation of Athelstane has been much criticised, as too violent a breach of probability, even for a work of such fantastic character. It was a *tour-de-force*, to which the author was compelled to have recourse, by the vehement entreaties of his friend and printer, who was inconsolable on the Saxon being conveyed to the tomb" ([HC.4, vol. 8], vol. 2, 287n15; cf. [EW.25A&B] n. pag.).

Far more important than Athelstane's resurrection is the section of *Ivanhoe* that Holt recognized as a source for Ethelred's confrontation with a hermit in "The Mad Trist." Holt's finding may be prefaced with Pollin's 1970 comment on the "veneer of medievalism" in this episode: its vocabulary, Pollin suggested, comes from "obsolete terms read in Scott and other historical novelists" (*Discoveries in Poe* 207). Readers of "Usher" are introduced to the vocabulary of "The Mad Trist" by a narrator who assumes they are familiar with Sir Launcelot Canning's narrative:

> I had arrived at that well-known portion of the story where Ethelred, the hero of the Trist, having sought in vain for peaceable admission into the dwelling of the hermit, proceeds to make good an entrance by force. Here, it will be remembered, the words of the narrative run thus:
> "And Ethelred, who was by nature of a doughty heart, and who was now mighty withal, on account of the powerfulness of the wine which he had drunken, waited no longer to hold parley with the hermit, who, in sooth, was of an obstinate and maliceful turn, but, feeling the rain upon his shoulders, and fearing the rising of the tempest, uplifted his mace outright, and, with blows, made quickly room in the plankings of the door for his gauntleted hand; and now pulling therewith sturdily, he so cracked, and ripped, and tore all asunder, that the noise of the dry and hollow-sounding wood alarummed and reverberated throughout the forest." (*Collected Works* 2: 413)

Remarkably, Holt is alone in recognizing that Poe based this "well-known portion" of "The Mad Trist" on the Black Knight's confrontation with a hermit in chapter 16 of *Ivanhoe*. When the Black Knight—Richard the Lionheart traveling incognito—wanders deep into the woods near the Derbyshire Hills after the tournament at Ashby, he seeks a bed and supper; encounters a ruined chapel; and, expecting "hospitality" from the hermit who occupies it, "leap[s] from his horse and assail[s] the door of the hermitage with the butt of his lance, in order to arouse attention and gain admittance" (Scott [HC.2] chap. 16, 257; cf. [EW.8] chap. [16], 140). When the hermit stubbornly refuses the knight's demands even after extended appeals, the latter threatens to "beat" the door down and "make entry" for himself. After continued defiance and "barking and growling" from the hermit's dogs, "the knight struck the door so furiously with his foot that posts as well as staples shook with violence" ([HC.2] chap. 16, 259; [HC.4, vol. 8], vol. 1, chap. 16, 187; cf. [EW.8] chap. [16], 141). At this point, the hermit grudgingly relents; the dogs are restrained; food, drink, and ballads are exchanged; and the hermit turns out to be the bearded, brawny, and convivial Friar Tuck ([HC.2] chap. 16–17; cf. [EW.8] chap. [16–17]). Clearly Holt had good reason for marking these passages as sources for the "well-known portion" of Sir Launcelot Canning's "The Mad Trist" in which "the hero . . . , having sought in vain for peaceable admission into the dwelling of the hermit, proceeds to make good an entrance by force" (*Collected Works* 2: 413). It hardly seems a coincidence that Poe gives the author of "The Mad Trist" a knighthood that recalls Sir Walter Scott's.[9]

7. Scott's Fiction in the United States

It seems certain that Poe would have expected readers of "The Mad Trist" to recognize this borrowing from *Ivanhoe*. As Hart noted in *The Popular Book: A History of America's Literary Taste*, Scott's "novels were the most popular of all American pleasure reading" from 1814, when *Waverley* was first published, until well beyond his death in 1832 (73, 77–78). Dekker argued that the publication of *Waverley* and its successors "must be reckoned one of the major intellectual events of the nineteenth century" because in them Scott "developed a model of historical narrative that transformed the writing of fiction and history" (29). More significantly for this essay, Dekker credited Scott with creating both "the genre [of the historical romance] as we know it and an immense international market for... books like *Rob Roy* and *Ivanhoe*" (1). William St. Clair's study of reading in the Romantic period concludes that Scott's novels outsold those of all other novelists in English combined (221–22). And Emily B. Todd pointed out that Scott was the favored target for pirating by American publishers in this era (496), a practice that, along with the lack of international copyright, helped create what McGill called a culture of reprinting in the United States (*American Literature* 76–79, 88–89).

The economic returns of this culture, especially for publishers of Scott's fiction, obviously sustained years of frequent reprintings of Scott works. Listings in the *American Imprint* series, as well as in William B. Todd and Ann Bowden's *Sir Walter Scott: A Bibliographical History 1796–1832*, record an average of fifteen separate U.S. imprints of Scott titles (counting collected sets with multiple volumes as only single works) in each of the years between 1820 (when *Ivanhoe* debuted in America) and the appearance of "The Fall of the House of Usher" in 1839 (Shoemaker et al., 1820–39; see also listings of U.S. reprints in Todd and Bowden chaps. 3–5, for individual novels, and chaps. 6–7, for collected editions). The same sources document that *Ivanhoe* alone enjoyed a minimum of twelve reprintings in the United States by seven different publishers in the first three years after its initial appearance in this country (Todd and Bowden 509–11; see also Shoemaker et. al, 1820–23). Indeed, to quote Jane Millgate's study of its publication, *Ivanhoe* achieved an "aura of the immense fame... on its first publication in [December] 1819 [which it] subsequently maintained through its role as model for innumerable works of historical fiction published in all parts of the world during the succeeding century" (795).

After suffering an 1826 bankruptcy fueled by his financial entanglements in publishing and advance commitments of his immense literary income,

Scott placed new emphasis on securing returns from his past work by re-editing collected editions of his writings. In 1829, he began to issue his "corrected and annotated [magnum opus] edition of the Waverley novels" with "new introductions . . . and extensive notes" through the Edinburgh publisher Robert Cadell (E. B. Todd 498; see also Todd and Bowden 885–87). Especially important here is that Scott's introduction to the "magnum opus" edition of *Ivanhoe* in 1830 called explicit attention to "the meeting of the King with Friar Tuck at the cell of that buxom hermit" and discussed the popularity of the motif, which involves "the rambles of a disguised sovereign," in "old romances" ([HC.4] vii–xii; cf. [EW.25A& B] n. pag.; cf. *The Prefaces* 140–44). Obviously, in 1830 Scott alerted a new generation of readers to the very section of his romance that Poe imitated in "The Mad Trist." And nine years later, when "Usher" was published, the listings in *American Imprints* show that the "magnum opus" version of *Ivanhoe* enjoyed four separate U.S. printings in the year 1839, two in stand-alone editions and two as parts of multivolume sets of the *Waverley Novels* (Shoemaker et al., 1839).

8. The Significance of the "Usher"-*Ivanhoe* Connection

To hypothesize about the function of "The Mad Trist" for an audience familiar with both Scott and the hermit episode in *Ivanhoe*, we must first grant that Canning's story shifts sharply away from the original after Ethelred noisily breaks through the hermit's door. Rather than facing a "maliceful" hermit, Ethelred confronts "a dragon of a scaly and prodigious demeanor" with "fiery tongue" and "pesty" breath, a beast that in turn guards "a palace of gold, with a floor of silver," on the wall of which hangs an enchanted "shield of shining brass" (*Collected Works* 2: 414). By altering his original with these magical and legendary elements, of course, Poe insures that Sir Launcelot Canning's "uncouth" imitation of *Ivanhoe* will include noisy events that correspond point for point with those leading to the end of "Usher." Thus, the noise of the knight's shattering of the door, followed by the "death-cry of the dragon" and "the terrible ringing sound" of the "brazen shield" as it falls to the silver floor, are echoed by the physical sounds of Madeline's escaping her coffin, opening the iron door of her prison, and struggling within "the copper archway of the vault" to reach the narrator's bedchamber, where, ironically, "The Mad Trist" itself is being read to calm down her troubled twin brother (2: 414–16). Madeline's entrance, of course, initiates the end of Poe's tale, when the separated Usher twins fall into one another in their "final death-agonies," mirrored by the corresponding death of their ancestral house as it, too, collapses into its reflection in the tarn (2: 416–17; 398).

Clearly, Poe adapted and altered the hermit episode in *Ivanhoe* so that "The Mad Trist" mirrors climactic plot events in its frame story. More significantly, I think Poe deliberately invokes Scott in this story within a story to locate his elegantly wrought Gothic tale, and himself as its author, in the literary marketplace. As we have seen, in 1839 that marketplace had long been heavy with reprints of Scott's popular historical romances, the imitators of which Poe had been reviewing since 1835. Scott Peeples pointed out that the text's description of "The Mad Trist" as a romance of "uncouth and unimaginative prolixity" (*Collected Works* 2: 413) implies to various critics that Poe saw it as "parodic" and "purposively ludicrous" (185), although the admiration Poe expressed for *Ivanhoe* suggests a more complex purpose than his simply making fun of a twenty-year-old book. In my view, an adequate formulation of "The Mad Trist" as parody must make sense of the relationship between this story within a story—with its transformation of the knight's assault on a hermit's door into a battle for entrance into a golden palace—and the generically different Gothic tale that frames it.

One approach to such an explanation is to expand Peeples's view of "The Fall of the House of Usher" as a self-referential "story about its own construction" (188). In light of Holt's findings, I think the tale should also be approached as a self-referential story about its own relationship to readers and the marketplace for Gothic fiction. In these terms, "Usher" encodes Poe's concerns about whether his demanding, symbolically intricate use of the Gothic can be competitive against the cruder appeal of work by imitators of Scott's historical romances. Thus, when Poe's narrator and title character turn from "por[ing] together over" the esoteric, "rare and curious" books in Usher's library (*Collected Works* 2: 408–9, 419–21nn15–25) and distract themselves with the "uncouth and unimaginative prolixity" of "The Mad Trist," Poe dramatizes how the audience for demanding books such as Usher reads had shifted its attention to the far-less-sophisticated pleasures of imitation "antique volume[s]" (2: 413), that is, historical romances in the Scott manner. To put the point in somewhat different terms, the story within a story in "Usher" ironically poses the question of how complex authors would fare with readers who were satisfied with such crude effects as the fiery-tongued dragon and exotic palace of gold in "The Mad Trist," or even with the improbable resurrection of Athelstane in the original *Ivanhoe*—whether or not one's printer felt it to be necessary.

Finally, Holt's source findings in *Ivanhoe* make possible a fuller marketplace-oriented reading of "The Fall of the House of Usher" as an allegory of the displacement of one of Poe's favorite literary genres, the Gothic, by another, the historical romance in the manner of Sir Walter Scott. In terms of context, this reading takes into account not only the *Ivanhoe* source for "The Mad Trist" but also the historic sequence of prose romance forms that Thompson and Link traced in *Neutral Ground* (82–100). It also recognizes, as has Poe criticism generally, that the 1839 "Usher" emerged at the end of a period in Poe's career in which he experimented, often ironically, with various genres in fiction ranging from the historical romance ("King Pest" [1835] and "Epimanes") and the "voyage of discovery" ("MS. Found in a Bottle" and *Pym*) to the Gothic, both in the earlier manner of Horace Walpole (1717–97; "Metzengerstein" with the 1836 subtitle "A tale in imitation of the German" [*Collected Works* 2: 15–17]) and in the more recent fashion of the 1820s *Blackwood* tale of terror (explicitly parodied in "Loss of Breath" [1835] and "How to Write a Blackwood Article" [1838], pushed to an extreme in "Berenice" [1835])—to name just a few. During much of this period, Poe could place his tales in magazines but not convince book publishers to issue them in the Folio Club framework that attributed their variety to fictional literary club members (Hammond, "Evolution of a Lost Book" 13, 24–38). When, at the end of the 1830s, Poe finally secured book publication for an unframed collection of his tales (Quinn 287–90), his preface would assert that most of the twenty-five stories were "the result of matured purpose and very careful elaboration" and "written with an eye to this republication in volume form," with a "certain unity of design" implied by the title, *Tales of the Grotesque and Arabesque* (*Collected Works* 2: 473–74).

Reprinted in this 1840 collection, "The Fall of the House of Usher" is clearly a self-conscious exercise in a long-established Gothic tradition by a writer who was, as Terence Whalen set forth at length, a professional student of the economy of the literary marketplace, particularly after the Panic of 1837 affected returns from both magazine and book publishing (see esp. 21–57). Thus Poe was certainly aware that, beginning with Scott's *Waverley* in 1814, the popularity of the historical romance had far exceeded that of fiction written in the conventions of the Gothic. The preface to *Tales of the Grotesque and Arabesque* offers a sign of such awareness, for in it Poe defended his fiction against charges of " 'Germanism' and gloom," charges that imply that a Gothic manner is out of step with the contemporary marketplace in fiction (*Collected Works* 2: 473; Thompson 19–20). In light of the context from which it emerged and Holt's recognition of its relationship to *Ivanhoe*, "The Fall of the House of Usher" can be read as a self-referential allegory of the marketplace fortunes of its Gothic mode, an allegory built into the contrast of Usher's entrapment in his ancestral home and Ethelred's quest for riches in "The Mad Trist."

Clark Griffith, it is relevant to point out here, read Poe's "Ligeia" of 1838 in similar terms. Building on Poe's self-consciousness of literary tradition, and on the fact that the author "shifted facilely and readily from one vein of prose fiction directly into another" in this period (8), Griffith found in "Ligeia" a sardonic allegory of a weak and "hopelessly uninspired" British Romanticism—figured in the character of a light-haired Rowena who owes her name to the conventional heroine in *Ivanhoe*—being overcome and then reanimated by German Transcendentalism—figured in the character of the learned, dark-haired Ligeia (9–13, 17–25). This essay argues for an analogous reading of "The Fall of the House of Usher" of 1839: a narrator-critic visits an ancient house emblematic of a decaying, ingrown Gothic literary tradition, a house that falls when the narrator calls attention to an alternative genre, the historical romance, by reading "The Mad Trist." Presiding over this house is the isolated, self-absorbed, self-referential author (and artist-musician) Roderick Usher—implicitly a Poesque figure trapped in "the vein" of "Germanism" longer than "for the time being," a manner that Poe himself acknowledged practicing in his preface to *Tales of the Grotesque and Arabesque*, a statement clearly composed in the same year (*Collected Works* 2: 473–74).

To elaborate this allegory briefly, it is from the collapse of Usher's literary domain that the narrator flees after failing to rescue the master whose control—like that of "the monarch Thought" over his "dominion" in the "Haunted Palace"—is "tottering" (*Collected Works* 2: 406). The intervention involves trying to turn Usher's attention away from his Gothic house (and his obsession with the unquiet double of himself buried in it) so that he can focus instead on "The Mad Trist"—as repeatedly noted, an imitation of the historical romance in the manner of Scott's *Ivanhoe*. Thus, the narrator plays a concerned critic, one who tries to aid an author frozen in the Gothic—able to write only such self-reflective works as "The Haunted Palace" (itself a mise en abyme for "The Fall of the House of Usher")—by pointing him toward an alternative (and more lucrative?) literary mode, a romance featuring an ironically appropriate story of a knight's impatient quest for fortune. The result is a spectacular failure: Usher hears only the sounds of his own house's buried secrets rather than the narrated noises of Ethelred's breaking down doors and fighting dragons in order to win "a palace of gold" with a "floor of silver." The point: while the literary marketplace may offer riches to "doughty" adventurers of romance such as Ethelred, for self-absorbed authors such as Usher who are trapped in the decayed house of their literary ancestors and unable to avoid the reduplications it produces (2: 398–400), the future promises only extinction when house and master collapse in upon themselves.

NOTES

1. Material from the Palmer C. Holt Poe Collection is quoted with permission of Manuscript, Archives, and Special Collections (MASC), Holland and Terrell Libraries, Washington State University, Pullman, WA. This project owes particular thanks to Trevor Bond and Pat Mueller of MASC for aid with the Holt materials. I have briefly reported Holt's source findings relative to Scott's fiction in papers at the American Literature Association conference in

Baltimore, May 1998, and at the Third International Edgar Allan Poe Conference in Philadelphia, October 2009. For use of the Holt archive in a recent study of Poe's borrowings from Edward Bulwer-Lytton's *Pelham; or, The Adventures of a Gentleman* of 1828, see Richard Kopley (esp. 109–10).

2. Pollin suggests that Bulwer-Lytton was the source of Poe's misspelling of "Lammermoor" as "Lammermuir" in "Bulwer-Lytton's Influence" 10.

3. See Holt, "[Mabbott Poe edition (*Poems*)]," "[Notes on Mabbott, Tales II]," and "[Notes on Trelawny, 'MS. Found,' Mabbott]."

4. Holt annotated individually published volumes of *Marmion* (1810) and *Lady of the Lake* (1810), as well as the contents of two collections and an anthology selection of Scott's poetry. His separate notes on Poe's poems are located in various folders, most unlabeled, in box 1 of the Holt Papers.

5. The known sources for Poe's long fiction (*Pym* [1838], "Hans Pfaall" [1835], and "Julius Rodman" [1840]) evidently do not include Scott. In the sources for these works recorded in volume 1 of Pollin's edition of Poe's *Collected Writings*, there is only one indirect reference to Scott (268n10.2A), a note to *Pym* that cites the account of the Flying Dutchman in Scott's footnotes to *Rokeby* (1813)—an account that Mabbott quotes as a thematic source for "MS Found in a Bottle" (1833; *Collected Works* 2: 132).

6. Parenthetical citations to annotated Scott works in the Holt Collection are coded "[HC.n]," with "n" designating an annotated volume or multivolume edition of Scott's writings as numbered in order in "Works Cited." To aid in locating the relevant passages in the standard scholarly edition of Scott's fiction, I accompany all parenthetical citations to Holt's annotated texts (which often have internal volume divisions with discontinuous pagination and chapter numbering) with equivalent citations to volumes in *The Edinburgh Edition of the Waverley Novels* (1993–present), coded "[EW.n]" and listed individually in "Works Cited" with "n" designating the volume number in that edition. In citations to volumes in the *Edinburgh Edition*, only their continuously numbered chapters [in square brackets] and pagination are used. For access to the latter edition, I wish to thank Dave Smestad, Interlibrary Loan/Access Services, Holland and Terrell Libraries, Washington State University, Pullman, WA, and Julie Monroe, Special Collections and Archives, University of Idaho Library, Moscow, ID. In the few references to Holt's annotations of Scott's poetry, citations are to HC.3 and accompanied by equivalents in an accessible modern collection, J. Logie Robertson's edition of Scott's *Poetical Works* for Oxford University Press.

7. Holt also notes occurrences of "levin" in his annotations to Scott's *The Lay of the Last Minstral* (canto 4, stanza 18; canto 6, stanza 25); *Rokeby* (canto 2, stanza 14; canto 5, stanza 33); "The Fire King" (stanza 8); and "The Dance of Death" (stanza 1)—[HC.3] 25, 41, 219, 252, 431, 472; cf. *Poetical Works* 26, 46, 327, 364, 638, 725.

8. Holt does overlapping annotations of two different editions of *Ivanhoe*, volume 8 of HC.4 and HC.2; because the former is less extensively marked, it is cited only when its findings do not overlap with those in HC.2.

9. The sources of Sir Launcelot Canning's name, and Poe's later use of it as a pseudonym, are discussed by Mabbott in *Collected Works* 1: 328 and 2: 422n30 and Pollin in *Discoveries in Poe* 206–29.

WORKS CITED

Allen, Michael L. *Poe and the British Magazine Tradition*. New York: Oxford UP, 1969. Print.

Alterton, Margaret. *Origins of Poe's Critical Theory*. University of Iowa Humanistic Studies 2.3. Iowa City: The University, 1925. Print.

Bell, Michael Davitt. *The Development of American Romance: The Sacrifice of Relation*. Chicago: U of Chicago P, 1980. Print.

Booth, Bradford A., and Claude E. Jones. *A Concordance of the Poetical Works of Edgar Allan Poe*. Baltimore: Johns Hopkins UP, 1941. Print.

Campbell, Killis. "Poe's Reading." University of Texas *Studies in English* 5 (1925): 166–96. Print.

Cobb, Palmer. *The Influence of E. T. A. Hoffmann on the Tales of Edgar Allan Poe*. Chapel Hill: U of North Carolina P, 1908. Print.

Dekker, George. *The American Historical Romance*. Cambridge, UK: Cambridge UP, 1987. Print.

Elmer, Jonathan. *Reading at the Social Limit: Affect, Mass Culture, and Edgar Allan Poe*. Palo Alto: Stanford UP, 1995. Print.

Griffith, Clark. "Poe's 'Ligeia' and the English Romantics." *University of Toronto Quarterly* 24.1 (1954): 8–25. Print.

Hammond, Alexander. "Edgar Allan Poe's *Tales of the Folio Club*: The Evolution of a Lost Book." *Poe at Work: Seven Textual Studies*. Ed. Benjamin Franklin Fisher IV. Baltimore: Edgar Allan Poe Soc., 1978. 13–55. Print.

———. "Further Notes on Poe's Folio Club Tales." *Poe Studies* 8.2 (1975): 38–42. Print.

———. "A Reconstruction of Poe's 1833 *Tales of the Folio Club*: Preliminary Notes." *Poe Studies* 3.2 (1972): 25–32. Print.

Hansen, Thomas S., with Burton R. Pollin. *The German Face of Edgar Allan Poe: A Study of Literary References in His Works*. Columbia, SC: Camden, 1995. Print.

Hart, James D. *The Popular Book: A History of America's Literary Taste*. 1950; Berkeley: U of California P, 1961. Print.

Holt, Palmer C. "Amenities of Seeking Poe Sources." Folder, MS 2010–06, box 1. Holt Papers on E. A. Poe. Manuscript, Archives, and Special Collections, Holland and Terrell Libraries, Washington State U, Pullman. MS.

———. "[Mabbott Poe edition (Poems)]." Folder, MS 2010–06, box 1. Holt Papers on E. A. Poe. Manuscript, Archives, and Special Collections, Holland and Terrell Libraries, Washington State U, Pullman. MS.

———. "[Notes on Mabbott, Tales II]." Folder, MS 2010–06, box 1. Holt Papers on E. A. Poe. Manuscript, Archives, and Special Collections, Holland and Terrell Libraries, Washington State U, Pullman. MS.

———. "Notes on Poe's 'To Science,' 'To Helen,' and 'Ulalume.'" *Bulletin of the New York Public Library* 63.11 (1959): 568–70. Print.

———. "[Notes on Trelawny, 'MS Found,' Mabbott]." Folder, MS 2010–06, box 1. Holt Papers on E. A. Poe. Manuscript, Archives, and Special Collections, Holland and Terrell Libraries, Washington State U, Pullman. MS.

———. "Poe and H. N. Coleridge's Greek Classical Poets: 'Pinakidia,' 'Politian,' and 'Morella' Sources." *American Literature* 34.1 (1962): 8–30. Print.

———. "[Pollin notes]." Folder, MS 2010–06, box 1. Holt Papers on E. A. Poe. Manuscript, Archives, and Special Collections, Holland and Terrell Libraries, Washington State U, Pullman. MS.

Jacobs, Robert D. *Poe: Journalist and Critic*. Baton Rouge: Louisiana State UP, 1969. Print.

Kopley, Richard. "Poe's Taking of *Pelham* One Two Three Four Five Six." *Poe Studies* 41 (2008): 109–16. Print.

McGill, Meredith. *American Literature and the Culture of Reprinting, 1834–1853*. Philadelphia: U of Pennsylvania P, 2003. Print.

———. "Poe, Literary Nationalism, and Author Identity." *The American Face of Edgar Allan Poe*. Ed. Shawn Rosenheim and Stephen Rachman. Baltimore: Johns Hopkins UP, 1995. 271–304. Print.

Millgate, Jane. "Making It New: Scott, Constable, Ballantyne, and the Publication of *Ivanhoe*." *Studies in English Literature, 1500–1900* 34.4 (1994): 795–811. Print.

Moore, John Robert. "Poe, Scott, and 'The Murders in the Rue Morgue.' " *American Literature* 8.1 (1936): 52–58. Print.
———. "Poe's Reading of *Anne of Geierstein.*" *American Literature* 22.4 (1951): 493–96. Print.
Newlin, Paul A. "Scott's Influence on Poe's Grotesque." *American Transcendental Quarterly* no. 2 (1969): 9–12. Print.
Peeples, Scott. "Poe's 'constructiveness' and 'The Fall of the House of Usher.' " *The Cambridge Companion to Edgar Allan Poe.* Ed. Kevin J. Hayes. New York: Cambridge UP, 2002. 178–90. Print.
Poe, Edgar Allan. *Collected Works of Edgar Allan Poe.* Ed. Thomas Ollive Mabbott. 3 vols. Cambridge, MA: Harvard UP, 1969–78. Print.
———. *The Collected Writings of Edgar Allan Poe.* Vol. 1. *The Imaginary Voyages: The Narrative of Arthur Gordon Pym, The Unparalleled Adventure of One Hans Pfaall, The Journal of Julius Rodman.* Ed. Burton R. Pollin. 1981. New York: Gordian, 1994. Print.
———. *The Collected Writings of Edgar Allan Poe.* Vol. 2. *The Brevities: Pinakidia, Marginalia, Fifty Suggestions, and Other Works.* Ed. Burton R. Pollin. New York: Gordian, 1985. Print.
———. *The Collected Writings of Edgar Allan Poe.* Vol. 3. *Writings in "The Broadway Journal": Nonfictional Prose, Part 1, The Text.* Ed. Burton R. Pollin. New York: Gordian, 1986. Print.
———. *The Collected Writings of Edgar Allan Poe.* Vol. 4. *Writings in "The Broadway Journal": Nonfictional Prose, Part 2, The Annotations.* Ed. Burton R. Pollin. New York: Gordian, 1986. Print.
———. *The Collected Writings of Edgar Allan Poe.* Vol. 5. *Writings in "The Southern Literary Messenger": Nonfictional Prose.* Ed. Burton R. Pollin and Joseph V. Ridgely. New York: Gordian, 1997. Print.
———. *The Complete Works of Edgar Allan Poe.* 17 vols. Ed. James A. Harrison. 1902. New York: AMS Press, 1965. Print.
———. *Essays and Reviews.* Ed. G. R. Thompson. New York: Lib. of America, 1984. Print.
———. *The Poems of Edgar Allan Poe.* Ed. Killis Campbell. Boston: Ginn, 1917. Print.
———. *The Short Fiction of Edgar Allan Poe: An Annotated Edition.* Ed. Stuart Levine and Susan Levine. 1976. Urbana: U of Illinois P, 1990. Print.
Pollin, Burton R. "Bulwer-Lytton's Influence on Poe's Works and Ideas, Especially for an Author's 'Preconceived Design.' " *Edgar Allan Poe Review* 1.1 (2000): 5–12. Print.
———. *Dictionary of Names and Titles in Poe's Collected Works.* New York: Da Capo, 1968. Print.
———. *Discoveries in Poe.* Notre Dame: U of Notre Dame P, 1970. Print.
———. "Poe's Use of the Name Ermengarde in 'Eleonora.' " *Notes and Queries* ns 17.9 (1970): 332–33. Print.
———. *Word Index to Poe's Fiction.* New York: Gordian, 1982. Print.
Quinn, Arthur Hobson. *Edgar Allan Poe: A Critical Biography.* 1941. New York: Cooper Square, 1969. Print.
Ringe, Donald A. "Poe's Debt to Scott in 'The Pit and the Pendulum.' " *English Language Notes* 18.4 (1981): 281–83. Print.
Savoye, Jeffrey. "Sinking Under Iniquity." *Edgar Allan Poe Review* 8.1 (2007): 70–74. Print.
Scott, Walter, Sir. [EW.22]. *Anne of Geierstein.* Ed. J. H. Alexander. *The Edinburgh Edition of the Waverley Novels.* Vol. 22. Edinburgh: Edinburgh UP, 2000. Print.
———. [EW.3]. *The Antiquary.* Ed. David Hewitt. *The Edinburgh Edition of the Waverley Novels.* Vol. 3. Edinburgh: Edinburgh UP, 1995. Print.
———. [EW.18A]. *The Betrothed.* Ed. J. B. Ellis, with J. H. Alexander and David Hewitt. *The Edinburgh Edition of the Waverley Novels.* Vol. 18A. Edinburgh: Edinburgh UP, 2009. Print.
———. [EW.7A]. *The Bride of Lammermoor.* Ed. J. H. Alexander. *The Edinburgh Edition of the Waverley Novels.* Vol. 7A. Edinburgh: Edinburgh UP, 1995. Print.
———. [EW.23A]. *Count Robert of Paris.* Ed. J. H. Alexander. *The Edinburgh Edition of the Waverley Novels.* Vol. 23A. Edinburgh: Edinburgh UP, 2006. Print.

———. *The Edinburgh Edition of the Waverley Novels.* 30 vols. Ed.-in-Chief David Hewitt. Edinburgh: Edinburgh UP; New York: Columbia UP, 1993–present. Print.

———. [EW.2]. *Guy Mannering.* Ed. P. D. Garside. *The Edinburgh Edition of the Waverley Novels.* Vol. 2. Edinburgh: Edinburgh UP, 1999. Print.

———. [HC.1]. *Guy Mannering.* Ed. William Allan Nielson. The Harvard Classics Shelf of Fiction. New York: Collier, 1917. Print.

———. [EW.25A&B]. *Introduction and Notes from the "Magnum Opus" Edition of 1829–33.* Ed. David Hewitt. *The Edinburgh Edition of the Waverley Novels.* Vol. 25A&B. Edinburgh: Edinburgh UP, 2011 [forthcoming]. Print.

———. [HC.2]. *Ivanhoe.* Ed. H. Ward McGraw. New York: Merrill, 1928. Print.

———. [EW.8]. *Ivanhoe.* Ed. Graham Tulloch. *The Edinburgh Edition of the Waverley Novels.* Vol. 8. Edinburgh: Edinburgh UP, 1998. Print.

———. [EW.11]. *Kenilworth: A Romance.* Ed. J. H. Alexander. *The Edinburgh Edition of the Waverley Novels.* Vol. 11. Edinburgh: Edinburgh UP, 1993. Print.

———. "On the Supernatural in Fictitious Composition: and Particularly in the Works of Ernest Theodore William Hoffmann." *Foreign Quarterly Review* 1.1 (1827): 60–98. Rpt. in *Sir Walter Scott On Novelists and Fiction.* Ed. Ioan Williams. London: Routledge, 1968. 312–53. Print.

———. [EW.14]. *Peveril of the Peak.* Ed. Alison Lumsden. *The Edinburgh Edition of the Waverley Novels.* Vol. 14. Edinburgh: Edinburgh UP, 2007. Print.

———. [EW.12]. *The Pirate.* Ed. Mark Weinstein and Alison Lumsden. *The Edinburgh Edition of the Waverley Novels.* Vol. 12. Edinburgh: Edinburgh UP, 2001. Print.

———. [HC.3]. *The Poetical Works of Sir Walter Scott, Bart.* London and New York: Warne, [1895]. Print.

———. *Poetical Works, With the Author's Introduction and Notes.* Ed. J. Logie Robertson. 1904; London: Oxford UP, 1971. Print.

———. *The Prefaces to the Waverley Novels.* Ed. Mark A. Weinstein. Lincoln: U of Nebraska P, 1978. Print.

———. [EW.15]. *Quentin Durward.* Ed. J. H. Alexander and G. A. M. Wood. *The Edinburgh Edition of the Waverley Novels.* Vol. 15. Edinburgh: Edinburgh UP, 2001. Print.

———. [EW.5]. *Rob Roy.* Ed. David Hewitt. *The Edinburgh Edition of the Waverley Novels.* Vol. 5. Edinburgh: Edinburgh UP, 2008. Print.

———. [EW.4B]. *The Tale of Old Mortality.* Ed. Douglas Mack. *The Edinburgh Edition of the Waverley Novels.* Vol. 4B. Edinburgh: Edinburgh UP, 1993. Print.

———. [HC.4]. *The Waverley Novels.* Lib. Ed. From the Last Rev. Ed., Containing the Author's Final Corrections, Notes, &c. 27 vols. Boston: Parker and Mussey; New York: Redfield and Francis; Philadelphia: Thomas, Cowperthwait; Cincinnati: Derby, 1852–53. [The majority of Holt's annotations are in this multivolume edition. A bookseller's note in the first volume states it lacked vol. 16 when purchased.] Print.

Shoemaker, Richard H., Gayle Cooper, Carol Rinderknecht, et al. *A Checklist of American Imprints for 1820–[39].* New York: Scarecrow, 1964–88. Print.

St. Clair, William. *The Reading Nation in the Romantic Period.* Cambridge, UK: Cambridge UP, 2004. Print.

Stovall, Floyd. *Poe the Poet.* Charlottesville: UP of Virginia, 1967. Print.

Thompson, G. R. *Poe's Fiction: Romantic Irony in the Gothic Tales.* Madison: U of Wisconsin P, 1973. Print.

Thompson, G. R., and Eric Carl Link. *Neutral Ground: New Traditionalism and the American Romance Controversy.* Baton Rouge: Louisiana State UP, 1999. Print.

Todd, Emily B. "Walter Scott and the Nineteenth-Century American Literary Marketplace: Antebellum Richmond Readers and the Collected Editions of the Waverley Novels." *Publications of the Bibliographical Society of America* 93.4 (1999): 495–517. Print.

Todd, William B., and Ann Bowden. *Sir Walter Scott: A Bibliographical History, 1796–1832.* New Castle, DE: Oak Knoll, 1998. Print.

Whalen, Terence. *Edgar Allan Poe and the Masses: The Political Economy of Literature in Antebellum America.* Princeton: Princeton UP, 1999. Print.

Wiley, Elizabeth. *Concordance to the Poetry of Edgar Allan Poe.* Selinsgrove, PA: Susquehanna UP, 1989. Print.

Wilson, James Southall. "The Devil Was In It." *American Mercury* 24.94 (1931): 215–20. Print.

W. D. Howells's Unpublished Letters to J. Harvey Greene

DONNA CAMPBELL
Washington State University

The relationship between W. D. Howells (1837–1920) and his boyhood friend James Harvey (or Hervey) Greene (1833–90)[1] is treated only briefly in biographies of Howells, an understandable situation given the extensive network of professional and personal relationships that Howells cultivated throughout his life.[2] But the two men maintained a friendly, if intermittent, correspondence until Greene's death in 1890, and Greene was an important presence during Howells's formative years, as Howells indicates in *Years of My Youth* (1916). Also supporting the idea of Greene's importance to Howells at this time are the scarce surviving letters, "one in 1852 and seven each in 1857 and 1858 [that] provide only a sketchy account of these years" (Howells, *Selected Letters* 1: xiv), of which one mentions Greene and another is written to Greene and his wife Jane. In 2008, seven newly discovered and previously unpublished letters from Howells to Greene were made available for publication by John T. Narrin, Greene's great-great-great-grandson, and William Griffing, a descendant of Greene's sister Cassie. The rarest of these is a letter from 1854, a year for which no other letter from Howells is known to exist. The Howells-Greene letters held by Narrin include, in addition to the 1854 letter, one from the 1860s, two from the 1870s, and three from the 1880s; another letter from Howells was reprinted in Greene's lengthy obituary in the *Medina County Gazette and News* in 1890 ("He Sleeps").

The Howells-Greene letters held by Narrin not only offer glimpses of Howells's attitudes about everything from the Young America movement to Leo Tolstoy (1828–1910) but also create a context for Howells's fascination with the narrative of Greene's life. In these letters and in Greene's memoir *Reminiscences of the War*, a more complex picture of Howells emerges through his relationship with Greene because Howells casts Greene as a character with two different personae. The first is an idealist whose active life in the service of his principles Howells admired as a contrast to his own; for the young Howells, Greene served as role model, mentor, friend, and critic. In recounting Greene's life in 1915 and 1916,

RESOURCES FOR AMERICAN LITERARY STUDY, Vol. 34, 2009.
Copyright © 2011 AMS Press, Inc.

however, Howells writes about the later Greene as a tragic figure in a real-life drama that Howells could not stop retelling: the story of Greene's unjust dismissal from the Army because of the prejudices of a superior officer. In *Years of My Youth*, Howells pinpoints the "defeat" of Greene's life (*Selected Letters* 6: 83n3) as arising from this episode, in the process implicitly contrasting Greene's early promise and later "defeat" with his own unpromising beginnings but later great success as a critic and author.

James Harvey Greene and W. D. Howells

The friendship between Howells and Greene began in 1847 when Greene, at age fourteen, became an apprentice at the *Hamilton* [OH] *Intelligencer* under Howells's father, the publisher William Cooper Howells (1807–94).[3] As W. D. Howells writes in *Years of My Youth*, Greene lived "with our family like one of ourselves, as brotherly as if he had been of our blood" until he "left us to live the wandering life of the journeyman printer . . . fighting and writing on the Free State side" in Kansas (122). By June 1856, Greene was working at the *Herald of Freedom*, the newspaper of the Emigrant Aid Society that had settled Lawrence, an antislavery stronghold in the contested territory of "bleeding Kansas" ([Destruction of the *Herald of Freedom* Office]). Its editor, George Washington Brown (1820–1915), may have known Greene when both lived in Jefferson, Ohio; a May 1 letter to Greene, then at the *Cleveland Leader*, from the abolitionist James Redpath (1833–91) suggests such a connection.[4] On May 21, Lawrence was attacked, the Free State Hotel was burned, and the newspaper's printing presses were destroyed by a force of eight hundred to one thousand proslavery Southerners. Greene reported on the destruction of the *Herald of Freedom* office in a letter published in the June 12, 1856, issue of the *New York Daily Times*, noting indignantly the arrest and imprisonment of G. W. Brown and others on charges of "*high treason!*" by the proslavery sheriff, Samuel J. Jones (1820–80; [Destruction of the *Herald of Freedom* Office]). Howells's comment about Greene's "fighting and writing" on the antislavery side is borne out by the public record, as well as by Greene's later recollections of his days as a "border ruffian" ("He Sleeps" 1).

By 1857, Greene had moved away from Lawrence, and if his activities on behalf of the abolitionist cause had slowed, his antislavery sentiments had not. From the offices of his new position at the Jefferson, Ohio–based *Ashtabula Sentinel*, he wrote on March 24 to John Brown offering aid and expressing admiration. By July, he was the editor of the *Prairie du Chien* [WI] *Leader*,[5] where he was to remain for a few years, and in August, he married Jane R. Harvey (1834/35–?). Within the next three years, the couple had two daughters, Ellen I. (Nellie; 1858–?) and Sarah C. (Clara; 1860–?) (see 1860 Census and 1870 Census);[6] yet when the Civil War broke out, Greene volunteered. In September 1861 he was commissioned Captain of Company F of the 8th Wisconsin Infantry Volunteers, known as the "Eagle Regiment" for its mascot, a live bald eagle called Old Abe that was carried into battle on a standard bearing the Union colors (Williams 121).[7] Greene was mustered out on February 27, 1865, settled in Ohio, and on July 1, 1869, purchased the newspaper he would publish for the rest of his career, the *Medina County Gazette* (Perrin et al. 292).[8] According to Harriet Taylor Upton and Harry Gardner Cutler in their *History of the Western Reserve*, Greene was a popular editor who during his tenure increased the "circulation and general influence" of the *Gazette*; they add that he was "not only a journalist of repute but an eloquent public speaker as well" (375). His oration on the U.S. Centennial, a history of the nation, is reprinted in full in the *History of Medina County* "at the repeated request of friends of this enterprise" (Perrin et al. 364). He died on May 31, 1890 (Upton and Cutler 374).

Howells's Letters to Greene

The first of Howells's extant letters to Greene was written during the summer of 1854, which was one of the worst years of Howells's life (Goodman and Dawson 27).

Sunday, June 4th, 1854
Jefferson, Ash[tabula] Co., O[H]

Dear Hervey:
  How naturally does one put off everything in the way of letter-writing till Sunday. My little library is filled from morning till late at night with eager and countless letter-writers: the printer-girls writing endless epistles to far off friends, Vic scratching notes to her acquaintance, and Joe answering correspondence from all quarters.[9] Truth to tell, I look with not a little envy on the many and gilt-edged notes which Joe receives. He has a dozen she-friends when I have none, and I have often marveled that he should be so popular with them, when I find no favor in their eyes at all. I console myself, however, when I reflect that the ladies are a giddy, superficial set, and are ridiculed by some of our most eminent writers.
  As I was saying, the library is besieged by scribblers all Sunday long, and I am not a little surprised, therefore, to find myself in peaceful possession of it at one o'clock. The view from the window at which I sit gazing, in the vacancy of don't-know-what-to-say-ness—is passing lovely! The most striking object in the foreground is a useful but not-to-be-named little building, embowered in the shade of the grandest of wild cherry trees. On either

hand stretches a tract of clay, facetiously up and planted with corn, from which the heat hazes upward, like it used to do from the stove at school. Chickens are making beds in the garden beds, and a solitary and sultry turkey gobbler is stalking thro' a thick growth of smart-grass, picking truculent insects therefrom. He has not even the ambition to gobble when I whistle at him. There is, however, an impotent old chicken cock in full chase of a coy and virtuous pullett [sic]. I am in no pain for her honor, however, for the old fellow is so wholly a prey to the weakness of age that he will never harm her. He reminds me of one [of] those worn-out gallants whom Addison describes in his Spectators, who without the power of gratifying their licentious desires, were forever losing their self-command, and the gravity of age in "the presence." However, I shall not stray off into an essay on chastity, but will come at once to your letter.

To your questions as to whether or no I am a progressive, etc., I hardly know what to say. I fear that in most things you will deem me a conservative. I hate Young America, brass, boots, collar and all. I eat meat. I drink coffee. I am not a believer in socialism and place very little faith in the "good time coming." Slavery, however, I abhor from the bottom of my heart, as the son of an Englishman[10] can and ought. I do not use tobacco, and thoroughly mislike the puppyism which vents itself in bad cigars. I am in favor (if you except the drinking of wine) of teetotalism. But withal, I have a great love for whatever is old and time hallowed, and in this love, I am more and more confirmed every day. I do not see that the world is a whit better now than it ever was. Nor do I see how it is to be improved by the disuse of meat-eating, and a perfection of table-tilting. However, I am open to conviction, and I should like to see some thoughts from you on the subject.

I am proud of the praise you bestow upon my attempts at poetizing. There is, perhaps, no admiration which is so welcome to one as that he receives in private from his friends, and to a young writer, you will agree with and understand me when I say, it is doubly so.

You speak of my coming to see you. I fear that is one of the not-to-be-dones of this life, though nothing would give me more pleasure. You, however, who are about withdrawing from business, might easily come to see us. What do you say to the Fourth of July as a day? I will be at the cars in readiness, if you will but come. I think you might. We all want to see you so much and there is to be the [illegible] kind of a blowout here on "the anniversary of our national independence." If you do not answer this straightaway, I shall conclude that you are coming.

Your friend,
    Will. D. Howells

At first glance, the letter shows little outward evidence of Howells's psychological crisis that summer, which took the form of what he called "*hypochondria*," a combination of depression with a fear of dying by rabies so paralyzing that he was forced to cease work in his father's printing office at the *Ashtabula Sentinel* (Goodman and Dawson 27). Instead, it mixes mildly risqué subjects (the outhouse, the impotent rooster chasing a pullet) and coy references to young women with an attempt to provide a vivid description of his surroundings. But Howells's decisive responses to the serious contemporary questions of the day, made apparently in response to a query of Greene's, suggest a young man determined to set down his ideas for a friend whose ethical as well as literary standards he values.

After thanking Greene for his "praise" for his "attempts at poetizing," Howells provides a comprehensive list of his beliefs. Not surprisingly, given Greene's fervent abolitionism, Howells asserts his abhorrence of slavery but rejects the expansionism (and what he sees as the boisterous exhibitionism) of the Young America movement. He also rejects vegetarianism, socialism, or spiritualism ("table-tilting") as a possible solution to the world's problems, although he would later become interested in Tolstoy's Christian socialism and would explore the supernatural in such works as *The Undiscovered Country* (1880), *The Shadow of a Dream: A Story* (1890), and *Questionable Shapes* (1903). Having dismissed socialism and other schemes for reforming the world, at this point in his life Howells speaks positively only of "whatever is old and time hallowed," a stance that discourages any possibility of social change except contemplation of the past. In contrast, Greene believed in actively pursuing social change: even before moving to Lawrence, he had been running a literary paper, but he changed its politics to promote the Free-Soil cause. When the Kansas-Nebraska Bill passed in 1854, Greene sold the paper and "went to Kansas to help make it a free state" ("He Sleeps" 1), putting his abolitionist beliefs before practical advancement. In referring to Greene's idealism, his "withdrawing from business" to fight for his principles, Howells may be hinting at a dissatisfaction with his own lack of action in comparison with Greene's fiery activism.

Howells's published letters from 1857 to 1865 further suggest the continuing friendship between Greene and the Howells family. Howells's brother Joe, who, like Greene, was older than Howells, apparently played matchmaker for Harvey and Jane Greene: in *Years of My Youth*, Howells asserts that Joe encouraged a correspondence between Greene and "a young girl of the village" who later became his wife (122). As Howells reports to his sister Vic on April 20, 1857, about the romance, "I have received two letters from Harvey this week. Poor, homesick soul! he's twice as 'bad took' as I—and after all the tossing about in the world that he has done, too!" (*Selected Letters* 1: 9). After Harvey and Jane Greene's marriage in August

1857, Howells writes to the newlyweds in November of that year, thanking them for their "husbandandwifely and exceedingly welcome letter" and humorously bemoaning the lack of news in "our charming hamlet" (*Selected Letters* 1: 15). As he had done with his mention of Joseph Addison's (1672–1719) *Spectator* papers in the 1854 letter, however, Howells makes it clear that this is a literary and intellectual, as well as a personal, friendship. He laments the loss of *Putnam's Magazine*, which had recently ceased publication, but professes himself "charmed with the 'Atlantic' " despite its being "a little too *Bostony* in its flavor" (*Selected Letters* 1: 17). The correspondence and friendship continued: on January 28 and 29, 1865, Howells wrote to his sister Anne from Venice, asking, "Why has Harvey Greene never a message to send me? You must remember me cordially to him" (*Selected Letters* 1: 208), perhaps forgetting that Captain J. H. Greene's actions in the Vicksburg campaign, the Red River campaign, and other crucial battles over the past four years might have made him too busy to write.

By 1868, Howells was himself a little "*Bostony*," since he had been for three years the assistant editor of the *Atlantic Monthly*, the magazine that had so charmed him in 1854.

Boston
January 29, 1868

My dear Harvey:

I got your paper, the other day, with the very kind notice of my Dall'Ongaro article, for which I thank you. After reading that, I read the whole paper, and whether it was really good, or seemed so from its relation to praise of me, I liked it very much, and felt like saying something about it in The Atlantic.

I hope that you and Jane and the little Harvies and Janes are well, and passing the winter comfortably. The winters here are a great trial to me, after Italy, and as soon as the leaves begin to fall, I feel like engaging my passage for Liverpool. However, unless Chase is elected President, and I am sent minister to Florence, I see no present chance of getting back there. Do go in for Chase, Harvey!

My wife not being very strong, we've shut up our house in Cambridge for a little while, and come into Boston to board—we have a lodging and dine at a restaurant. Winny enjoys this arrangement immensely, and won't hear of going back to Cambridge.

Harvey, is there anything in your army experience or observations that would make into a poem or a small romance? I can't get a "subject" and it's money out of pocket every day I remain in this state.

Give Elinor's and my own love to Jane and the little ones, and believe me as ever,

Your affectionate,
W. D. Howells.

This 1868 letter suggests both the personal bonds of friendship that the two had maintained after the war and Howells's respect for Greene's literary acumen. The humorous exhortation to vote for Salmon P. Chase (1808–73) so that the Howells family could return to Venice asks Greene to back a favorite son candidate over the interests of Greene's staunchly Republican paper, the *Fremont Journal*.[11] The mention of family members would be a constant in the letters exchanged between the two from this point on: Howells had married Elinor Mead (1837–1910) in Paris on Christmas Eve, 1862, and by January 1868 the couple had one child, Winifred (Winny), born on December 17, 1863. Two others would follow: John Mead on August 14, 1868, and Mildred (Pilla), on September 26, 1872.

The letter further testifies to Howells's treatment of Greene as a professional writer and editor. Since at this stage of his career Howells sometimes worried about whether a given article would be successful, he thanks Greene for the notice of the "Dall'Ongaro" article, an essay on Francesco Dall'Ongaro (1808–73) first published in the January 1868 *North American Review*, but he goes on to praise Greene's piece as something he wishes to mention in *The Atlantic*. The request for "subjects" from Greene's army experiences further demonstrates that Greene is not only a friend but also a fellow writer. Although Howells did not yet depend entirely on the fiction he could write, since he would not leave *The Atlantic* until March 1, 1881, the pressure he felt to make money by means of his pen existed already, and he characterized himself at this time as "a mill, ceaselessly grinding" (Goodman and Dawson 129). The letter demonstrates both a parallel and a contrast between the two careers, given Howells's recognition that Greene, as an editor, had the power to promote Howells's writing, albeit on a smaller stage than Howells could command with a mention of Greene's paper in *The Atlantic*.

Another reference to Greene's editorial boosting of Howells's work occurs in Howells's letter to his father dated October 31, 1868. Howells praises Greene's thoughtful notice about Howells's mother's death, which had appeared earlier that month, but he continues to be preoccupied about the success of his articles: "Much will depend upon the success of Gnadenhütten: if that is generally liked, I shall feel encouraged to go on in the same direction" (*Selected Letters* 1: 303). Published in the *Atlantic Monthly* in January 1869, "Gnadenhütten" was hardly calculated to be a popular choice for a nation still feeling the emotional and physical wounds of the recent war. It tells of the 1782 massacre at Gnadenhütten in eastern Ohio, in which ninety-six Christian Indians at prayer were bludgeoned to death and scalped by white militiamen. On April 12, 1869, Howells wrote to his brother Joe, "Thank you for the scrap from Harvey's paper. It was very pleasant of him to mention my article, which hasn't been too successful. Please give him my love when you write him" (*Selected Letters* 1: 322). Despite its subject matter, or perhaps because of its local historical interest, Greene apparently helped to promote the article even if it was not "too successful" elsewhere.

Howells continued to share his literary interests with Greene, sending him books of interest to both, as a November 12, 1870, letter and those from the 1880s demonstrate.

Office of the Atlantic Monthly
No. 124 Tremont Street
Boston
November 12, 1870
My dear Harvey:

I arranged your affair with Messrs. Fields, Osgood & Co. so that they should send you an advertisement by which you could pay for Bryant's Homer without any outlay. I hope that this was to your satisfaction and that you now have the books.

We are all well, but I'm horribly busy, or I should have answered you before. Besides my Atlantic work I've been seeing a book through the press and giving a course of lectures in Boston.

We should have been much glad to see you last summer and if it hadn't been so hot, I should have gone to Medina, I believe. But I had a sort of heat-stroke in New York and I thought it best to be cautious.

Are you never coming to Boston? I should like so much to have you here.

Elinor joins me in love to Jane.

Yours affectionately,
    Will.

The lectures to which Howells refers are his well-attended course on "New Italian Literature" at the Lowell Institute in the fall of 1870 (Goodman and Dawson 135), and the book to which Howells refers is probably *Suburban Sketches*, first published in book form in 1871 but based on a collection of *Atlantic* articles that had appeared from 1868 to 1870. Howells's reference to his "heat-stroke" is but one instance of his sporadic bouts of ill health, and he would fear the recurrence of his heat-stroke in 1871. His illnesses, however, were rarely as severe as Elinor's and Winifred's intermittent but chronic invalidism, as mentioned in the letter of May 14, 1885.

There was apparently a slight rift between the friends in the 1870s. In an 1873 letter to his father, Howells wrote, "I'm sorry that Harvey bought my books—for I should [have] been so glad to send him a set, if I hadn't rather stupidly supposed that he had them. I wrote to him last week in reply to a letter which I got a long time ago. I'm glad to hear that he feels friendly towards me, for he had some reason to feel otherwise . . . " (*Selected Letters* 2: 14). As George Arms and Christoph K. Lohmann suggest, the reason for Howells's speculation about Greene's possible coolness is not known (*Selected Letters* 2: 14n4).

By the end of the decade, however, Howells writes warmly from his new home, Redtop, to congratulate Greene on the marriage of his daughter.

Editorial Office of
The Atlantic Monthly
Winthrop Square,
Boston
October 20, 1879

Dear Harvey:
You gave me your kind message when I was at Jefferson [Ohio] and if I had been at all master of my time while I was in Cleveland, I should have let you know my whereabouts. But I was there only a day and a half, and had to be too much at the disposal of others to make an appointment with you. Of course I could not let you come all the way from Medina and take your chances of finding me. But can't you make all this even by coming some time to Boston, and paying us a visit? That seems much simpler, and would be [illegible] pleasanter. We have a lovely little place here in the country (5 miles out), and could make you have a good time.

Elinor joins me in congratulations to you and Jane on your daughter's marriage. Joe told me about the wedding-feast, and what a pleasant affair it was. I wish we could have been there. Remember me to the young people, and wish them joy from me.

Our hope is to see Jane here with you. My wife joins me in cordial regards to you both.
Yours affectionately,
    W. D. Howells

The "lovely little place here in the country (5 miles out)" was the Howells family's new house in Belmont, Massachusetts, which was designed in part by William Rutherford Mead (1846–1928; Elinor Mead Howells's brother). Called "Redtop" for its redwood shingles and red-painted roof, it had been built with substantial input from Elinor Howells. Howells and his family had moved there on July 8, 1878, and it proved to be a good place for family life as well as for Howells's writing (Goodman and Dawson 203–5). The "daughter" to whom Howells refers is probably Sarah C. (Clara) Greene, the younger of the Greenes' two daughters.[12] That he did not mention her by name suggests that the primary relationship existed between Howells and the two elder Greenes, rather than a family friendship in which Howells had come to know the Greene children as individuals.

When Howells next wrote to Greene, on May 14, 1885, *The Rise of Silas Lapham* was appearing in serial form in *Century Magazine*.

302 Beacon Street
Boston
May 14, 1885

Dear Harvey:
　I don't know how you will take the turn that the love-affairs have taken in Silas Lapham but I hope you won't think them too recreant to tradition. You old-fashioned novel-readers will have to be treated like "offensive partizans" in the reform of fiction. I shall look to Jane to defend me, in any event.
　I should like dearly to see you both, and I hope sometime soon to do so. But I am a slave to my trade, and I hardly see the hour when I can have off long enough to enjoy myself.
　I am sorry to hear of your sickness. I am very well myself, but Elinor is a standard invalid, and Winifred has no health. Mildred and John are [tough?]. With our love to Jane. Yours ever,
　Will

The principal "love-affair" in *The Rise of Silas Lapham*, to which Howells refers, is doubly unconventional: first, Tom Corey, the young scion of an old Boston family, behaves unconventionally by wanting to go into Silas Lapham's paint business instead of spending his days in genteel idleness; and second, he falls in love with Penelope Lapham, the less beautiful and more outspoken of Silas's two daughters. The affectionate tone with which Howells addresses both Greenes is similar to that of his earlier letters of the 1850s; and, as he had done in the letter to Harvey and Jane Greene in 1857, Howells includes Jane as a figure with decided literary opinions of her own, since she is to "defend" his realism against what he teasingly calls Harvey's defense of traditional novels. As part of his humor, Howells uses the same terms for enemies in the "realism war" that had been applied to those whom Greene had fought at Vicksburg and in the Red River campaign. Perhaps inevitably, the letter returns to the topic of the Howells family's illnesses, for at this time the mysterious nervous malady that had plagued Winifred since she was sixteen was intensifying. In 1885 and 1886, as she stubbornly refused to eat or exercise, the Howells family moved from city to city throughout the Northeast in a desperate search for a cure. Winifred ended up a patient of S. Weir Mitchell (1829–1914) in 1889, the year she died of heart failure in Mitchell's care (Goodman and Dawson 295).

In 1886, Greene sent Howells *Reminiscences of the War*, a privately printed volume in an edition of fifty copies, based on letters he had written home during the Civil War. Howells had begun writing the "Editor's Study" columns for *Harper's New Monthly Magazine* in January of that year, and for the next six years he would continue to champion realism in this forum. The positions of the two as writer and critic were now clearly reversed. Instead of a young poet pleased by Greene's praise or a tentative author hoping for a good notice of "Gnadenhütten" from his editor friend, Howells was now the most influential literary critic in the country and in a position to pass judgment on the memoir of Greene, his former critic and mentor.

302 Beacon Street
Boston, Aug. 29, 1886

Dear Harvey:

I got your book yesterday, and read it through last night. Even if it had not been yours, I should have found it intensely interesting. That long letter of Jane's was excellent; how well she writes. I thank you heartily for the book, in which I was amused to find a bit of my own history embalmed. Do you think you could spare me a copy for the Boston Public Library?

You have done the right thing in printing your reminiscences just as they were written; they have a wonderful freshness and vitality.

I am just going to write to father who is to return to Jefferson [Ohio] in October. It's a great relief to have him going back to be near Joe. I suppose I shall visit him before winter, and then I'll get Joe to show me the way to Medina. Joe spent Friday with me. You never [saw?] such a change in a man. He's actually well and making [illegible].[13]

My own family are in the country so you both must receive my love for all. It's a big lump. Yours ever,
Will.

Howells's praise of the book, which he reinforces with a request for a copy for the Boston Public Library, should be taken at face value, for *Reminiscences of the War* is indeed "intensely interesting." It contains sharp observations and balances the action-filled descriptions of engagements with vivid sensory evocations of the reality of war, such as the "zip" and "thug" of the bullets, by which the men know whether their comrades were safe or hit (68). Greene describes the daring of Colonel Joseph Anthony Mower (1827–70), the brigade commander, who escapes from his captors despite the bullet that hits him "in the face, going into one cheek, through his mouth, knocking out his teeth, and out on the other side" (32), as well as a grotesque moment when Greene, having slipped under a blanket next to a sleeping soldier on a bitterly cold night, finds himself huddled next to a Confederate corpse. Although Greene devotes much space to the fighting, he pauses to sketch brief, illuminating portraits of individuals, such as the rendering of Ulysses S. Grant (1822–85) before the siege of Vicksburg in his "slouch hat, a torn blouse, and an eye glass slung over his shoulder" (55) and vignettes such as the sight of "our boys [emptying] their haversacks" for the starving Confederate troops until "every rebel you see is going about munching a hard tack" (65) after the siege was over. He has a keen eye for the effects of war on civilians, which affected the "fine looking old man" who, as the Union troops set fire to his mill, "put his hand to his head and slowly walk[ed] away as if his heart" were breaking (54), as well as the " 'poor cuss' standing disconsolately by a dilapidated old cabin, watching the soldiers steal his cabbage and onions" (51).

As befits Greene's antislavery politics, *Reminiscences* has much to say about the "mildew of human slavery" as a "blasting curse to a country" (16). At Bate's plantation in Mississippi, he learns that female slaves were made to line up three times a year and those who were not pregnant received twenty lashes (53). He notes frankly the ways in which treating human beings as property leads to other repellant practices, such as incest, when he observes a "young white woman," a slave, whose master was both her father and her child's father (36). When discussing the injustices of slavery, Greene wrote openly about following his strong principles rather than army regulations. He describes at length his company's helping a slave, Jimmy, to escape to Illinois in defiance of General Henry Wager Halleck's (1815–72) order that escaped slaves should not be harbored in the camps (7–8), and he rounds out this story by relating his later accidental meeting with a free and relatively prosperous Jimmy years later on a riverboat (86). Greene was equally, if injudiciously, frank when giving his opinions of those in command. He praised Grant for his steady judgment and effective tactics but called George B. McClellan (1826–85) a "great puffed up toad" (7), stated that General Nathaniel Banks (1816–94) was "totally deficient in every element of military talent" (79), and heaped scorn on "our brilliant Lt. Col. J. W. Jefferson," who was drunk at Vicksburg and shot himself in the finger to avoid active duty thereafter, and who "would injure me in any way he could, if he could do so stealthily" (82).[14]

But Greene spares time in his book for glimpses of family and home life as well, including a letter from Jane detailing her visit to the regiment's encampment in Tennessee. On January 6, 1863, he comments on the marriage of his old friend Howells, the "bit of . . . history embalmed" mentioned in Howells's 1886 letter:

> Your news from home is delightfully interesting; not the least bit of the information is that of the marriage of our dear friend Will D. Howells. Quite a little romance, wasn't it, his betrothed going all the way to Paris, where they were married, and then going to that paradise of lovers, Venice. How glad I am that Will got the appointment as Consul to Venice. It was the opportunity he had long wanted; and he will make good use of it in gathering materials for future literary efforts. I wonder often how he must feel, away from home while this war is going on. (40)

It was not the first time that Greene had found himself in the thick of action in pursuit of a moral cause while Howells observed from a safe distance, and the contrast between the choice of a life of action versus one of contemplation could not have been lost on Howells. Greene concludes *Reminiscences* with an account of his decision to leave the service after three and a half years as the war was winding down, heading north "with several other officers who had likewise been mustered out, with our honorable discharges and a record of our services inscribed on them, in our pockets" (84)—a picture at odds with one that Howells would give in *Years of My Youth*.

The last of the unpublished letters to Greene reflects Howells's growing interest in Tolstoy.

Lee's Hotel, Auburndale, Massachusetts
May 14, 1887
Dear Harvey:

I got your letter yesterday morning, and the Gazette came in the evening. I read your printed notice through to the first-rate "ad." of the close. It made me yell, and it had the same effect on Elinor, whom I tried it on instantly. But your words about my sketch were most touching to me and I felt your kind heart in every one. It's perfectly delightful to think of your coming with Jane to meet me at Jefferson. I start—or intend to start—tomorrow, and I shall be overjoyed to see you both.

The old Hamilton days have often commended themselves to me as extremely good material, and I suppose I shall use them yet, tho' just how, I don't know.

I'm glad you find Tolstoi so great. For me, he's a test; I find that no fool or liar likes him. His books have changed my whole way of looking at life; I can't see myself or others as I once did.

But I hope soon to talk all these things out with you, and many others.

Yours affectionately,
  Will

Upset at the injustice of the legal system in the case of those accused in the Haymarket Riots of 1886, Howells sought solace in Tolstoy's works, reading *War and Peace* (1869) in January 1887, although he found Tolstoy's Christian socialism naive (Goodman and Dawson 286). But the "change" Howells speaks of is nonetheless genuine, and on August 12 he sent Greene other works by Tolstoy: *Anna Karenina* (1875–77), *Childhood* (1852), *Boyhood* (1854), *Youth* (1856), *My Religion* (1884), *My Confession* (1882), and *Iván Ilyitch* (1887), with *What to Do?* (1886; also known as *What Is to Be Done?*) to follow upon its publication.[15] The timing is significant: in March, two months before his letter to Greene, Howells had been called "the moral writer, the idealist, Howells," at a gathering of literary celebrities in honor of Henry Wadsworth Longfellow (1807–82; see Goodman and Dawson 276). As the Haymarket prisoners were tried and sentenced in August, the month in which he sent Greene a shipment of books by Tolstoy, Howells moved from idealism to action, writing private letters to those with jurisdiction over the case and then a public appeal on behalf of those condemned to death that was printed in the *New-York Tribune* and the *Chicago Tribune*. For taking this unpopular stand, Howells found himself "demonized in the press," as even the *New-York Tribune* tried to distance itself from his letter (Goodman and Dawson 283). Like Greene, he had acted upon his beliefs, and, like Greene, he had earned little but the satisfaction of knowing he was right for doing so.

But Howells also sounded a happier note in the letter by referring to the men's early days in Ohio. The "printed notice through to the first-rate 'ad.' " is Greene's notice of Howells's "My Year in a Log Cabin," which appeared in the May 12 *Youth's Companion*. In the May 13, 1887, issue of the *Medina County* [OH] *Gazette*, Greene reviews Howells's "bit of autobiography" and reminisces about the boyhood pastimes he enjoyed with Will and Joseph Howells:

> We remember that a spear hurled from the hands of one of the braves in a close quarter conflict struck the future poet and novelist

near one of the eyes, breaking up the battle in a panic, and the swolen [*sic*] face surgically treated and bound up by his dear mother.... Will spent many years in Venice and Italy, gathering the honey of literature, and reaching the topmost round in the ladder of fame in America as a novelist; "the oldest brother" works as hard getting out the Ashtabula "Sentinel" every Thursday as he did in getting out the Hamilton "Intelligencer" or Dayton daily before he had a beard, and the writer after two years in Kansas in "border ruffian" times and four years in Dixie, has for nearly twenty years been getting out the Medina GAZETTE every Thursday, terms $1.50 per year. ("Howells' Autobiography")

If Greene felt any regrets that Howells had surpassed him by "gathering the honey of literature" and "reaching the topmost round in the ladder of fame" while he, despite his active service, had settled for the life of a small-town editor, the sting of the comparison is muted by the humor of the close of the "first-rate ad."

The final letter from Howells to Greene, that of May 27, 1890, appeared in the June 6, 1890, issue of the *Medina County* [OH] *Gazette and News* ("He Sleeps" 4; ellipses in original):

Boston
May 27, 1890
My Dear Harvey:
I have just got home and found your letter to Joe, which he had forwarded to me. I wish I could give you by hand and mouth some touch of the sympathy I feel with you in your trials. Life is not what we saw it when we were boys; but at least it has love in it, and love is but at times. I have glimpses of a kind of future man as much above me as I am above a "dragon of the prince," who will not always suffer in suffering, but will know that it is all to some end and what the end is.... I have not forgotten the talk we had in those trouser-tearing rustic chairs under father's spruce trees and your frank censure of some of my tendencies. I think that what you said helped me to get a new and true start....
Your affectionate friend,
    Will.

In addition to the general consolation the letter offers, Howells refers once again to their boyhood days and Greene's "frank censure" of Howells's "tendencies," those that inclined him to hypochondria and self-doubt. As he explains in *Years of My Youth*, Greene gave him "specific instructions . . . for my entry into the great world; as if he would realize in my prosperous future the triumphs which fortune had denied him in his past," including advice to "face the proudest down and make audacity do the part of the courage I was lacking in" (128). In praising Greene's giving him a "new and true start," Howells pays tribute to Greene and the importance of the mentoring received at his hands in those "trouser-tearing rustic chairs," even as he credits Greene with a degree of precognition of their opposing fortunes in the future.

A quarter of a century later, as Howells began to write *Years of My Youth*, Greene's role was transformed from that of important (if apparently brusque) mentor to that of a suffering innocent as Howells began to focus on another part of Greene's story: the tale of a man unjustly accused by a superior officer. In a letter to his sister Aurelia dated July 21, 1915, Howells writes of an incident he had not discussed in any of the letters to Greene:

> Another thing: Did either of you know of poor Harvey Greene's being forced out of the army in dishonor by his superior officer who lied against him? I used to hear of it from Joe, who said that Harvey always meant to kill the wretch if they met. But of course this didn't happen; the man died. (*Selected Letters* 6: 83)

In their note to this passage, Arms and Lohmann explain that, "In a later letter to Aurelia, 4 February 1916 (MH), Howells wrote that 'Harvey was a fine fellow, intense and brave; but his life seems to have been a defeat; and poor Jane's' " (*Selected Letters* 6: 83).[16] Howells continues in this vein in *Years of My Youth*, which he was writing at the time: "H. G. was among the first to volunteer for the great war, and quickly rose from the ranks to be captain, but somehow he incurred the enmity of a superior officer who was able to have him cashiered in dishonor from the army" (122). The retelling in *Years* is more dramatic, since being cashiered, unlike simply resigning from the service, involves public disgrace.

Greene's service record provides the missing context for the circumstances for Howells's story of his "defeat." Greene had held several positions of responsibility during his tour of duty, including Acting Inspector General for the "District of North East Louisiana" on June 19, 1863, with duties that included inspecting the arms, clothing, and other equipment of the regiments under his jurisdiction. Whether a misunderstanding arose from Greene's reporting a deficiency in a regimental commander or from some other cause, on July 23, 1864, Special Orders No. 246, section 35, states that Greene "is hereby dishonorably dismissed [from] the service of the United States, with loss of all pay and allowances, for habitual drunkenness on duty; defrauding the government by selling public property, and appropriating the proceeds to his own use." That Greene, who was so idealistic about the antislavery cause that he had given up his business and gone to Kansas in 1854, and so earnest that he had written scathing comments about those who sought to defraud the army and its soldiers in letters home, would betray the Union cause seems highly unlikely; it is more probable that he incurred the wrath of a superior officer who lied against him, as Howells claimed. Further evidence that Greene had been unjustly accused appears in the reversal of his dismissal on January 13, 1865, in Special Orders No. 20, section 11, which states that Greene "is, upon the recommendation of his Commanding General, hereby restored to his command, with pay from the date at which he rejoins his regiment for duty." Greene rejoined his company on February 26, 1865, and was "Honorably Mustered out of U. S. Service" the next day. Of this contretemps, he mentions only the honorable discharge and its date in *Reminiscences* (84).

Despite this experience and the bitterness that might have been its logical consequence, a bitterness at which Howells hints in his late letters, Greene remained involved with the military and veterans' affairs after the war. He attended at least one later encampment of the regiment, in 1889 (Williams 123), and his obituary provides an extensive record of his service.[17] Upton and Cutler state that "it seems pathetically fitting that his death should occur soon after he had officiated so tenderly in the decoration of the soldier graves of the Medina veterans" (375), a circumstance noted in his obituary, which quotes Greene as saying "I can now die more easily" after the visit of his army comrades to his sickroom ("He Sleeps" 1). Greene remained an eminent man in his own sphere: he plays a prominent role in the *History of Medina County* (Perrin et al.), gave the "sketch of national history" oration at the July 1876 dedication of the Soldiers' Monument of Medina, and was called upon to speak at local ceremonies marking the death of General Grant (Perrin et al. 364).

Given Greene's record, then, why did Howells see his life as a "defeat"? The unjust treatment Greene apparently received at the hands of a dishonest superior does not seem to have soured him on the institution of the Army, if public sources are to be believed, nor are there intimations in the existing letters that he wanted a more active literary career or a wider degree of recognition than he had as a respected small-town editor. Howells did not provide Greene with the extensive literary suggestions that he regularly gave to young aspiring writers, so presumably Greene did not ask for this kind of advice. Greene's chronic illness, which his service record dates from the earliest years of the war, evoked sympathy from Howells in at least one letter, yet despite—or perhaps because of—his family's perennial ill health, Howells seems not to have focused on this as a cause of the "defeat."[18] Although Howells reports that Greene wanted to kill the "wretch" who had injured his reputation, he did not report Greene as saying that his life had been ruined thereby, although that is the interpretation that Howells put on the incident. Since the narrative of defeat emerges late in Howells's account of Greene's life, another possibility is that, as Howells assessed his own early life and subsequent career for *Years of My Youth,* he compared it with that of Greene: the timid young reporter writing letters about chickens and the dashing "border ruffian" fighting injustice in bleeding Kansas had fulfilled their early promise in very different ways, with one exceeding all expectations by becoming the foremost literary critic and realist novelist of his day and the other, his life blighted by an unjust accusation, confounding those early hopes by submerging himself in running a small-town newspaper, as Howells's father and brother Joseph had done.

What emerges most strongly from Howells's late account of James Harvey Greene is the portrait of a brave man unjustly accused by those in power over him. Greene was a friend; an intellectual companion; and, in an ironic reversal of the role Howells usually played for others, an editor who was able to support and promote Howells's works. He played a role hitherto unexplored in Howells's life and work: that of the impetuous man of action who sacrificed much for his intense idealism, consistently stood up for his principles, and paid the price. As Howells writes in *Years of My Youth,* "[R]omance for romance, I think their [Harvey and Jane Greene's] romance of the greatest pathos of any I have known, and it has phases of the highest tragedy" (122). The "highest tragedy" may be that, after such an auspicious beginning, Greene had been wronged by circumstances in such a way that his life never regained the momentum of his early promise. It is also possible that, in comparing the idealistic youth and wise mentor who gave Howells "a new start" with the small-town editor and memoir writer that Greene became, Howells looked back on Greene's life in *Years of My Youth* with a mixture of nostalgia for that world and relief that he had escaped from it.

ACKNOWLEDGMENTS

I want to thank John T. Narrin and William Griffing for making W. D. Howells's letters available and for permitting them to be published, Ross Campbell for research assistance in the National Archives, and the anonymous readers for *Resources for American Literary Study* whose excellent suggestions improved this article.

NOTES

1. Greene's name appears in various forms and spellings both in Howells's letters and in print sources. Howells usually spells the name "Harvey Green" in writing to others (see the letter to Anne T. Howells of January 28, 1865 [*Selected Letters* 1: 208]), but he addresses some envelopes to "J. H. Green" (omitting the final *e*) and includes the salutation "Dear Hervey" (rather than "Harvey") in his earliest letter to Greene. Greene's memoir *Reminiscences of the War: Bivouacs, Marches, Skirmishes and Battles* (1886) was published under the name J. H. Greene, the name by which he was also known as an editor; his wife's letter included in that volume identifies him as "Harvey," so presumably that was the preferred spelling. Greene's service record lists him as "Capt. James H. Greene." He is listed as "James Hervey Greene"

in William Coyle's *Ohio Authors and Their Books: Biographical Data and Selective Bibliographies for Ohio Authors, Native and Resident, 1796–1850* and as "Harvey Green" in Goodman and Dawson's *William Dean Howells: A Writer's Life.*

2. See, for example, the sole reference to Greene in Goodman and Dawson: "A family friend, Harvey Green, cashiered for incurring the wrath of a senior officer, would, like Sam, drag out his life in one long 'defeat' " (101).

3. James Harvey Greene was born in Middletown, Butler County, Ohio, on June 2, 1833 (Upton and Cutler 374).

4. Redpath was in Boston in the spring of 1857, and later that year he expressed similar sentiments about "free-state settlers, such as George W. Brown and others" who supported Kansas Governor Robert J. Walker (1801–69), calling them "miserable dough-faces and sycophants" (McKivigan 35). The envelope is addressed to Greene at the *Cleveland Leader*, where Greene worked during the winter of 1856 ("He Sleeps" 1).

5. The WorldCat detailed record for the *Prairie du Chien Leader* lists Greene as an editor, with "W. Hill," from July 18, 1857, to February 12, 1859, and Greene alone as editor from March 12 to December 8, 1859. The 1860 Census lists his occupation as "Publisher." "W. Hill" is William Hill (1831–1918); he later moved to Neodesha, Kansas, and worked in a bank ("Neodesha in 1873" 243n1).

6. Although she is referred to as "Jane" in *Reminiscences* and in Howells's letters, Jane signs herself "Rachel Jane" in the letter interpolated into *Reminiscences*, and the 1890 U.S. War Department's "Special Schedule—Surviving Soldiers, Sailors, and Marines, and Widows" lists her as "Rebeca [*sic*] Jane."

7. See "He Sleeps in Peace" for Greene's account of his Army service.

8. Greene is listed in WorldCat as the editor of the *Fremont Journal* from October 12 to December 28, 1866, and Howells addresses the 1868 letter to "Mr. J. H. Greene, (Editor, Journal), Fremont, Sandusky County, Ohio."

9. "Vic" is Victoria, Howells's younger sister (1838–86). "Joe" is Joseph, Howells's oldest brother (1832–1912). The manuscript of the letter has double hyphens (=), a printer's mark, instead of single hyphens.

10. Howells was "the son of an Englishman" because his grandfather, Joseph Howells (1783–1858), had moved his family from Hay (Hay-on-Wye) in Wales in 1808 when William Cooper Howells was one year old (Cady 1). Strongly opposed to slavery, as was his father, W. D. Howells may also have been alluding approvingly to England's earlier abolition of the slave trade in 1807 and of slavery throughout the Empire in 1833, in contrast to the continuing support for slavery in the United States shown by the Fugitive Slave Act (1850). On May 24, 1854, a few weeks before Howells wrote this letter, a former slave named Anthony Burns (1834–62) had been arrested in Boston under this legislation, and two days later, a crowd of abolitionists tried to free him before he could be sent back into slavery, an event much in the news and possibly on Howells's mind as well.

11. A fellow Ohioan, Secretary of the Treasury under Lincoln, and (at the time of Howells's letter) the Chief Justice of the U.S. Supreme Court, Chase was among the first to invite Howells into the social circles of Columbus, Ohio, when both men lived there in 1858. Having failed to gain the Republican nomination for president in 1860, Chase switched parties for the 1868 election but was equally unsuccessful in seeking the Democratic nomination for the presidency, and Howells did not get to return to Italy as minister to Florence.

12. Sarah C. is called "Clara" in the 1870 census. That she is the daughter referred to here is suggested by the fact that the 1880 census lists the Greenes' older daughter Ellen (Nelly) as still living at home.

13. In the early 1880s, after several years as consul at Toronto, Howells's father, William C. Howells, resigned his post and bought a farm in Virginia, an ill-fated venture. Joseph Howells's illness was thought to be due to overwork, and, given William C. Howells's age,

having both family members near one another was a relief to Howells (Goodman and Dawson 265–66 and passim).

14. It is not clear from the service record whether Jefferson is the superior officer who had Greene dismissed from the Army, although this statement seems to hint at such a connection. Before the regiment advanced to Corinth, Jefferson was relieved of command on January 7, 1863, at the suggestion of Brigadier General Charles S. Hamilton and on the order of General Grant (Simon 237). However, John Melvin Williams's *"The Eagle Regiment"* reproduces letters written in November 1864 from Grant and General William Starke Rosecrans (1819–98) praising Jefferson's conduct in battle (155–56).

15. A note from T. Y. Crowell to Howells dated August 12, 1887 (and sent on to Greene with the annotation "With love, Will"), states that these books have been sent to Captain J. H. Greene at Howells's request.

16. This letter is not at the Houghton Library as the notation "MH" suggests, according to Heather Cole, Assistant Curator of Modern Books and Manuscripts (personal communication to the author, Aug. 21, 2009).

17. Although Greene is not given a full biographical sketch in Williams's *"The Eagle Regiment,"* as are the other company commanders, he is singled out for his bravery during the skirmishes at the Battle of Young's Point in June 1863 (18).

18. Greene had suffered intermittently from "purulent cystitis, or . . . inflammation of the bladder" since 1861 and was intermittently in "excruciating pain" for many years with this illness, including the months before his death from it ("He Sleeps" 1).

WORKS CITED

Cady, Edwin H. *The Road to Realism: The Early Years 1837–1885 of William Dean Howells.* Syracuse: Syracuse UP, 1956. Print.

Cole, Heather. "Howells Letter to J. Harvey Greene at Houghton Library." Message to the author. Aug. 21, 2009. E-mail.

Coyle, William. *Ohio Authors and Their Books: Biographical Data and Selective Bibliographies for Ohio Authors, Native and Resident, 1796–1850.* Cleveland: World, 1962. Print.

Crowell, T. Y. Letter to W. D. Howells. Aug. 12, 1887. MS. Private Collection of John T. Narrin and William Griffing.

[Destruction of the *Herald of Freedom* Office]. *New York Daily Times* June 12, 1856: 1. *ProQuest Historical Newspapers.* Web. Aug. 10, 2009.

1860 Census. Prairie du Chien, Crawford, WI. Roll M653_1402, p. 833, image 108. *Ancestry.com.* 1860 Federal Census. Provo, UT: Generations Network, 2004. [Original data: United States of America, Bureau of the Census. *Eighth Census of the United States, 1860.* Washington, DC: National Archives and Records Administration, 1860. M 653, 1438 rolls.] Web. Aug. 10, 2009.

1870 Census. Medina. Medina [County], OH. Roll M593_1241, p. 367, image 309. *Ancestry.com.* 1870 Federal Census. Provo, UT: Generations Network, 2003. [Original data: United States of America, Bureau of the Census. *Ninth Census of the United States, 1870.* Washington, DC: National Archives and Records Administration, 1870. M 593, RG29, 1761 rolls.] Web. Aug. 11, 2009.

1880 Census, Medina, Medina [County], OH. Roll T9_1047. Family History Film 1255047, p. 361B: Enumeration District 195; image 0293. *Ancestry.com and The Church of Jesus Christ of Latter-day Saints. 1880 United States Federal Census* [database online]. Provo, UT: Ancestry.com, 2010. [Original data: United States of America, Bureau of the Census. *Tenth Census of the United States, 1880.* Washington, DC: National Archives and Records Administration, 1880.] Web. Dec. 10, 2010.

Goodman, Susan, and Carl Dawson. *William Dean Howells: A Writer's Life.* Berkeley: U of California P, 2005. Print.

[Greene, J. H.] "Howells' Autobiography." Rev. of "My Year in a Log Cabin." *Youth's Companion* May 12, 1887. *Medina County* [OH] *Gazette* May 13, 1887: 4. Print.
———. Letter to John Brown. Mar. 24, 1857. MS. John Brown Collection, #299, box 1, folder 21. Kansas State Hist. Soc., Topeka. *Territorial Kansas Online.* Kansas State Hist. Soc. and U of Kansas, June 15, 2006. Web. Jan. 20, 2011. <http://www.territorialkansasonline.org/~imlskto/cgi-bin/index.php?SCREEN=show_document&SCREEN_FROM=kansas_question&document_id=102600>.
———. *Reminiscences of the War: Bivouacs, Marches, Skirmishes, and Battles, Extracts from Letters Written Home from 1861 to 1865.* Medina, OH: Gazette, 1886. Print.
———. [Sketch of National History]. July 4, 1876. Perrin et al. 364–75. Print.
"He Sleeps in Peace" [Obituary of J. H. Greene]. *Medina County* [OH] *Gazette and News* June 6, 1890: 1, 4. Print.
Howells, W[illiam] D[ean]. "Francesco Dall'Ongaro." *North American Review* Jan. 1868: 26–42. Print.
———. "Gnadenhütten." *Atlantic Monthly* Jan. 1869: 95–115. Print.
———. Letter to J. Harvey Greene. June 4, 1854. MS. Private Collection of John T. Narrin and William Griffing.
———. Letter to J. Harvey Greene. Jan. 29, 1868. MS. Private Collection of John T. Narrin and William Griffing.
———. Letter to J. Harvey Greene. Nov. 12, 1870. MS. Private Collection of John T. Narrin and William Griffing.
———. Letter to J. Harvey Greene. Oct. 20, 1879. MS. Private Collection of John T. Narrin and William Griffing.
———. Letter to J. Harvey Greene. May 14, 1885. MS. Private Collection of John T. Narrin and William Griffing.
———. Letter to J. Harvey Greene. Aug. 29, 1886. MS. Private Collection of John T. Narrin and William Griffing.
———. Letter to J. Harvey Greene. May 14, 1887. MS. Private Collection of John T. Narrin and William Griffing.
———. "My Year in a Log Cabin." *Youth's Companion* May 12, 1887: 313–15. Print.
———. *Questionable Shapes.* New York: Harper, 1903. Print.
———. "The Rise of Silas Lapham." *Century Magazine* Nov. 1884: 1–13; Dec. 1884: 242–67; Jan. 1885: 370–84; Feb. 1885: 581–92; Mar. 1885: 663–77; Apr. 1885: 858–73; May 1885: 15–28; June 1885: 241–56; July 1885: 353–73; Aug. 1885: 513–26. Print.
———. *The Rise of Silas Lapham.* Boston: Ticknor, 1885. Print.
———. *Selected Letters.* Ed. George Arms, William M. Gibson, and Christoph K. Lohmann. 6 vols. Boston: Twayne, 1979–83. Print.
———. *The Shadow of a Dream: A Story.* 1890. New York: Harper, 1903. Print.
———. *Suburban Sketches.* New York: Hurd, 1871. Print.
———. *The Undiscovered Country.* Boston: Houghton, 1880. Print.
———. *Years of My Youth.* New York: Harper, 1916. Print.
McKivigan, John. *Forgotten Firebrand: James Redpath and the Making of Nineteenth-Century America.* Ithaca: Cornell UP, 2008. Print.
"Neodesha in 1873; From a Letter of William Hill, Pioneer Banker." *Kansas Historical Quarterly* 13.4 (1944): 243–48. Print.
Perrin, William Henry, J. H. Battle, and Weston Arthur Goodspeed. *History of Medina County and Ohio.* Chicago: Baskin, 1881. Print.
"*Prairie du Chien Leader.*" [1857–61. Crawford County, WI: Hill & Green[e]. Notes: Publisher varies. Editors: W. Hill & J. H. Greene, July 18, 1857–<Feb. 12, 1859>; J. H. Greene, <Mar. 12, 1859–Dec. 8, 1859>.] WorldCat Detailed Record; Keyword Search: J. H. Greene. *WorldCat.org.* Online Computer Lib. Center, Inc. (ONLC), 2001–11. Web. Jan.

20, 2011. <http://www.worldcat.org/title/prairie-du-chien-leader/oclc/12618904&referer=brief_results>.

Redpath, James. Letter to J. H. Greene. May 1, [1856]. MS. Private Collection of John T. Narrin and William Griffing.

Simon, John Y., ed. *The Papers of Ulysses S. Grant. Volume 7: December 9, 1862–March 31, 1863.* Carbondale: Southern Illinois UP, 1979. Print.

Tolstoï, Count L[yof] N. *Anna Karenina.* 1875–77. Trans. Nathan Haskell Doyle. New York: Crowell, 1886. Print.

———. *Childhood, Boyhood, Youth.* 1852–56. Trans. Isabel F. Hapgood. Boston: Crowell, 1886. Print.

———. *Iván Ilyitch, and Other Stories.* Trans. Nathan Haskell Doyle. New York: Crowell, 1887. Print.

———. *My Confession.* 1882. New York: Crowell, 1887. Print.

———. *My Religion.* 1884. Trans. L. M. Smith. New York: Crowell, 1885. Print.

———. *War and Peace: An Historical Novel Translated into French by a Russian Lady, and from the French by Clara Bell.* New York: Gottsberger, 1869. Print.

———. *What to Do? Thoughts Evoked by the Census of Moscow.* 1886. Trans. Isabel F. Hapgood. Boston: Crowell, 1887. Print.

United States. War Department. Adjutant General's Office. *Service Record of James H. Greene.* Special Orders No. 246. Extract. No. 35. Signed by E. D. Townsend, Assistant Adjutant General, July 23, 1864. Washington, DC: National Archives and Records Administration, 1864. DVD. Accessed Aug. 31, 2009.

———. ———. ———. *Service Record of James H. Greene.* Special Orders No. 20. Extract. No. 11. Signed by W. A. Nichols, Assistant Adjutant General, Jan. 13, 1865. Washington, DC: National Archives and Records Administration, 1865. DVD. Accessed Aug. 31, 2009.

———. ———. "Special Schedule—Surviving Soldiers, Sailors, and Marines, and Widows, etc." 1890 Veterans Schedules, roll 72, p. 2, Enumeration District 277. Print.

Upton, Harriet Taylor, and Harry Gardner Cutler. *History of the Western Reserve.* Vol. 1. Chicago: Lewis, 1910. Print.

Williams, John Melvin. *"The Eagle Regiment," 8th Wis. Inf'ty. Vols. A Sketch of Its Marches, Battles and Campaigns from 1861 to 1865. With a Complete Regimental and Company Roster, and a Few Portraits and Sketches of Its Officers and Commanders by a "Non-Vet" of "Co. H."* Belleville, WI: "Recorder," 1890. Print.

Young Edith Jones:
Sources and Texts of Early Poems by Edith Wharton

IRENE C. GOLDMAN-PRICE
Independent Scholar

Although we usually think of Edith Wharton (1862–1937) as a fiction writer, she also had a lifelong engagement with poetry. Her earliest publications were poems, and her final book, *Eternal Passion in English Poetry*, published posthumously in 1939, was an anthology of love poems, which she edited with her friends Robert Norton (c. 1866–c. 1946) and Gaillard Lapsley (1871–1949). In between, there were three volumes of poetry: *Verses*, published privately by her family in 1878, when Edith Jones was just sixteen; *Artemis to Actæon, and Other Verse*, published at the height of her creativity in 1909; and *Twelve Poems*, published toward the end of her career, in 1926. Throughout her long writing career, she frequently "warbled," as she described it to her editor, William Crary Brownell (1851–1928; Wharton to Brownell, Oct. 16, 1908), sometimes for publication and sometimes to relieve and express her deepest emotions.

Recently recovered letters from a teenaged Edith Jones to her governess, Anna Catherine Bahlmann (1849–1916), reveal a passionate engagement with poetry on the part of a precocious student.[1] In the letters, written between 1875 and 1880, when Edith was thirteen until she was eighteen, we can observe her reading and responding to numerous English and American poets, translating poetry from the German, writing poems of her own, and successfully seeking publication. The letters reveal two poems of which scholars were not previously aware: "Counting the Stars," published here for the first time, and "St. Martin's Summer," published here for the first time in 120 years. They also mention by name several poems that were published but have not been collected, along with four other poems that may have been lost forever (or may be lurking in an attic or an archive awaiting discovery), and they reference several other, unnamed poems. These early letters chronicle an intense literary apprenticeship in language, cadence, poetic subject, and tone that might well have pointed to a career as a poet rather than one as a novelist.

On November 13, 1875, Edith Jones wrote to her teacher from her parents' summer home in Newport, Rhode Island, where things had been

RESOURCES FOR AMERICAN LITERARY STUDY, Vol. 34, 2009.
Copyright © 2011 AMS Press, Inc.

quiet since the social season ended. Recalling Hamlet's speaking to his closest friend, she writes, "Today is what the poets call 'halcyon' weather, a word which 'brings to my mind's eye, Horatio' a vision of becalmed ships in blue seas with white birds swooping overhead...." She had been reading Henry Wadsworth Longfellow's (1807–82) new book, *The Masque of Pandora, and Other Poems* (1875), and she reviewed it for her teacher, not altogether favorably:

> I like "Pandora" quite well. It is a dramatic poem in blank verse, with Greek choruses, but it is too short—it has not substance enough, & it wants, as I think all Longfellows [*sic*] do, fire & passion & reality. His poetry always reminds one of a chilly sculpture, it is so lifeless. I think his characters want vigour. They are passionless & collected as if they were walking in a trance, or beneath the influence of a calming spell. Such at least is the impression that he gives me, but I judge merely from my own feelings. Some parts, however, of "Pandora" are very beautiful, & I think these two lines run very smoothly.
> "Who would not love, if loving she might be
> Changed like Callisto[2] to a star in Heaven?"
> I don't want to fill my letter with a review, but I must send you the last three lines spoken by Pandora, for I ~~very~~ think them very fine & I want to know if you agree with me. She says: "Only through punishment of our evil deeds,
> Only through suffering are we reconciled to the Immortal Gods & to ourselves"—I hope that I have not bothered you with all this, but when I get on one of my pet subjects, I never feel inclined to leave it off, & I do like occasionally to have a discussion about poetry.

At thirteen, Edith Jones was already well-schooled in verse form and in Greek and Roman (as well as German and Norse) mythology. As a critic (and perhaps as a vibrant teenager), she preferred passion and high drama in her poetry. She admired poetry and stories that engaged with myth, and she liked to allude to what she had read. Ignoring the common estimate of Longfellow as the greatest living American poet, she cut right to what she considered his crucial weakness: his want of passion, a quality she links, interestingly, with realism. She would surely have agreed with what one twentieth-century critic said of him: "Longfellow's once-great popularity was not the effect of his literary quality, but of his perfect identification of the average taste" (Abel 321). Edith Jones would never be average in her tastes.

The chief weakness in Longfellow, for Edith, was his reluctance (or inability) to reach deeply enough into the imaginative and emotional life that she herself possesses. As a grown woman, Wharton would refer variously to her imagination, her source of inspiration, as "teeming visions," "the furious Muse" (*Backward Glance* 35), her "secret garden" (197), and "a wild wingèd thing" ("La Folle du Logis" 98). This inner passion was the thing that drove her to make up stories, that comforted and entertained her on sleepless nights, that urged her to freedom when she felt confined by her life. At age thirteen, she may have believed that all people possessed such a store of treasures; certainly she can be forgiven for expecting America's supposed greatest poet to have a deep well of passion and imagination, and therefore for being disappointed when he didn't reveal it in his poetry.

During the summer and fall of 1876, Edith was reading another iconic American poet, James Russell Lowell (1819–91), whose poems "Prometheus" (1843), "Rhoecus" (1843), and "Columbus" (1844), in blank verse, she found "very beautiful indeed." She was also translating poems from the German, particularly Johann Wolfgang von Goethe (1749–1832), and she confers via letter with Anna, in August 1876, for confirmation of her translations of Goethe's "Mignon" poems from *Wilhelm Meister's Lehrjahre* (1795–96):

> I wish that you would help me to correct it. "Still stands the myrtle & the laurel high" bothers me because it is so absurdly literal—but "calm grows the myrtle" is just as bad, & as I can only use a word of one syllable, I am at a loss how to correct it. Then—"What" "O thou poor child, what hath man done to thee?" does not satisfy me. Yet what can I put in the place of "man"? "The cloud-ridged mountain" is a difficult line, for Wolkensteg is not very easily translated. Then again, "The mule <u>ascends</u> with ease" is not a literal rendering of what, correctly, would be "The mule seeks his way through the fog." Please, if it be not troubling you too much, tell me which lines you do not like in your next letter. "So laßt mich scheinen, bis ich werde" is much more difficult, & consequently my translation is much worse. Is "so let me seem until I be" good English, or would "am" be better?

Edith Jones here engages with questions of connotation and denotation, the imperative to convey the feeling of the poem beyond the literal language. She is sensitive to rhythm and to problems of compression in poetry, as well as to the double difficulty of translating someone else's words. As a working writer, she wants criticism, not just praise, a rare quality in someone just fourteen years old but one that she would retain throughout her career. She would have a lifelong love of Goethe, particularly his poetry and poetic drama, in which she found expressed the passion that Longfellow lacked.

A month later she was still engaged with these two Goethe poems and with another, unnamed translation she was preparing for Anna. She also talked about a poem she had written, "Friederike," about Goethe's lover.

This was such a lengthy poem that she dramatized, "I should expire before I had copied her," and therefore she planned to show Anna the poem when they came together in New York (Wharton to Bahlmann, Sept. 23, 1876). It is too bad that she did not copy and send it; "Friederike" is the first of four poems she mentions to Anna that have not survived, or perhaps have yet to be found.

In the fall of 1878, several letters indicate that Edith continued her active engagement in reading and writing poetry and in preparing her work for publication. Ever the critic, she responded to an inquiry by Anna about *Clytemnestra* (1855), a long verse-play by Owen Meredith (Sir Edward Robert Bulwer-Lytton [1831–91]):

> You ask if I remember a certain part in Klytemnestra. . . . No! I confess I remember nothing but the plagiarisms. One from Marlowe's Faustus & one or more from Shakespere. But how can one look for high tragedy in a vers au société writer? "Aux Italiens" & "Chess" will survive Klytemnestra I imagine. (Wharton to Bahlmann, Sept. 2, 1878)

Although she enjoys and appreciates long poems based on myths and ancient stories, Bulwer-Lytton's treatment meets with her disdain.

Edith also criticizes Robert Browning (1812–89) in this letter, although she admits to liking one of his poems:

> By the way I have discovered a new poem in Browning & even in that wretchedest of books "Dramatis Personae" [1864]. It is called "May & Death." Do you know it? There is not a single quote-able (what a word!) line in it but the whole is "round and perfect as a star." (Wharton to Bahlmann, Sept. 2, 1878)

"May and Death" is a short poem in which the speaker mourns a friend who died in May, wishing at first that spring would not come again, then reconciling himself to it so that other friends might still enjoy the season. The final two stanzas turn the poem again, finding an image to link the speaker's pain to a woodland plant whose green leaves show a streak of red, symbolizing for him his heart's blood spilled at the death of his friend. We can imagine that the union of nature and human suffering is what attracted the young Edith Jones to this particular verse.

Now that Edith was sixteen, she appeared to have internalized to some degree her society's imperative that emotion, particularly pain or sadness, be restrained. The Browning poem evinces this emotional restraint without being "lifeless," and its turns are indeed graceful. Her approbation of the poem as "round and perfect as a star" comes from Alexander Smith's (1830–67) "A Life Drama" (1852). Smith's poetry was widely acclaimed when it appeared in London in 1852 and in America the following year; it was compared favorably to the work of John Keats (1795–1821), Percy Bysshe Shelley (1792–1822), and Alfred, Lord Tennyson (1809–92). This letter, with its references to Christopher Marlowe (1584–93), William Shakespeare (1564–1616), Bulwer-Lytton, Browning, and Smith, demonstrates the breadth of Edith's reading at a very young age.

The same letter of September 2, 1878, indicates that Edith had sent Anna another of her poems, "I met my love," in a prior letter, and that Anna had said kind things about it. Thus we have the title of a second lost poem. On the basis of Anna's positive reception, Edith enclosed several other poems, requesting Anna's criticism. While we do not know the names of these poems, we can see that Edith was actively writing and that she relied on Anna as a critical audience for her work.

Indeed, Edith's "furious Muse" must have been at work because just nine days later she sent Anna "my last effusion which, if it reminds you of anything, ought to suggest 'Violet Fane.'" That poem, "Counting the Stars," appears here for the first time in print:

> Counting the Stars
> Have you forgotten, Love, the night
> We sat & counted the stars together?
> The Autumn moon o'erhead was bright
> And soft calm the blue September weather.
>
> ———————————
>
> The stars came peeping, faint & pale,
> Thro' drifts of cloud fleece torn & riven,
> That swept, like a thin & tattered veil,
> Across the violet vault of Heaven.
>
> ———————————
>
> And as we counted, one by one,
> The mystic nine in the sky a-quiver,[3]
> I breathed a wish to the silent stars,—
> A wish my heart will hold forever.
>
> ———————————
>
> Ah, half in jest, & half in love,
> We sat & counted the stars together.
> The Autumn moon was bright above
> And soft the blue September weather.
>   (Wharton to Bahlmann, Sept. 11, 1878)

Clearly influenced by the Romantics, the poem is sweet but not overly sentimental. It demonstrates a feel both for rhythm, using a loose iambic tetrameter, and for the sound of words, and it also shows the judicious use of rhyme and repetition to deepen meaning. Her selection of strong verbs in stanzas 2 and 3 is perhaps the most telling trait for an author-in-training. The subject of the poem, love recollected in tranquility many years past, is a conventional one. She may have recognized this in comparing herself to Violet Fane in a characteristic gesture of self-irony. Fane was the literary pseudonym of Lady Mary Montgomerie Lamb Singleton Currie (1843–1905), a British baroness who was a novelist, poet, and essayist who published four slim, well-received volumes of poetry between 1872 and 1878. A number of the poems concern mutability and regret.

Although she does not mention it in these letters, Edith Jones was preparing a volume of poetry that would be published privately at the end of 1878. "Counting the Stars" was not included in the volume, but "June and December," one of two poems she sent Anna Bahlmann in an October letter that has not survived, was included, along with twenty-one other poems of her own authorship and a handful of translations from the German. In subject, "June and December" is akin to "Counting the Stars," but here the speaker addresses a current love, speculating on what it will be like to remember, when they are old, the moments they share together now, in their youth. And yet another poem in her collection, "What We Shall Say Fifty Years Hence, of Our Fancy-Dress Quadrille" (1878), begins with the same cadence and sentiment of "Counting the Stars": "Do you remember, long ago, / Our Fancy-Dress Quadrille?" "What We Shall Say" bears the epigraph "Danced at Swanhurst, August 1878," so we can speculate that Edith was, at sixteen, having romantic experiences that she felt deeply enough to wish to express in verse.

Edith's spurt of poetic creativity continued through the fall of 1878. On October 17 she wrote to Anna about a Thomas Bailey Aldrich (1836–1907) poem she admired, "The Lady of Castelnoire" (1865), the last stanza of which she called "perfect." (In Wharton's library at The Mount, her restored home in Lenox, Massachusetts, the stanza is marked in her copy of Aldrich with a light pencil line.) She mentioned several of her own poems by name, including "June & December," which was supposed to appear in print somewhere, but she did not know when. While I have not found it in any contemporary journal, "June and December" survives in *Verses* and in subsequent collections of Wharton's poetry. The other two poems she mentions to Anna, "Phantoms" and "Sensuchtsroman," have not been located.

By the end of 1878, probably for Christmas, Edith Jones's volume *Verses* had been published by Newport mapmaker, bookseller, and publisher Charles E. Hammett Jr. (1822–1902) in a small private edition. According to Wharton's account in her unpublished fragment "Life and I," her mother "took an odd inarticulate interest" in her poems and kept "a blank book in which she copied many of them." It was her mother (Lucretia Stevens Rhinelander Jones [1824–1901]) who "perpetrated the folly" of having an edition of them printed ("Life and I" 1090). In a deathbed reminiscence, however, Wharton credited her father (George Frederic Jones [1821–82]) for this publication (Benstock 36). The letters to Anna indicate that Edith's father took an active interest in her work: it was he who copied out several of her poems to send to Anna and others. Her brother Harry (Henry Edward Jones [1850–1922]) took enough interest to show her poems to a friend, thus facilitating her first important publication, in *The Atlantic*, in 1880. Although we cannot be sure which family member arranged the publication of *Verses*, evidence in these letters thus belies the common belief, perpetrated by Wharton herself in *A Backward Glance*, that her family did not encourage her literary aspirations.

On October 16, 1879, Edith told Anna she had written "two sonnets and a long piece," but she did not name them, nor did she mention *Verses*. She did, however, brag about four poems that would be coming out in *The Atlantic*, and she quoted the editor, William Dean Howells (1837–1920): "If I can think of any good name I will print them in a little group. They strike me as having a fresh, delicate and authentic quality. It is something very uncommon to find so young a writer reminding you so little of other writers." The poems, "The Parting Day," "A Failure," "Patience," and "Wants," were published in the February, April, and May 1880 issues of *The Atlantic*. Ironically, Edith owed her success to Longfellow, the man whom she had so blithely denigrated at thirteen. Allen Thorndike Rice (1853–89), who had recently purchased the *North American Review*, was the friend to whom her brother had shown her poems, and he in turn showed them to Longfellow, who gave them to Howells. In her autobiography, *A Backward Glance*, Wharton acknowledged her debt to Longfellow, calling him "her first literary protector" and naming chapter 4 of her memoir "Unreluctant Feet," from a line in his poem "Maidenhood" (1842; see Wharton, *Backward Glance* 74–77). In her letters to Anna, she failed to mention that she had also published two poems, "Only a Child" and "The Constellation's Last Victory," in the *New York World* under the pseudonym Eadgyth, or that a fifth poem was published by *The Atlantic* in March, "Areopagus."[4]

These five poems from *The Atlantic*, only two of which were included in Louis Auchincloss's collection of Wharton's poetry for the Library of America, are available in their original form online at the Web site of *The Atlantic* (http://www.theatlantic.com). They are also available, with several small errors, online at the University of Virginia Library's Modern English

Collection, a Web site maintained by the University of Virginia, and in the Dodo Press volume, *Edith Wharton's Verse.*

Some of the *Atlantic* poems resemble, in subject, the earlier ones about love. "The Parting Day" concerns a woman who chooses to remain silent when a man she loves makes a farewell visit to her. Her love remains unspoken, and the tension of the poem is in the speaker's emotional restraint. In this it can be said to resemble Aldrich's "The Lady of Castelnoire," which Edith had read and admired more than a year earlier. She had troubled herself to copy out for Anna the last stanza of Aldrich's poem, to accompany the October 17, 1878, letter:

"And they called her cold. God knows . . .
Underneath the Winter snows
The invisible hearts of flowers grew ripe for blossoming!
And the lives that look so cold, if their stories could be told
Would seem cast in gentler mould, would seem full of love & Spring[.]"

We see in this Edith's then-interest in the hidden world of passion that may live underneath a seemingly cool exterior, a more mature response than finding restraint "lifeless." The necessity and pain of keeping feelings hidden is a theme she would continue to explore many times in her fiction.

"A Failure" is also about failed love, this time the regrets of a woman who feels she might have been a better person had the man she loved chosen to marry her. Was Edith trying on these topics, or had she already experienced a disappointment? In "A Failure," the idealized person whom the speaker feels she could have been is a conventional portrait of a Victorian wife:

> Ah, yes, to you I might have been
> That happy being, past recall,
> The slave, the helpmeet, and the queen,—
> All these in one, and one in all.

A reader today, having been exposed to feminist criticism of the Victorian ideal of a woman as slave, helpmeet, and queen, might be tempted to feel, not regret for the speaker, but rather relief that she was not in fact chosen by this man. But it would not be a reading the poet seems to have intended.

"Wants" and "Patience" are poems that we now might call feminist. In both, the speaker contemplates a woman's life and finds it trying and disappointing. "Wants" begins, "We women want so many things," and it goes on to list the never-ending compromises a woman must make as the things she really wants become impossible to achieve: happiness, love, friendship, children (who will leave home so quickly), duty, and, finally, "With sudden weariness oppressed, / We leave the shining goal unwon, /

And only ask for rest." A woman's life cannot lead to self-fulfillment, but only to partial and temporary successes based on her service to others. "Patience," in the same vein, describes a woman who longs to cry, who seeks to fly, who wanders helplessly, all the while guided by Patience, who, with "wisdom stern" yet "compassion sweet," tutors her in acceptance. The life to which this speaker seems to look forward is one of long disappointment and chastening. It is as though Edith Jones's inner visions, her desires for her own life, are battering against her society's restrictive expectations for young women. These are issues that, as a mature woman, she would explore in depth in her fiction even as she lived them.

The final poem mentioned by Edith Jones during this six-year period of creativity is "St. Martin's Summer," by far the most accomplished of the juvenilia, and it is a poem that Wharton scholars have so far missed. It was published in *Scribner's Monthly* in November 1880, and again in a volume by Scottish editor William Sharp (1856–1905) called *American Sonnets* in 1889, and it is published here for the first time since then. Edith was proud of having earned seven dollars for it, which, she says to Anna, "is doing very well for 14 lines" (Wharton to Bahlmann, Aug. 26, 1880):

> ST. MARTIN'S SUMMER
> After the summer's fierce and thirsty glare,
>   After the falling leaves and falling rain,
>   When harsh winds beat the fields of ripened grain
> And autumn's pennons from the branches flare,
> There comes a stilly season, soft and fair,
>   When clouds are lifted, winds are hushed again,—
>   A phantom Summer hovering without pain
> In the veiled radiance of the quiet air;
> When, folding down the line of level seas,
>   A silver mist at noonday faintly broods,
> And like becalmèd ships the yellow trees
>   Stand islanded in windless solitudes,
> Each leaf unstirred and parching for the breeze
>   That hides and lingers northward in the woods.

This is a far more accomplished poem than any of the five printed in *The Atlantic*. Her use of the sonnet form is easy and relaxed, neither rhythm nor rhyme seeming forced. The subject ("St. Martin's Summer" is an English expression akin to our "Indian Summer") offers a close view of nature and weather, and in this Edith is more successful than in regarding the young female heart. Metaphor is more organic to the poem, and words are chosen for their sound as well as their meaning ("the realm of words" was "my own native country," she wrote in "Life and I" [1080]). The final quatrain seems to look forward to America's poet of New England weather, Robert Frost (1874–1963), with trees "standing islanded" and a breeze that "hides and lingers northward in the woods." She has written a sonnet, like Frost's brilliant "Silken Tent" (1939), so skillful that we hardly notice that it is one long sentence.

Allen Rice visited the Jones family in August 1880, and he suggested to eighteen-year-old Edith that she undertake a long, rhymed narrative version of one or more of the old German "Volksaggen," an idea that she contemplated with excitement. In her letter about it to Anna, she recalled works by Wolfram von Eschenbach (c. 1170–c.1220) and Hartmann von Aue (c. 1160–c. 1210–20), William Morris (1834–96), Matthew Arnold (1822–88), Richard Wagner (1813–83), and Owen Meredith (Edward Robert Bulwer-Lytton). Not wishing to compete with their works, she proposed rewriting the Parcival story, finding von Aue's rendition of it unsatisfactory (Wharton to Bahlmann, Sept. 23, 1880). She read Matthew Arnold's lectures *On Translating Homer* (1861, 1862; see *Essays in Criticism*) to better understand the complex demands of translation and the multiple accomplishments of great epic poetry.

But another, more exciting opportunity was also coming Edith's way: her parents had decided to return to Europe, and they successfully engaged Anna Bahlmann to travel with them as Edith's companion. It was a prospect that thrilled Edith, and her letters to Anna were filled with excitement—"I am continually on the verge of explosion now," she wrote on August 26, 1880—and also with her careful intellectual preparation for what they would see. She read travel books, books about European art and architecture, and lots of poetry, noting where certain poems were written and expressing the desire to stand on the spot and read the poem. This European trip would be critically important in her emotional and creative life. It would also be the occasion of the death of her beloved father, in Cannes, in March of 1882. When Edith and her mother returned to New York, Miss Edith Jones took her place in society as a *jeune fille à marier*. The poetry project was set aside, and Edith's literary career was suspended until several years after her marriage. Her first story, "Mrs. Manstey's View," appeared in *Scribner's Magazine* in July 1891. She was twenty-nine years old.

ACKNOWLEDGMENT
The author is grateful to the Edith Wharton Restoration at The Mount and its staff for access to Wharton's library.

NOTES
1. Edith Jones Wharton's letters, written over a period of forty years to her governess/secretary, Anna Catherine Bahlmann, include thirteen letters written when she was a teenager; of the thirteen, ten mention poetry, and I quote from nine of these here. The letters from Edith Jones Wharton to Bahlmann remained in the Bahlmann family's possession until

June of 2009, when they were sold at auction to Yale University's Beinecke Library. More than 130 letters from Wharton, as well as many other documents from Bahlmann's life, are now available for study in The Anna Catherine Bahlmann Papers Relating to Edith Wharton in the Yale Collection of American Literature, Beinecke Rare Book and Manuscript Library. The letters are quoted here by permission of the estate of Edith Wharton and the Watkins/ Loomis Agency. As far as we know, Bahlmann's letters to Wharton do not survive.

2. This is an interesting reference on Longfellow's part, since Callisto, in Greek myth, is supposed to have been raped by Zeus rather than to have submitted lovingly. Surely Edith, who knew her mythology well, would have known that, though she might not yet have understood the concept of rape.

3. "The mystic nine" probably refers to the constellation Pleiades, said to be the seven sisters of Greek mythology and their parents, Atlas and Pleione. The constellation is linked with mourning and loss because it rises at sunset during the fall, at the time of Samhain, the Gaelic festival of remembrance of the dead. A possible argument against this interpretation is that the action of the poem occurs in November, and Samhain is in late October.

4. See Millicent Bell on "Only a Child." A copy of "The Constellation's Last Victory," published in the *New York World* on March 28, 1880, can be found in the Auchincloss section of the Edith Wharton Archives at the Beinecke Library, YCAL 42, box 64.

WORKS CITED

Abel, Darrell. "Henry W. Longfellow." *American Literature*. Vol. 2. New York: Barnes, 1963. 307–22. Print.

Aldrich, Thomas Bailey. "The Lady of Castelnoire." *Poems*. Boston: Ticknor, 1865. 83–87. Print. [Wharton copy.]

Arnold, Matthew. *Essays in Criticism*. 1865. New York: Macmillan, 1877. Print. [Wharton copy.]

Bell, Millicent. " 'Eadgyth' Wharton in the *New York World*, 1879." *Yale University Library Gazette* 30.2 (1955): 64–69. Print.

Benstock, Shari. *No Gifts from Chance: A Biography of Edith Wharton*. New York: Scribner's, 1994. Print.

Browning, Robert. *Dramatis Personae*. London: Chapman, 1864. Print.

Frost, Robert. "The Silken Tent." *The Poetry of Robert Frost*. Ed. Edward Connery Lathem. New York: Holt, 1975. 331–32. Print.

Goethe, Johann Wolfgang von. *Wilhelm Meister's Lehrjahre*. Stuttgart: Cotta, 1875. Print. [Wharton copy.]

Longfellow, Henry Wadsworth. "Maidenhood." *Ballads and Other Poems*. Cambridge: Owen, 1842. 125–28. Print.

———. *The Masque of Pandora, and Other Poems*. Boston: Osgood, 1875. Print.

Lowell, James Russell. *The Poetical Works of James Russell Lowell*. Boston: Ticknor, 1858. Print.

Meredith, Owen [Edward Robert Bulwer-Lytton]. *Clytemnestra, The Earl's Return, The Artist, and Other Poems*. London: Chapman, 1855. Print.

Modern English Collection. Digital Scholarship Services, U of Virginia Lib., Charlottesville. Web. Jan. 13, 2011. <http://etext.lib.virginia.edu/modeng/modeng0.browse.html>.

Smith, Alexander. "A Life-Drama." 1852. *A Life-Drama and Other Poems*. 1853. Boston: Ticknor, 1859. 5–160. Print.

Wharton, Edith. "Areopagus." *The Atlantic* Mar. 1880. Web. July 12, 2010. <http://www.theatlantic.com/past/docs/issues/1880mar/areopagus.htm>.

———. *Artemis to Actæon, and Other Verse*. New York: Scribner's, 1909. Print.

———. *A Backward Glance*. 1933. New York: Scribner's, 1964. Print.

———. "The Constellation's Last Victory." *New York World* Mar. 28, 1880. Print.

———. "Counting the Stars." MS accompanying Wharton, letter to Bahlmann, Sept. 11, 1878. Anna Catherine Bahlmann Papers relating to Edith Wharton. Yale Collection of American Literature, Beinecke Rare Book and Manuscript Lib., New Haven.

———. *Edith Wharton: Selected Poems*. Ed. Louis Auchincloss. New York: Lib. of America, 2005. Print.

———. *Edith Wharton's Verse*. N.p.: Dodo, n.d. Print.

———. "A Failure." *The Atlantic* Apr. 1880. Web. July 12, 2010. <http://www.theatlantic.com/past/docs/issues/1880apr/failure.htm>.

———. "La Folle du Logis." 1909. Wharton, *Selected Poems* 98–101. Print.

———. "June and December." 1878. Wharton, *Selected Poems* 17–18. Print.

———. Letters to Anna Catherine Bahlmann. Nov. 13, 1875; Aug. 1876; Sept. 23, 1876; Sept. 2, 1878; Sept. 11, 1878; Oct. 17, 1878; Oct. 16, 1879; Aug. 26, 1880; Sept. 23, 1880. MSS. Anna Catherine Bahlmann Papers relating to Edith Wharton. Yale Collection of American Literature, Beinecke Rare Book and Manuscript Lib. New Haven.

———. Letter to William Crary Brownell. Oct. 16, 1908. MS. William Crary Brownell (AC 1871) Papers, box 2, folder 3. Amherst College Archives and Special Collections, Amherst College Lib., Amherst, MA.

———. "Life and I." *Edith Wharton: Novellas and Other Writings*. Ed. Cynthia Griffin Wolff. New York: Lib. of America, 1990. 1069–96. Print.

———. "Mrs. Manstey's View." *Scribner's Magazine* July 1891: 117–22. Print.

———. "Only a Child." *New York World* May 30, 1879. Print.

———. "The Parting Day." *The Atlantic* Feb. 1880. Web. July 12, 2010. <http://www.theatlantic.com/past/docs/issues/1880feb/parting.htm>.

———. "Patience." *The Atlantic* Apr. 1880. Web. July 12, 2010. <http://www.theatlantic.com/past/docs/issues/1880apr/patience.htm>.

———. "St. Martin's Summer." *Scribner's Monthly* Nov. 1880: 138. Print. Rpt. in *American Sonnets*. Ed. William Sharp. London: Scott, 1889. Print.

———. *Twelve Poems*. London: Medici Soc., 1926. Print.

———. *Verses*. Newport: Hammett, 1878. Print.

———. "Wants." *The Atlantic* May 1880. Web. July 12, 2010. <http://www.theatlantic.com/past/docs/issues/1880may/wants.htm>.

———. "What We Shall Say Fifty Years Hence, of Our Fancy-Dress Quadrille." 1878. Wharton, *Selected Poems* 15–16. Print.

Wharton, Edith, Robert Norton, and Gaillard Lapsley, eds. *Eternal Passion in English Poetry*. New York and London: Appleton-Century, 1939. Print.

New Information on Hemingway's "3 very fine weeks" in Constantinople in 1922

DAVID ROESSEL
The Richard Stockton College of New Jersey

Ernest Hemingway (1899–1961) spent "3 very fine weeks" in Constantinople in October 1922 as a reporter covering the end of the Greco-Turkish War of 1919–22 (*Selected Letters* 86). Charles Fenton suggested that this experience became "a crucible for his writing" (183), and Jeffrey Meyers has said that it was "immensely important for his development as a writer" (22). Malcolm Cowley reported that Hemingway told him that it was during this trip that he came to "really understand war" (49). The role this trip to the Near East played in his emergence as a writer could be debated. What is beyond dispute is the fact that, in an otherwise quite well-documented life, we know very little about Hemingway during those three weeks in Constantinople. There are the journalistic dispatches that Hemingway wrote, but, besides telling us that he interviewed Hamid Bey (1870–1943), head of the Turkish Red Crescent, and Afghan diplomat Shere Mohamet Khan, they provide few personal details beyond the fact that upon arrival he stayed at the Hotel de Londres (Hemingway, *Dateline* 227); was bitten by insects while sleeping (*Dateline* 239); was told a story about the Greek army in Anatolia by a Captain Wittal (*Dateline* 244); and met a cameraman named Shorty Wornall in Thrace (*Dateline* 249). Wornall is almost certainly the "Shorty" mentioned by Esther Lovejoy, who took pictures of the destruction of Smyrna (see Lovejoy 139 and Humphries 89).

Nor do Hemingway's letters provide much information. None survive that were written during the period that Hemingway was in the Near East. In a letter to John R. Bone (1877–1928) on October 27, 1922, written just days after his return to Paris, he mentioned that he caught malaria: "After I picked up the fever I felt very depressed about my work and when I felt too bad to go on the destroyer to Mytilene everything looked very black." However, when he discussed the trip to Constantinople in letters written long after the journey, he would often lay stress on details that we know are not true. He wrote to James Gamble (1882–1958) just over a year after his trip, "I went out to Constantinople, Smyrna, Thrace etc. as war correspondent for the Toronto Star and the International News Service"

RESOURCES FOR AMERICAN LITERARY STUDY, Vol. 34, 2009.
Copyright © 2011 AMS Press, Inc.

(*Selected Letters* 107). In a letter to William Dodge "Bill" Horne (1892–1986), dated June 17–18, 1923, Hemingway said that he "was with the Greek army in the big retreat and then three weeks in Constant itself, 3 very fine weeks when just as it was getting light you'd all get into a car and go to watch the sunrise and wonder whether there was going to be a war that would set the whole world on fire again—and there damn nearly was. And then came home across Thrace in a car, on horseback, and walked and then went through Bulgaria and Serbia and finally hit Trieste," where he caught a train straight to Paris and Hadley (*Selected Letters* 86). Just a year after his return, he wrote his father on November 7, 1923, in an account of some hunting that he had done, that he had killed twenty-two quail in one day in Thrace with a "borrowed double barreled twelve gauge" (*Selected Letters* 100). The first two letters seem to imply that Hemingway was present at the burning of Smyrna and had been with the Greek army in Anatolia, not, as he actually was, an observer of the evacuation—of the Greek army and much of the population—from Eastern Thrace before it was to be handed over to the Turks. Later, and even more outrageously, Hemingway would say in a letter to Gustavo Durán Martínez (1906–69) in 1940 that he had commanded a platoon under Mustafa Kemal (1881–1938) with the conquering Turkish army (Reynolds, *Final Years* 33).

There is also the fiction, notably the flashbacks in "The Snows of Kilimanjaro" (1936), in which the dying protagonist recalls being with the Greek army in Anatolia, spending a night with a hot Armenian whore, and writing a letter to a first love (*Short Stories* 64). At least one of these reflects biographical truth. Hemingway did write a letter to Agnes von Kurowsky (1892–1984) on his return to Paris, but he never went to Anatolia with the Greek army, and whether the Armenian whore is real or imagined is anyone's guess (see Lynn 189–90; the response that Agnes sent to Hemingway after his late October 1922 letter is published in Villard and Nagel 164–68). Finally, there is "On the Quai at Smyrna," added as an introduction to the 1930 edition of *In Our Time*. J. M. Harrison, noting that the speaker uses many English expressions, has said of this piece that "we can envision the Britisher telling his story to the 'author' over a glass in some quiet bar" (141). Yet if someone did tell Hemingway such a story of Smyrna when he was in Constantinople, as a Captain Wittal recounted the Greeks' bombing their own troops in Anatolia (see *Dateline* 244), it seems odd that he did not use the information until eight years later. Could that conversation "over a glass," as Harrison imagines it, have occurred in Paris some years after Hemingway's trip to the Levant? For the present purposes, it is sufficient to note that "On the Quai at Smyrna" provides no information about Hemingway's activities in Constantinople in 1922.[1]

Recent biographies have added little to Hemingway's own record, most emphasizing only the fact that the writer contracted malaria during his stay.

Fig. 1. Admiral Mark Bristol (right) in front of the American Embassy in Pera where the press conferences with the journalists were held.
Photo courtesy the U.S. Naval Historical Center and Gerald L. Vincent

Carlos Baker says that Hemingway was "too ill to join other correspondents aboard a British destroyer on a briefing trip to Mytilene" (98). Kenneth S. Lynn also comments that the young writer "came down with malaria. Although doses of quinine made him feel better, he was unable to attend press conferences for a week" (181). Michael Reynolds notes that Hemingway went to a British military hospital on October 13 and adds that "for the most part Hemingway's information came from the British [military] briefings and what he picked up at the bar" (*Paris Years* 76).

There is, however, a previously unknown source for Hemingway's stay in Constantinople, the war diary of the American High Commissioner in the city, Admiral Mark Lambert Bristol (1868–1939; see fig.1). In the years immediately after World War I, Constantinople was occupied by the Allied Powers and the High Commissioners of Britain, France, Italy, and the United States functioned as the government of the city and the surrounding area. Bristol's policy in Constantinople has elicited some criticism, since he saw opportunities for American influence by supporting the Nationalist Turks over the Greeks and other Christians in the region. The historian Bruce Clark notes:

> Bristol is generally treated as a hero by Turkish historians, and demonized in Greek and Armenian accounts. It is certainly true that during and after the capture of Izmir, he took trouble to suppress

accounts of the story which showed Turks in a bad light.... He was a person of robust views on racial questions. He was an Anglophobe who also regarded the Greeks as "about the worst race in the Near East" and did not care much for the other religious minorities of the region. (136)[2]

As Marjorie Dobkin notes, "Bristol took special pains with the writers of the press" during his entire time as High Commissioner, often using the newsmen to express his views (62). Bristol's practice of holding regular press conferences began on Tuesday, September 26, 1922, as the number of reporters for American papers in the city increased after the burning of Smyrna and the possibility of war grew between Turkey and the Allies, especially Britain. Bristol's diary, now in the Library of Congress Manuscript Division, includes a record of all press conferences he gave, along with who was present and what matters were discussed. Bristol records how the practice of holding press conferences started:

Tuesday, 26 of September
Upon the suggestion of one of the American newspaper representatives here and upon recommendation of my staff I decided to receive all the representatives of American newspapers now here in Constantinople once a day, at about half past twelve, immediately after our daily staff conference.

In accordance with the above idea I received Col. Sweeney, representing the New York World, Dr. Henry Wales, representing the Chicago Daily Tribune, Mr. C. Brown, representing the Chicago Daily News, Mr. Carl von Wiegand, representing the Hearst papers, Mr. F. M. America, representing the New York Times, and Mr. J. A. Mills, representing the Associated Press. I told them that I had had no idea that they would like to come in or I would have arranged this conference for them before. When they left they all thanked me very much for allowing them to come in. I did not give out anything of particular importance. We really had only a quiet talk about what we had heard, etc. The fact was I did not really have any news to give them, except about what our relief organizations were doing and what money had been appropriated by the different associations for this relief work. Likewise, I gave them a general idea of the conference I had had the day before with the Allied High Commissioner in regard to the joint plan for relief of refugees.

From that point on, Bristol held conferences on most weekdays and Saturdays with the American correspondents in Constantinople and conscientiously recorded everyone who attended the meetings. Hemingway's name appears seven times. The first entry is on Tuesday, October 3, and the last is on Wednesday, October 11. The entries in the diary concerning press conferences for the period when Hemingway attended are given below (misspellings and other accidentals have been retained).

Tuesday, 3 of October

The representatives of the American Press were received for a conference. Present were: Mr. C. Brown, Mr. Charles Sweeny, Mr. Henry Wales, Dr. E. J. Bing, Mr. D. von Wiegand, Mr. B. J. Kospoth, Mr. Ernest Hemingway, representing the International News and Toronto Star, Mr. J. A. Mills, F. M. America. Colonel Sweeny related to me his experiences with Colonel Cornwall, of the British army, who is the censor. He complained of the personal abuse of Colonel Cornwall in talking to him, and I asked Colonel Sweeny to give me a memorandum of his experiences. All the correspondents were indignant at the treatment they were receiving from the British censor. They complained that they were not treated in a gentlemanly way and that their despatches were censored in an absurd manner, and in some cases military news was censored out of one despatch and allowed to go in another, whereas in other cases news was censored out simply because it was political or claimed to be not true. I assured the press representatives that I would do all that I could to assist them to have this condition ameliorated.

Wednesday, 4 of October

I received the representatives of the American press. Present were: J. A. Mills, C. Brown, F. M. America, Henry Wales, Carl von Wiegand, E. M. Hemingway, B. J. Kospoth, C. Sweeny. I informed them that I had little or no news this morning and then went on to explain to them the relief work that we had been doing at Smyrna, Moudania, and Rodesto. I pointed out that practically everything that had been done was done by America. I suggested that they should look over the diary of Commander Powell, Commanding Officer of the EDSALL, and they might find there information upon which to prepare a good story. In the same way the report of the Disaster Relief Committee of Smyrna could be seen, and this would give, I believed, some interesting information. Of course I was not a newspaper man and only made those suggestions as to where to find information on this subject. In view of the great interest that our Americans at home took in relief work it had occurred to me that news on this subject would be desirable for our press representatives. The press men still complained of the censorship and stated that there was a new grievance. They hand their press despatches in to the censor and he apparently passes everything and sends them on to the clerk, but it seems that later he sends for them again, and so the press men do not know what has been censored out. I told Colonel Sweeny that I decided I could not send his despatch by our code. I felt that this would be liable to stir up feeling between the Allies and myself without my being justified in taking this step. Further that I felt there were two sides to the story and without hearing the other side I could not properly and squarely act. I stated that I had sent a copy of Sweeny's memorandum to General Harington and General Harington could obtain the other side of the story. I further stated that it was my opinion that such things if possible should be arranged here among ourselves. Sweeny thanked me and was evidently satisfied with my decision. I remarked that of course he had ways of sending out the despatch himself, and probably it had already gone. Everyone smiled at this idea. I asked them what they thought of the official communiqué that had gone out by the conference in Moudania, and they were quite disgusted with this sort of news, and stated that it amounted to nothing.

Thursday, 5 of October

I received the representatives of the American press. Present: C. Sweeny, Carl von Wiegand, Ernest M. Hemingway, E. J. Bing, B. J. Kospoth, Henry Wales, C. Brown, F. M. America, J. A. Mills. I told them that I had very little news for them, except that practically all of the refugees had been evacuated from Smyrna, and our latest report was that we had evacuated 220,000. It was my belief that our naval ships, with the use of Greek merchant ships, had practically done all of this work, and that it was not until the 26 of September that the British Navy lying in Smyrna sent an offer to assist us. Our senior officer present, Commander Halsey Powell, called on British Admiral Nicholson and arranged for British assistance, and then went ashore and got permission from the Turkish authorities for the British to land. This permission was granted on condition that the British officers and men were not armed and that they did not go beyond the immediate vicinity of the point of embarkation on the railway pier. In half an hour a hundred and thirty British officers and men were ashore, and from that time to the present worked with our people, rendering very valuable assistance. Further there had been some British ships assisting in the evacuation but some of these were chartered by the Greek Committee and therefore not furnished by the British. Rumbold informed me that the British Board of Trade was going to send fifteen British ships to assist in evacuating the refugees from Smyrna. I had sent a telegram to find out if any of these ships had assisted and thus far I had received no answer to my radio. Yet I was firmly convinced that the Allies, Britain, France, and Italy, had rendered little or no assistance in the evacuation of refugees, except for the benefit of their own citizens. All of the press men were very amused at the official communiqués that were being given out by the British Headquarters. One of the press men stated that it was practically only "Some points have been decided upon and other points are yet under consideration."

"The Greek officers that came to the conference were seasick." However, they all stated that my interceding in behalf of better censorship had undoubtedly improved matters very much. At the present time they have no difficulty in getting off their despatches and practically nothing is cut out by the censor.

Friday, 6 of October

I had the usual conference of the American press representatives. Present: C Brown, C. M. Hemmingway, B. J. Kospoth, Henry Wales, Carl von Wiegand, John Clayton, H. A. Bradstreet (an Australian recently arrived and this was his first conference. He represents the New York Times), E. J. Bing, C. Sweeny, and J. A. Mills. I told them I had little or no news for them except the news from one of their colleagues which, of course, according to newspaper etiquette I was not at liberty to give them. They all then asked Clayton, who had been to Moudania and got back the night before, to tell his story. He said he would next day when he was sure it had gotten out. This created a bit of amusement. They all said that the military censorship was now very wide open and they were having no trouble at all, and practically all of their despatches were going through. I may add here that later in the evening one of the newspaper men showed me despatches from their papers stating the pressure was being brought upon the Premiers of the Allied countries and telegrams were being sent to Harington about the censorship, and they need not worry but that the difficulties would be cleared away. This shows the foolishness of the British, especially here, in trying to shut down on the press. It only puts them in bad with the press when the friendliness of the press is especially desirable. This is exemplified by one of the Secretaries of the British High Commission remarking to one of my officers that they would be all right if they only had the press back of them. They realize that the people in England are not behind them in their present policy and I am sure that if they could get the people behind them they would go to war with Turkey. It is a very remarkable situation. I am reminded of the information from our Embassy at London that the British cabinet contemplated abandoning the patrol of Constantinople in order to defend the Straits and then if a massacre or disturbances or other atrocities were committed in Constantinople, that would get their people behind them. The more I dip into European politics, the more disgusted I become. It is incomprehensible to me that politicians seem to have such a lack of moral character when it comes down to politics.

Saturday, 7 of October

I had the usual conference with the press representatives. Present: Carl von Wiegand, E. M. Hemmingway, Henry Wales, Frazier Hunt (who is a magazine writer for the Hearst press), C. Brown, C. Sweeny, J. A. Mills, B. J.

Kospoth. We hadn't very much to talk about and I told them the only news I had was some I had just received from Dr. Nansen. I had been to call on him at the hotel and he had just returned from seeing General Pelde. The latter had told Dr. Nansen that he felt cheered up in regard to the conference at Moudania and believed that a settlement would be reached tonight. One of the press men stated that he had received more pessimistic news from the British High Commissioner. I was not surprised at this, because all the information we have gotten from there, and generally directly from members of the High Commission, indicated that they are anti-Turk and even direct information came from Rumbold that he proposed a boundary of Thrace in accordance with the old Enos-Media line. This is an indication of how he is living in the past or else he is trying to play the Oriental game of bartering. In either case he is playing a poor game at the present time.

Monday, 9 of October
The press representatives were received. Present: J. A. Mills, Henry Wales and C. Brown. I had practically no news to give them and we simply had a rather pleasant little chat.

Tuesday 10 of October
The regular conference with the press men was held. Present: Henry Wales, C. Brown, E. M. Hemmingway, B. J. Kospoth, Frazier Hunt and Carl von Wiegand. The press men had another complaint about censorship. Some of them had filed their despatches in the morning so as to get them off in time to reach their papers before they went to press, but the censors claimed that these despatches could not be given out until after Major Johnson, at the British headquarters, had a conference with the newspaper men. When they went to this conference it was delayed and their despatches were delayed. The press men were again stirred up by this foolish sort of ruling. I must say also that I sympathized with them. However, I suggested to Mr. Brown, who was one of those who had suffered, that he see Colonel Cornwall and see what could be done to fix it up and then let me know and I would see what I could do to help them.

Wednesday, 11 of October
Only two of the press representatives appeared at the conference, E. M. Hemmingway and C. Brown.

Because of other business, Bristol was unable to hold any press conferences from the 12th to the 16th, the day on which, according to Reynolds, Hemingway left the city for Thrace (*Paris Years* 77). So during the time that Hemingway was in Constantinople, he missed only one of the press

Fig. 2. The American Embassy in the Pera section of Constantinople. Photo courtesy the U.S. Naval Historical Center and Gerald L. Vincent

conferences, on Monday, October 9, that Bristol held at the American Embassy (see fig. 2). This challenges the claim that Hemingway was so sick with malaria that he missed all of the press briefings by British military headquarters for an entire week. Further, the idea that Hemingway would somehow have had to find a way to deal with his illness in a strange city with no assistance is hard to balance with the fact that he was a regular and welcome visitor at the American Embassy. As many of the American reporters in Constantinople had traveled around the region on American naval vessels, we might consider that Carlos Baker should not have been so definitive in stating that the destroyer traveling to the island of Mytilene (where Hemingway was too ill to go) was British. Indeed, given the fact that the British had a hostile attitude toward the press, it seems possible that Bristol would have arranged such a trip on an American destroyer. The fact that Hemingway attended Bristol's press conferences also calls into question Reynolds's assertion that Hemingway's information came from the "British briefings and what he picked up at the bar" (*Paris Years* 76). Hemingway clearly got a lot of information from these discussions between Bristol and the journalists.

Unfortunately, on October 11, the day only Constantine Brown (1899–1966) and Hemingway attended the press conference, Bristol gives no indication of the topics discussed. But the other entries indicate that Hemingway picked up a good deal of background about the situation in the Near East from these gatherings. Some of the discussions at the press conferences seem to have made their way into his dispatches, notably, but

Fig. 3. A street in Pera, the foreign section of Constantinople.
Photo courtesy the U.S. Naval Historical Center and Gerald L. Vincent

not only, the account of the censorship of dispatches in "Near East Censor Too 'Thorough' " (*Dateline* 237–38). The discussion of the Moudania conference and the British policy toward the Turks in "Russia Spoiling the French Game," which ends, "then we can fight the Gallipoli over again" (*Dateline* 234), reflects Bristol's thinking that the British were living in the past. And, while Hemingway certainly heard stories about the burning of Smyrna from other reporters and British officers, he would also have heard accounts from the American naval personnel who had been present. No evidence exists that Hemingway took advantage of Bristol's offer to look at the diary of Commander Halsey Powell (1883–1936) of the *Edsall* concerning events in Smyrna (nor have I yet been able to discover whether this diary exists), but it is intriguing to know that the offer was made. How much of Hemingway's background information came from Bristol himself, how much from his staff, and how much from his fellow journalists is, of course, impossible to determine.

The record of attendees at the press conferences expands our knowledge of Hemingway's acquaintances in Constantinople; indeed, it probably records the circle of journalists that he interacted with while in the city. The one best known to Hemingway scholars is Charles Sweeny (1882–1963), who became a friend for several decades. Nearly all of the biographers mention that Hemingway met the colorful Sweeny in Constantinople, presumably at the press briefings or at one of the places in Pera where foreign correspondents gathered (see fig. 3). Sweeny, according to some, acted as

Fig. 4. A photograph taken at a picnic hosted by the Bristols and attended by Hemingway's friend Charles Sweeny (far right).
Photo courtesy the U.S. Naval Historical Center and Gerald L. Vincent

a mentor to Hemingway while he was in the Orient and became a longtime friend. Richard Deacon, Sweeny's biographer, says that "[w]hen Hemingway went down with malaria it was Sweeny who advised him how to cope, when he was racing against time to write a dispatch it was Sweeny who supplied the fact to pad out the narrative" (121). Deacon makes much of Sweeny as a French secret agent, which he well might have been, but he certainly was not as secretive in his movements as Deacon suggests. Nor did the Colonel keep himself "away from all correspondents except Hemingway and Larry Larue" (121; the latter name is actually Larry Rue [1893–1965], the author of *I Fly for News* [1932]). Even as he had regular attendance at Admiral Bristol's news conferences, Sweeny became a good friend of Constantine Brown, who later recommended Sweeny as a pilot for the French in Morocco, and John Clayton (1893–1979), with whom, along with Brown, he made a long trip into Anatolia. And Sweeny went to several social functions hosted by the Bristols, including a picnic at which his photograph was taken (see fig. 4). Further, the fact that Sweeny's sympathies were "on the Turkish side" (Deacon 120) might have made him suspicious to the British military, but certainly not at the American Embassy where Bristol's support of the Turks was well known.

Brown's memoir, *The Coming of the Whirlwind* (1964), features a section dealing with his time as a foreign correspondent based in Constantinople and sheds useful light on Bristol and his attitudes. On his arrival as the correspondent for the *Chicago Daily News*, Brown recalls, "the Admiral invited me to make myself at home at the Embassy.... I took him at his word and dropped in at the Embassy almost every day to talk to the Admiral or one of his aides." Brown describes Bristol as "an old-fashioned rough-and-ready seadog who had been converted into a rough-and-ready diplomat.... He made no secret of his admiration for Mustafa Kemal [1881–1938] and his national liberation movement. 'I don't know much about the man really,' Admiral Bristol admitted, 'but anybody who is willing to challenge such odds out of love for his country has my respect'" (128–29). Bristol continually urged reporters to go to Ankara and get the "Turkish" side of the story, and he also advised that stories of atrocities deal with acts committed by both Greeks and Turks: "It was Admiral Bristol who proposed that I work my way into Asia Minor to visit Mustafa Kemal at his headquarters in Ankara, he 'wanted to convey to Kemal an unofficial assurance that, whatever might be the intentions of the British, French, Italians, and Greeks, the United States had no designs on Turkish territory or Turkish interests.' For this I seemed an appropriate messenger, for if I were stopped by the British I could protest quite truthfully that I was a reporter in search of news" (137). Later, Brown notes, "[I] made several later visits to Angora and on my return to Constantinople would report what I had seen and heard to Admiral Bristol. He was more than ever persuaded that the United States should lend its support to Kemal and continued to urge this view in his despatches to Washington" (143). Brown summered in the resort town of Therapia on a houseboat, the *Nelly*, which was anchored next to the USS *Scorpion*, which served as Bristol's flagship and summer home. Because Prohibition extended to American naval vessels through an edict by Secretary of the Navy Josephus Daniels (1862–1948), whenever the Bristols held a party a plank was put between the two boats so that Bristol's guests could leave American soil and get a drink (see fig. 5).

In his memoir, *Of the Meek and the Mighty* (1939), Edward J. Byng (1894–1962; Bristol consistently spells it as Bing) says that the correspondents for the American papers had a daily routine, which Hemingway seems to have followed. They would begin the day with the briefing at British Headquarters, and then proceed to the press conference at the American Embassy at half past noon: "Each morning we correspondents—there were about two dozen of us in all—would drive to the British G.H.Q., where Major Johnson of the British General Staff would read out

Fig. 5. The USS *Scorpion*, Admiral Bristol's summer home where he hosted the parties mentioned by Constantine Brown.
Photo courtesy the U.S. Naval Historical Center and Gerald L. Vincent

the official statement, giving a short résumé of the events of the past twenty-four hours, including Turkish troop movements. Admiral Mark Bristol was most helpful and obliging to the representatives of the American Press. . . . Out of business hours the Admiral was also a charming host, on his flagship the Scorpion and in the rooms of the Embassy" (208).

Frazier Hunt's (1885–1967) *One American and His Attempt at Education* (1938) is of special interest since the title appears in Reynolds's *Hemingway's Reading, 1910–1940*. Hunt would have had a particular reason for wanting to meet Hemingway, for just before both men left for the Near East, Hunt, a literary scout for Hearst publications, had sent Hemingway a letter from London dated September 21, praising his story "My Old Man" (1923) and offering advice and encouragement, noting that "if you do some more stories and if you can just as easily do a bright and 'sweet' yarn as you can do a tragic one, you will find your market 50% easier to make" (qtd. in Reynolds, *Paris Years* 78). According to Reynolds, Hemingway did not receive the letter until he returned to Paris at the end of October, but he clearly met Hunt in Constantinople as they attended two press conferences together, and Hunt would have realized that this was the Ernest Hemingway with whom he had just communicated. Yet, like Brown and Byng, Hunt never mentions meeting the young author in Constantinople in October 1922. Hunt had at least one private meeting with

Bristol, on October 10, and also made the Bristol-advised trip into Anatolia with Art Wills, "a one-time naval officer" (267), and Larry Rue in a car acquired and driven by John Clayton. Of Kemal's soldiers, he says, "[T]hey were Washington's men at Valley Forge" (268), and he also describes Turkish villages burned by the Greeks.

While these three memoirs provide interesting background about the journalistic circle in Constantinople with which Hemingway associated, one odd fact stands out. All of these books were published well after 1930, by which time Hemingway had become famous, yet not a single one of them mentions that they had met Hemingway as a young reporter there. Reading their accounts, we get some understanding of why Hemingway created stories of a trip to Anatolia. Bristol urged, and tried to facilitate, trips by American journalists to the Turkish nationalists to counter the supposed pro-Greek and pro-Armenian bias in the American press and, according to Brown, to send messages to the government of Kemal. Brown, Byng, Sweeny, Clayton, Hunt, Rue, and almost all the other American reporters went into Anatolia. Hemingway may have been too sick, or spent too little time in the Near East, to be able to make the journey, but he certainly knew it was one of the things that nearly all of his colleagues had done. Indeed, one of the American reporters who made the trip was Clare Sheridan (1885–1970), the famous "girl" reporter for the *New York Tribune*. She was in Constantinople at the same time as Hemingway, and, according to Bristol's diary, met with Bristol on October 6:

> Mrs. Clare Sheridan, who went to Smyrna, from there to Athens and returned to Constantinople, called and asked to see me before the conference of press men. I saw her for a few minutes and found that her real object was to get permission to go to Moudania on one of our destroyers. I told her there were no accommodations at Moudania for a woman, it was a little fishing village, and it would be impossible for her to stay on board one of our destroyers. Jokingly I said I thought that I could not allow scandal in our navy. She laughed, and asked if she could get on a British ship, saying, "I suppose not, because our people (meaning the British) are very down on the press." I asked her why they were down on the press and she said she didn't know but that they didn't want any of the press around. I told her that on British light cruisers they had extra quarters so they might take care of her, but on destroyers we had nothing of the kind. I excused myself in order to have my conference with the newspaper men and she asked to be present. I told her that she might, but when she heard that Dr. Nansen was sitting outside to see me, she immediately left to see an old friend, and later when I joined Dr. Nansen she had gone.

Fig. 6. The quai at Smyrna, September 1922.
Photo courtesy the U.S. Naval Historical Center and Gerald L. Vincent

Sheridan, who had gotten an interview with Mustafa Kemal after the capture of Smyrna (Sheridan, *West and East* 141–48) and wrote about the horrors on the quai (see figs. 6 and 7), pooled together with John Clayton, E. J. Byng, and Harold Albert Bradstreet (1895–1933) to hire a boat and get to Moudania to cover the deliberations about the armistice (*West and East* 167–68).[3] Again, Hemingway might have been fighting malaria, but he could not have been pleased to be scooped by Mrs. Clare Sheridan. Hemingway might have met Sheridan in Constantinople even though she did not attend any of Bristol's press conferences, but if so she does not record a meeting in either of her accounts of her trip to Turkey, *West and East* (1923) or *The Naked Truth* (1928). Hemingway certainly knew of her in Constantinople, for when he was in Lausanne covering the peace agreement between Turkey and Greece and Sheridan arranged the only private interview with Benito Mussolini (1883–1945), he slightingly referred to her as someone "who smiled her way into many interviews" (*Dateline* 256). The Lausanne Conference, which lasted from late November 1922 until February 1923, was also the last time Bristol and Hemingway met (according to Baker [102–4], Hemingway arrived in Lausanne on November 22 and left on December 16). Bristol noted on November 28: "I met Mr. Hemmingway in the corridor. He was in Constantinople representing the Hearst papers and is here for the same purpose. He asked if I was going to be quoted in the papers and I told him, 'No,' that I was acting in the same way that I had acted in Constantinople. He was very cordial in

Fig. 7. Flotsam in Smyrna harbor, September 1922.
Photo courtesy the U.S. Naval Historical Center and Gerald L. Vincent

appreciating the situation." This is also the only time that Hemingway mentions the admiral, saying in a letter to Hadley, "Admiral Bristol's come and they want to meet Mummy" (*Selected Letters* 74).

There remains one question to ponder. As we can see from what Constantine Brown said, Bristol liked to influence reporters toward certain kinds of stories in order to shape the opinion back home and counteract what he saw as an American partiality for the Greeks and Armenians. Was Bristol able to influence Hemingway in this way? At first glance it might appear so, as Bristol repeatedly urged reporters to balance any reports of atrocities committed by the Turks with those committed by the Greeks. Bristol began this practice well before Hemingway arrived in the city, for in his diary for July 20, 1921, he records a meeting with John Dos Passos (1896–1970) of the *New York Tribune* and the *Metropolitan Magazine*. Bristol says that Dos Passos was

> thinking of going to Rodosto where the [Greek] refugees from Ismidt are now located. I told him I thought it would be better for him to go to Ismidt where those refugees came from and get a proper background for a visit to Rodosto. Also to Yalova and Guemlik where the Greeks had murdered and burned the Turkish villages; and then visit these refugees where they are located in and around Constantinople. I suggested that he might then write one story bringing out the savagery of both the Greeks and Turks against each other. Mr. Dos Passos liked this idea.

This was vintage Bristol; when a reporter wanted to do a story of Turkish atrocities, the admiral would suggest that it be balanced with an account of Greek atrocities. His suggestion was not because he was neutral, but rather because he thought it was a good way to counteract what he saw as the pro-Greek slant of the American press (on Bristol and Dos Passos, see my "Rewriting Reminiscences").

"Constantinople, Dirty White, Not Glistening and Sinister," one of Hemingway's reports from the city, dated October 18, seems to deal with the matter of the atrocities in the region in the manner that Bristol encouraged. He states that "it is an uncontested fact that the Greek army in its retreat across Anatolia laid waste and burned Turkish villages, burnt their crops, the grain on the threshing floors and committed atrocities. These facts are testified to by American relief workers and Christians who were in the country before, during, and after the Greek defeat." He then concludes that he will "take up the question of Greek atrocities later when I have the evidence and testimony of both Christians and Turks and will try to give a complete presentation of the matter to the *Star* readers" (*Dateline* 229). If Hemingway does not have all of the evidence and testimony, how can he declare that the actions of the Greek army are an "uncontested fact," especially when the dispatches never mention any conversations with American relief workers? Indeed, the only relief worker that Hemingway interviewed for an article was the head of the Turkish Red Crescent, Hamid Bey, and Hemingway himself said that "Turkish Red Crescent (equivalent to the Red Cross) reports on Greek atrocities in Thrace must be discounted as the leader of Red Crescent is Kemal's head in Constantinople and Red Crescent official reports are used as propaganda to force the immediate occupation of Thrace by the Turks" (*Dateline* 219). Between these last words, dated October 4, sent just after his arrival in Constantinople, and his comments about uncontested Greek atrocities, Hemingway had spent several press conferences with Bristol, who would have been glad to provide Hemingway with some carefully selected testimony of American relief workers.

Hemingway's attitude toward the Greeks and the Turks in his dispatches offers the moral balance between Greeks and Turks that Bristol had urged on Dos Passos, particularly in his reports of the Greek evacuation from Thrace. This comes across perhaps best in Hemingway's conversation with Madame Marie, the innkeeper in Adrianople in "Refugees from Thrace":

> "I won't care when the Turks come," Madame Marie said, sitting her great bulk down at a table and scratching her chin.
> "Why not?"
> "They're all the same. The Greek and the Turks and the Bulgars. They're all the same." She accepted a glass of white wine. "I've seen them all. They've all had Karagatch."
> "Who are the best?" I asked.
> "Nobody. They're all the same." (*Dateline* 251)

Hemingway's views were based on the lessons of the Great War, and for him "the key to understanding the postwar Near East ran through the western front. When every soldier and every civilian could be seen as a victim, national identities seemed insignificant" (Roessel, *In Byron's Shadow* 215). Bristol, at bottom, thought the Turks were better than the Greeks, and his encouragement of balanced reporting was a public relations ploy. For Hemingway, however, the experience and the new myth of the Great War had shown that it did not matter who won because in the end all were losers. Indeed, despite Hemingway's youth, and perhaps because of the short length of his stay in Constantinople, Bristol seems to have had no success in getting Hemingway to subscribe to the position that the Turks were fighters for independence like Washington at Valley Forge. And it would be Hemingway, not Bristol, who made the Smyrna disaster and the Greek defeat part of modern American literature (see Roessel, *In Byron's Shadow* 210–21).

But there is one place where Bristol may well have influenced Hemingway's opinion. In "The Snows of Kilimanjaro," the dying narrator remembers the following incident:

> Now in his mind he saw the railway station at Karagatch and he was standing with his pack and that was the headlight of the Simplon-Orient cutting the dark now and he was leaving Thrace. That was one of the things he had saved to write about, with, in the morning at breakfast, looking out the window and seeing snow on the mountains of Bulgaria and Nansen's Secretary asking the old man if it were snow and the old man looking at it and saying, No, that's not snow. It's too early for snow. And the Secretary repeating to the other girls, No, you see, It's not snow, and them all saying, It's not snow we were mistaken. But it was snow all right and he sent them on into it when he evolved the exchange of populations. And it was snow they tramped along in until they died that winter. (*Short Stories* 55)

Fridtjoff Nansen (1861–1930), the famous Norwegian Arctic explorer and director of international relief efforts in Constantinople in late 1922, hardly deserves this accusation. Whatever Nansen's controversial role in helping to promote the mandatory exchange in 1923 of Greeks in Turkey and Turks in Greece at the Lausanne Conference, he was not responsible for the plight of the Greek refugees in Thrace that Hemingway saw in late October. Their departure was a result of the Moudania conference, which gave Eastern Thrace to the Turks and allowed the Greek army fifteen days to evacuate (Clark 48–49). Fears by the local Greek population that they would experience a repeat of the horrors of Smyrna if they stayed in their homes prompted them to leave. In his dispatches, Hemingway acknowledges that the Greek civilians of Eastern Thrace chose to leave with the Greek army (*Dateline* 232). Hemingway did not witness any of the mandatory exchange of populations in 1923 that Nansen helped arrange (see Clark 93–96), in which more than a million civilians were forcibly moved between Greece and Turkey. Further, Nansen, who received the Nobel Prize in 1922 for his relief work, was considered a hero by some at the time, including E. J. Byng. Jeffrey Meyers notes that Hemingway needed "a scapegoat for everything" and "unfairly blames the humane Fridtjoff Nansen" (31).

Bristol, however, had a completely different opinion of Nansen and his activities. In his diary for October 6, 1922, Bristol records that he had a call from Nansen, "the noted explorer and now the High Commissioner of the League of Nations for the relief of refugees. He is a typical Norwegian type, with a personality that is not particularly pleasing and at the same time not displeasing. . . . Their attitude towards doing relief in this part of the world, together with what has appeared in the press, indicates that they expect large contributions from America and that the League of Nations will direct the expenditure of the funds." As can be seen from his comments on the efforts to help at Smyrna, Bristol thought that America had done the most work and had not been given full credit. Bristol attempted to impress upon Nansen that that greatest need was now in Greece, which was full of refugees from Asia Minor. But it was evident that Nansen "did not sympathize with the idea of their taking up work in Greece."

On October 7, Bristol returned Nansen's call by visiting him at the Pera Palace Hotel: "I could not help but think, when I was ushered into his suite of rooms that relief money was being used for these expenses, and also called to mind that one of our Americans who came on the steamer with Dr. Nansen when he arrived a few days ago in Constantinople stated that Dr. Nansen was accompanied by fifteen to twenty clerks and assistants." Despite the increasing problems in Greece, Nansen's whole attitude, according to Bristol, was that "the League of Nations would be charged with looking out for Christian minorities in Turkey and therefore his Committee would take up this question at once." Bristol concluded his entry: "This interview with Dr. Nansen convinced me more than ever that we are absolute fools to give our money to the League of Nations or any of those other foreign organizations to spend for relief work."

On October 15, the question of the exchange of the populations of Christians and Muslims in Thrace was raised, and Bristol noted, "It seemed to me more at this conference that Nansen was sort of injecting himself into affairs in the Near East without any justification." In the weeks that followed, Bristol continued to think that Nansen was injecting the explosive issue of population exchange into discussions, with drastic consequences in 1923 when the exchange was made nearly comprehensive and mandatory. In Nansen, Bristol found a sentiment for wanting to carry on relief work for the political effect it might have (Oct. 6). Hemingway may have heard some of Bristol's views about Nansen during his time in Constantinople, but it seems likely that the admiral passed on some more information when the two men met at the peace congress in Lausanne. Hemingway could, of course, have come to his view of Nansen on his own; still, it is curious that Bristol and Hemingway shared such a vitriolic view of a man whom others saw as a tireless and effective aid worker. But as an observer in Thrace, Hemingway would have known that it was not Nansen who sent the Greeks of Eastern Thrace out into the snow—or rather, as Hemingway indicated in his dispatches at the time, rain (*Dateline* 232).

While this essay has sketched in some of the background of Hemingway's stay in Constantinople, there remain a number of blank spots and questions. Why did the young Hemingway make so little impression on those around him during his stay in the Near East that he never gets a mention from anyone, even after he was one of the most famous authors on the planet? Why, unlike Dos Passos, Brown, Hunt, and nearly every other journalist who came to Constantinople, does Hemingway never mention meeting Bristol in anything written for publication at the time, or later? Why, again unlike Dos Passos, Sweeny, Brown, Hunt, and even Clare Sheridan, does Bristol never record having a private meeting, either professionally or socially, with Hemingway during those three weeks in Constantinople? Was Hemingway too ill? Did he never request a meeting with Bristol? What should be clear is that Hemingway went to the American Embassy nearly every day in the company of most of the other American reporters in the city to meet with the highest American official in the region. And yet, despite that, Hemingway's "3 very fine weeks" remain something of a mystery; indeed, they seem a bit more mysterious. At the end of 1922, Agnes von Kurowsky, the nurse whom Hemingway fell in love with in Milan during World War I, responded to news of the impending publication of his first book: "How proud I will be in the not-very-distant future to say 'Oh, yes, Ernest Hemingway. Used to know him quite well during the war' " (Villard and Nagel 167). But in those "3 very fine weeks," perhaps for the last time in his life, the people who met the writer apparently would not feel it important and memorable that they had met Ernest Hemingway.

NOTES

The photographs included with this essay (figs. 1–7) are from the scrapbooks of Admiral Thomas C. Kinkaid (1888–1972), who served under Admiral Mark Bristol in 1922. The scrapbooks are housed in the U.S. Naval History and Heritage Command Center, formerly the U.S. Naval Historical Center, Washington Naval Yard, Washington, DC. I wish to thank Gerald L. Vincent, who has done research on Kinkaid, for providing the illustrations. I also wish to thank the Manuscript Division of the Library of Congress for providing assistance in using the Mark L. Bristol Papers.

1. Of course, if there were a more concrete answer to the question "who is the 'he' of the introducing sentences" (Harrison 141), then we might have a better idea of whether this conversation took place in Constantinople. I admit that it is tempting to suppose that it did; indeed, I think that it is tempting to suppose that it was no other than Shorty Wornall, who had been in Smyrna before he met Hemingway in Thrace. Then the final version of *In Our Time* would open and close with reports by Wornall. But, beyond such speculation, there is no record of when, or even if, the conversation in "On the Quai at Smyrna" took place.

2. See also the comments about Bristol by Marjorie Dobkin (56–62). Her conclusion on Bristol's character and views are similar to Clark's, although she demonizes him for his position on the Asia Minor Disaster. The earliest attack on Bristol from supporters of the Greek side was Edward Hale Bierstadt's *The Great Betrayal* in 1924.

3. The connection between the accounts about Smyrna by Sheridan and Hemingway deserves more attention. Sheridan writes about "the filthy water that was stagnant and stinking of corpses of men and beasts" (*West and East* 150) and of "cases of childbirth on the quai" (152). This does not necessarily mean that Hemingway had read or seen Sheridan's *West and East* (1923); perhaps both writers were drawn to the most dramatic situations of the Greek refugees in both Smyrna and Thrace. In the only discussion of Sheridan and Hemingway to date, I find that, while they both present a similar view of the state of Europe "in our time," Sheridan lacked the language and style to shape the literary record of the period as Hemingway did (*In Byron's Shadow* 221–22).

WORKS CITED

Baker, Carlos. *Ernest Hemingway: A Life Story.* New York: Scribner's, 1969. Print.
Bierstadt, Edward Hale. *The Great Betrayal.* New York: McBride, 1924. Print.
Bing, Edward J. *Of the Meek and the Mighty.* London: Nicholson, 1939. Print.
Bristol, Mark Lambert. War diary: 1919–27. MS. Mark L. Bristol Papers, 1882–1939. Manuscript Div., Lib. of Congress, Washington, DC.
Brown, Constantine. *The Coming of the Whirlwind.* Chicago: Regnery, 1964. Print.
Clark, Bruce. *Twice a Stranger: How Mass Migration Forged Modern Greece and Turkey.* London: Granta, 2006. Print.
Cowley, Malcolm. "A Portrait of Mister Papa." *Ernest Hemingway: The Man and His Work.* Ed. John K. M. McCaffery. Cleveland: World, 1950. 34–56.
Deacon, Richard. *One Man's War: The Story of Charles Sweeny, Soldier of Fortune.* London: Barker, 1972. Print.
Dobkin, Marjorie. *The Smyrna Affair.* New York: Harcourt, 1971. Print.
Fenton, Charles. *The Apprenticeship of Ernest Hemingway: The Early Years.* New York: Farrar, 1954. Print.
Harrison, J. M. "Hemingway's *In Our Time.*" *Critical Essays on "In Our Time."* Ed. Michael Reynolds. Boston: Hall, 1983. 141–44. Print.
Hemingway, Ernest. *The Complete Short Stories of Ernest Hemingway.* New York: Scribner's, 1987. Print.
———. *Dateline, Toronto: The Complete "Toronto Star" Dispatches, 1920–1924.* Ed. William White. New York: Scribner's, 1985. Print.
———. *Ernest Hemingway: Selected Letters, 1917–1961.* Ed. Carlos Baker. New York: Scribner's, 1981. Print.
———. *In Our Time.* New York: Scribner's, 1930.
———. Letter to [John R.] Bone, Oct. 17, 1922. TC [Typed Cable]. Ernest Hemingway Personal Papers. John F. Kennedy Presidential Lib. and Museum, Boston.

Humphries, David. *Different Dispatches: Journalism in American Modernist Prose.* New York: Routledge, 2006. Print.
Hunt, Frazier. *One American and His Attempt at Education.* New York: Simon, 1938. Print.
Lovejoy, Esther. *Certain Samaritans.* New York: MacMillan, 1933. Print.
Lynn, Kenneth S. *Hemingway.* New York: Simon, 1987. Print.
Meyers, Jeffrey. "Hemingway's Second War." 1984. *Hemingway: Life into Art.* New York: Cooper Square, 2000. 21–33. Print.
Reynolds, Michael. *Hemingway: The Final Years.* New York: Norton, 1999. Print.
———. *Hemingway: The Paris Years.* Oxford, UK: Basil Blackwell, 1989. Print.
———. *Hemingway's Reading, 1910–1940: An Inventory.* Princeton: Princeton UP, 1981. Print.
Roessel, David. *In Byron's Shadow: Modern Greece in the English and American Imagination.* New York: Oxford UP, 2001. Print.
———. "Rewriting Reminiscences: Hemingway, Dos Passos and the Greco-Turkish War of 1920–1922." *Hellenism and the U.S.: Constructions/Deconstructions.* Ed. Savas Patislides. Thessaloniki: Aristotle U, 1994. 33–40. Print.
Rue, Larry. *I Fly for News.* New York: Boni, 1932. Print.
Sheridan, Clare. *The Naked Truth.* New York: Harper, 1928. Print.
———. *West and East.* New York: Boni, 1923. Print.
Villard, Henry Serrano, and James Nagel. *Hemingway in Love and War: The Lost Diary of Agnes Von Kurowsky, Her Letters, and Correspondence of Ernest Hemingway.* New York: Hyperion, 1989. Print.

"To Weave the Whole Thing Together": Thomas Wolfe's Revisions of *From Death to Morning*

PARK BUCKER
University of South Carolina Sumter

From 1932 to 1934, while composing his lengthy second novel, Thomas Wolfe (1900–1938) excised episodes from the vast work-in-progress as marketable short stories, almost all of them published by *Scribner's Magazine*. After months of intense revision and aborted proofreading, Wolfe completed his novel, *Of Time and the River*, and on December 26, 1934, signed a contract with Scribner's for a yet-to-be-titled volume of short stories. Wolfe's editor Maxwell Perkins (1884–1947) scheduled the book for a fall 1935 publication and in late spring issued a salesman's dummy advertising the author's "versatility, precision and economy" (Wolfe, *Stories* front paste-down endpaper)—adjectives not often ascribed to Thomas Wolfe. The dummy reprinted the first six pages of "The Web of Earth," a 1932 novella composed separately from *Of Time and the River*. Although Perkins compiled the stories and directed that galley proofs be prepared, he could not release the book until Wolfe returned from his wanderings in Europe and the American West to perform the final revision—a stipulation upon which the author had insisted. On May 20, 1935, Wolfe cabled Perkins from Berlin: "NO TITLE STORIES YET DEATH PROUD BROTHER SHOULD BE INCLUDED WAIT FOR ME" (Bruccoli and Bucker 158). "Death the Proud Brother," a meditative novella on death, became the second story in the volume. Wolfe did not intend the collection merely to reprint his magazine stories. On May 23, 1935, the author wrote Perkins:

> Please don't go too far with the stories before I get there. There are things I can do that will make them much better and if you will only wait on me I will do them and we will have a fine book of stories and unlike any I know of. (Bruccoli and Bucker 162)

Although most of the collected stories evolved out of episodes deleted from *Of Time and the River*, the volume is not simply an assembly of leftover material. Wolfe believed it to include some of his most ambitious and successful fiction, and he wanted to craft the volume, through revision, into a unified whole. On September 1, Wolfe wrote that he intended to inject "so many things bearing upon death and night and morning that could be put in to weave the whole thing together" (Bruccoli and Bucker 177). Part of the impetus for Wolfe's efforts derived from his desire to answer negative criticisms of his effusive prose style. When Wolfe finally returned to New York in late September, he made significant revisions in all of the fourteen collected stories, except for "The Web of Earth," the volume's final and longest narrative. Scribner's published the book, titled *From Death to Morning*, on November 14, 1935. Unfortunately, Wolfe's revised galleys—for this and his other Scribner's books—have not survived. In the absence of such evidence, the extent of authorial and/or editorial revision can be determined only through a comparison of the magazine and book versions of each story. A concordance and collation of the stories published in *From Death to Morning* with their original magazine texts documents Wolfe's efforts to "weave" his stories together and reveals the author's careful and deliberate methods of revision. Although Wolfe could be infantile and chimerical in his reaction to adverse criticism, the changes he made for the book of short stories illustrate his evolving skills as a literary craftsman. A genius writes the first draft; a craftsman perfects the final one.

Slightly less than one-half of the 1,102 revisions in *From Death to Morning* may be termed accidentals, spelling and punctuation changes, as opposed to substantive word revisions or additions that affect meaning. "Accidental" is a misnomer, as punctuation can also affect meaning, as well as rhythm. Although *Scribner's Magazine* and the Charles Scribner's Sons book publisher shared the same building, they apparently had different house styles. Some of the stylistic revisions include: towards/toward, grey/gray, court house/court-house, and work room/work-room. Also, many more commas appear in the book version than in the magazine. Most of these may have been added by Perkins, assistant editor John Hall Wheelock (1886–1978), or other house editors while they waited for the author to return to New York. On September 16, Perkins wrote to Wolfe's English publisher, A. S. Frere-Reeves, that he had corrected the galleys "so far as I dared, and returned them to the press to be sent back in revised galleys. The moment Tom gets here, I am going to try to make him read them" (Perkins 106). Even before Wolfe's revisions, Perkins regarded the stories as a significant departure for the author from his previous novels. In his letter to Frere-Reeves, Perkins continued: "I think these stories will make a very favorable impression, because most of them are not autobiographical in the sense in which the novels are, and they are objective, and are relatively free from those extravagant characteristics which are regarded as Tom's defects" (106). Perkins feared that in his desire to unify the book Wolfe would add more stories, thereby causing further delay. "I shall fight against this," he wrote Frere-Reeves, adding that Wolfe "seems to feel a certain shame at the idea of turning out a book of reasonable dimensions" (106). Many reviewers had publicly balked at the 912-page length of *Of Time and the River*. (*From Death to Morning* is 304 pages.)

Wolfe did not add any new stories to *From Death to Morning*. Conversely, the collation reveals that Wolfe, the much-maligned "putter-inner," famous for repetition and hyperbole, actually cut more than 2,000 words from the magazine texts of his stories. In the case of "The Four Lost Men," he deleted more than 1,400 words, particularly the long sequence in which the men catalog women of regional America (106.II.21–107.I.51). For the complete transcription of Wolfe's story, see *Four Lost Men: The Previously Unpublished Long Version, Including the Original Short Story*, edited by Matthew J. and Arlyn Bruccoli (2008). Contrary to the popular legend that depicts Wolfe cutting 4,000 words out of *Look Homeward, Angel* (1929), only to put in 40,000 new ones (repeated by John Chamberlain in the *New York Times* on March 8, 1935), Wolfe inserted only 900 new words into *From Death to Morning*. In a November 3, 1935, interview with the *New York Herald Tribune*—granted as part of the publicity for the story collection—Wolfe confessed, "My tendency is to put in rather than to take out.... But the editors told me we ought to give the readers a break and give them a book like this" (Magi and Walser 57). The newspaper paraphrases Wolfe's new perspective as "the goat-cry wells less frequently in his throat" (54).

With *From Death to Morning*, Wolfe literally silenced his "goat-cry." He deleted all "goat-cry" descriptors in the *Scribner's Magazine* stories collected in *From Death to Morning*. The author employs the "goat-cry" phrase three times in the *Scribner's Magazine* text of "The Four Lost Men," a story in which W. O. Gant evokes the presidents of his youth: "Garfield, Arthur, Harrison, and Hayes." Yet for the story's book publication, Wolfe eliminated all three references. Wolfe changed the presidents' "savage goat-cry of their pain and joy" (101.I.9) to a "savage cry" (114.9). In *Scribner's Magazine*, the men "cry out the fierce goat-cry of ecstasy and exultancy..." (105.II.21); in *From Death to Morning*, they "cry out in ecstasy and exultancy..." (126.31) without the barnyard descriptor. In the original magazine text, the presidents feel "the goat-cry swelling in their throats" (106.I.36); in the book, Wolfe deleted the entire phrase. This specific excision may have been at Perkins's suggestion. When the compositors in 1933 first set the story to appear in *Scribner's Magazine*, Wolfe reported to the magazine's editor, "Max asked me to cut out references to whores and brothels in reference to Our Presidents" (Bruccoli and Bucker 123). A "goat-cry," with its sexual connotations, could have similarly disturbed Perkins.

Wolfe's desire to muzzle his "goat-cry" stemmed not so much from his editors but rather from published criticism of his recent novel as too long and plotless, and his style as wild and undisciplined. Although Wolfe labored over *Of Time and the River* for many months, he believed that Perkins sent the book to the printers prematurely. On March 31, 1935, he angrily wrote to Perkins, "I was not ready to read proof, I was not through writing" (Bruccoli and Bucker 143). The novel received generally favorable notices and enjoyed excellent sales, yet Wolfe characteristically fixated on the few negative comments that attacked his effusive style and autobiographical material. Both Wolfe and Perkins believed that the short story volume, with its "objective stories," could effectively refute these criticisms by showcasing the author's versatility. Writing to Wolfe in England, the editor assuaged Wolfe's anger at reviewers with plans for *From Death to Morning*. On April 20, 1935, Perkins explained:

> As for the book of stories, I am very anxious to get this done rapidly, and we must tackle it as soon as you get back. These stories refute some of the criticism of you as being a too subjective writer. The woman's story ["In the Park"] and "Web of Earth" are entirely objective. And that is true of several of the other stories. You have completely imagined whole natures of people totally unlike yourself. I think these stories will show them a few things more you can do and will give them another surprise. This is the way to answer critics. (Bruccoli and Bucker 156)

Yet Wolfe remained in Europe until midsummer. Perkins met Wolfe's boat when the author returned from Europe on July 4, 1935, with hopes that Wolfe would finally read the prepared galleys. The two men celebrated their reunion, but Wolfe traveled west for a writers conference in Colorado, leaving the galley proofs unread. He refused to allow his short story collection to be released without his final revision. He obviously feared that the unrevised stories committed many of the "literary sins" exhibited by his novel. On August 12, Wolfe wrote Perkins from Colorado:

> ... I will not consent this time to allow the book to be taken away from me and printed and published until I myself have had time to look at the proofs, and at any rate to talk to you about certain revisions, changes, excisions, or additions that ought to be made.... I propose rather to prepare my work in every way possible to meet and refute, if I can, some of the very grave and serious criticisms that were made about the last book, and as my friend and the person whose judgment I trust most, you must help me to do this. (Bruccoli and Bucker 172)

Wolfe's desire to revise the stories may have been as much practical as aesthetic. He was greatly angered by the many typographical errors in both

Look Homeward, Angel and *Of Time and the River* that he properly thought should have been caught by Scribner's editors. Significantly, *From Death to Morning* has only one such error: "knapack" for "knapsack" in "The Face of the War" (86). Perkins apparently did not appreciate Wolfe's urgent desire to attempt a revision of the stories. He had already read and corrected the stories in galleys and believed that their current state was sufficient to demonstrate Wolfe's talent and versatility. But the editor acceded to his author's wishes, replying on August 20, 1935, "How you can think badly of [the stories] I cannot imagine, but they are waiting for you anyhow" (Bruccoli and Bucker 173).

The artistic charges to which Wolfe refers, and to which both author and editor wished to respond, came primarily from New York City reviewers. In his popular *New York Herald Tribune* column, "The Conning Tower," F.P.A. (Franklin Pierce Adams [1881–1960]) charged Wolfe with "lyricitis" and advised him to "discipline himself to write less repetitiously and not get carried away, as he seemeth to be by the sound of his own voice." *New York Herald Tribune* critic Burton Rascoe (1872–1957), who infuriated Wolfe by accusing him of being humorless, mildly disparaged Wolfe's use of repetitious adjectives, charging the author with using the word "lovely" 20,000 times (1). Literary columnist Isabel M. Paterson (1885–1961) expressed the same sentiment more strongly: "[I]t might be an interesting experiment to take one of his chapters and eliminate all the superlatives, the adjectives, indicating altitude, volume, and violence.... Step it down again to life size, and see what would remain." Clifton Fadiman (1904–99), reviewer for the *New Yorker* and longtime Wolfe critic, announced: "It is open to debate whether [Wolfe] is a master of language or language is a master of him." Fadiman described *Of Time and the River* as a "frenzied anti-intellectual" book and reminded Wolfe that "it is the blue pencil that creates the purple patch" (79). In a March 1935 letter to Perkins, Wolfe raged: "The Fadimans say take away his apostrophes, declamations, lyrics, dreams, incantations—and where would he be?... Apparently, I would be a good writer if I would only correct 3,264 fundamental faults, which are absolutely, profoundly, and utterly incurable and uncorrectable" (Bruccoli and Bucker 146). Probably the cruelest critique came from Evelyn Scott (1893–1963) in *Scribner's Magazine*; she described Wolfe—a celebrated Scribner's author—as "reflective without the mental discipline to illuminate his own blindness" and as a writer who dilutes his fiction with "literary banalities" (2). Professional reviewers were not the only readers to complain of Wolfe's verbosity. In April 1935, F. Scott Fitzgerald wrote Perkins criticizing Wolfe's short story "His Father's Earth" (*Modern Monthly*, April 1935—a story not selected by Wolfe or Perkins for *From Death to Morning*). Fitzgerald commented on Wolfe's redundant use of superlatives: "He who has such infinite power of suggestion and delicacy has absolutely no right to glut people on whole meals of caviar" (280).

As early as September 1934, Wolfe and his Scribner's editors planned to issue a book of his short stories to follow *Of Time and the River*, published in March 1935. While revising the novel, Wheelock urged Wolfe "to cut out of that part of the book the Harrison and Hayes passage in the boy's memory of his father on the porch. It isn't needed in the book and if it were used there it would spoil it for a story which should go into the book of stories" (Bruccoli and Bucker 126). This passage became "The Four Lost Men," story 6 in *From Death to Morning*. Despite its early inception, the volume did not have a title or precise table of contents until late summer 1935. On September 1, Wolfe wrote Perkins that he wished to dedicate the story collection to his dead brother Ben "because of the nature of the book of stories, and the subject matter involved" (Bruccoli and Bucker 176). *From Death to Morning* is dedicated by the author to "THE MEMORY OF HIS BROTHER / BENJAMIN HARRISON WOLFE / AND TO THE PROUD AND BITTER BRIEFNESS OF / HIS DAYS" (ix). Wolfe's original dedication—which was cut at the suggestion of Perkins and Wheelock—continued in his September 1 letter, "the writer dedicates this book, believing that of all his work which has been published, the present volume may offer both to death and life, the matter worthiest of such commemoration" (Bruccoli and Bucker 178).

In the same letter, Wolfe urged Perkins on

> ... the desirability of getting a good order in the arrangement of the stories—... the arrangement really should, so far as we make it do so, illustrate the title, From Death to Morning—that is, they should progress in a general way beginning, say, with Death The Proud Brother, and ending perhaps, with such a piece as The Web of Earth. (Bruccoli and Bucker 176)

The story sequence fulfills Wolfe's intention for the book to exhibit both dual and progressive themes: moving from death to life, from darkness to light, from despair to hope. The stories evolve from the anonymous deaths described in "Death the Proud Brother," through the disappointed wanderings of "Only the Dead Know Brooklyn," "Dark in the Forest, Strange as Time," and "The Bums at Sunset," to the invigorating nostalgia of "In the Park," "The Men of Old Catawba," and "Circus at Dawn." The volume ends with "The Web of Earth," a 33,000-word novella—essentially the last third of the book—in which Eliza Gant evokes the eternal permanence of familial bonds.

A concordance of *From Death to Morning*—when used in conjunction with a collation of the book/magazine stories—documents Wolfe's intentional injection of recurring images and motifs. As with much of Wolfe's fiction, the stories juxtapose silence and frozen moments of time with scenes of great speed and exhilarating movement. *From Death to Morning* teems with modes of transportation: trains, speeding cars and trucks, horses, and Spanish galleons. Even in the confining "No Door," Wolfe describes the narrator's dismal Brooklyn apartment as shaped like a "pullman car" (4). The "No Door" of *From Death to Morning* originally appeared as the first segment of a four-part novella (also titled "No Door") published in *Scribner's Magazine* (July 1933), most of which was incorporated into *Of Time and the River*. Who selected this part of "No Door" for the opening story of *From Death to Morning* remains unclear, but it works well as an introduction to the volume's themes and images.

"No Door" begins and ends with an ardent and mournful wish inspired by ships in New York Harbor. The narrator notices the ships from a penthouse apartment—not his: "[T]here are ships there—there are ships—and a wild intolerable longing in you that you cannot utter" (2). Back in his small Brooklyn apartment, the narrator remembers: "[W]e know that we are lost, and cannot stir . . . and there are ships there! there are ships!" (14). "Death the Proud Brother" similarly evokes ships in its concluding paragraphs: "They come! Ships call!" (69). Wolfe resisted Wheelock's suggestion that he delete this reference as repetitive of *Of Time and the River*. "The Web of Earth" concludes with Eliza's urging her son to return to his homeland as ships sound in New York Harbor. Her closing words—"*Ships again!*" (304)—offer not only a means of escape from the alienating atmosphere of New York City, but also a passage home—Wolfe's most primal and recurring theme. The final story, with this concluding image, serves both as the book's literal destination—"the morning" of the title—and as its thematic anchor in its affirmation of home and family.

Before beginning revision, Wolfe postulated creating stories that would "lead right into The Web Of Earth and by doing a few things like this I know the whole book could be woven together and given a tremendous feeling of unity and cumulative effect that you almost never find in a book of stories" (Bruccoli and Bucker 177). Wolfe achieved this effect, not by creating new stories that would have delayed the book against Perkins's wishes, but by selecting the sequencing and revising previously written stories. Wolfe's substantive revision of the stories preceding "The Web of Earth"—a story in which he significantly did not make major changes—documents not only his craftsmanship and professional versatility but also his desire to recast formerly disparate episodes into a thematic progression.

In "No Door," Wolfe describes one of the narrator's few moments of beauty and happiness in Brooklyn as "an iridescent web of light and color" (6) blazing on the side of a ship. This image introduces the "web" imagery that Wolfe employs throughout the book. One of the words he deleted from the magazine version of "No Door" is "unweave" (11.I.48). In "Death the Proud Brother," he describes light shining through an elevated train's "rusty iron webbing" (19) and the light reflected off the tall buildings as "a swarming web of iridescent and crystalline magic" (29). In the same story, he describes the girders of a building under construction as "spare webbing" (34). In "The Four Lost Men," he again connects web imagery to New York in describing the masts of nineteenth-century ships as a "soaring web" (129). Wolfe also employs web images in his descriptions of crowds, for example, "the great crowd which swarmed and wove unceasingly on the street" (29) and "the everlasting web and weaving of the crowd" (131). For Wolfe, a "web" serves as an evocative metaphor for the hidden connections among characters and their past. The image of a web suggests not only a linkage but also a pattern. In "Dark in the Forest, Strange as Time," Wolfe muses on the dark side of the Germanic national soul as "the infinite strange weavings . . . . so sorrowfully and unalterably woven and inwrought with all the blind brute hunger of the belly and the beast of man" (107–8). Wolfe ultimately and appropriately places this image in the voice of Eliza, the Earth Mother of the Gant cycle. As the narrator of "The Web of Earth," Eliza describes the reach and interconnections of her father's progeny:

> All these children that he had went out and had big families of their own, those that didn't die early or get killed, until now there are hundreds of them living down there in Catawba in the mountains, and in Georgia and Texas and out west in California and Oregon until now they are spread all over like a web. (221–22)

A "web" may also be seen as an image for Wolfe's fiction itself, linking his seemingly disparate narratives into a patterned whole. The most obvious unifying revision that Wolfe makes is in connecting the volume's three major stories—"Death the Proud Brother," "The Four Lost Men," and "The Web of Earth"—with his fictional universe in *Look Homeward, Angel* and *Of Time and the River*, specifically the Gant family. Although Perkins viewed these stories as objective and marketed the books as a "different side" of Thomas Wolfe, they form chapters in the author's lifelong epic. Wolfe may write from a variety of perspectives, but all his fiction can be seen as episodes in the same narrative. Beginning with the book's dedication, the memory of Ben pervades *From Death to Morning*. Wolfe obviously links the "proud and bitter briefness" of Benjamin Harrison Wolfe/Gant to "Death the Proud Brother." Wolfe further emphasizes this connection in his new 884-word introduction to the story (first published in *Scribner's Magazine* in June 1933). The original story begins with a nameless narrator recalling the times that he has "looked upon the visage of death in the city" (17). Wolfe's added prologue serves not only as an apostrophe to Night and Death but also as a specific reference to Eugene Gant's experiences, marking the narrator as the hero from Wolfe's previous novels. The narrator remembers: "As a child, when I had been a route boy on a morning paper, I had seen them on the streets of a little town—that strange and lonely company of men who prowl the night" (15). The introduction concludes with references to the deaths of both Ben and W. O. Gant: "I had watched my brother and my father die in the dark mid-watches of the night, and I had known and loved the figure of proud Death when he had come" (17). This new introduction documents Wolfe's stated intention to inject images of "death and night and morning" to unify the stories.

Despite the critics' complaints of excessive language, Wolfe resisted cutting the story's ending apostrophe to Sleep. He did cut one paragraph in which he imagines the deathlike darkness of "polyped spores," but kept the rest, explaining to Wheelock in a letter written during his revisions of the galleys:

> ... the passage that follows to the end of the story is really one of my most ambitious apostrophes—to Loneliness, and Death and Sleep—It is the kind of thing that some of the critics have gone gunning after me for—but it is also the kind of thing that many people have liked in my writing, and that some say they hope I never lose—This passage in particular—about Sleep and Death, etc—has made [friends]—Now, what do you think—It's a pretty serious matter to me, because if it really is better that I cut out this <u>kind</u> of writing entirely, it is a fundamental thing and I must seriously change my whole method and style everywhere.... (Bruccoli and Bucker 181)

Apparently Wheelock agreed with Wolfe; the passage was retained.

As Wolfe's letters indicate, he viewed "The Web of Earth" as the companion piece to "Death the Proud Brother." The only significant revision that Wolfe made to the concluding novella is the change of the narrator's name from Delia Hawke to Eliza Gant; the other family names are similarly changed to conform to the Gant mythology. Like the revision to "Death the Proud Brother," this change inextricably links "The Web of Earth" to *Look Homeward, Angel* and *Of Time and the River*. According to Wolfe's correspondence, he received galley proofs for "The Web of Earth," but unlike with the other stories, he never returned them to Wheelock. On October 18, 1935, Wheelock reported to Wolfe:

> All the proofs of "From Death to Morning" are in the printer's hands, and publication is scheduled for November 15. This means that there can be no delay anywhere along the line. In the case of the final story, "Web of Earth", I have sent the printer duplicate galleys from our files, and if there are any corrections you wish to make, they can be made in page proof, which I hope to have tomorrow. (Bruccoli and Bucker 184)

Wolfe may have had other reasons for not revising the novella besides obvious time constraints. It is the oldest story in the volume (originally published in July 1932) and had been highly praised by the Scribner's editors. He may not have wished to return to a story that old. It is the narrative that Wolfe prized as the best example of his work in the volume, demonstrating his ability to create a non-Eugene central character and voice. Also, most of Wolfe's substantive revisions elsewhere in the story collection occur in the descriptions or apostrophes of an omniscient narrator. The success of "The Web of Earth" depends entirely on the consistent voice of Eliza. *From Death to Morning* begins on the dedication page with Wolfe's lyric: "*Up on the mountain, down / in the valley, long, long / in the hill, Ben, cold, / cold, cold*" (ix). The volume ends with Eliza's narrative—interrupted by many digressions—of the birth of Ben and his twin brother, Grover. Working backward in chronological time, the stories progress from isolated death scenes to a vivid memory of birth. Whereas Wolfe purposefully connects "Death the Proud Brother" and "The Web of Earth" with the Gant family of Altamont, he makes the opposite revision in "The Face of the War." The young boy who visits the makeshift bordello is from Pulpit Hill in "Catawba" ("The Face of the War" 228). Wolfe revises this to read Hopewell in Georgia (*From Death to Morning* 83), perhaps so as not to cast Eugene Gant as the prostitute's customer.

Although overtly defensive about critical attacks, Wolfe revised the stories in *From Death to Morning* in an obvious attempt to reduce his rhetoric. Wolfe did not completely rewrite the galleys, as Fitzgerald famously did with *The Great Gatsby* (1925), nor did he often rewrite sentences. Instead, he inserted or eliminated entire passages, or he changed or deleted a single word—almost always an adjective. He also altered a word if he had used it recently in a sentence. Throughout the book, the author deleted many descriptive words such as "immense" and "exultant" that critics had labeled as examples of Wolfian overstatement. In the magazine versions of his stories, Wolfe employs the description "immense and lonely skies" three times—in "The Face of the War" (225.II.6), in "Dark in the Forest, Strange as Time" (276.I.25), and in "The Bums at Sunset" (30.II.7–9). He obviously recognized this repetition and altered two of the occurrences. In "The Face of the War," Wolfe revised "the desolation of immense and lonely skies" to "the desolation of the skies" (76.8), placing the emphasis on "desolation" rather than on "immense" and "lonely." Wolfe retained the description in "Dark in the Forest, Strange as Time," but deleted it from "The Bums at Sunset." In the magazine stories, "immense" occurs thirty-six times; in *From Death to Morning*, thirty. Wolfe also severely cut back on his use of "exultant"—a favorite word. A form of "exultant" appears twenty-seven times in the magazine stories; in *From Death to Morning*, Wolfe reduced that number by nine to a final total of eighteen, cutting five of the six occurrences from one story: the 2,000-word sketch "Circus at Dawn" (*Modern Monthly*, Mar. 1935). In the two instances when Wolfe did not just delete "exultant" from the story, he changed it to "thrilling":

19.I.8 cool exultant darkness [205.6 cool and thrilling darkness
19.II.5 of exultant joy [205.16 of joy
20.I.13 furiously and exultantly in the [206.20 furiously in the
21.I.20 strong exultant excitement, [209.1 strong excitement,
21.I.43 and exultant life [209.18 and thrilling life

Wolfe retained one occurrence of "exultant" in "Circus at Dawn," thereby strengthening the image with its singularity. After describing the sounds of a train depot, Wolfe writes: "And to all these familiar sounds, filled with their exultant prophecies of flight, the voyage, morning, and the shining cities . . . " (206.6–8). With this single use, Wolfe reserves "exultant" for the possibility and joy of wandering.

Many of the revisions in *From Death to Morning* are in the recasting of dialect speech, which can be presumed to be authorial, as the writer attempts to replicate the specific sounds of a foreign or pronounced accent. The revised stories show a great refinement of these dialect spellings, specifically in the speech of the German characters in "Dark in the Forest, Strange as Time" and "One of the Girls in Our Party," as well as in the vagabond's speech in "Bums at Sunset." Twenty of the twenty-one revisions made in "Only the Dead Know Brooklyn" were subtle improvements in Brooklyn dialect: "you" becomes "yuh," "forget" becomes "forgit," and "things" becomes "t'ings." In 1933, John O'Hara—a master of dialogue—complained to *Scribner's Magazine* editor Kyle Crichton of the characters' speech in Wolfe's novella "Death the Proud Brother" (June 1933): "The dialog was so incredibly bad that it should have embarrassed everyone, beginning with Woofie himself. Look Around, Angel" (75).

The revised "Only the Dead Know Brooklyn" also demonstrates Wolfe's use of stronger vulgarities than he was allowed in most magazines; the story originally appeared in the *New Yorker* on June 15, 1935. For book publication, Wolfe changed "duh goddam town" (13.I.4) and "whole goddam place" (13.III.1) to "duh f- - - - town" (91.3) and "whole f- - - - place" (93.23). After revising "The Face of the War," Wolfe wrote Wheelock, "Will you please observe Galley 26—and the words screw and puss which I have written in, and tell me if we can use them" (Bruccoli and Bucker 183). Scribner's allowed Wolfe to use "puss" but not "screw." The *Modern Monthly* (June 1935) version of the story reads "I'll come back here and smack yuh rightin duh - - - - - yuh" (227.29). Scribner's allowed Wolfe to replace the blank with "puss" (80.4). The magazine version of the story employs "f- - - - -" as an expletive. Wolfe apparently wanted to replace this construction with "screw" but *From Death to Morning* retains "f- - - -." Wolfe even allows Eliza Gant some salty language in "The Web of Earth" that was denied her in *Scribner's Magazine*: He replaced the blank in "Tell 'em your - - is your own" (51.II.30) with "ass" (254.26).

Wolfe's attention to revision and detail even extended to the briefest of the stories. He made substantive changes in character and mood in both "The Bums at Sunset" and "The Far and the Near." An examination of the revisions Wolfe made in these short short stories reveals that even a minor change can significantly affect a story's meaning. In the original version of "The Bums at Sunset" (*Vanity Fair*, Oct. 1935), Wolfe uses the adjective "brutal" five times; in the book, he uses it twice. Part of this revision may have been to eliminate repetition, but it also diminishes the vagabonds' rough nature: a "seamed brutal face" (30.I.61) becomes merely a "seamed face" (151.15); "a powerful and brutal gesture" (30.II.23) becomes "a powerful gesture" (151.32); and "brutal friendliness" (30.III.9) becomes "coarse friendliness" (152.14). In the book, the small bum no longer snarls "viciously" (62.I.19). Yet Wolfe subtly increases the animalistic menace of Bull, the head bum, at the end of the story by changing Bull's "cupped hand" (62.II.19) to a "cupped paw" (154.13). In making the vagabonds less threatening at the beginning, Wolfe makes the boy's ultimate pairing with Bull more frightening and sinister.

Although Wolfe did not significantly rewrite an entire sequence, he did recraft—or add on—passages that began or ended a story. The changes that Wolfe made in the second paragraph of "Dark in the Forest, Strange as Time" reveal the author's ability to "deflate" his rhetoric without damaging the description's delicacy or tone:

Scribner's Magazine	*From Death to Morning*
The woman, who was about thirty-five years old, was at the flawless summit of a mature and radiant beauty. She was a glorious creature, packed to the last red ripeness of her lip with life and health, a miracle of loveliness in whom all the elements of beauty had combined with such exquisite proportion and so rhythmical a balance that even as one looked at her he could scarcely believe the evidence of his eyes, so magically did her beauty melt into a thousand forms of loveliness, so magically did it change and yet remain itself.	The woman was at the flawless summit of a mature and radiant beauty, packed to the last red ripeness of her lip with life and health, a miracle of loveliness in whom all the elements of beauty had combined with such exquisite proportion and so rhythmical a balance that even as one looked at her he could scarcely believe the evidence of his eyes.
Thus, although . . . (273.I.11–20)	Thus, although . . . (98.8–14)

The author no longer must describe to the reader how the woman is a "glorious creature" or that her beauty "magically" melts and "magically" changes "into a thousand forms of loveliness" because he renders her fully in the middle of the passage—the section that Wolfe retains. Wolfe also alters the end of the story by reordering the final paragraphs. He moves a meditative passage on the transitory nature of human contact closer to the end of the story, placing it precisely when the boy leaves the dead man behind in the train compartment, rather than as a contemplative digression while the boy rides in the train during the night. As the youth moves away from the dead man, the narrator wonders:

> Was it not well to leave all things as he had found them, in silence, at the end? Might it not be that in this great dream of time in which we live and are the moving figures, there is no greater certitude than this: that, having met, spoken, known each other for a moment, as somewhere on this earth we were hurled onward through the darkness between two points of time, it is well to be content with this, to leave each other as we met, letting each one go alone to his appointed destination, sure of this only, needing only this—that there will be silence for us all and silence only, nothing but silence, at the end? (113.7–19)

The questions posed in the paragraph gain greater meaning as the boy literally, as well as emotionally, moves away from the "spectral figure of the cadaver" (113). Rather than interrupt the narrative, Wolfe moves this apostrophe to deathly silence appropriately to the end. The only other story for which Wolfe similarly rearranges paragraphs is "In the Park" (*Harper's Bazaar*, June 1935). Like "The Web of Earth," this "subjective" story has a female narrator, the unnamed Esther Jack, and is based on the memories of Wolfe's lover Aline Bernstein (1881–1955). Esther also appears in the magazine version of "Death the Proud Brother," but Wolfe deleted all references to her name, revising it instead to "a woman that I loved" (31). Wolfe moves an expository paragraph from sixth place to first. The paragraph's first line—"That year I think we were living with Bella" (169)—immediately places the story in the far past. Wolfe may have been returning the story to its original form. His literary agent, Elizabeth Nowell, had made substantive changes to the story in an effort to sell it to a high-paying commercial magazine such as *Harper's* (Kennedy xiii–xv).

The last story Wolfe revised for *From Death to Morning* was "The Cottage by the Tracks" (*Cosmopolitan*, July 1935). The magazine's editors provided the title. Wolfe's original title was "The Other Side of the House" (Kennedy 20). For the story volume, Wolfe changed the title to "The Far and the Near," reflecting the duality and juxtaposition demonstrated throughout the entire volume. In a letter to Wheelock, Wolfe described his revisions, "which have been done with a view to changing the attitude of the two women to a <u>timid</u> and <u>uneasy unfriendliness</u> rather than surly hostility" (Bruccoli and Bucker 183). Wolfe altered the woman's "surly tongue" (176.II.10) to an "unfriendly tongue" (167.23). Instead of admitting the retired engineer "surlily" (176.II.21) into her house, she allows him to enter "almost unwillingly" (167.32). Wolfe transforms her "bewildered unfriendliness, a sullen and restrained mistrust" (176.II.26), to a "bewildered hostility, a sullen, timorous restraint" (168.2). These alternative descriptors significantly transform the story's meaning. They establish a regretful and sad meeting, rather than one of abrasion and overly harsh confrontation. In the magazine version, Wolfe ridicules the women as stupid and unfeeling; in the book, they emerge as ignorant and pitiful. The original story ends with the engineer "sick with doubt and horror as it saw the strange and unsuspected visage of an earth which had always been within a stone's throw of him, and which he had never seen or known" (176.II.37–39). For *From Death to Morning*, Wolfe added this final line: "And he knew that all the magic of that bright lost way, the vista of that shining line, the imagined corner of that small good universe of hope's desire, was gone forever, could never be got back again" (168). The last image no longer evokes doubt and horror but rather the man's original bright vision. With this final addition, the engineer changes from experiencing sickness to having a reverie of a lost but cherished memory.

Most critics did not appreciate or recognize Wolfe's many revisions in *From Death to Morning*. Several of the reviews repeated past accusations of excess and formlessness. One notable exception was Peter Monro Jack's commentary in the *New York Times Book Review*. The article's subtitle—drawn from the review—surely gratified Wolfe: "In These New Stories It Is Noted How Remarkably Controlled Is His Superabundance and How Successful Is His Excess." In assessing Wolfe's career, Malcolm Cowley (1898–1989) observed that the author's "unit of construction was the episode, not the scene, the chapter, or novel" (175). Wolfe did write in episodes; their connective tissue emerges when viewed as facets of one lifelong narrative. The revisions that Wolfe made in *From Death to Morning* serve as an indication of the author's awareness of and talent for complicated narrative construction. In a letter written two weeks after Wolfe's death, Perkins observed: "I always thought that at bottom he did have a sense of form, and some of the things he wrote like 'Web of Earth' showed it. Not a word in that was ever changed" (Bruccoli and Bucker xviii).

A contemporary evaluation of Wolfe's *From Death to Morning* may be informed by his inscription in a presentation copy of the volume that "[a] well-known 'reaction' has set in against me, and that I will take a pounding on this book. . . . I believe that as good a writing as I have ever done is in this book, and because my faith has always been that a good thing is indestructible and that if there is good here—as I hope and believe there is—it will somehow survive" (*Letters* 494).

A Collation of Short Stories in Thomas Wolfe's *From Death to Morning* with their Original Magazine Appearances

* = accidental

"No Door"

Scribner's Magazine July 1933: 7–12, 46–56 [*FDTM* 1–14

   7.I.1 OCTOBER: 1931 [[deleted]
* 7.I.6 know, and [1.5 know—and
   7.I.7 period in my life, a few [1.6 period, a few
* 7.II.15 evidences [2.1 evidence
   8.I.12 the old red light [2.17 the red light
   8.I.13 painted without violence or heat upon the river [2.18 painted upon the river
   8.I.24 is living in [2.28 is burning in
   8.II.7 moment this old [3.17 moment the old
* 8.II.11 have known in [3.21 have known, in
* 9.I.17 offal; mixed [5.13 offal, mixed
   9.II.10 remembered [6.26 remember
   9.II.23 then.¶ Yes, [7.5 then.¶ [space break] Yes,
* 10.I.24 before he inherited [8.12 before, he inherited
   10.II.27 each other's [10.1 one another's
   10.II.37 my three dollehs [10.11 my t'ree dollehs
   11.I.1 If yah don't [10.30 if yuh don't
* 11.I.27 dismisses it, and [11.15 dismisses it and
   11.I.48–II.5 night. It lies beside us in the darkness while the river flows, it fills as with wild secret song and the unmeasured desolations of gray time, and it abides with us forever, and is still, until we cannot root it from our blood or pluck it from our soul or unweave it from our brain. Its taste is acrid, sharp, and bitter at the edges of our mouth, and it is with us, in us, and around us all the time, our jail, our captive, and our master, all in one; whose dark visage we cannot decipher from our own, whom we have fought, loved, hated, finally accepted, and with whom we must abide now to our death forever.¶ So what [12.2 night.¶ So what
   11.II.42 Dhat's [12.34 Dat's

11.II.46 otheth [13.4 oddeh
11.II.52 since [13.10 sinct
11.II.53 in soft tragic [13.11 in soft soft tragic
* 12.I.3 constraint inviting [13.15 constraint, inviting
12.I.40 the old red light [14.17 the red light
12.I.43 atoms on the [14.20 atoms in the

"Death the Proud Brother"

Scribner's Magazine June 1933: 333–38, 378–88 [*FDTM* 15–70

333.1 Three times already [15.1–17.26 The face of the night, the heart of the dark, the tongue of the flame—I had known all things that lived or stirred or worked below her destiny. I was the child of night, a son among her mighty family, and I knew all that moved within the hearts of men who loved the night. I had seen them in a thousand places and nothing that they ever did or said was strange to me. As a child, when I had been a route boy on a morning paper, I had seen them on the streets of a little town—that strange and lonely company of men who prowl the night. Sometimes they were alone, and sometimes they went together in a group of two or three, forever in mid-watches of the night in little towns prowling up and down the empty pavements of bleak streets, passing before the ghastly waxen models in the windows of the clothing stores, passing below hard bulbous clusters of white light, prowling before the façades of a hundred darkened stores, pausing at length in some little lunchroom to drawl and gossip quietly, to thrust snout, lip, and sallow jowl into the stained depths of a coffee mug, or dully to wear the slow gray ash of time away without a word. ¶ The memory of their faces, and their restless prowling of the night, familiar and unquestioned at the time, returned now with the strangeness of a dream. What did they want? What had they hoped to find as they prowled past a thousand doors in those little, bleak, and wintry towns? ¶ Their hope, their wild belief, the dark song that the night awoke in them, this thing that lived in darkness while men slept and knew a secret and exultant triumph, and that was everywhere across the land, were written in my heart. Not in the purity and sweetness of dawn with all the brave and poignant glory of its revelation, nor in the practical and homely lights of morning, nor in the silent stature of the corn at noon, the drowsy hum and stitch of three o'clock across the fields, nor in the strange magic gold and green of its wild lyric wooded earth, nor even in the land that breathed quietly the last heat and violence of day away into the fathomless depth and brooding stillness of the dusk—as brave and glorious as these times and lights had been—had I felt and found the mystery, the grandeur, and the immortal beauty of America.¶ I had found the dark land at the heart of night, of dark, proud, secret night: the immense and lonely land lived for me in the brain of night. I saw its plains, its rivers, and its mountains spread out before me in all their dark immortal beauty, in all the space and joy of their huge sweep, in all their loneliness, savagery, and terror, and in all their immense and delicate fecundity. And my heart was one with the hearts of all men who had heard the strange wild music that they made, filled with unknown harmonies and a thousand wild and secret tongues crying to men the exultant and terrible music of wild earth, triumph and discovery, singing a strange and bitter prophecy of love and death.¶ For there was something living on the land at night. There was a dark tide moving in the hearts of men. Wild, strange and jubilant, sweeping on across the immense and sleeping earth, it had spoken to me in a thousand watches of the night, and the language of all its dark and secret tongues was written in my heart. It had passed above me with the rhythmical sustentions of its mighty wing, it had shot away with bullet cries of a demonic ecstasy on the swift howlings of the winter wind, it had come softly, numbly, with a dark impending prescience of wild joy in the dull soft skies of coming snow, and it had brooded, dark and wild and secret, in the night, across the land, and over the tremendous and dynamic silence of the city, stilled in its million cells of sleep, trembling forever in the night with the murmurous, remote and mighty sound of time. ¶ And I was joined in knowledge and in life with an indubitable certitude to the great company of men who lived by night and had known and loved its mystery. I had known all joys and labors and designs that such men know. I had known all things living on the earth by night, and finally, I had known by night the immortal fellowship of those three with whom the best part of my life was passed—proud Death, and his stern brother, Loneliness, and their great sister, Sleep. I had lived and worked and wrought alone with Loneliness, my friend, and in the darkness, in the night, in all the sleeping silence of the earth, I had looked a thousand times into the visages of Sleep, and had heard the sound of her dark horses when they came. And I had watched my brother and my father die in the dark mid-watches of the night, and I had known and loved the figure of proud Death when he had come.¶ [space break] Three times already

333.I.7 morning, and when the whole world reeled about me its gigantic and demented dance—I [17.32 morning—I
333.I.12 cession [18.2 cessation
333.I.20 seen before I saw this one had come [18.10 seen had come
333.I.23 have.¶ [space break] The [18.12 have.¶ The
333.II.2 swarming with their violent [18.28 seething with the violent
333.II.4 forth, uncountably, innumerably, [18.30 forth, innumerably,
333.II.5 with a tidal [18.31 with the tidal
333.II.8 design that the lives [18.33 design characteristic of the lives
333.II.8 peoples have—like [18.34 peoples—like
333.II.10 itself beneath an infinite and cruel sky—are fractured [19.1 itself—are fractured
333.II.14 dreams of madness, terror, and drowning, even [19.4 dreams, even
333.II.15–19 street. For this reason, Thomas de Quincey remarked that if he were forced to live in China for the remainder of his days, he would go mad.¶ Upon [19.5 street.¶ Upon
333.II.25 harsh, broken, driven, beaten, groping, violent, [19.12 harsh, driven, beaten, violent,
333.II.28 cart or wagon which [19.14 cart which
* 333.II.31 greasy looking [19.17 greasy-looking
334.I.1 so large, powerful, and cumbersome [19.24 so powerful and cumbersome
334.I.17 truck in front of it, and [19.31 truck, and
334.I.27 instant and exploding fountain [20.6 instant fountain
334.I.31 crowd of swarming, shouting, excited, dark-faced people [20.10 crowd of shouting, dark-faced people
* 334.II.38 brains, and [22.1 brains and
* 334.II.39 flesh was almost [22.2 flesh were almost
334.II.55 the immense and [22.17 the vast and
335.I.21 light. A few feet away, upon [23.3 light a few feet away. Upon
335.I.43 of immense and lonely [23.24 of lonely
335.I.46 wild, savage, cruel and lonely earth was [23.26 wild and savage earth, was
335.I.52 terrible and gaping [23.32 terrible, gaping
* 335.I.52 wound, which [23.32 wound which
* 336.I.7 and which made [25.16 and that made
* 336.I.14 reality as [25.23 reality, as
* 336.I.39 meagre [26.12 meager
336.I.51–II.3 assured.¶ He had the look of something prized, held precious by æsthetic women; I had also seen his kind among the art-theatre crowd who sometimes went to Esther's house.¶ "Oh, swell!" [26.19 assured.¶ "Oh,

* 336.II.18 too! . . . . I [26.33 too! . . . I
  336.II.42 flaw of laughter [27.22 flow of laughter
  336.II.43 he said softly [27.23 he spoke softly
  336.II.46 his soft dark mouth [27.26 his dark mouth
  336.II.50 you mean?" She said reproachfully, "I think [27.30 you mean!" she said reproachfully. "I think
  337.I.1 said softly. [28.1 said.
  337.I.51 but yet seemed [29.18 but that yet seemed
  337.II.6–12 I thought I knew all the people, to have the warm and palpable substance of their lives in my hands, and to know and own the street as if I had created it. [29.23–26 I felt I knew all the people, that I had the warm and palpable substance of their lives in my hands, and knew and owned the street itself as if I had created it.
* 337.II.16 towards [29.28 toward
  337.II.17 curb, a uniformed [29.28 curb, and a uniformed
  337.II.22 few cold incisive [29.34 few incisive
* 337.II.40 fine spun [30.17 fine-spun
  337.II.46 she came by. [30.22 she passed by.
* 337.II.48 meagre, [30.24 meager,
  338.I.14 of being crushed down and smothering beneath [31.10 of feeling crushed and smothered beneath
  338.I.16 it, like a helpless, hopeless, penniless, and nameless atom, [31.13 it, a nameless atom,
  338.I.20 certitude, exultancy, and power as one [31.16 certitude as one
  338.I.23 trees, with their [31.19 trees, in their
  338.I.38–39 For Esther's sister was vice-president of this mighty shop, second-in-command, [31.33–34 For the sister of a woman that I loved was a director of this mighty shop, its second-in-command,
  338.I.40 from Esther's merry [32.2 from that woman's merry
  338.II.11 for Esther's sister, [32.26 for her sister,
  338.II.28 of Esther and [33.7 of the woman and
  378.I.8–12 Fair. Here was the Fair: here were fixed flow and changeless change, immutable movement, the eternity of the earth haunted by the phantasmal briefness of our days.¶ Therefore. [34.4 Fair.¶ Therefore
  378.II.17 accustomed art, [35.13 accustomed arc,
  378.III.13 of sick horror. [36.16 of horror.
* 378.III.14 fallen like a [36.16 fallen, like a
  378.III.51 began again, [37.8 began anew,
  379.I.14 What'll he say [37.21 What'll *he* say
  379.I.18 what is going to happen [37.23 what's gonna happen
  379.I.32 everything was [38.1 everything on earth was

* 379.III.34 moment and in a quietly confidential tone he [40.18 moment, and in a quietly confidential tone, he
  379.III.36 fourth [40.20 fourt'
  379.III.58 fourth one which I will now describe to you, was this: That where [41.1 fourth one, was this: That, where
  380.I.40 we rushed and [41.30 we thrust and
  380.I.51 and thrust on [42.4 and passed on
  380.II.23 gray, and yet no one would say so. By [42.25 gray. By
* 380.II.24 people out of [42.26 people, out of
  380.II.28 standing there, just [42.29 standing here, just
  380.II.40 comrade, had walked [43.3 comrade, walked
  380.II.44 searched his pockets [43.6 searched the man's pockets
  380.III.2 streets, but cannot [43.20 streets, and cannot
  380.III.23 and flung [43.34 and to be flung
* 380.III.36 mouth the ghost [44.9 mouth, the ghost
* 380.III.59 whine with [44.25 whine, with
* 381.I.4 I'd a-let [44.30 I'd 'a' let
  381.I.5 minute. Yuh know [44.30 minute. *You* know
  381.I.17 courtesy. "Yuh know [45.5 courtesy. "*You* know
* 381.I.30 meagre, [45.14 meager,
  381.II.13 tenement of bright blood and agony in which [46.9 tenement in which is written
  381.II.35 slender resource which he built [46.26 slender resources which he had built
  381.III.1 were legible, and [47.9 were revealed, and
  381.III.11 Meanwhile, the [47.16 And now the
  381.III.15 dead man seem [47.19 dead seem
* 381.III.47 know" with [48.7 know," with
* 382.I.54 hurry on knowing [49.21 hurry on, knowing
  382.II.10 boy had looked [49.32 boy looked
  382.II.19–21 sallow, and pitted skin, and black hair and eyes, who wore a cap, a leather jacket, [50.5–6 sallow, pitted skin, black hair and eyes, a cap, a leather jacket,
  382.II.37 one doesn't call [50.18 one don't call
* 382.II.39 by himself saying [50.19 by himself, saying
  382.II.42–43 understanding or belief.[space break] Meanwhile the boy [50.24–25 understanding or consent. [space break] The boy
  382.II.45 a dull fascinated eye [50.25 a fascinated eye
* 382.II.54 meagre [50.32 meager
* 382.III.38 continued, "I knew [51.31 continued. "I knew
  383.I.25 emotion of surprise, interest, or excitement any longer. As [52.33 emotion. As
  383.I.46 read upon the doctor's face the [53.14 read there the

383.II.38 with the maddening [54.13 with maddening
* 383.III.6 hair, all three [54.33 hair—all three
* 383.III.17 centre [55.7 center
* 383.III.32 contempt, "For [55.17 contempt. "For
* 384.I.40 kick-off [56.34 kick off
384.I.48 goes—but there was [57.5 goes—but *there* was
* 384.II.31 says, 'yuh'd [58.4 says, 'Yuh'd
384.II.56 on a carrion, [58.20 on carrion,
* 384.III.9 shining fragile-looking [58.29 shining, fragile-looking
384.III.19 stiff greasy spines, [59.1 stiff oily spines,
* 384.III.29 meagre [59.9 meager
384.III.41 Meanwhile, the Italian [59.17 The Italian
384.III.47 eye and livid face feeding [59.21 eye feeding
385.I.2 with his glittering [59.32 with glittering
385.I.4 with the girl in [59.33 with her in
385.I.16 a stolid, weary, and impassive calm. [60.7 a stolid and impassive calm.
385.I.28 Meanwhile, the people [60.16 The people
* 385.I.46 him, undergo [60.28 him undergo
385.I.53 around him. The [60.33 around him grow tremendously. The
* 385.II.28 smile, as [61.24 smile—as
385.III.18 were followed, and [62.24 were observed, and
385.III.42 man of the stretcher [63.8 man on the stretcher
385.III.43 raised his white [63.8 raised a white
* 385.III.49 body which [63.13 body, which
386.I.2 it. Then they started [63.23 it. They started
* 386.I.17 wide showing [63.33 wide, showing
386.I.43 breast below, and [64.17 breast beneath, and
386.I.53 away to almost nothing. [64.24 away almost to nothing.
* 386.II.10 side opening [65.2 side-opening
* 386.II.18 "O.K. John [65.8 "O.K., John
386.II.28 the gulf of night, a [65.15 the darkness, a
* 386.III.12 taxi man: [66.10 taxi-man:
386.III.15 Then the policeman, still laughing, saying "Jesus!" tossed [66.12 Then, still laughing, saying "Jesus!" he tossed
* 386.III.17 stretcher men [66.14 stretcher-men
386.III.18 body. Then one [66.14 body. One
* 386.III.24 "O.K. John [66.19 "O.K., John
386.III.37 Meanwhile, the jesting [66.28 The jesting
* 386.III.46 taxi drivers [66.34 taxi-drivers
386.III.53 river, a great ship baying at the harbor's mouth. And [67.6 river. And
* 386.III.61 dark, I knew [67.10 dark. I knew

387.I.3–III.28 and morning. [space break] The face of the night, the heart of the dark, the tongue of the flame—I had known all things that lived or stirred or worked below her destiny. I was the child of night, a son among her mighty family, and I knew all that moved within the hearts of men who loved the night. I had seen them in a thousand places and nothing that they ever did or said, was strange to me. As a child when I had been a route boy on a morning paper, I had seen them on the streets of a little town—that strange and lonely company of men who prowl the night. Sometimes they were alone, and sometimes they went together in a group of two or three, forever in mid-watches of the night in little towns prowling up and down the empty pavements of bleak streets, passing before the ghastly waxen models in the windows of the clothing stores, passing below hard bulbous clusters of white light, prowling before the facades of a hundred darkened stores, pausing at length in some little lunchroom to drawl and gossip quietly, to thrust snout, lip, and sallow jowl into the stained depths of a coffee mug, or dully to wear the slow gray ash of time away without a word.¶ The memory of their faces, and their restless prowling of the night, familiar and unquestioned at the time, returned now with the strangeness of a dream. What did they want? What had they hoped to find as they prowled past a thousand doors in those little, bleak, and wintry towns?¶ Their hope, their wild belief, the dark song that the night awoke in them, this thing that lived in darkness while men slept and knew a secret and exultant triumph, and that was everywhere across the land, were written in my heart. Not in the purity and sweetness of dawn with all the brave and poignant glory of its revelation, nor in the practical and homely lights of morning, nor in the silent stature of the corn at noon, the drowsy hum and stitch of three o'clock across the fields, nor in the strange magic gold and green of its wild lyric wooded earth, nor even in the land that breathed quietly the last heat and violence of day away into the fathomless depth and brooding stillness of the dusk—as brave and glorious as these times and lights had been—had I felt and found the mystery, the grandeur, and the immortal beauty of America.¶ I had found the dark land at the heart of night, of dark, proud, secret night: the immense and lonely land lived for me in the brain of night. I saw its plains, its rivers, and its mountains spread out before me in all their dark immortal beauty, in all the space and joy of their huge sweep, in all their loneliness, savagery, and terror, and in all their immense and delicate fecundity. And my heart was one with the hearts of all men who had heard the strange wild music that they made, filled with unknown harmonies and a thousand wild and secret tongues crying to men the exultant and terrible music of wild earth, triumph and discovery, singing a strange and bitter prophecy of love and death.¶ For there was something living on the land at night. There was a dark tide moving in the hearts of men. Wild, strange and jubilant, sweeping on across the immense and sleeping earth, it had spoken to me in a thousand watches of the night, and the language of all its dark and secret tongues was written in my heart. It had passed above me with the rhythmical sustentions of its mighty wing, it had shot away with bullet cries of a demonic ecstasy on the swift howlings of the winter wind, it had come softly, numbly, with a dark impending prescience of wild joy in the dull soft skies of coming snow, and it had brooded, dark and wild and secret, in the night, across the land, and over the tremendous and dynamic silence of the city, stilled in its million cells of sleep, trembling forever in the night with the murmurous, remote and mighty sound of time.¶ And always, when it came to me, it had filled my heart with a wild exultant power that burst the limits of a little room, and that knew no stop of time or place or lonely distances. Joined to that dark illimitable energy of night, like a page to the wind, and westward, my spirit rushed across the earth with the wild post of the exultant furies of the dark, until I seemed to inhabit and hold within my compass the whole pattern of the earth, the huge wink of the enormous seas that feathered its illimitable shores, and the vast structure of the delicate and engulfing night.¶ And I was joined in knowledge and in life with an indubitable certitude to the great company of men who lived by night and had known and loved its mystery. I had known all joys and labors and designs that such men know. I had known all things living on the earth by night, and finally, I had known by night the immortal fellowship of those three with whom the best part of my life was passed—proud Death, and his stern brother, Loneliness, and their great sister, Sleep. I had watched my brother and my father die in the dark mid-watches of the night, and I had known and loved the figure of proud Death when he had come. I had lived and worked and wrought alone with Loneliness, my friend, and in the darkness, in the night, in all the sleeping silence of the earth, I had looked a thousand times into the visages of Sleep, and had heard the sound of her dark horses when they came.¶ [space break] Therefore, immortal [67.15 and morning. ¶ [space break] Therefore, immortal

388.I.50 to me again the old [69.1 to me once more the old
* 388.II.5 heart beats [69.7 heartbeats
388.II.13–37 We call!¶ [space break] As from dark winds and waters of our sleep on which a few stars sparely look, we grope our feelers in

the sea's dark bed. Whether to polyped spore, blind sucks or crawls or seavalves of the brain, we call through slopes and glades of night's dark waters on great fish. Call to the strange dark fish, or to the dart and hoary flaking of electric fins, or to the sea-worms of the brain that lash great fish to bloody froth upon the seafloor's coral stipes. Or, in vast thickets of our sleep call to blue gulphs and deep immensities of night, call to the cat's bright blazing glare and ceaseless prowl; call to all things that swim or crawl or fly, all subtlest unseen stirs, all half-heard, half-articulated whisperings, O forested and far!—call to the hooves of sleep through all the waste and lone immensity of night: "Return! Return!" ¶ [space break] They come: [69.15 We call!¶ [space break] They come:

* 388.II.50 night time, [69.24 night-time,
* 388.III.2 we lay all [69.26 we lie all
* 388.III.26 hungers, great [70.9 hungers; great

388.III.32 flow with lapse and reluctation of their breath, with glut [70.13 flow with glut

388.III.47 all-engulfing sleep. [70.22 all-engulfing Sleep.

"The Face of the War"

Modern Monthly June 1935: 223–31, 247 [*FDTM* 71–90

223.I.1 year of the war [71.1 year the war
223.I.8 ready to crouch [71.8 ready to leap
223.I.10 he retreated warily under [71.9 he retreats under
223.I.17 who advanced upon [71.14 who advances upon
223.I.18 hand, and screaming [71.16 hand, screaming
* 223.I.27 meagre [71.23 meager
* 223.I.33 aid, [71.27 aide,
* 223.II.4 squawt [72.3 squat
223.II.14 his arms blindly, [72.9 his arms thrust blindly,
* 223.II.34 centre [72.27 center
* 224.I.14 hear now, but [73.5 hear now but
* 224.I.19 Again: the [73.9 Again, the
* 224.I.24 authority—As here:—Three [73.13 authority, as here. Three
224.I.25 boys, himself among them, all employed [73.13 boys, all employed
* 224.I.42 grey, [73.27 gray,
* 224.II.3 chubby, red-cheeked [73.33 chubby red-cheeked
* 224.II.4 fair-haired blue-eyed [74.1 fair-haired, blue-eyed
* 224.II.5 speech attempts [74.2 speech, attempts
224.II.9 filthy-tips [74.5 filthy finger-tips

- * 224.II.11 loathesome [74.6 loathsome
  224.II.14 outa ya [74.9 out a ya
  224.II.18 dull reptilian wink [74.11 dull wink
  224.II.28 Anuddeh [74.20 Annuddeh
- * 224.II.31 ya p- - - - get [74.21 ya p- - - -! Get
- * 224.II.38 shame, the the brutal [74.27 shame, the brutal
  224.II.43 harsh need [74.32 harsh pang
  225.I.8 unhoused, lonely men [75.7 unhoused men
- * 225.I.26 thin, meagre mummers—act [75.21 thin and meager mummers, act
- * 225.I.36 hoboes jungle [75.29 hoboes' jungle
- * 225.I.43 meagre [75.34 meager
  225.II.6 the immense and lonely skies [76.8 the skies
- * 225.II.9 grimy, grey and dingy brown [76.11 grimy gray and dingy brown,
- * 225.II.10 brake rods [76.11 brake-rods
- * 225.II.16 waste and [76.16 waste, and
- * 225.II.17 distances in [76.17 distances, in
- * 225.II.18 aften [76.18 often
- * 225.II.26 ties or [76.24 ties, or
  225.II.27 ragged brown [76.25 soiled brown
- * 225.II.27 grey [76.25 gray
  225.II.30 ragged bone now cold [76.27 rags and bone, now cold
- * 225.II.30 lifeless to [76.28 lifeless, to
- * 225.II.36 waiting, calculation [76.32 waiting calculation
- * 226.I.2 extravavagance [77.9 extravagance
- * 226.I.15 knid [77.19 kind
  226.I.20 rasping, strident voices [77.24 rasping voices
  226.I.24 interlocked [77.27 interlarded
  226.I.24 raving speech [77.27 strident speech
- * 226.I.26 monotony, such [77.28 monotony—such
  226.I.29 with [77.31 wit'
  226.II.1 the customary [78.12 a customary
- * 226.II.10 with, a [78.19 with a
- * 226.II.13 yourself? . . . [78.22 yourself . . .
- * 226.II.15 hoarsely with [78.23 hoarsely, with
  226.II.26 little board compartment [79.2 little compartments
- * 226.II.39 Said [79.8 said
- * 227.I.2 humour, [79.16 humor,
  227.I.3 whatchya [79.17 whatcha
  227.I.15 dah Marines [79.26 duh Marines
- * 227.I.25 tenderly drawing [80.1 tenderly, drawing
  227.I.29 in duh - - - - - yuh [80.4 in duh puss, yuh

227.I.34 impatient and shouted demands [80.8 impatiently shouted demands
227.I.37 Christ's sake [80.10 Chris' sake
* 227.II.25 moment a woman's [81.4 moment, a woman's
* 227.II.27 moment dear [81.5 moment, dear
227.II.35 you, kid? [81.12 yuh, kid?
228.I.35 distant tone, [82.13 distant way,
228.I.35 as if someone [82.14 as of some one
228.II.3 painly [82.25 plainly
228.II.4 Catawba! [82.27 'Georgia'!
* 228.II.11 well-known [82.33 well known
* 228.II.17 everyone [83.4 every one
228.II.17 Pulpit Hill [83.4 Hopewell
* 228.II.18 smoke-grey [83.5 smoke-gray
* 228.II.28 someone [83.12 some one
* 228.II.32 anyone [83.17 any one
228.II.37 Catawba, [83.22 'Georgia,'
* 228.II.46 again "I [83.28 again, "I
229.I.7 Catawba. [84.1 'Georgia.'
* 229.I.15 buy, to solicit [84.7 buy; to solicit
229.I.20 war, the million threaded web of chance and of dark time, the huge [84.12 war, the huge
229.I.24–26 land, beneath whose single law of perilous, fatal, million-visaged chance we all have lived, where all [84.14 land, where all
* 229.I.35 humour [84.21 humor
229.I.36 sweltering room [84.22 sweltering noon
229.I.39 sweltering heat [84.25 suffocating heat
* 229.II.6 sort,—canned [84.33 sort—canned
229.II.17 the whole compacted [85.10 the compacted
* 229.II.19 savour [85.11 savor
229.II.20 abundance has slowly [85.12 abundance had slowly
229.II.22 timbers of the pier. [85.14 timbers.
229.II.40 Meanwhile, the Negro [85.28 The Negro
* 230.I.7 shipside, [86.5 ship-side,
* 230.I.26 everyone's [86.20 every one's
* 230.I.30 knapsack [86.23 knapack
* 230.I.31 everyone [86.25 every one
* 230.I.37 complaint, into [86.29 complaint; into
* 230.II.12 exasperation: As [87.13 exasperation: as
230.II.15 strangling, stamps [87.15 strangling, and stamps
230.II.17–19 toothache, and finally hurls his cap down on the floor and stamps on it, cursing bitterly. [87.17 toothache.
* 230.II.35 throat—"Oh you [87.31 throat—"Oh, you

* 230.II.42 ink complected [88.2 ink-complected
  230.II.43 now shouted [88.3 now shouts
  231.I.14 *he chokes.* [88.17 he chokes.
* 231.II.3 Dey-ain't [89.12 Dey ain't
* 231.II.23 him weeping [89.27 him, weeping
  231.II.26 hands on to his ears [89.29 hands to his ears
* 231.II.29 son of a bitch [89.32 son-of-a-bitch
* 231.II.40 red faced [90.7 red-faced
  231.II.42 great roll of [90.8 great wall of
  231.II.44 Negroes cavorting [90.11 Negroes are cavorting
  247.II.16 but the far [90.25 but far
  247.II.18 on-coming ondulous stride [90.27 on-coming, undulant stride

"Only the Dead Know Brooklyn"

New Yorker June 15, 1935: 13–14 [*FDTM* 91–97

13.I.4 duh goddam town. [91.3 duh f---- town
13.I.23 Bensenhoist. [91.15 Bensonhoist.
13.I.31 Bensenhoist. [91.21 Bensonhoist.
* 13.II.12 someone's [92.21 some one's
13.II.27 Bensenhoist?" [92.31 Bensonhoist?"
13.II.39 name"—Bensenhoist, y'know—"so I [93.6 name—Bensonhoist, y'know—so I
13.II.53 if you neveh [93.15 if yuh neveh
13.III.1 whole goddam place wit all [93.23 whole f---- place with all
13.III.2 pahts. Mahked out, you know—Canarsie [93.23 pahts mahked out. You know—Canarsie
13.III.4 Bensenhoist, [93.25 Bensonhoist,
13.III.22 at things, y'know [94.2 t'ings, y'know
14.I.55 neveh forgit it. [96.5 neveh forget it.
14.I.56 stays with yuh [96.6 stays wit yuh
14.I.60 a regular fish [96.8 a regulah fish
14.I.62 duh odeh kids [96.10 duh oddeh kids
14.I.63 would yuh do [96.11 would you do
14.II.8 befoeh anyone could [96.18 befoeh any one could
14.II.11 dey have [96.19 dey've
14.III.8 Bensenhoist [97.5 Bensonhoist
14.III.17 to 'm, anyway [97.12 to 'im, anyway
* 14.III.18 if someone knocked [97.12 if some one knocked

"Dark in the Forest, Strange as Time

Scribner's Magazine Nov. 1934: 273-78 [*FDTM* 98-113

273.I.11-20 The woman, who was about thirty-five years old, was at the flawless summit of a mature and radiant beauty. She was a glorious creature, packed to the last red ripeness of her lip with life and health, a miracle of loveliness in whom all the elements of beauty had combined with such exquisite proportion and so rhythmical a balance that even as one looked at her he could scarcely believe the evidence of his eyes, so magically did her beauty melt into a thousand forms of loveliness, so magically did it change and yet remain itself. ¶ Thus, although [98.9-14 The woman was at the flawless summit of a mature and radiant beauty, packed to the last red ripeness of her lip with life and health, a miracle of loveliness in whom all the elements of beauty had combined with such exquisite proportion and so rhythmical a balance that even as one looked at her he could scarcely believe the evidence of his eyes.¶ Thus, although
273.I.26 was full, lavish [98.19 was ripe, lavish
273.I.29 fashionably, smartly, and expensively dressed; [98.23 fashionably dressed;
273.II.11 his expensive overcoat [99.12 his overcoat
* 274.I.55 fräuleins [101.21 Fräuleins
* 274.II.2 fräuleins [101.25 Fräuleins
* 274.II.8 somewhat one [101.31 somewhat, one
* 274.II.40 towards [102.30 toward
* 274.II.52 departure that [103.7 departure, that
275.I.16 the barrier of an alien [103.18 the guise of an alien
* 275.I.22 strangely [103.23 strangly
* 275.I.30 arms clasped him [103.29 arms clasped him
* 275.I.48 spectre's [104.13 specter's
275.I.53 walked slowly [104.21 walked on slowly
* 275.II.14 embrace devouring [104.26 embrace, devouring
275.II.36-38 "That was my wife. Now in the winter I must go alone, for that is best. But in the spring when I am better she will come to me." [105.9-10 "Zat vas my vife. Now in ze vinter I must go alone, for zat iss best. But in ze spring ven I am better she vill come to me."
276.I.24 the lonely, naked men, [106.16 the naked men,
276.I.26 us, and ten [106.17 us, ten
* 276.I.29 captured memory? [106.20 captured, memory?
276.I.31 elfin, [106.22 elfish,
276.I.44 old swarm-haunted brain [107.1 old brain
276.I.50 of brutal and barbaric [107.6 of barbaric

276.I.54 as all the haunting, strange, and powerful [107.10 as the strange and powerful
276.II.4 with a brutal, smouldering, and unsated lust. [107.14 smouldering and unsated lust.
276.II.5 hated that great [107.15 hated the great
276.II.9 drink, a whole [107.18 drink, whole
276.II.13 the great belly [107.23 the huge belly
276.II.15 his blood, his life, his spirit. [107.24 his blood, his spirit, and his life.
276.II.18 was soaring, glorious, haunting, strange and beautiful: [107.27 was magical, glorious, strange and beautiful:
276.II.21 the old swarm-haunted and Germanic [107.29 the old Germanic
276.II.22 cruel, teaming, strange [107.30 cruel, baffling, strange
276.II.29 beast.¶ [108.2 beast of man.¶
276.II.35 that haunting and lonely [108.8 that lonely
* 276.II.43 spectre, [108.16 specter,
* 277.I.9 spectre [108.31 specter
* 277.I.16 dry: The spectre [108.34 dry: the specter
277.I.25 Zat is right— [109.6 Zat iss right—
277.I.26 "Zat will all [109.7 "Zat vill all
277.I.29 again. "And dat iss [109.10 again. "Und zat iss
277.I.31 everyvere [109.12 eferyvere
277.I.32 eferyt'ing—and I [109.12 eferyt'ing—und I
277.I.33 iss de same," [109.13 iss ze same,"
277.I.35 rifers, [109.16 riffers,
* 277.I.36 peoples—You vish [109.16 peoples—you vish
277.I.36 One field, one hill, one rifer," [109.17 Vun field, vun hill, vun riffer,"
277.I.39 inaudible—"One life, one place, one time." [109.20 inaudible—"Vun life, vun place, vun time."
* 277.I.45 spectre [109.27 specter
* 277.I.53 spectre [109.34 specter
* 277.II.4 magic light, as [110.3 magic light as
277.II.23 the haunting and phantasmal radiance [110.14 the phantasmal radiance
* 277.II.51 express which [111.7 express, which
* 278.I.2 towards [111.12 toward
* 278.I.13 culture, and [111.24 culture and
* 278.I.15 And instead [111.26 And, instead
278.I.17–21 train and sees the lonely, savage, and illimitable earth that strokes past calmly and imperturbably like the visage of time and eternity, one feels [111.27 train, one feels

* 278.I.29 spectre [112.3 specter
  278.I.32 an atom and [112.7 an inch, and
* 278.I.33 some subtle fatal [112.8 some subtle, fatal
  278.II.5–18 end.¶ Was it not well to leave all things as he had found them in silence at the end? Might it not be that in this great dream of time in which we live and are the moving figures, there is no greater certitude than this: that having met, spoken, known each other for a moment, as somewhere on this earth we were hurled onward through the darkness between two points of time, it is well to be content with this, to leave each other as we met, letting each one go alone to his appointed destination, sure of this only, needing only this—that there will be silence for us all and silence only, nothing but silence at the end?¶ And [112.24 end.¶ And
  278.II.25 the windows. [112.34 the window.
  278.II.33 him. In [113.4 him. Then, for a moment, still unsure, he stood there looking back. In
  278.II.35 move. Already [113.7–19 move.¶ Was it not well to leave all things as he had found them, in silence, at the end? Might it not be that in this great dream of time in which we live and are the moving figures, there is no greater certitude than this: that, having met, spoken, known each other for a moment, as somewhere on this earth we were hurled onward through the darkness between two points of time, it is well to be content with this, to leave each other as we met, letting each one go alone to his appointed destination, sure of this only, needing only this—that there will be silence for us all and silence only, nothing but silence, at the end?¶ Already
  278.II.36 stop. Then the boy [113.19 stop. The boy
* 278.II.41 towards [113.24 toward
* 278.II.42 towards [113.25 toward
  278.II.44 that one day he [113.27 that he

"The Four Lost Men"

Scribner's Magazine Feb. 1934: 101–8 [*FDTM* 114–33

* 101.I.8 great-starred night the [114.8 great-starred night, the
  101.I.9 savage goat-cry of their pain [114.9 savage cry of all their pain
  101.I.33–101.II.12 of noon, in the warm dusty stir and flutter and the feathery clucking of the sun-warm hens at noon. One felt it in the ring of the ice-tongs in the street, the cool whine of the ice-saws droning through the smoking block. One felt it poignantly somehow, in the solid lonely liquid leather shuffle of men in shirt-sleeves coming home to lunch in one direction in the brooding hush and

time-enchanted spell of noon, and in screens that slammed and sudden silence. And one felt it in the humid warmth and hungry fragrance of the cooking turnip greens, in leaf, and blade and flower, in smell of tar, and the sudden haunting green-gold summer absence of a streetcar after it had gone.¶ In all these ancient, most familiar things and acts and colors of our lives, one felt, with numbing ecstasy, the impending presence of the war. The war had got in [115.3–116.1 of noon, in the ring of the ice-tongs in the street, the cool whine of the ice-saws droning through the smoking block, in leaf, and blade and flower, in smell of tar, and the sudden haunting green-gold summer absence of a street-car after it had gone. ¶ The war had got in

* 101.II.26 cow bells [115.21 cow-bells
* 101.II.27 wild wailing [115.22 wild, wailing
  101.II.30–32 full June. The war was in the ancient red-gold light of fading day, that fell without violence or heat upon the streets of life, the houses where [115.25 June, and in the houses where
* 101.II.35 valleys, fading [115.28 valleys fading
  102.I.1–4 It was in the whole earth breathing the last beat and weariness of day out in the huge hush and joy and sorrow of oncoming night.¶ Finally, the war had got into all sounds [115.31–116.1 It was in the whole huge mystery of earth that, after all the dusty tumult of the day, could lapse with such immortal stillness to the hush, the joy, the sorrow of oncoming night.¶ [page break] The war had got into all sounds
* 102.I.5 hunger, and wild [116.2 hunger and wild
  102.I.14–16 familiar, remote as time, as haunting as the briefness of our days.¶ And suddenly, [116.11–12 familiar.¶ And suddenly,
* 102.I.23 flesh, and yielding [116.19 flesh and yielding
  102.I.24 the low, rich, sensual welling [116.20 the rich, sensual welling
* 102.I.25 tender from the [116.21 tender, from the
* 102.I.52 to us his life [117.12 to us, his life
* 102.II.11 of it had under this [117.26 of it, had, under this
* 102.II.12 and war returned in [117.27 and war, returned in
  103.I.2 Hayes.¶ "Ah, Lord!" [119.4 Hayes.¶ [space break] "Ah, Lord!"
* 103.II.2 backbone as sure [120.26 backbone, as sure
* 103.II.3 heaven before [120.27 heaven, before
* 104.I.13 court-house [122.16 courthouse
* 104.I.25 rich-fibred, [122.28 rich-fibered,
* 104.I.27 silence, slily lowered [122.30 silence, slyly lowered
* 104.I.45 after battles and the [123.13 after battles, and the
* 104.II.8 fibre [123.20 fiber
  104.II.34 rock-bright sallows of [124.12 rock-bright shallows of

* 104.II.40 familiar plain, [124.18 familiar-plain,
* 104.II.55 plain familiar [124.33 plain-familiar
  105.I.1 and tomorrow will be [124.34 and who to-morrow will be
* 105.I.5 again, at one [125.3 again—at one
* 105.I.10 us and the [125.7 us, and the
* 105.I.11 distances, shape [125.8 distances; shape
* 105.I.15 now, engulf [125.12 now; engulf
* 105.I.22 always as it [125.19 always, as it
* 105.I.36 wheat field [125.33 wheatfield
  105.I.44 the west forever— [126.7 the West forever—
* 105.I.46 Wilson's Mill where [126.9 Wilson's Mill, where
  105.II.18 the Thirties, the Forties, and the Fifties? Did [126.28 the 'Thirties, the 'Forties, and the 'Fifties? Did
  105.II.21 cry out the fierce goat-cry of ecstasy and exultancy, as [126.31 cry out in ecstasy and exultancy, as
* 105.II.26 gas lamps [127.2 gas-lamps
  105.II.44–45 funnels, the racketing clack of wheels upon the light, ill-laid, ill-joined rails? Had they [127.20 funnels? Had they
* 106.I.3 heart beats [127.23 heartbeats
  106.I.4 as they waited, waited, waited in the [127.24 as they waited, waited in the
* 106.I.21 the huge lonely earth [128.6 the huge, lonely earth
* 106.I.21 night time [128.6 night-time
  106.I.24 network of the light, [128.9 network of light,
  106.I.36 then waited, feeling the goat-cry swelling in their throats, feeling wild joy and sorrow [128.21 then waited, feeling wild joy and sorrow
* 106.I.44 little towns with [128.28 little towns, with
  106.I.46–II.10 in the darkness?¶ Were they not burning with the wild and wordless hope, the incredible belief that all young men have known before the promise of that huge mirage, the deathless dupe and invincible illusion of this savage, all-exultant land where all things are impending and where young men starve? Were they not burning in the enfabled magic, mystery, and joy of lilac dark, the lonely, savage, secret, everlasting earth on which we lived, and wrought, and perished, mad with hunger, unfed, famished, furious, unassuaged? Were they not burning, burning where a million doors of glory, love, unutterable fulfilment, impended, waited in the dark for us, were here, were here around us in the dark forever, were here beside us in the dark forever, were ready to our touch forever, and that duped us, mocked forever at our hunger, maddened our hearts and brains with searching, took our youth, our strength, our

love, our life, and killed us, and were never found? ¶ Had Garfield, Arthur, [128.31 in the darkness?¶ Had Garfield, Arthur,
- 106.II.13 they waited in the [128.34 they stood in the
* 106.II.14 lighted, certain, [129.1 lighted—certain,
- 106.II.17–19 of the town, the lonely, wild and secret earth, the lilac dark, the huge starred visage of the night—did they not [129.4 of the town, did they not
- 106.II.21–107.I.51 Soon, soon, soon!" ¶ And then as Garfield, Arthur, Harrison, and Hayes prowled softly up and down in the dark cobbled streets hearing the sudden shrill departure of the whistle in the night, the great wheels pounding at the river's edge, feeling the lilac dark, the heart-beats. Of the sleeping men, and the attentive silence, the terror, savagery, and joy, the huge mystery and promise of the immense and silent earth, thinking, feeling, thinking, with wild, silent joy, intolerable desire, did they not say: ¶ "Oh, there are women in the West and we shall find them. They will be waiting for us, calm, tranquil, corn-haired, unsurprised, looking across the wall of level grain with level eyes, looking into the flaming domains of the red, the setting sun, at the great wall and the soaring vistas of the western ranges. Oh, there are lavish, if corn-haired women in the West with tranquil eyes," cried Garfield, Arthur, Harrison, and Hayes, "and we shall find them waiting in their doors for us at evening!"¶ "And there are women in the South," they said, "with dark eyes and the white magnolia faces. They are moving beneath the droop of tree-barred levels of the South. Now they are moving on the sweep of ancient lawns, beside the great slow-flowing rivers in the night! Their step is light and soundless as the dark, they drift the white ghost-glimmer of their beauty under ancient trees, their words are soft and slow and hushed, and sweeter far than honey, and suddenly their low and tender laugh, slow, rich, and sensual, comes welling from the great vat of the dark. The perfume of their slow white flesh is flower-sweet, magnolia strange, and filled with all the secret languors of desire! Oh, there are secret women in the South," they cried, "who move by darkness under drooping trees the white ghost-glimmer of magnolia loveliness, and we shall find them!"¶ "And there are women in the North," cried Garfield, Arthur, Harrison, and Hayes, "who wait for us with Viking eyes, the deep breast and the great limbs of the Amazons. There are powerful and lovely women in the North," they said, "whose eyes are blue and depthless as a mountain lake. Their glorious hair is braided into ropes of ripened grain, and their names are Lundquist, Neilsen, Svensen, Jorgenson, and Brandt. They are waiting for us in the wheat-fields of the North, they are waiting for us at the edges of the

plains, they are waiting for us in the forests of great trees. Their eyes are true and level, and their great hearts are the purest and most faithful on the earth, and they will wait for us until we come to them." ¶ "There are ten thousand lonely little towns at night," cried Garfield, Arthur, Harrison, and Hayes, "ten thousand lonely little towns of sleeping men, and we shall come to them forever in the night. We shall come to them like storm and fury, with a demonic impulse of wild joy, dark chance, dropping suddenly upon them from the fast express at night-leaving the train in darkness, in the dark mid-watches of the night, and being left then to the sudden silence, mystery, and promise of an unknown little town. Oh, we shall come to them forever in the night," they cried, "in winter among howling winds and swirling snow. Then we shall make our tracks along the sheeted fleecy whiteness of an empty silent little street, and find our door at length, and know the instant that we come to it that it is ours." ¶ "Coming by storm and darkness to the lonely, chance and secret towns," they said, "we shall find the well-loved face, the longed-for step, the well-known voice, there in the darkness while storm beats about the house and the white mounting drifts of swirling snow engulf us. Then we shall know the flower-whiteness of a face below us, the night-time darkness of a cloud of hair across our arm, and know all the mystery, tenderness, and surrender, of a white-dark beauty, the fragrant whiteness, the slow bounty of a velvet undulance, the earth-deep fruitfulness of love. And we shall stay there while storm howls about the house," they said, "and huge drifts rise about us. We shall leave forever in the whitened silence of the morning, and always know the chance, the secret and the well-beloved will be there waiting for us when storms bowl at night, and we come again through swirling snow, leaving our footprints on whitened, empty, silent streets of unknown little towns, lost at the heart of storm and darkness upon the lonely, wild, all-secret mystery of the earth." ¶ And finally did not Garfield, Arthur, Harrison, and Hayes, [129.8 Soon, soon, soon!" ¶ Did not Garfield, Arthur, Harrison, and Hayes,

* 107.I.54 street with [129.10 street, with
  107.II.5 in all the intolerable [129.16 in the intolerable
  107.II.34–108.I.10 dancing morning-gold—and feel, with an unspeakable sorrow and delight, that there are ships there, there are ships—and something in our hearts we cannot utter. ¶ "And we shall smell the excellent sultry fragrance of boiling coffee, and think of silken luxury of great walnut chambers in whose shuttered amber morning-light proud beauties slowly stir in sensual warmth their lavish limbs. Then we shall smell, with the sharp relish of young

hunger, the grand breakfast smells: the pungent bacon, crisping to a turn, the grilled kidneys, eggs, and sausages, and the fragrant stacks of gold-brown wheat cakes smoking hot. And we shall move, alive and strong and full of hope, through all the swarming lanes of morning and know the good green smell of money, the heavy leathers and the walnut of great merchants, the power, the joy, the certitude and ease of proud success."¶ "We shall come at furious noon to slake our thirst with drinks of rare and subtle potency in sumptuous bars of swart mahogany in the good fellowship of men, the spicy fragrance of the lemon rind and angostura bitters. Then, hunger whetted, pulse aglow and leaping with the sharp spur of our awakened appetite, we shall eat from the snowy linen of the greatest restaurants in the world. We shall be suavely served and tenderly cared for by the pious unction of devoted waiters. We shall be quenched with old wine and fed with the rare and priceless honesty, the maddening succulence of grand familiar food and noble cooking, fit to match the peerless relish of our hunger!" ¶ "Street of the day, [130.11 morning-gold.¶ "Street of the day,
108.I.12 "Streets of the [130.14 "Street of the
108.I.12 noon, streets of the [130.14 noon, street of the
108.I.15–17 swarming feet, the man-swarm ever passing in its million-footed weft—street of the jounting [130.18 swarming feet,—street of the jounting
108.I.22–23 come!"¶ "Street [130.23–24 come!¶ "Street
108.I.39–40 merit!"¶ "Street [131.6–7 merit!¶ "Street
* 108.II.15 city we shall [132.2 city, we shall
* 108.II.25 night time [132.13 night-time
* 108.II.34 hope, and [132.22 hope and
* 108.II.38 been, who have [132.25 been who have
* 108.II.42 water and one [132.29 water, and one

"Gulliver"

Scribner's Magazine June 1935: 328–33 [*FDTM* 133–49

"Gulliver, The Story of a Tall Man" ["Gulliver"
* 328.I.9 shirts, and [134.4 shirts and
328.I.26 all its joy and pain and strangeness of an incommunicable loneliness, [134.18 all the joy and pain and strangeness of its incommunicable loneliness,
* 328.II.14 palpable and [135.2 palpable, and
328.II.15 away if we could utter, [135.4 away if we could span it, only a word, a wall, a door away if we could utter,

  329.I.22 lived, if thinking, seeing, makes it so, and in [136.9 lived, and in
* 329.I.32 eight and nine foot Titans, [136.18 eight- and nine-foot Titans,
  329.I.46 in the interesting [136.33 in an interesting
* 329.I.48 Lady, and piquant [137.1 Lady and piquant
  329.II.29 Thus, when this tall man was alone, he never thought [138.3 Thus, there was a tall man once and when he was alone he never thought
  330.I.2 of astonished disbelief [138.31 of astounded disbelief
  330.I.28 average man, that [139.24 average men, that
* 330.I.31 flame in such [139.27 flame, in such
  330.II.11 and little aging, a [140.27 and bitter anguish, a
  330.II.32 consonance of his rut.¶ It never changed, [141.14 consonance of his wit.¶ For one such man, at least, it never changed,
  330.II.35 streets all around [141.17 streets around
  330.II.36 countries, among a [141.19 countries, amid a
* 331.I.26 Such then were [142.22 Such, then, were
  331.I.27 the national humor [142.22 the popular humor
  331.I.37 "You're ver-ree tall, [142.29 "You're ver-ee tall,
* 331.I.41 [with hasty correction] [142.33 (with hasty correction)
  331.I.44 ... *I mean* [142.34 ... *I* mean
  331.I.46 ... *I mean,* [143.7 ... *I* mean,
  331.I.50 ... *Reelee,* I [143.8 ... *Ree-lee,* I
  331.II.16 rotting birch: within, [143.22 rotting brick: within,
  331.II.23 jowled, squatty face [143.26 jowled, swart face
* 331.II.33 Grogan, wit by nature [143.32 Grogan—wit by nature
  331.II.41 still crowding): "*Je-sus* ... [144.6 still crouching): "*Je-zus* ...
  331.II.51 a lookut 'im, [144.16 a look ut 'im,
  332.I.23 t' laff ... [145.12 t' laugh ...
* 332.I.50 metallically stamped and [145.34 metallically stamped, and
  332.I.55 natural tensity of [146.5 natural tension of
  332.II.30 yuh? (lustily) ... Now [147.1 *yuh?* ... (hastily). Now
  332.II.47 eight (reflectively). ... Six [147.18 eight ... (reflectively). Six
* 333.I.4 wallop ... and [147.31 wallop. ... and
* 333.II.12 theaters [148.29 theatres

"The Bums at Sunset"

Vanity Fair Oct. 1935: 30, 62 [*FDTM* 150–54

* 30.I.23 procession towards the [150.18 procession toward the
  30.I.28 was indeterminate. He [150.21 was indeterminable. He
* 30.I.40 pin striped suit [150.30 pin-striped suit

* 30.I.43 his trousers pocket [151.3 his trouser pocket
   30.I.61 seamed brutal face [151.15 seamed face
   30.II.7–9 shambles, of immense and lonely skies, the savage wildness, the wild, cruel and lonely distance of America. [151.21 shambles, of the savage wilderness, the wild, cruel and lonely distances of America.
   30.II.17 his hard cupped hand [151.28 his cupped hand
   30.II.23 a powerful and brutal gesture [151.32 a powerful gesture
   30.II.25 the quality of [151.33 the fragrance of
   30.II.26 and fragrant relish [151.34 and pungent relish
   30.II.30 the rare qualities [152.3 the thrilling qualities
   30.II.33 behind the man [152.6 behind this man
   30.II.34 back of the vagabond. Now, [152.6 back. Now,
   30.III.9 of brutal friendliness: [152.14 of coarse friendliness:
* 30.III.10 goin' kid?" [152.16 goin', kid?"
   30.III.10 "To the big town?" [152.16 "To duh Big Town?"
   30.III.25 by the way [152.29 by duh way
   30.III.28 to the Big [152.31 to duh Big
   30.III.28 goin' that way [152.31 goin dat way
   62.I.5 fawning insinuation. "You [153.6 fawning insinuations. "You
* 62.I.11 like you?—Dat's [153.11 like you—Dat's
   62.I.13 kids began to [153.12 kids begin to
* 62.I.17 a noice maid or [153.14 a noice-maid or
   62.I.19 snarled viciously, and [153.15 snarled once more, and
* 62.I.22 yuh! . . G'wan, now. . Get [153.18 yuh! . . . G'wan, now. . . . Get
* 62.I.27 quietly in a [153.22 quietly, in a
   62.I.28 leave the kid alone. The kid [153.23 leave duh kid alone. Duh kid
* 62.I.35 "A-a-ah t'hell [153.28 "A-a-ah, t'hell
   62.I.37 duh cradle [153.29 duh - - - - cradle
   62.I.39 Bull said in [153.31 Bull replied in
   62.I.44 said the kid [153.34 said duh kid
* 62.II.7 a tool house on [154.5 a tool-house on
   62.II.18 tough scarred face [154.13 tough seamed face
   62.II.19 cupped hand, and [154.13 cupped paw, and
* 62.II.42 off, half-heard and half-suspected, there [154.30 off, half heard and half suspected, there

"One of the Girls in Our Party"

Scribner's Magazine Jan. 1935: 6–8 [*FDTM* 155–63

* 6.I.3 American middle west— [155.3 American Middle West—
  6.I.7 metallic, could be heard lifted in a united clamor of [155.7 metallic, were united in a clamor of
  6.I.12 luncheon, she called [155.12 luncheon, called
  6.II.24–25 same."¶ [space break] Miss [157.3–4 same."¶ Miss
  7.II.8 named Mr. Vogelsang, and [158.33 named Singvogel, and
* 7.II.10 party, asked [158.34 party asked
  7.II.12 of Mr. Vogelsang, no [158.37 of Mr. Singvogel, no
  7.II.15 of Mr. Vogelsang. [159.2 of Mr. Singvogel.
  7.II.16 Vogelsang iss [159.3 Singvogel iss
  7.II.21 is all uff golt [159.8 is uff golt
  7.II.27 de platform, turn [159.14 de blatform, turn
* 7.II.30 see?—So! Now! *two!* [159.17 see?—so! now! *two!*
  7.II.34 has efer been [159.21 has effer been
  7.II.35 a voman. [159.22 a vooman.
  7.II.36 Mr. Vogelsang, [159.23 Mr. Singvogel,
  7.II.40 guilders witch iss [159.27 guilders vich is
* 7.II.46 shtair case [159.33 shtair-case,
  7.II.46 for efery day [159.33 for effery day
* 7.II.47 year engrafed [159.33 year, engrafed
  7.II.52 Mr. Vogelsang [160.6 Mr. Singvogel
  7.II.54 Mr. Vogelsang [160.7 Mr. Singvogel
  8.I.1 Mr. Vogelsang [160.11 Mr. Singvogel
  8.I.4 year comes dere [160.13 year gomes dere
  8.I.8 Mr. Vogelsang. [160.17 Mr. Singvogel.
  8.I.14 Mr. Vogelsang. [160.22 Mr. Singvogel.
* 8.I.29 Arc de Triumph, [160.35 Arch de Triumph,
* 8.I.37 buses [161.6 busses
* 8.I.52 group and do [161.20 group, and do
* 8.II.2 went, I believe [161.34 went; I believe
* 8.II.5 book?"—it's [161.37 book?"—It's
* 8.II.12 tonight. [162.8 to-night.
* 8.II.40 "enamorata"? [162.35 "inamorata"?
* 8.II.51 slope, nights [163.8 slope; nights

"The Far and the Near"

Cosmopolitan July 1935: 48–49, 176 [*FDTM* 164–68

"Cottage by the Tracks" ["The Far and the Near"
* 48.I.20 a breathing space at [164.14 a breathing-space at
* 176.I.30 up the path, and [167.10 up the path and
  176.II.3 harsh and mean and meager; [167.18 was harsh and pinched and meager;
  176.II.6 with suspicion and dislike. All [167.20 with timid suspicion and uneasy doubt. All
* 176.II.8 her gesture vanished [167.22 her gesture, vanished
  176.II.10 her surly tongue. [167.23 her unfriendly tongue.
  176.II.21 him surlily into [167.32 him almost unwillingly into
  176.II.26 bewildered unfriendliness, a sullen and restrained mistrust. ¶ And [168.2 bewildered hostility, a sullen, timorous restraint.¶ And
  176.II.39 known. [168.12 known. And he knew that all the magic of that bright lost way, the vista of that shining line, the imagined corner of that small good universe of hope's desire, was gone forever, could never be got back again.

"In the Park"

Harper's Bazaar June 1935: 54–55, 104, 106, 108 [*FDTM* 169–84

54.I.1 When the show was over [169.1–10 That year I think we were living with Bella; no, we weren't, I guess we were living with Auntie Kate—well, maybe we were staying with Bella: I don't know, we moved around so much, and it's so long ago. It gets all confused in my mind now; when Daddy was acting he was always on the go, he couldn't be still a minute; sometimes he was playing in New York, and sometimes he went off on a tour with Mr. Mansfield and was gone for months.¶ Anyway, that night when the show was over
* 54.I.13 everyone seemed [169.22 every one seemed
  54.I.14 as exultant and happy as we were [169.22 as happy and elated as we were
* 54.I.25 April now [170.6 April, now
* 54.II.4 Des-o-la-tion into [170.15 Des-o-la-tion, into
  54.II.8–18 laugh.¶ That year I think we were living with Bella: no, we weren't, I guess we were living with Auntie Kate—well, maybe we were staying with Bella: I don't know, we moved around so much, and it's so long ago. It gets all confused in my mind now; when Daddy was acting he was always on the go, he couldn't lie still a

minute; sometimes he was playing in New York, and sometimes he went off on a tour with Mr. Mansfield and was gone for months.¶ I think that must [170.19 laughed.¶ I think that must
* 54.II.20 cream--¶ In those [170.21 cream----¶ In those
  54.II.23 eat. There was [170.23 eat. *There* was
* 55.I.13 show with two [171.10 show, with two
* 55.II.9 hurry because [171.29 hurry, because
* 104.I.5 everyone else [172.14 every one else
* 104.I.6 someone would [172.15 some one would
* 104.I.23 Irish voice: it [172.26 Irish voice; it
* 104.I.47 Church as well [173.9 Church, as well
* 104.I.75 the pontifical palate [173.28 the pontifical palate
  104.II.18 on his back [174.27 on the back
* 104.II.22 so handsome: there [174.31 so handsome; there
  104.II.47 was a great [175.15 was another great
* 104.II.64 them or what [175.27 them, or what
  104.II.84 a marvelous meal [176.7 a wonderful meal
* 104.II.86 place cooked [176.8 place, cooked
* 104.II.88 most marvelous oysters [176.9 most marvellous oysters
  104.II.93 up his glass [176.13 up the young fellow's glass
* 106.I.29 everyone in [177.8 every one in
* 106.I.63 flying, I suppose [177.34 flying. I suppose
  106.I.74 you!"¶ But the [178.7 you!"¶ [space break] But the
* 106.I.80 night with [178.13 night, with
  106.I.92 car was some [178.21 car were some
  106.I.99 motor cars we ever saw. Somehow [178.25 motor cars. Somehow
  106.II.2–3 although now I know they would look crude and funny and old-fashioned, it [178.28–29 although I know they would look crude and funny and old-fashioned now, it
* 106.II.10 and strange as [178.33 and strange, as
  106.II.25 way that old [179.10 way the old
* 106.II.26 looked so well [179.10 looked, so well
  106.II.44 earth belong to them. [179.23 earth belonged to them.
* 106.II.50 cop was going [179.27 cop were going
* 106.II.88 said well, [180.21 said, well,
  106.II.95 would. I never knew just what did happen, I guess [180.26 would. I guess
* 108.II.25 man! How noble in reason! How infinite in faculty! in form [183.6 man! how noble in reason! how infinite in faculty! in form
  108.II.46 sing. Now broke the birdsong in first light, [183.21 sing. And now the bird-song broke in the first light,

108.II.48–55 the birdsong made: like a flight of shot, the sharp fast skaps of sound arose. With chitterling bicker, fast-fluttering skiffs of sound, the palmy honied birdcries came. Smooth drops and nuggets of bright gold they were. Now sang the birdtree filled with lutings in bright air: the thrum, [183.23–34 the bird-song made. It came to me like music I had always heard, it came to me like music I had always known, the sounds of which I never yet had spoken, and now I heard the music of each sound as clear and bright as gold, and the music of each sound was this: at first it rose above me like a flight of shot, and then I heard the sharp, fast skaps of sound the bird-song made. And now they were smooth drops and nuggets of bright gold, and now with chittering bicker and fast-fluttering skirrs of sound the palmy, honied bird-cries came. And now the bird-tree sang, all filled with lutings in bright air; the thrum,

108.II.56 chirrs arose now. The little brainless cries arose and fell with liquorous liquefied lutings, [184.1 chirrs arose. And now the little brainless cries arose, with liquorous, liquefied lutings,

* 108.II.60–62 And now there was the rapid kweet kweet kweet kweet of homely birds, [184.3 And now I heard the rapid kweet-kweet-kweet-kweet-kweet of homely birds,

108.II.63 others with thin [184.5 others had thin

108.II.65–66 stitch, a mosquito buzz, while some with rusty creakings, high shrew's caws, [184.6 stitch, and high shrew's caws,

108.II.67 with harsh far calls—all birds that are awoke [184.7 with harsh, far calls—these were the sounds the bird-cries made. All birds that are awoke

108.II.69 passed whirr [184.9 passed the whirr

108.II.73 mingled.¶ "Sweet [184.12 mingled. "Sweet

* 108.II.76 that and [184.14 that, and
* 108.II.85 ago that [184.19 ago, that

108.II.85 think of it [184.20 think about it

* 108.II.86 confused, and [184.20 confused and

"The Men of Old Catawba"

"Old Catawba" *Virginia Quarterly Review* Apr. 1935: 228–38; "Polyphemus" *North American Review* June 1935: 20–26 [*FDTM* 185–204

"Old Catawba" ["The Men of Old Catawba"
* 228.3 American state of [185.3 American State of
* 228.4 the state might [185.4 the State might

* 228.5 the states of the union: its [185.5 the States of the Union: its
* 228.8 coastal states [185.8 coastal States,
* 228.9 populated states of [185.9 populated States of
  228.11 live about three million [185.12 live three million
  228.12 whom about the third [185.12 whom the third
* 228.15 The state possesses [185.15 The State possesses
  228.17 than that of [185.17 than those of
  228.18 of her critics to [185.18 of her cities to
* 228.23 habit, between [185.23 habit between
  229.1 and number. The [186.3 and numbers. The
* 229.4 that state where [186.6 that State where
  229.6 the tribes that [186.8 the tribe that
  229.8 to a tribe that [186.10 to a group that
* 229.10 that state. People [186.13 that State. People
* 229.11 the state have [186.13 the State have
* 229.16 the state: it [186.19 the State: it
* 229.36 Anyone who [187.6 Any one who
* 229.36 the state for [187.6 the State for
* 230.3 that state inspires [187.9 that State inspires
  230.15 this is all the men [187.22 this includes all the men
  230.18 A one-eyed Spaniard, [187.25 Catawba got discovered in this way: a one-eyed Spaniard,

"Polyphemus" ["The Men of Old Catawba"
* 20.10 the cruellest and [188.2 the cruelest and
* 20.15 pearl-grey water [188.7 pearl-gray water
* 20.21 and desolate looking. [188.13 and desolate-looking.
* 20.21 cool grey water [188.13 cool gray water
* 21.8 the grey stuff [189.1 the gray stuff
* 21.25 "marvelous [189.20 "marvellous
* 21.28 in towards the [189.22 in toward the
* 21.29 on shore a [189.23 on shore, a
* 21.36 the shore pointing [189.31 the shore, pointing
  22.1 now, he was not [189.33 now, and he was not
* 22.13 the marvelous moon [190.11 the marvellous moon
* 22.31 without whose intervention [190.30 without Whose intervention
* 22.33 of Spain and [190.33 of Spain, and
* 22.34 read today of [190.34 read to-day of
  22.35 arrogance touches us [191.1 arrogance touch us
* 23.3 these men. For [191.6 these men? For
  23.4 possesses.¶ At any [191.7 possesses.¶ [space break] At any

- * 23.11 ran away yelling into [191.15 ran away, yelling, into
  23.34 in considerable quantity [192.8 in abundant quantity
- * 24.19 the marvelous clay [192.31 the marvellous clay
  25.2 ground.¶ It [193.20 ground.¶ [space break] It
- * 25.20 Indians and [194.8 Indians, and
- * 26.1 Westward in great [194.27 Westward, in great
  26.4 broken bowl of [194.30 broken boil of

  "Old Catawba" ["The Men of Old Catawba"
  231.23 "By d-*damn!*" one of [196.14 "*'Od-damn!*" one of
  231.28 community, accompanied by roars and whoops of laughter. It may [196.20 community. It may
- * 231.30 usage so that [196.22 usage, so that
- * 232.12 there," someone suggests, [197.6 there," some one suggests,
- * 232.19 pausing, and lifting [197.13 pausing and lifting
- * 232.32 someone says, [197.27 some one says,
- * 233.3 horizon, "who [198.1 horizon, who
- * 233.9 someone asks. [198.7 some one asks.
- * 233.31 someone helpfully [198.31 some one helpfully
  234.7 an' hundred [199.9 and a hundred
- * 234.15 someone said. [199.19 some one said.
- * 234.18 someone else [199.21 some one else
- * 234.20 says, "The *legal* [199.24 says, "the *legal*
- * 234.36 the damnedest logic [200.7 the damndest logic
  235.10 Jim!" another one says [200.19 Jim!" yet another says
  235.36 there is one [201.11 there are one
- * 235.36 warriors who [201.11 warriors, who
- * 236.19 'foreign' [201.32 "foreign"
- * 236.20 other states, [201.33 other States,
- * 236.20 'foreign-born' [201.34 "foreign-born"
- * 236.21 the state has [202.1 the State has
- * 236.29 long loping stride, [202.9 long-loping stride,
- * 236.31 the state. In [202.11 the State. In
  237.33 that goes back [203.19 that runs back
  238.7–11 still live, waiting until the unspeakable thing in them shall be spoken, until they can unlock their hearts and wreak out the dark burden of their spirit—the legend of loneliness, of exile, and eternal wandering that is in them.¶ The real history [203.30 still live.¶ The real history
  238.19 the immense and eternal earth, [204.5 the eternal earth,
  238.23 of the sea that with lapse and reluctation of its breath, feathers eternally [204.10 of the sea that feathers eternally

238.26 wilderness; it is a history of time, dark time, strange secret time, forever flowing like a river.¶ The history [204.11 wilderness.¶ The history
238.34 terrible American earth [204.18 terrible earth

"Circus at Dawn"

Modern Monthly Mar. 1935: 19–21, 52 [*FDTM* 205–11

    19.I.1 were the times [205.1 were times
* 19.I.5 paper. On [205.4 paper, on
* 19.I.7 in, I would [205.5 in I would
    19.I.8 cool exultant darkness [205.6 cool and thrilling darkness
* 19.I.12 towards [205.11 toward
* 19.I.14 greyed [205.12 grayed
    19.II.1 light of the day that seems [205.13 light of day which seems
* 19.II.4 stillness and one [205.15 stillness, and one
    19.II.5 of exultant joy [205.16 of joy
    19.II.7–15 done (to see this happen—to see Virginia so at first light from the windows of a Pullman berth—as later I would do so many times, to see the lonely, the glorious, the beautiful and everlasting earth emerge so in that still incredible purity of light—is one of the things that men will remember out of life forever and think of as they die).¶ Then, having reached the sculptural [205.17–20 done, for to see this happen is one of the things that men will remember out of life forever and think of as they die.¶ At the sculptural
* 19.II.17 light my father's [205.21 light, my father's
* 19.II.22 someone we knew who [205.25 some one we knew, who
* 19.II.24 Then having [205.27 Then, having
* 19.II.34 prophesies [206.7 prophecies
    19.II.37 aerial smoke [206.9 acrid smoke
    19.II.38 cars, clean pine board of [206.10 cars, the clean pine-board of
* 20.I.7 sumptuous looking cars [206.16 sumptuous-looking cars
    20.I.10 in great strings [206.18 in long strings
    20.I.13 furiously and exultantly in the [206.20 furiously in the
    20.I.14 the great receding [206.21 the receding
* 20.I.24 trains there [206.28 trains, there
    20.I.32 be this tremendous [207.1 be the tremendous
* 20.I.32 confused hurried, [207.1 confused, hurried,
* 20.I.34 iron-grey [207.3 iron-gray
* 20.I.39 tracks and [207.7 tracks, and
    20.I.42 the great horses [207.9 the big horses
* 20.II.26 grey [207.34 gray

* 20.II.27 two and then [207.34 two, and then
* 20.II.40 with swarth rich [208.12 with swart rich
* 20.II.42 reply.¶ "He [208.14 reply:¶ "He
* 20.II.45 say 'wait [208.17 say 'Wait
* 21.I.3 towards [208.20 toward
  21.I.4 others, making [208.22 other, making
* 21.I.9 Har!"—And [208.27 Har!"—and
  21.I.12 described the elephant's prowess to each other. [208.29 described to each other the elephant's prowess.
* 21.I.19 they ate,—mixed [208.35 they ate—mixed
  21.I.20 strong exultant excitement, [209.1 strong excitement,
* 21.I.35 husky looking [209.12 husky-looking
  21.I.36 on great loaded [209.13 on loaded
* 21.I.40 food—there [209.16 food, there
  21.I.41 fragrance—which somehow [209.17 fragrance—that somehow
  21.I.43 and exultant life [209.18 and thrilling life
* 21.I.44 see, sending [209.20 see sending
* 21.II.2 fine looking [209.24 fine-looking
* 21.II.18 hair, and the [210.3 hair and the
  21.II.18 the figures of [210.3 the figure of
  21.II.19 and powerfully-built, [210.3 and a powerfully-built,
* 21.II.20 responsible looking [210.5 responsible-looking
* 21.II.41 me whispering: [210.21 me, whispering:
* 21.II.43 head. W-w-ell [210.23 head? W-w-ell
* 21.II.44 knowingly "He's [210.24 knowingly. "He's
* 52.I.6 said "D-d-one [210.30 said. "D-d-one
* 52.I.8 vigorously "It's [210.32 vigorously. "It's
* 52.I.11 s-s-s-stuff!" My brother said "w-w-w-why," [210.34 s-s-s-stuff!" my brother said. "W-w-w-why,"
* 52.I.12 solemn conviction "It [211.1 solemn conviction, "it
  52.II.12 grounds reluctantly and [211.10 grounds and
  52.II.14 seen, heard and smelled that [211.11 seen and heard that
  52.II.15 and finally the memory [211.12 and the memory
  52.II.16 its glorious smells would [211.13 its wonderful smells, would
* 52.II.19 lunch rooms [211.16 lunch-rooms
* 52.II.21 ham and egg [211.17 ham-and-egg
* 52.II.24 doughnuts and [211.20 doughnuts, and

"The Web of Earth"

Scribner's Magazine July 1932: 1–5, 43–64 [*FDTM* 212–304

* 1.I.1 ... in the [212.1 ... In the
* 1.I.11 and, "Twenty [212.10 and "Twenty
  1.I.18 Mr. Hawke?" I [212.17 Mr. Gant?" I
  1.II.1 Mrs. Hawke," your [212.23 Mrs. Gant," your
* 1.II.11 "Oh! don't go!" [213.1 "Oh, don't go!"
* 1.II.18 happened to the [213.7 happened, to the
* 1.II.21 "But, say [213.11 But, say
  1.II.21 then!—Ed—Gil—Lee—pshaw! Boy! John! I mean—I reckon Lee is [213.11 then!—Ben—Steve—Luke—pshaw! Boy! Gene! I mean—I reckin Luke is
* 1.II.24 say?"¶ "You [213.14 say?¶ "You
  2.I.1 tell about [213.15 tell me about
* 2.I.2 time."¶ "Oh, yes! [213.17 time."¶ Oh, yes!
* 2.I.4 Hah?"¶ "Those [213.18 Hah?¶ "Those
* 2.I.5 harbor, mama."¶ "What say? [213.19 harbor, Mama."¶ What say?
* 2.I.7 yon way?"¶ "No, mama, it's [213.21 yon way?¶ "No, Mama, it's
* 2.I.9 there."¶ "Hah? [213.24 there."¶ Hah?
  2.I.22 I'd a let him [214.1 I'd let him
  2.I.24 you mustn't be [214.3 you musn't be
* 2.I.30 back again." [214.8 back again.
* 2.I.31 "Well, now, [214.10 Well, now,
* 2.I.38 countries, England, [214.16 countries: England,
  2.I.38 all your folks [214.17 all our folks
* 2.I.43 "Say ... [214.21 Say ...
* 2.I.45 that night?" [214.23 that night?
* 2.II.3 about, the [214.29 about—the
* 2.II.14 and mother singin' and the [215.5 and Mother singin', and the
* 2.II.16 rained. The [215.6 rained? The
* 2.II.28 boy: there's [215.18 boy, there's
* 2.II.39 owned—Oh, Lord! [215.28 owned—oh, Lord!
* 2.II.41 as father said, [215.29 as Father said,
* 2.II.41 would a left [215.30 would 'a' left
* 2.II.45 black nigger smell that [215.34 black nigger-smell that
  3.I.3 "they're goin' to [216.7 "they're going to
* 3.I.4 screamed—why I [216.8 screamed—why, I
* 3.I.11 course, father always [216.14 course, Father always
* 3.I.18 "Why," mother said, [216.21 "Why," Mother said,
* 3.I.27 told mother she [216.30 told Mother she
* 3.I.32 everything that [216.34 everything—that

* 3.I.36 stolen as [217.3 stolen, as
* 3.I.37 could as [217.4 could, as
* 3.I.38 mind today as [217.5 mind to-day as
* 3.II.1 says mother, wringin' [217.15 says Mother, wringin'
  3.II.1 hands, "here they [217.15 hands, "there they
* 3.II.4 know, screaming [217.17 know screaming
* 3.II.5 And grandfather's down [217.18 And Grandfather's down
* 3.II.11 But law! the [217.23 But Law! the
  3.II.43 man Dockery. I reckon [218.19 man Mackery? I reckon
  4.I.2 you goin' to [218.28 you going to
  4.I.6 man Dockery, running [218.32 man Mackery, running
  4.I.9 perspiration, Dockery, you [218.34 perspiration, Mackery, you
* 4.I.18 pass, father and mother and [219.9 pass, Father and Mother and
  4.I.20 and Woodsend tribes [219.10 and Pentland tribes
  4.I.23 Bill Woodsend that [219.13 Bill Pentland that
* 4.I.26 saw, why, don't [219.16 saw, why don't
  4.I.29 Bill Woodsend made [219.18 Bill Pentland made
  4.I.33 Billy Woodsend was [219.22 Billy Pentland was
  4.I.37 Bill Woodsend was [219.27 Bill Pentland was
* 4.I.38 who'd a gone [219.27 who'd 'a' gone
* 4.II.3 it, father? What's [220.6 it, Father? What's
* 4.II.6 he says, says, "I've [220.9 he says, "I've
* 4.II.8 "Why, father," Sam [220.11 "Why, Father," Sam
* 4.II.20 "Why, father," says [220.21 "Why, Father," says
* 4.II.31 dinner, and [220.31 dinner and
* 4.II.31 more, and [220.32 more and
* 4.II.38 said, "Good bye, Sam: [221.4 said, "Good-bye, Sam:
* 4.II.41 of will power and [221.7 of will-power and
* 4.II.45 it, father went [221.9 it. Father went
* 4.II.48 no, father," I [221.12 no, Father," I
* 4.II.50 *very day*, sir [221.14 *very day* sir
* 5.I.1 whispered "Six": [221.16 whispered, "Six":
  5.I.2 knew.¶ [space break] But [221.17 knew.¶ But
  5.I.4 Bill Woodsend standin' [221.19 Bill Pentland standin'
* 5.I.8 course father was [221.22 course Father was
* 5.I.21 mountains and [221.34 mountains, and
* 5.I.30 to father at [222.8 to Father at
  5.I.31 Bill Woodsend died [222.8 Bill Pentland died
  5.I.34 Bill Woodsend was [222.11 Bill Pentland was
  5.II.5 was goin' to [222.30 was going to
  5.II.15 you in these days: fried [223.5 you nowadays: fried
* 5.II.24 away—why, [223.12 away, why,
* 5.II.24 as mother said [223.13 as Mother said

* 5.II.24 you'd a thought [223.13 you'd 'a' thought
* 5.II.29 here—yes, [223.17 here yes,
* 5.II.45 with mother plucking [223.32 with Mother plucking
* 43.I.17 "Well, now [224.15 Well, now
* 43.I.36 his work room lettering [224.27 his work-room lettering
* 43.II.1 the work room, sir, [224.31 the work-room, sir,
* 43.II.1 papa said, "You're [225.8 papa said. "You're
* 43.II.11 words, "It's [225.15 words. "It's
* 43.II.13 up: You've [225.17 up: you've
* 43.II.18 I'd studied [225.20 I'd 'a' studied
  43.II.21 Mr. Hawke would [225.22 Mr. Gant would
* 43.II.22 fine lawyer with [225.22 fine lawyer, with
  44.I.1 Mr. Hawke!" I [227.20 Mr. Gant!" I
* 44.I.22 Temperance arm [227.34 Temperance, arm
  44.I.39 Mr. Hawke!" I [228.12 Mr. Gant!" I
* 44.I.57 him again: he [228.23 him again; he
  44.II.13 Mr. Hawke, I'll [229.1 Mr. Gant, I'll
* 44.II.14 says, "You did [229.2 says, "you did
* 44.II.15 says, "The only [229.2 says, "the only
* 44.II.27 could a wrung [229.11 could 'a' wrung
* 44.II.29 I said, "Let [229.12 I said. "Let
* 44.II.35 to support and [229.16 to support, and
* 44.II.52 then but child! [229.28 then, but child!
* 44.II.54 . . . That nigger [229.29 . . . that nigger
* 44.II.55 You know that [229.30 You know, that
* 44.III.22 he'd a been [230.14 he'd 'a' been
  44.III.25 "Why, Delia! We [230.16 "Why, Eliza! We
  44.III.34 Mr. Hawke took [230.22 Mr. Gant took
* 44.III.36 lived—Yes [230.23 lived—yes
* 44.III.59 is,' "he [231.6 is,' he
* 44.III.60 hollers, " 'There! . . . [231.6 hollers, 'there! . . .
* 45.I.5 'Yes she is [231.10 'Yes, she is
* 45.I.5 damn you, you're [231.10 damn you you're
  45.I.39 says, "Why Delia! Surely [231.32 says, "Why, Eliza! Surely
* 45.II.13 I'd a had [232.21 I'd 'a' had
* 45.II.14 I'd a been [232.22 I'd 'a' been
  45.II.33 "Oh, Delia, I'll [233.2 "Oh, Eliza, I'll
* 45.II.58 came south from [233.19 came South from
  45.III.18 at Columbia, South Carolina [233.32 at Columbus, South Carolina
* 45.III.32 right!¶ Well, [234.7 right.¶ Well,
* 45.III.53 sir: when [234.21 sir; when
* 45.III.57 fire. Now, he [234.24 fire. Now he

* 46.I.48 up. "Now he's [235.26 up. "Now, he's
* 46.I.58 come home, you [235.33 come home you
* 46.II.11 at him: "Well," [236.6 at him. "Well,"
* 46.II.41 the divorce?" I [236.27 the divorce," I
* 46.II.41 said, "You or [236.27 said, "you or
   46.III.2 he had to [237.8 he *had* to
   46.III.7 won't work. Now [237.11 won't wash. Now
* 46.III.14 You'd a got [237.16 You'd 'a' got
* 46.III.16 him: he couldn't [237.18 him; he couldn't
* 46.III.45 "Well now [238.5 "Well, now
* 46.III.55 Greenwood hotel now [238.12 Greenwood Hotel now
* 46.III.58 a schoolteacher that [238.14 a school-teacher that
* 47.I.2 county, I got [238.15 county. I got
* 47.I.12 sir, why yes, wasn't [238.22 sir, why, yes, wasn't
* 47.I.16 a tax-payer like [238.25 a taxpayer like
* 47.I.24 yes: Don't I [238.30 yes: don't I
* 47.I.61 I'd a died [239.22 I'd 'a' died
   47.II.4 she tell *me?* "Oh, [239.24 she *tell* me? "Oh,
   47.III.1 a dam Yankee [240.29 a damn Yankee
* 47.III.16 saller complection, you [241.5 saller complexion, you
* 47.III.39 but law! they [241.21 but Law! they
* 48.I.33 dark black and white sort [242.23 dark black-and-white sort
* 48.I.47 creamy-white complection without [242.33 creamy-white complexion without
   48.III.31 you, Delia, it [245.2 you, Eliza, it
* 49.II.3 know. "I'll cut [246.33 know, "I'll cut
* 49.II.26 you *certainly* know [247.16 you certainly know
   49.II.28 Mistah Hawke,' says [247.17 Mistah Gant,' says
* 49.II.51 my deathrattle,' he [247.32 my death-rattle,' he
* 49.II.56 didn't let-on to [248.1 didn't let on to
* 49.II.57 all—"Do you [248.2 all—"do you
* 49.III.24 bitterness—"Now see [248.22 bitterness— "now see
   49.III.25 Mr. Hawke, surely [248.23 Mr. Gant, surely
* 49.III.53 after that you [249.8 after that, you
* 50.I.23 their mouth, the [249.27 their mouths, the
* 50.I.44 him, "Now my [250.6 him, "now my
   50.I.48 Mr. Hawke, by [250.9 Mr. Gant, by
* 50.I.53 Lord," he said, "You know [250.12 Lord!" he said, "you know
   50.II.11 that's all that he'd a-been [250.26 that's all he'd a-been
   50.II.17 same Perfessor Truman [250.30 same Perfesser Truman
* 50.II.18 Truman (why, [250.30 Truman, why,
* 50.II.20 about, and [250.32 about (and
   50.II.57 bring Delia and [251.23 bring Eliza and

* 50.II.58 you,' "your [251.24 you,' your
* 50.III.8 man—now, boy, [251.30 man—now boy,
* 50.III.14 eye—Oh! that [251.33 eye—oh! that
  50.III.18 Mr. Hawke and [252.3 Mr. Gant and
  50.III.38 see Perfessor Truman? [252.16 see Perfesser Truman?
* 50.III.43 Of course, I wanted [252.19 Of course I wanted
* 51.I.12 said. "Proud," she [253.5 said. "Proud?" she
* 51.I.20 Of course, she [253.11 Of course she
  51.II.30 your—is your [254.26 your ass is your
  51.II.51 with him—Lee and Ed—I tell [255.8 him—Luke and Ben—I tell
  51.II.54 Mr. Hawke to [255.10 Mr. Gant to
* 51.II.54 any minute when [255.11 any minute, when
  51.II.55 and *Ed—Ed* was the one! [255.11 and *Ben—Ben* was the one!
  51.III.61 told Lee he'd [256.22 told Luke he'd
* 52.I.26 of course Eliot [257.7 of course, Eliot
  52.II.9 Mrs. Hawke," your [258.2 Mrs. Gant," your
* 52.II.12 window. Why the [258.4 window. Why, the
  52.II.32 house he was in [258.17 house that he was in
* 52.II.37 her night gown and [258.21 her night-gown and
  52.II.38 Mrs. Hawke," she [258.21 Mrs. Gant," she
* 52.II.44 her children, you [258.25 her childern, you
  52.II.49 halls. Ed was [258.28 halls. Ben was
  52.III.39 "Why, mama," Ed says, [259.29 "Why, Mama," Ben says,
  52.III.54 one," Ed said, [260.5 one," Ben said,
* 52.III.58 thing."¶ So [260.8 thing." ¶ 'So
  53.I.9 to Lee and Ed, "we're [260.16 to Luke and Ben, "we're
* 53.I.28 we'd a found [260.29 we'd 'a' found
* 53.I.33 on, children," I [260.33 on, childern," I
  53.I.36 Mr. Hawke, we'll [261.1 Mr. Gant, we'll
  53.I.48 "Why, mama," Lee says, [261.9 "Why, Mama," Luke says,
  53.II.1 toper Ben Tolly [261.16 toper Gus Tolly
* 53.II.3 house,—here, he [261.18 house—here, he
* 53.II.6 papa had and [261.20 papa had, and
  53.II.9 old Ben Tolly," [261.22 old Gus Tolly,"
  53.II.11 says Lee, "I'll [261.23 says Luke, "I'll
  53.II.19 at Ben Tolly's [261.29 at Gus Tolly's
  53.II.20 heard Ben Tolly [261.29 heard Gus Tolly
  53.II.25 moment Ben Tolly [261.32 moment Gus Tolly
  53.II.29 Mrs. Hawke," he [262.1 Mrs. Gant," he
* 53.II.31 says. "Well, now [262.3 says. "Well now
  53.II.33 "Mr. Hawke is [262.4 "Mr. Gant is
* 53.II.45 could a cut [262.12 could 'a' cut

	53.II.48 says Lee, "and [262.14 says Luke, "and
	53.III.9 said Lee, "you're [262.30 said Luke, "you're
	53.III.11 and Ed will [262.31 and Ben will
	53.III.12 said Ed, "I'll [262.32 said Ben, "I'll
	53.III.15 said Lee, "if [262.34 said Luke, "if
	53.III.18 said Ed, "if [263.2 said Ben, "if
	53.III.46 with Lee and [263.22 with Luke and
*	53.III.49 some night-shirts, shirts, [263.24 some nightshirts, shirts,
	54.I.11 "Why, mama," Lee said, [264.3 "Why, Mama," Luke said,
*	54.I.14 "why, I took [264.5 "why I took
	54.I.29 with Lee, and Ed stayed [264.17 with Luke, and Ben stayed
	54.I.30 course, Ed was [264.18 course, Ben was
*	54.I.32 with mama," he [264.20 with Mama," he
	54.I.34 matter?" Lee said, [264.21 matter?" Luke said,
	54.I.38 said Ed—that [264.24 said Ben—that
*	54.I.42 damned nurse maid," says [264.26 damned nursemaid," says
	54.I.52 said Lee, "this [264.34 said Luke, "this
*	54.I.58 says, "tickee, tickee" [265.3 says, "Tickee, tickee"
	54.II.1 Mr. Hawke had [265.4 Mr. Gant had
*	54.II.12 you know, easy-like [265.11 you know easy-like
*	54.II.27 feller, and [265.22 feller and
	54.II.34 Mr. Hawke," I [265.26 Mr. Gant," I
	54.II.41 to Lee later [265.32 to Luke later
*	54.II.51 say." "Yes," he [266.4 say," "Yes," he
*	54.II.53 right. "tickee, [266.6 right, "tickee,
*	54.II.54 I said, winkin' [266.7 I said winkin'
	54.II.59 Mr. Hawke," I [266.10 Mr. Gant," I
	54.III.6 has," Lee said [266.16 has," Luke said
	54.III.19 "Mr. Hawke has [266.25 "Mr. Gant has
*	54.III.31 there: Your [266.33 there: your
	54.III.40 Well, Ed and Lee got [267.6 Well, Ben and Luke got
*	54.III.52 he'd a ruined [267.14 he'd 'a' ruined
	54.III.53 on: Lee shook [267.15 on: Luke shook
	55.I.8 Mr. Hawke a [267.25 Mr. Gant a
	55.I.14 eye Lee then, [267.30 eye Luke then,
	55.I.26 Captain," Lee says [268.5 Captain," Luke says
*	55.I.31 father accidently mislaid [268.8 father accidentally mislaid
	55.I.33 "would *you* know the [268.9 "would you *know* the
	55.I.45 what you do," [268.18 what to do,"
	55.I.56 us, I tell you [268.29 us, I'll tell you
	55.II.4 to Lee later [268.32 to Luke later
	55.II.8 the eye of [269.1 the eyes of
	55.II.9 flesh crawl." "Yes," [269.2 flesh crawl!" "Yes,"

        55.II.38 "Why, Delia," he [269.22 "Why, Eliza," he
        55.III.14 you swallowed any [270.12 you swallered any
        55.III.49 Mr. Hawke. "Dock [271.3 Mr. Gant. "Dock
*   55.III.58 and, of course, [272.5 and of course,
        56.II.8 Zeb Woodsend's address [272.26 Zeb Pentland's address
*   56.II.8 today"—of [272.27 to-day"—of
        56.II.20 what Woodsend said [273.2 what Pentland said
        56.II.25 Zeb Woodsend proved [273.5 Zeb Pentland proved
*   56.II.38 to ravin' and [273.14 to ravin and
        56.II.50 Mr. Hawke said [273.23 Mr. Gant said
*   56.II.57 your papa I [273.27 your papa, I
*   56.III.7 refinement I said [273.32 refinement, I said
*   56.III.7 your papa than [273.33 your papa, than
*   56.III.18 bite, when [274.6 bite. When
*   56.III.18 got out your [274.6 got out, your
*   56.III.34 new court house and [274.17 new courthouse, and
*   56.III.37 brick," says, [274.19 brick"; says,
*   56.III.46 longer. Why didn't [274.26 longer. Why, didn't
        56.III.47 tell Jenny way [274.27 tell Daisy way
*   57.I.5 but, of course, [275.24 but of course,
        57.I.34 my dealings with [275.26 my dealin's with
*   57.II.26 of course, then, I said [276.28 of course, then I said
*   57.II.48 that trial in [277.10 that trial, in
        57.III.13 Mr. Hawke said [277.27 Mr. Gant said
        57.III.17 Mr. Hawke," he [277.30 Mr. Gant," he
*   57.III.31 he did it looked [278.5 he did, it looked
        57.III.33 Mr. Hawke a [278.6 Mr. Gant a
        57.III.49 Mr. Hawke didn't [278.18 Mr. Gant didn't
        58.I.18 we are about [279.4 we're about
*   58.I.45 they'd a spent [279.25 they'd 'a' spent
*   58.I.47 about, "Look [279.27 about. "Look
*   58.I.51 they'd a stopped [279.30 they'd 'a' stopped
        58.I.57 same Perfessor Truman, [279.34 same Perfesser Truman,
        58.II.1 married Perfessor Truman's [280.1 married Perfesser Truman's
*   58.II.9 today they're [280.7 today, they're
*   58.II.13 enough blood shed already [280.9 enough bloodshed already
*   58.II.15 head, "No," [280.11 head. "No,"
*   58.III.20 harm through [281.21 harm, through
        58.III.47 Mr. Hawke had [282.6 Mr. Gant had
*   59.I.2 course—saloon keeper though [282.15 course—saloon-keeper though
        59.I.28 Major Woodsend," I [282.32 Major Pentland," I
        59.I.49 Mr. Hawke, "there [283.13 Mr. Gant, "there

* 59.II.1 that court-house bell [283.22 that courthouse bell
* 59.II.12 know, says "I [283.29 know, says, "I
* 59.II.42 the flower beds outside [284.17 the flower-beds outside
* 59.II.45 the sitting room door [284.19 the sitting-room door
* 59.III.10 along towards the [284.34 along toward the
  59.III.43 "No, Delia," he [285.25 "No, Eliza," he
* 59.III.43 I'm not and [285.25 I'm not, and
  60.I.33 "No, Delia, you're [286.27 "No, Eliza, you're
* 60.I.42 out towards South [286.33 out toward South
  60.I.56 said, "Delia, I've [287.9 said, "Eliza, I've
* 60.I.57 mountains tonight, and [287.10 mountains to-night, and
* 60.II.5 bare feet and [287.13 bare feet, and
* 60.II.23 his getaway except [287.26 his get-away except
  60.II.38 you, Delia. I [288.3 you, Eliza. I
  60.II.44 Mr. Hawke. Now [288.7 Mr. Gant. Now
* 60.II.54 taking blood-money—"but [288.14 taking blood money—"but
* 61.I.2 reckon towards the [289.28 reckon toward the
* 61.I.29 him, "Ed [290.14 him. "Ed
* 61.I.49 California Truman [290.29 California, Truman
* 62.I.10 he'd a come [293.23 he'd 'a' come
* 62.I.38 the saloon keepers—he [294.10 the saloon-keepers—he
  62.II.49 didn't Lee get [295.23 didn't Luke get
* 62.III.26 woman myself when [296.15 woman myself, when
* 62.III.27 that time eat [296.15 that time, eat
* 63.I.28 and Oh! to [297.26 and oh! to
* 63.I.31 other women when [297.29 other women, when
  63.I.59 and Gil and Jenny were [298.14 and Steve and Daisy were
  63.II.6 got Gil to [298.18 got Steve to
* 63.II.9 says "Damn [298.20 says, "Damn
* 63.II.25 so towards sunset [298.31 so toward sunset
* 63.II.30 the soldiers band a playin' and [299.1 the soldiers' band a-playin' and
* 63.II.43 music, in January [299.10 music. In January
  63.II.46 had tore loose [299.12 had torn loose
  63.II.49 "it's tearing me [299.14 "it's tearin me
* 63.III.1 "My God, My God! What [299.23 "My God! My God! What
* 63.III.10 blossoms—Oh! the [299.29 blossoms—oh! the
  63.III.35 everything standing up [300.14 everything standin' up
* 63.III.37 among it like [300.15 among it, like
* 63.III.38 says "Oh! [300.16 says, "Oh!
* 63.III.47 Lord! You could [300.22 Lord! you could
  63.III.48 them popping from [300.22 them poppin' from
* 63.III.49 worst come to [300.23 worst comes to

* 63.III.52 earth perduce for [300.25 earth produce for
* 63.III.55 Coal company here [300.27 Coal Company here
  64.I.6 shaking, "Delia, it's [300.34 shaking "Eliza, it's
  64.I.9 "Oh, Delia, everything [301.2 "Oh, Eliza, everything
  64.I.16 but Delia, Delia," he [301.8 but Eliza, Eliza," he
  64.I.23 "but Delia, what [301.12 "but Eliza, what
* 64.I.40 is"—why didn't [301.23 is"—why, didn't
  64.I.41 grow up within [301.24 grow old within
* 64.I.60 said. "Why I [302.4 said. "Why, I
* 64.I.61 a flash: Now [302.4 a flash. Now
* 64.II.8 . . . if I'd [302.10 . . . If I'd
* 64.II.19 it did and [302.18 it did, and
* 64.II.22 Mediterranean fruit fly down [302.19 Mediterranean fruit-fly down
* 64.II.22 more fruit fly there [302.20 more fruit-fly there
* 64.II.37 I said, "they may [302.29 I said. "They may
* 64.II.37 have but [302.30 have, but
  64.II.45 you come on [303.1 you can come on
  64.II.47 but Delia," he [303.3 but Eliza," he
* 64.II.58 Nelson, I lay [303.11 Nelson. I lay
  64.III.18 born—Ed and Arthur were [303.28 born—Ben and Grover were
  64.III.30 Mr. Hawke. "You [304.2 Mr. Gant. "You
* 64.III.33 "By God it is!" [304.5 "By God, it is!"
* 64.III.38 I work the [304.9 I work, the
* 64.III.48 this alone [304.18 this, alone

WORKS CITED

A[dams], F[ranklin] P[ierce]. "The Conning Tower." *New York Herald Tribune* Mar. 9, 1935: 11. Print.
Bruccoli, Matthew J., and Park Bucker, eds. *To Loot My Life Clean: The Thomas Wolfe–Maxwell Perkins Correspondence.* Columbia: U of South Carolina P, 2000. Print.
Chamberlain, John. "Books of the Times." *New York Times* Mar. 8, 1935: L19. Print.
Cowley, Malcolm. "Wolfe: Homo Scribens." *A Second Flowering: Works and Days of the Lost Generation.* New York: Penguin, 1973. 156–90. Print.
Fadiman, Clifton. "Thomas Wolfe." *New Yorker* Mar. 9, 1935: 79–82. Print.
Fitzgerald, F. Scott. *A Life in Letters.* Ed. Matthew J. Bruccoli. New York: Scribner's, 1994. Print.
Jack, Peter Monro. "The Turbulence of Mr. Wolfe." *New York Times Book Review* Nov. 24, 1935: BR6. Print.
Kennedy, Richard S., ed. *Beyond Love and Loyalty: The Letters of Thomas Wolfe and Elizabeth Nowell.* Chapel Hill: U of North Carolina P, 1983. Print.
Magi, Aldo P., and Richard Walser, eds. *Thomas Wolfe, Interviewed.* Baton Rouge: Louisiana State UP, 1985. Print.
O'Hara, John. *Selected Letters of John O'Hara.* Ed. Matthew J. Bruccoli. New York: Random, 1978. Print.

Paterson, Isabel M. "Turns with a Bookworm." *New York Herald Tribune Books* Feb. 24, 1935: 18. Print.
Perkins, Maxwell. *Editor to Author: The Letters of Maxwell Perkins*. Ed. John Hall Wheelock. New York: Scribner's, 1950. Print.
Rascoe, Burton. "The Ecstasy, Fury, Pain and Beauty of Life: Thomas Wolfe Sings and Shouts in His New Gargantuan Novel." *New York Herald Tribune Books* Mar. 10, 1935: 1–2. Print.
Scott, Evelyn. "Colossal Fragment." *Scribner's Magazine* June 1935: 2–4. Print.
Wolfe, Thomas. "The Bums at Sunset." *Vanity Fair* Oct. 1935: 30, 62. Print.
———. "Circus at Dawn." *Modern Monthly* Mar. 1935: 19–21, 52. Print.
———. "The Cottage by the Tracks." *Cosmopolitan* July 1935: 48–49, 176. Print.
———. "Dark in the Forest, Strange as Time." *Scribner's Magazine* Nov. 1934: 273–78. Print.
———. "Death the Proud Brother." *Scribner's Magazine* June 1933: 333–38, 378–88. Print.
———. "The Face of the War." *Modern Monthly* June 1935: 223–31, 247. Print.
———. "The Far and the Near." *Cosmopolitan* July 1935: 48–49, 176. Print.
———. "The Four Lost Men." *Scribner's Magazine* Feb. 1934: 101–8. Print.
———. *Four Lost Men: The Previously Unpublished Long Version, Including the Original Short Story*. Ed. Matthew J. Bruccoli and Arlyn Bruccoli. Columbia: U of South Carolina P, 2008. Print.
———. *From Death to Morning*. New York: Scribner's, 1935. Print.
———. "His Father's Earth." *Modern Monthly* Apr. 1935: 99–104. Print.
———. "In the Park." *Harper's Bazaar* June 1935: 54–55, 104, 106, 108. Print.
———. *The Letters of Thomas Wolfe*. Ed. Elizabeth Nowell. New York: Scribner's, 1956. Print.
———. *Look Homeward, Angel*. New York: Scribner's, 1929. Print.
———. "No Door." *Scribner's Magazine* July 1933: 7–12, 46–56. Print.
———. *Of Time and the River*. New York: Scribner's, 1935. Print.
———. "Only the Dead Know Brooklyn." *New Yorker* June 15, 1935: 13–14. Print.
———. *Stories* [Salesman's Dummy for *From Death to Morning*]. New York: Scribner's, 1935. Print.
———. "The Web of Earth." *Scribner's Magazine* July 1932: 1–5, 43–64. Print.

The Magic Tower: An Unpublished One-Act Play by Tennessee Williams

NICHOLAS MOSCHOVAKIS
Independent Scholar

DAVID ROESSEL
The Richard Stockton College of New Jersey

Introduction

On April 21, 1936, Tennessee Williams (1911–83)—then twenty-five years old and still using his given name, Thomas Lanier Williams—received the following letter, as transcribed by his mother, Edwina Dakin Williams (1884–1980), in her memoirs:

My dear Mr. Williams,
  It gives me great pleasure to tell you that your play "The Magic Tower" has been awarded the prize in the Webster Groves Theatre Guild Contest. The decision of the judges was unanimous.
  My warmest congratulations to you, and may your pen continue to flow freely!
Very Truly Yours,
Mary Gaylord Cobb
Contest Chairman
Webster Groves Theatre Guild
(73)

The Webster Groves Theatre Guild was an amateur group in a wealthy St. Louis suburb. For winning its playwriting contest, Williams received an inscribed sterling-silver plate—and, far more welcome, "a promised fall production" (Leverich 168). That amateur production of *The Magic Tower*, on October 13, 1936, was the first recorded staging of any play composed entirely by the man later known as Tennessee Williams.
  To be sure, *The Magic Tower* was not the first time Williams saw words that he had written performed. In the summer of 1935, staying with his grandparents in Memphis, he wrote a short play with Bernice Dorothy

Shapiro titled *Cairo! Shanghai! Bombay!* for a neighborhood dramatic group (Leverich 152-53). Looking back, Williams would claim to have written the whole thing himself (except for "a quite unnecessary and, I must confess, an undistinguished prologue"), and remembering its performance on a lawn in Memphis, he would say, "Then and there the theatre and I found each other for better or for worse" (*Memoirs* 41-42).

But if Williams and the theater found each other in the summer of 1935, it would be some time before they realized they were meant for each other. When Williams returned home to St. Louis in September 1935, he devoted himself to poetry and short stories. As Donald Spoto observes, "[I]n 1936 and 1937, seven poems by T. L. Williams were published in *College Verse*, four in *Poetry*, and nine in the [Washington University] *Eliot*" (51). His mother would later claim responsibility for pushing him toward drama:

> I take some credit for launching Tom on his career as a playwright, although he has said "My conversion to the theatre arrived as mysteriously as those impulses that enter the flesh at puberty." Perhaps his "conversion" was not quite as mysterious as he would make it, but rather, achieved in large part by hard work. At any rate, twenty-six years ago, in the spring of 1936, I noticed in the newspaper that the Webster Groves Theatre Guild ... was offering a prize for the best one-act play. I suggested to Tom, "Why don't you enter this contest?"
>
> "Look at the deadline, Mother," he said, reading the announcement. "I'll never make it. It's nearly here."
>
> "You can do it," I urged him, remembering the speed with which he often wrote.
>
> The next thing I knew, he was in his room and I heard the typewriter going like mad.... (E. D. Williams 72-73)

Nevertheless, Williams's notebooks and journals of the period fail to mention the Webster Groves contest or the award. Similarly, his few references to the production of *The Magic Tower* show scant enthusiasm. After seeing a rehearsal on October 9, he writes: "Disappointed in the play. Too sugary." And the night before the play's first performance on October 13, he notes: "Tomorrow night my play – feel absolutely no interest – Isn't that silly?" (*Notebooks* 63).

A paradoxical reason for Williams's lackluster feelings about *The Magic Tower* may be that, well before it opened, the local publicity resulting from the Webster Groves prize had already helped Williams gain a foothold in an edgier and more compelling segment of the St. Louis dramatic scene. In September 1936 he had met with Willard Holland—director of a "progressive" local theater group, the Mummers—about a socially conscious full-length script by Williams titled *Candles to the Sun* (Mitchell 95, 97).

Holland wanted to direct a rewritten version (*Selected Letters* 93). When in March 1937 the play opened, it was positively reviewed (Mitchell 99). Writing in a later essay that "[t]he Mummers of St. Louis were my professional youth," Williams would eulogize the troupe's wild spirit and claim that their audiences never left the theater "without a disturbing kink in their nerves or their guts" ("Something Wild . . . " 44, 45).

In addition, before *The Magic Tower* opened in 1936, Holland had asked Williams to write a prologue for an upcoming Mummers antiwar production (Irwin Shaw's [1913–84] *Bury the Dead*). On the day of the first performance—November 11, Armistice Day—Williams wrote of his own contribution: "Holland has made something very clever out of it. He's a genius I think – a real genius – though I can't say I like him especially as a person. He's too slippery. I enjoy working with 'The Mummers'. A delightful bunch of young people. Nothing snotty or St. Louis 'Social' about them" (*Notebooks* 65). Does that last, snide allusion sum up Williams's views of the Webster Groves Theatre Guild? One cannot be sure, but given Williams's general silence about his work with the Guild, it is safe to infer that he was never much impressed by the group or its members. In contrast, he would continue working with Holland's group for three years in what became his true theatrical apprenticeship. Yet without the recognition of *The Magic Tower* by the Webster Groves Theatre Guild, this crucial link between Williams and the Mummers might never have been forged.

If Williams was less than enchanted with *The Magic Tower* as staged by Webster Groves, his disappointment does not detract from the play's interest for us as an early example of the young author's characteristic preoccupations and a document of his technical progress in the playwright's art. In the words of a 1936 reviewer, Anne H. Jennings (*Notebooks* 60), *The Magic Tower* "treats of the love of a very young, not too talented artist and his ex-actress wife, a love which their youthful idealism has translated into a thing of exquisite white beauty. They call the garret in which they live their 'magic tower' and are happy there until the artist's belief in his star fails. Then the magic tower becomes a drab garret once more" (qtd. in E. D. Williams 74). The same romantic theme of the necessity of illusion will reappear in the desperate compulsion of later, greater Williams characters—such as Blanche DuBois—to conceal reality's pitiful bare lightbulb with the colorful paper lanterns of fantasy. In *The Magic Tower*, when Jim asks Linda, "It's all just make-believe, isn't it?" she responds, "Of course it isn't! It's absolutely real." But in fact their tower will not endure. Linda gives up on her life with Jim when he, disappointed by a prospective patron and suddenly disgusted by the squalor around him, lashes out at the fantasy and destroys it: "Magic tower, boloney!" Linda replies, "I thought you said—in this state of enchantment—in which we lived—nothing ever happened—nothing ever mattered except our having each other!" Jim:

"These were pretty words!" Linda: "You didn't mean them? . . . I see—just words!" Linda, who has spent years successfully creating illusion on the stage, cannot manage to make the real world cohere with her hopes. But that is only because Jim proves unequal to those hopes, hopes that Linda has managed to sustain for him and his artistic future—until now. To quote Harold Arlen's (1905–86) lyrics from the 1933 hit "It's Only a Paper Moon," sung by Blanche in scene 7 of *A Streetcar Named Desire* (1947): "[I]t wouldn't be make-believe If you believed in me."

Williams must have been brooding on his own insecurities as he developed these archetypal romantic themes—the vital illusion and the broken spell—into a one-act play about the artist's paramount need for faith in his vocation. As he halfheartedly awaited its production in October 1936, he confided to himself: "If only I could always love my work – then I would be a great artist" (*Notebooks* 63). At this time the future Tennessee saw ruefully that much of his own apprentice work, like Jim's in *The Magic Tower*, was "all wet," that he still needed years to "master [his] technique." Moreover, until the end of his life, Williams would be dogged by a fear of such double-edged dismissals as the one Jim hears from the connoisseur and impresario in *The Magic Tower*: that "the world wasn't ready quite yet for my kind of art." Despite such fears, Williams would forever challenge himself to keep building his magic towers under conditions that were—inwardly, if not materially or financially—every bit as adverse as Jim's.

For all the inadequacy of *The Magic Tower* in Williams's eyes, its production gave him his first chance to see one of his serious dramatic efforts undergo the refining process of rehearsal and performance. Certainly the resulting script is reasonably well wrought, both in its fundamental stagecraft and also in its thematic use of symbols and allusions. From the dramaturgical perspective, the central "bay window" upstage allows actors to orient all their movements around what will become the focal point of the play's decisive action (when Linda jerks up the window shade, signaling her intent to leave Jim). And from the poetic point of view, the season is "late winter" to evoke endings: those of a belief, a love, and a couple's shared vision for the future. Opposed to these bleak foreshadowings, and figured in the play's central image of the magic tower, is the vain hope of inhabiting a timeless "state of enchantment" (a phrase used as the title on one of Williams's early drafts) in which "people are never concerned about endings. They just go on and on and on."[1] The same tension between enchanted innocence and disenchanted experience consistently informs the protagonists' dialogue, either consciously or perhaps through dramatic irony. Jim's passing allusions to "Melisande" and "Macushla" become significant if we trace the names to their sources in drama and music. Melisande was a woman who violated her marriage vows in a tragedy by the influential symbolist writer, Maurice Maeterlinck (1862–1949);[2] and

Macushla, in a sentimental parlor song popular during Williams's youth, was the name of an Irishman's lost beloved.[3]

Such fine points suggest that *The Magic Tower* was handled by Williams with considerable care between its first conception and its production. In a sense the play's gestation had begun long before its submission to the Webster Groves contest. Even if it is the case, as Edwina Williams claimed, that her son wrote the prizewinning script on short notice after learning of the contest deadline, that need not mean that he made it up on the spot. On the contrary, such rapid writing can be accounted for partly by Williams's perpetual willingness to cannibalize his previous writings for narrative and thematic elements. In 1931, while at the University of Missouri, Williams had written a story titled "Something By Tolstoi" about two mismatched young lovers who marry: the boy "timid and spiritual and contemplative," his sweetheart "something of a hoyden—full of animal spirits, life, and enthusiasm" (*Collected Stories* 18). As the wife puts it when she tells her husband "their" story after an absence of many years,

> They lived together in a few rooms over a small bookshop which had been left to the boy by his father. They would always have been exquisitely happy together except for one thing; the shop provided little more than a living and the girl was ambitious. She adored the boy—but her discontent grew on her and she was continually urging her husband to enter some more profitable business.... After a time, she received an offer from a vaudeville agent to exercise her talent for music upon the stage. Blinded with the glittering prospect of a theatrical career, she decided to accept the proposition of the vaudeville agent. She returned to the bookshop and told her husband that she was going to leave him. He was too proud to make any effort to keep her, but he handed her a key to the shop and told her that she would be wanting it someday—and that he would always be waiting for her. (*Collected Stories* 24)

After a successful career, she finally comes home to use her key. But her husband, on hearing her tell "their" story, does not seem to remember it and can only murmur that it seems like "something by Tolstoi." Dropping the key, his wife flees the shop. Clearly, Williams had this story in mind when he wrote *The Magic Tower*, although he made adjustments. Linda has already had a vaudeville career, one that still beckons to her. Jim lives the life of an artist, not a bookshop owner (making his dominant concerns much closer to Williams's own). And the couple's difference is not just in temperament but also in age—Linda being some years older, and so more worldly-wise.

Further similarities to early works by Williams may be noted. By March 1936, Williams had completed a version of his one-act play *Moony's Kid*

Don't Cry, about a young man whose adolescent dreams are choked by early marital and familial obligations—a theme that Mitch and Babe skillfully use in persuading Linda that Jim is "tied up" by her love more than he can ever be gratified by it (*Notebooks* 25; see also 20n33).[4] The same fundamental conflict between domesticity and desire would motivate the allegorical action of Williams's 1941 full-length play, *Stairs to the Roof*.[5] Another work of 1941, the one-act play *Thank You, Kind Spirit!*, would reprise the general topic of people's shared belief in a magical world and the indispensability of that shared belief to human happiness. More specific analogies to the plot of *The Magic Tower* can be found in the one-act play *The Fat Man's Wife*, probably completed in late 1937 or 1938; here a woman confronts what is almost certainly her last chance to desert her husband and embark on a life of adventure. Finally, Williams would reuse the metaphor of the magic tower itself in a key scene of *Spring Storm*, a full-length play he wrote for the Mummers under Holland's direction in 1937 and 1938.[6]

In the end, although Williams says almost nothing about the October 13 performance of *The Magic Tower* at Webster Groves High School by the Webster Groves Theatre Guild, he may have come away from that performance with a significant insight. The reviewer of the play concluded:

> Exquisitely written by its poet author and beautifully directed by David Gibson, this play evoked the emphatic response of the audience throughout, in spite of the fact that Elizabeth Rush should *not* have been cast in the role of the heroine. Her nervous acting and hurried speeches failed to convince, largely, we believe, because hysterical parts are her métier. (qtd. in E. D. Williams 74)

Lyle Leverich speculates that the "nervous" actor's performance may have turned the playwright's thinking about stage heroines in a new direction: "Apparently, as acted, the character was the prototype of numerous Tennessee Williams heroines to come, and what he regarded as 'too sugary' would soon become astringent in the plays taking shape in his mind" (185). It would be ironic, indeed, if an overwrought performance by a socialite in an affluent St. Louis suburb helped set Williams on the way to creating Blanche DuBois.

Our copy-text is a typed draft apparently used as a production script by the Webster Groves Theatre Guild. Preserved at the Harry Ransom Humanities Research Center at the University of Texas at Austin (Tennessee Williams Collection, box 24, folder 4), this typescript differs from others filed with it in that it bears numerous handwritten stage directions—in most cases brief blocking directions. It also bears corrections to the dialogue written in Williams's hand. In several places, lines are drawn through Williams's original, typed speeches and stage directions, presumably indicating material deleted from the production.

The edition presented here omits all the passages deleted in the typescript, on the principle that, whoever made these deletions, Williams must be considered to have approved them for the Webster Groves production. The edition similarly includes all the passages of added handwritten dialogue. However, the edition does not reproduce any of the handwritten additions to the stage directions. Such contingent and changeable details of production are not generally retained in plays published as reading texts—and, in any event, many of the handwritten directions clearly were not written by Williams. (Others may appear to be in Williams's hand, though the resemblance is difficult to judge in such brief additions. Generally the interest attaching to matters of staging and blocking is chiefly historical, of secondary importance even to the average scholarly reader.)

The handwritten alterations offer glimpses of the process whereby changes were introduced, for better or for worse, into *The Magic Tower* as the production took its course. Among the improvements one may number most of the deletions; in general these are judicious, and they help to make the action and dialogue less cluttered. There is one regrettable exception—the loss of a stage direction that was typed, then struck through in the copy-text, appearing below Linda's indictment "You're just trying to ruin everything!" (her last line of defiance to Mitch and Babe). At this point, Williams had originally typed "(Babe and Mitch close in upon her like predatory birds, both talking at once)." This deleted direction captures the sinister, almost devilish quality of the two figures as they work their worldly wiles on Linda—successfully tempting her away from a conventional life of marital self-abnegation onto a path that promises greater rewards for her, but only through serving the show business Mammon. Wholly different in motivation, yet interesting at times, are such finicky-seeming changes as the replacement of "before" with "ere ever" in Mrs. O'Fallon's line, "I made him show me the license ere ever I gave him permission to bring you in." This attempt at improving the landlady's Irish dialect reflects a wider cultural interest in ethnicity that, however clumsily practiced by Williams in 1936, would eventually contribute to the complex significance of a character such as Stanley Kowalski.

However, it is among changes for the worse that one must place the last lines: "Goodbye, Jim. Goodbye." These lines are written in, apparently as an afterthought, beneath the final stage direction and before the typewritten "CURTAIN." But the ending seems far stronger without the superfluous addition. Might this ill-considered change have been the cause of the cloying feeling that Williams reported after opening night, when he wrote that his play seemed "too sugary"? Here as elsewhere—though not without reluctance—we have adhered to our editorial principles by including the lines. We have added square brackets to indicate four minor interpolations, either to spell out information that the script indicates (a New York setting is implied by the mention of the Waldorf-Astoria Hotel) or to clarify stage directions in the copy-text.

THE MAGIC TOWER

Characters of the Play

Linda	An ex-vaudeville actress
Jim	A young artist
Mrs. O'Fallon	[An Irish] landlady
Molly	Landlady's daughter
Babe	A chorus girl
Mitch	A vaudeville hoofer

TIME: A rainy Sunday evening in late winter.

SCENE: A [New York City] garret converted into the living quarters of an unsuccessful young artist and his wife. It is a single room, evidently used for all domestic purposes as well as the artist's work. There is a large bay window in the center of the back wall. The door is to the left. In the right hand corner is a table bearing a wash-tub and electric grill, partly concealed by an ornamental screen. In front of the screen (or any other convenient position) is a studio couch with a bright assortment of pillows. About the wall are colorful batiks and watercolors. Facing the bay window is an easel over which is hung an artist's smock, hat and cane. The room has an ingenious, very inexpensive charm.

(As the curtain rises Linda is discovered at the ironing board, front center. She is moving the iron slowly up and down in one spot, her eyes fastened broodingly on Jim. Jim is reading a magazine.

Linda is more mature than Jim. She is still young and fresh but in voice and movement she has an air of quiet wisdom. Her rather cryptic smile is suggestive of emotional reserves and undiscovered depths of experience. There is something of the Mona Lisa about her.

Jim is still a bit adolescent. He is highly intelligent, even brilliant, but hasn't outgrown the impulsive naivete of less experienced youth.

As the play begins a thin curl of smoke is seen rising from Linda's iron.)

JIM: (dropping magazine and sniffing) Do I smell something burning?
LINDA: (with startled gesture) Oh! I'm afraid you do. It's your shirt.
JIM: (jumping up) My white shirt? My _only_ white shirt? Linda, how _could_ you?
LINDA: It was very simple, Jim. I was just looking at you and I completely forgot what I was doing.
JIM: Simple is right! Did it burn very much?
LINDA: Just the tail of it, darling!
JIM: Thank Heavens for that! Hmmm. Maybe I'd better get out of the room when you're ironing my shirts.
LINDA: Please don't! I don't want you to!
JIM: Why not?
LINDA: I like so much having you here.
JIM: (naively flattered) Do you really?
LINDA: (impulsively hugging him) Of course I do, my lord and master! I feel so warm and snug and protected when you are in this little room with me! (She goes over to the bureau and places his shirt in a drawer) It is just as though I were locked up in the top room of a tower with the stairs so long and steep that nobody but you could ever come near me again.
JIM: What a poetic idea that is! I think I'll paint a picture of you, Linda, in your magic tower. . . .
LINDA: (smiling with sudden pleasure) In OUR magic tower!
JIM: Yes, and with your long black hair flowing out of the window like Melisande's. . . .
LINDA: Oh, no. Not out of the window. I never look out of the window if I can help it. It's all so hopelessly ugly out there, those awful billboards and filling stations and delicatessens! I like to think of our—our magic tower—as being surrounded by wonderful green forests. . . .
JIM: Yes, that's it. Green forests! Forests of pine trees!
LINDA: Yes, and lovely clear blue lakes!
JIM: (suddenly laughing as the vision explodes) With crocodiles to eat the bill collectors up!
LINDA: Oh, yes! And a dragon to breathe fire in Mrs. O'Fallon's face every time she comes up for the rent! Oh, no! There wouldn't be any rent or any bill collectors or Mrs. O'Fallons, would there? That's the marvelous thing about living in a magic tower, Jim. There's only two people. The knight and the lady!
JIM: The enchanted prince and princess!

LINDA:	And they're always together. She won't let him leave her.
JIM:	Can't he even go hunting for supper?
LINDA:	No, he can't leave her a single moment because when he's gone the magic tower starts to crumble. If he stays away very long it falls to pieces and turns to a desert island. . . . So even if she moons over him so much that she burns the tail of his only white shirt he has to forgive her and stay right here in the magic tower looking perfectly happy about it!
JIM:	(laughing and returning to the couch with his magazine) Poor old Linda! It's all just make-believe, isn't it?
LINDA:	Make-believe? Of course it isn't! It's absolutely real.
JIM:	You can't tell me you don't find this life pretty dull after the excitement of the show business. Moving around from place to place all the time. . . .
LINDA:	What makes you think I found moving around from place to place exciting?
JIM:	Didn't you? I should think you'd have found it terribly exciting!
LINDA:	Terribly is right. Just like being tied to the tail of a runaway horse.
JIM:	Hmmm. I'd have liked it. Do you know, I've never been outside this city. I've grown up in the middle of it. All this ugliness. Mmmm. I'd give anything to have been the places you've been. At least you've got that. Memories. Things to look back on. . . .
LINDA:	Memories. Yes. I have lots of those. Some of them aren't so swell.
JIM:	And now it's all narrowed down to just this one little room. You must get awfully tired of it. . . .
LINDA:	If I tell you something very seriously will you promise to take my word for it?
JIM:	What?
LINDA:	In this little room I've been completely happy for the first and only time in my life! (She sets the iron on its end) Pull the cord out, will you, Jim. The iron's getting too hot.
JIM:	(obeying this direction) Hmmm. You really mean that, Linda?
LINDA:	Of course I mean it. I'm completely happy here.
JIM:	(stretching out on couch) Why?
LINDA:	I don't know.
JIM:	It isn't a very handsome room.
LINDA:	No.
JIM:	The wall paper is atrocious.

LINDA:	Yes.
JIM:	Nothing very grand about the furnishings.
LINDA:	No.
JIM:	Too hot in summer. Too cold in winter. The roof leaks in (counting wet spots on floor) one, two, three places!
LINDA:	Yes.
JIM:	(filling his pipe) What is it then?
LINDA:	(smiling to herself) I think you know.
JIM:	Something very supernatural I suppose.
LINDA:	No. Something very natural. (She places more ironed pieces in bureau drawers)
JIM:	(laughing) Well, I give up.
LINDA:	I'm surprised at your stupidity. What else could make me completely happy but just—our being here together like this. You and I. A few feet of space between us, that's all!
JIM:	So that's why you're happy!
LINDA:	Yes. That's why I'm happy. So you see it wasn't just make-believe about the magic tower. When two people make their own world there is something rather magical about it, don't you think?
JIM:	And did you mean it about the tower falling to pieces when I go out?
LINDA:	Yes, I meant that, too. When you go out—when you just go out of this room for a moment—something happens.
JIM:	(laughing) The spell is broken!
LINDA:	Yes. The spell is broken. I begin to look around me and I say to myself, "What atrocious wall paper! How damp the air is! If the roof continues to leak at this rate I shall have to learn how to swim before dark!"
JIM:	And what the devil are we going to have for supper tonight!
LINDA:	Oh, yes. That is the most immediate problem. What do we eat and when?
JIM:	I know. Mrs. O'Fallon had chicken for dinner. I'm going to raid the frigidaire right now. (He gets up and runs a comb through his hair)
LINDA:	And leave me up here by myself? I might drown before you get back. No. I'm going with you.
JIM:	I'll say you aren't! If Mrs. O'Fallon caught you in her frigidaire it would be grand larceny.
LINDA:	(sadly) I know. She doesn't approve of me. She thinks I married you for your family fortune. (She gives him a shove toward door) Go on, swipe a drum-stick for me!

	(When Jim goes out Linda's happy manner vanishes. She shrugs her shoulders as though trying to dismiss some oppressive thought. Goes over to the window)
LINDA:	(disgustedly) Rain . . . all the time!
	(She places washbowl under one of the leaking places. Footsteps are heard and rapping at door)
MRS. O:	Mrs. Flynn?
LINDA:	(anxiously) Oh, Mrs. O'Fallon! How charming of you to come up! Just when I was feeling so lonesome. . . .
	(Enter Mrs. O'Fallon. An Irish landlady in acid humor)
MRS. O:	Hmmm. No doubt. Hmmm. I see yer doin' yer wash up here.
LINDA:	(brightly) Oh, yes. I'm quite domestic these days. . . .
MRS. O:	Well, it ain't allowed. It's against the rules o' the establishment, Mrs. Flynn. Roomers ain't allowed to do their wash in the rooms!
LINDA:	(desperately) But Mrs. O'Fallon—Jim and I—we have to save every way that we can. . . .
MRS. O:	Hmmm. No doubt. I should think yer would. Yer five weeks behind on yer rent right now. I've turned out many a roomer in the dead o' winter fer bein' less than that, Mrs. Flynn! This ain't no charitable institution. . . .
LINDA:	I know, I know! I was just saying to Jim this morning—"Dear Mrs. O'Fallon, she's been so patient with us. . . ."
MRS. O:	(acidly) It's yer husband that I've been patient with, Mrs. Flynn. I always have a great deal o' sympathy fer young men like Jim who don't know properly how to take care o' themselves. . . .
LINDA:	I know. Jim has told me how lovely you were to him, Mrs. O'Fallon. Just like a mother, he said!
MRS. O:	Just like a mother, is it? Well, I like that! I'm hardly as old as all that, Mrs. Flynn!
LINDA:	(suppressing a smile) Oh, no! How stupid of me! It was an older sister, he said. Just a like an older sister!
MRS. O:	Hmmm! Yer a bit older than Jim is yerself, ain't you, Mrs. Flynn!
LINDA:	(confused) Why, yes, I am a little bit older than Jim is. . . . but what are you driving at, Mrs. O'Fallon?
MRS. O:	I'll tell yer what I'm driving at! Yer an able-bodied young woman—why don't yer go back to work?
LINDA:	Go back with the show?
MRS. O:	Oh, so it was show business you was workin' in, was it?
LINDA:	(a little defiantly) Yes, it was.

MRS. O:	(significantly) Humph! Well, well! An actress! And did you git fired?
LINDA:	(restraining) Why, no, I did not.
MRS. O:	Then take my advice. Go back to yer show business, girl. Jim Flynn ain't hardly a grown man, yit....
LINDA:	(quietly) He's my husband, Mrs. O'Fallon.
MRS. O:	Oh, I'm aware of that. I made him show me the license ere ever I gave him permission to bring you in. I know these young people!
LINDA:	(desperately) Oh, Mrs. O'Fallon! Jim and I are so happy here. So completely happy. Don't you see—if I went back to the show—all of this would end—we'd be separated—we'd lose each other! (Covers her face with her hands) This wonderful thing that we've made together—this magic tower—would fall to pieces—it would all be ruined!
MRS. O:	What kind o' nonsense is this!
LINDA:	(recovering her poise) I'm sorry.
MRS. O:	You show people! Always putting on an act! I had one before. A Shakespearean actor, he was! Started recitin' Hamlet's solitary ev'ry time I ast him for the rent! Couldn't get a word in edgewise! Humph! I finally had to throw his stuff out the window! Well, I just wanted to warn you, Mrs. Flynn. I have to be more strict about payments from married couples than from single young men—good night! (She starts to leave. Just then Jim enters. He playfully slaps at Mrs. O'Fallon. She instantly thaws)
JIM:	Hello, old sour puss! What's up?
MRS. O:	Git along with you, Jimmy! Always fooling around, you are! You oughta be trounced! (Exit Mrs. O'Fallon, rather mincingly. Jim thumbs his nose at her back as she closes the door)
LINDA:	(after a moment) Oh, that horrible woman! She gives me the creeps!
JIM:	What was it about? The rent? Poor old Linda! She's always picking on you! Lookit here! (From under his coat he produces a drumstick and an evening paper) Success! Here! That's for you!
LINDA:	You eat it, Jim. I'm not hungry.
JIM:	Aren't you really? Well, I am, all right. (Lies on couch reading paper and gnawing drumstick. Linda picks up some sewing. Her face resumes its former quiet smile.)

LINDA:	(softly) I'm glad that you're back. It's so much nicer now.
JIM:	(absorbed in paper) Hmmm.
LINDA:	In a minute I'll forget everything that she said!
JIM:	(jumping up suddenly, his face ecstatic) He's here, Linda, he's here!
LINDA:	(startled and amused) What on earth are you howling about? The new chimpanzee at the zoo?
JIM:	A fine way to speak of our future patron!
LINDA:	(aroused) Our future patron?
	(Jim springs toward her, brandishing paper)
JIM:	T. Anthony Wescott, the most famous art dealer in Europe. The man who discovered half the modern masters. Arrived this morning aboard the Ile de France. Stopping at the Waldorf-Astoria. (Reads from paper) "I am here on business," says Mr. Wescott, "My business is to review the best of contemporary American art. I am especially interested in the work of struggling young men of talent who have not yet acquired a reputation. I shall be the Christopher Columbus of modern art!"
LINDA:	Good Heavens!
JIM:	(grandiloquently) And I . . . I, Mr. Wescott, shall be your Virgin Islands!
LINDA:	What on earth do you mean?
JIM:	I'm going to see him at once!
LINDA:	Going to see him—in all this rain—at the Waldorf—how do you know they'll let you in, darling?
JIM:	Let me in? I'll break the door down! Where's my hat! My cane?
LINDA:	Here.
	(Linda hands him his wide-brimmed hat)
JIM:	Yes, and my cane! All art dealers have canes! I'll break it over his head if he says he's not in! Oh, he'll see me! Won't he, Linda!
LINDA:	Of course he'll see you, darling!
	(She hands him his cane)
	But don't get so excited over it. Act very nonchalant. As though you didn't give a tinker's damn! As though every art dealer in America were simply clamoring for your work! Hadn't you better call him first?
JIM:	Call him? Yes, of course! I'll make an appointment. I'll tell him I'm President of the National Academy. . . .
LINDA:	Oh, no. Tell him you're a millionaire. . . .

JIM:	A multi-millionaire who wants an old master to match his new mistress! That's it! That will make him foam at the mouth—at least till he sees me and the truth comes out! Say, have you got a nickel?
LINDA:	Not a penny, darling.
JIM:	Neither have I. How ghastly poor we are! It should be very easy for us to get into the kingdom of Heaven!
LINDA:	I think we're already there.
JIM:	We will be, Linda. If Wescott gives me a break we'll be made! Never mind the appointment. I'll take him by surprise!
LINDA:	But what will you do for carfare?
JIM:	(ruefully) Suppose I'll have to walk.
LINDA:	Through all this rain!
JIM:	Would you rather I borrowed a dime from Mrs. O'Fallon? Maybe I'd better do that. I'll call her Macushla....
LINDA:	Please don't! Perhaps you'd better wait till tomorrow morning. He'll still be in town.
JIM:	No. Not on your life. Rain brimstone for all I care—I'm going right NOW—I'll think of you all the way—Linda.... (Pulling up collar and turning down hat-brim) That will keep me warm and dry!
LINDA:	I'll think of you, too.
LINDA:	Aren't you forgetting something?
JIM:	(turning back) Oh, I haven't kissed you!
LINDA:	(laughing) I meant your pictures!
JIM:	(snapping fingers) Of course. My pictures. (Dashes around room selecting canvases) Which ones shall I take? I know! The ones of you! I'll take them to bring me good luck!
LINDA:	I've brought you nothing but bad luck, Jim.
JIM:	(gaily) Don't be silly. You're my lucky star.
LINDA:	Your evil star!
JIM:	(selecting pictures) This one and this one ... ah! This one of you in your dancing costume! (Humming to herself, Linda [goes to] portable)
JIM:	What are you doing, Linda? This is no time for music.
LINDA:	It's always time for music. (She puts a Strauss waltz on—"The Artist's Life")
LINDA:	See! He doesn't deny it. I am his evil star.... Dance with me, darling, before you go.
JIM:	(taking her in his arms) Linda! You're so indifferent![7]
LINDA:	Indifferent? Oh, if you only knew! How excited I am!

JIM:	Worried?
LINDA:	Not a bit! Why should I be? There's not a doubt in my mind, I'm so sure of you, Jim!
JIM:	(beaming with pride) Are you really? (They dance gaily around the room)
LINDA:	Remember to ask him for an advance payment, Jim. We're five weeks behind on the rent!
JIM:	Five weeks? Ho, ho! That's nothing!
LINDA:	And guess what we're having for supper tonight?
JIM:	Nightingale tongues! We'll have nightingale tongues!
LINDA:	(shouting) Half a loaf of stale bread!
JIM:	(breaking away and clasping his ears) Well, half a loaf is better than none!
LINDA:	(burying her head on his shoulder and hugging his) But it's such stale bread, darling. So dreadfully stale. It would ruin your dental work!
JIM:	Remember the Bishop of Bingen?[8] While everyone else was stricken with famine he locked himself up in a tower filled with good grain. Alas, poor fellow! The rats ate him up.
LINDA:	(laughing) What's the moral, please?
JIM:	We'll never be eaten by rats! (Picking up canvases) The filthy little rats of greed will never get into this magic tower of ours, will they, Linda?
LINDA:	(smiling) Of course they won't!
JIM:	There is something magical about it, isn't there?
LINDA:	This little room of ours?
JIM:	Yes. Our magic tower. With stairs so long and steep that nobody but you and I can ever reach it! (Goes to door smiling raptly) It's like living in a state of enchantment, isn't it, Linda? (opening door) Don't you feel that way about it sometimes, Linda?
LINDA:	(softly) Of course I do. I feel it so strongly sometimes that I'm frightened!
JIM:	Why frightened?
LINDA:	I wonder where it will end.
JIM:	(laughing) Then you aren't really enchanted. In a state of enchantment people are never concerned about endings. They just go on and on and on. Nothing ever happens. Nothing, I mean, that really matters.
LINDA:	How thrilling that sounds! I wonder if it's true?
JIM:	I'll prove it to you, Linda!

LINDA:	(gently) I'm sure that you will.
	(She kisses him and he goes out the door)
JIM:	(going down stairs) And nightingale tongues for supper! Remember that. Walking in wet weather gives me such an appetite! So long. . . .
LINDA:	(standing in doorway) I wish you weren't going.
JIM:	(from the stairs) Why?
LINDA:	When you're gone the magic tower isn't safe. I have such awful thoughts!
JIM:	About me?
LINDA:	No. About me. I think what a bother I am. How happy you'd be without me. Just think, if it wasn't for me you'd still be a gay young student without a care in the world!
JIM:	You lovely fool! I'd be the world's most miserable man! So long. . . .
LINDA:	Goodbye, Jim. Good luck!
	(She stands in the opened doorway until he is out of sight. Then she closes the door. She leans against it a moment with a faint, brooding smile)
LINDA:	(advancing to the center of the room and looking slowly around) Our magic tower! Our lovely, leaking tower!
	(At this point the stage is briefly darkened to indicate the passing of a few hours' time. During this interval Linda has undergone a transformation. With Jim absent she is no longer the self-contained young woman that she appeared to be in the beginning of the play. The romantic spell is lifted so that she can see more clearly the darker aspects of their situation. She is pacing restlessly around the room, now and then glancing toward the window with a fretful gesture as the lights go on. Someone knocks at the door)[9]
LINDA:	(slightly cringing) You, Mrs. O'Fallon?
MOLLY:	Naw, it's me!
LINDA:	(slightly relieved) Oh, Molly. Come in.
	(Enter Molly, a gangling, freckle-faced girl of 15)
MOLLY:	There's company to see yuh, Mizz Flynn.
LINDA:	(with sudden apprehension) SHHH!
MOLLY:	(loudly) Whatsamatter?
	(Linda softly closes the door)
LINDA:	Is it a big fat man with a brief case?
MOLLY:	A brief case o' what?
LINDA:	(desperately) Oh, a satchel, a leather case—you know—is he a bill collector or something like that?

MOLLY: (giggling) Oh! I thought you meant a case o' measles or something! Oh, my! Guess what he called you, Mizz Flynn? He called you the Duchess. He says tell the Duchess. . . .
LINDA: (delighted) It's Mitch!
(Throws open door and runs out on landing)
MITCH! Is it you?
MRS. O: [(from downstairs, offstage)] Molly! Molly!
MITCH: (from below) Me and the Babe!
MOLLY: Well, I will be seeing you, Duchess. [(exit)]
LINDA: Oh, BABE!
BABE: Yeah. It's me. We're waitin' for the elevator.
LINDA: (terribly agitated) How — — — are you!
(She [comes] back into the room with both hands pressed to her face. Babe and Mitch are heard climbing the stairs)
BABE: (puffing) Seventy-eight, seventy-nine, eighty! Whew! My stars and fallen arches! I wouldn't climb another five flights to Heaven!
(Enter Babe and Mitch. They are a flashily dressed young couple, good-looking and good-natured but not too sensitive: distinctly theatrical types)
BABE: Duchess! Fer cryin' out loud!
(She drops a large, paper-wrapped bundle and flings arms around Linda's sobbing figure)
MITCH: Say, what kind of a reception is this, I'd liketa know. I've played to some pretty dead pans in my time, but never, never have they busted out crying the moment I walked on the stage. Not even when me and Sarah Bernhardt. . . .
BABE: Can it, Mitch!
(He laughs and throws an arm around Linda)
LINDA: I'm sorry! It just struck me all of a sudden. . . .
MITCH: What the devil! Didja think we wasn't gonna play this town any more? Lookit here, Duchess! A wedding present!
(He picks up package Babe dropped)
LINDA: (taking it) Oh, how sweet!
(Still crying a little she kneels on the floor to unwrap the package)
Oh!
BABE: Yeah. A traveling bag!
MITCH: (significantly) Show people can always use an extra piece of luggage oncet a while. . . .
LINDA: (slightly embarrassed) It's beautiful! Jim and I will use it on our honeymoon. We're planning to have one some day.

BABE: (surveying the room) Criminently, what a dump! Parlor, bedroom and bath all in one!
LINDA: (laughing) There isn't any bath. Jim says that baths are an affectation of the idle rich!
BABE: A what? Hmmm. What kind of a guy is this husband of yours?
MITCH: No bath-tub? Gosh, Duchess, what do you make your gin in? Well—(he looks at leaking places in roof) I see you got plenty of running water, anyway!
LINDA: Isn't it awful? It's been leaking all afternoon! But when the sun comes out it's really very pleasant in here!
(Mitch seats himself on the floor beside her)
MITCH: So this is where you've been hiding out since you quit the show?
LINDA: This is it!
(Takes Mitch's handkerchief to wipe her eyes)
Oh, it really isn't as bad as it looks! It's what they call a—a studio apartment! All young artists have places like this!
BABE: I getcha. Bohemian, huh? Sure. This is really the stuff. Atmosphere. Color. Cockroaches and a leaking roof—well, where's the master of the house?
LINDA: (proudly) He's calling on T. Anthony Wescott at the Waldorf-Astoria. He just arrived this morning aboard the Ile de France.
BABE: The Eel de Frawnce? Well, fawncy that! Don't you remember, my dear, that's where we met the Count and Countess De Tootsie! It was simply ripping, you know, how the Count dunked his monocle in Lady Clamfeather's soup!
LINDA: Oh, Babe! Crazy as ever—Wescott's an art-dealer—Jim's gone to show him some of his pictures and if he'll just take an interest in Jim's work it will mean everything for us! It will mean—
([Goes or turns] to window)
Just everything!.... Oh—I wish this rain would stop! Poor Jim will get soaking wet!
MITCH: So Jim's the name. What's the rest of it?
LINDA: Mr. and Mrs. James Oliver Flynn!
MITCH: Fancy monicker, that! Look good on a billboard. Mr. and Mrs. Flynn and the Five Little Flying Flynns! How about it, Duchess? What can he do? Dance, patter, croon—adagio?
LINDA: He's an artist, you nut! Haven't you ever head of an artist before?

MITCH:	Sure. An artist is a guy that's out of a job and don't give a damn. (He opens a cigaret case and offers to Linda. Linda and Babe take cigarets) Seriously, Duchess, how are you fixed?
LINDA:	Okay.
BABE:	Come on. No stalling. What's the real situation. On the rocks, huh?
LINDA:	(smiling bravely) Everything is okay.
BABE:	Yeah. Everything including the roof. You look like you haven't had a square meal in a couple of weeks!
MITCH:	Come on, Duchess! You don't have to put on an act with us!
LINDA:	(walking back to the window) Oh, he works so hard, poor Jim! It's pitiful how hard he works. And nothing ever comes of it! Nothing at all!
MITCH:	(harshly) Just as I thought! He's a ham! Come on, Duchess, pack up this new traveling bag and let's get going!
LINDA:	What on earth do you mean?
BABE:	You know that you can get your old job back.
LINDA:	You two must be crazy!
MITCH:	You're going out on tour with us, Duchess. Bergmann said so. He sent us out here to get you. All is forgiven, come home, he said!
LINDA:	Give Mr. Bergmann my regrets. I'm not available this season—Say—what do you all think I am? Do you think I'd walk out on Jim just because things are a little tough right now? I'm not any quitter!
BABE:	You walked out on the show pretty quick!
LINDA:	(smiling) I wasn't in love with the show.
BABE:	So you're in love with this sap?
MITCH:	Of course she ain't. Not the Duchess. She always had too much sense. The smartest girl in the show, Bergmann used to say—
LINDA:	I am in love with him! Of course I am. (Turns her back to them) And if you're going to talk about him like that—
MITCH:	(good humoredly) The same old Duchess! Always on the high horse about something—
BABE:	Be sensible, kid—!
LINDA:	(seating herself on the couch) Oh, it's like the show business and everything else. You have to work your way up.
MITCH:	Yeah, but in the show business even the back row hoofers get regular pay. What do you folks live off of, huh? Love and a dime?

LINDA:	(laughing) Love and thirty cents!
BABE:	(sitting beside Linda) Thirty cents!
LINDA:	He gets thirty cents an hour posing at the art school where he used to study.
MITCH:	Posies, posies, who will buy my posies?
LINDA:	Once in a while he paints an advertising poster—that helps out some.
MITCH:	Swell. You can give him a job some day painting your signs on Broadway!
BABE:	And so that's how you live? How do you do it, honey?
LINDA:	I don't know. Really I don't. We just get along somehow. Oh, you needn't feel so terribly sorry for me. I've changed. I'm not the girl that I used to be. Something has happened to me since I've been with Jim. Something terribly funny.
MITCH:	I can see that!
LINDA:	There's something mysterious about this little place of ours—we call it our magic tower—when we're in it together we're perfectly happy. We haven't a care in the world. You'd think that we were millionaires!
MITCH:	Poor Duchess! She's gone off her nut!
LINDA:	You think I'm crazy?
MITCH:	Crazy? I'll say so! Bergmann's little pet she was! He pays her fifty a week and like that (snapping fingers) she walks out on the show! Marries a poor punk in a red beret....
LINDA:	(rising indignantly) He doesn't wear a red beret!
MITCH:	Marries a poor punk that stands up naked for thirty cents an hour....
LINDA:	He doesn't stand up naked!
MITCH:	Well, anyway, you married him, didn't you?
LINDA:	Yes, I married him! I was <u>crazy</u> about him!
BABE:	Hear that, Mitch? She WAS crazy about him, but she ain't any more!
LINDA:	(smiling and walking over to window) Was, am, and always will be! (looks out) Still raining—My heavens! Jim will be drowned!
BABE:	(winking at Mitch while Linda's back is turned) Honey, if you're so <u>crazy</u> about this artist guy, why don't you give him an even break?
LINDA:	What do you mean, an even break? I do everything that I can do to help Jim out! I wash his clothes, pose for him, mix his paints....
BABE:	I don't mean that. You know what I mean—he'll never get nowhere tied to your apron strings!

LINDA:	(her face darkening) Tied to my apron strings?
BABE:	These artists never get married, honey, until they've made a success. They can't afford to. It ruins their ca-<u>reer</u>!
MITCH:	Funny she ain't thought of that herself! The Babe is right, Duchess! You gotta look at it that way—you don't want to be a rock around this guy's neck!
LINDA:	A rock around Jim's neck? (There is a minute of silence. Babe and Mitch eagerly studying the gathering darkness on Linda's face)
LINDA:	(as if to herself) A rock—No, I couldn't be that! (She walks distractedly about the room)
BABE:	(harshly) That's what you'll be! Mark my word!
MITCH:	(following Linda) Babe's right about it, Duchess! That's the way you got to look at it! If you really love this guy....
BABE:	(eagerly) You don't want to spoil his chances!
LINDA:	(clasping her ears) Stop! I won't listen to any more of it! You're just trying to ruin everything!
BABE:	Think of the future, Duchess!
MITCH:	Yeah, the future!
BABE:	You're making an awful mistake, Honey, if you don't consider....
MITCH:	You've got too much sense—
LINDA:	Oh, stop! Please....
BABE:	Just think! If he wasn't tied up what he could do!
LINDA:	Tied up? No!
BABE:	If he wasn't tied up like this he could go to Europe and study in one of them fancy schools over there! That's where all the real artists go!
MITCH:	Sure! They ain't got a chance if they don't!
BABE:	How old is he, Duchess? I bet he's just a kid!
MITCH:	Listen! A smart young feller who ain't tied up with no dame—
BABE:	He can always make his own way!
LINDA:	No, no! I couldn't go on without Jim!
BABE:	Yes, you could, and you will. The show's pulling out tonight. You're going with us!
LINDA:	Oh, please—you're making me dizzy!
MITCH:	We open tomorrow in Chicago. Play there one week. Then South to St. Louis. New Orleans for Mardi Gras time. After that we go West. A coast to coast tour!
BABE:	We play the Palace in Los Angeles. That's just a couple of hops from Hollywood, kid! Say, with your talent and brains—

MITCH:	And her good looks!
BABE:	Bergmann always said—
MITCH:	She'll <u>wow</u> them!
BABE:	You bet she will. Good old Duchess. She always did. You should've seen Bergmann, Honey, the night you pulled out of the show. There was tears in his eyes. Honest to God, tears in his eyes! Wasn't there, Mitch?
MITCH:	He was all broken up!
LINDA:	Bergmann....
	(Linda shivers and covers her face with her hands)
BABE:	(harshly) Lookit her hands, Mitch! She's got dishwater hands!
MITCH:	Imagine that! The Duchess with dishwater hands!
BABE:	(softening) Never mind, honey, a little cold cream rubbed in every night....
LINDA:	Don't!
MITCH:	(glancing at wristwatch) Come on, Linda. Pack up. The train pulls out at seven.
BABE:	(nudging him) Give her time, give her time! Let her think it all over. Maybe she'd rather have him throw it up to her some day how she spoiled all his chances!
LINDA:	(gasping) Spoiled his chances!
	No, no, I'll never do that! I'll do anything but that!
BABE:	(again winking at Mitch) Just give her time. She has to think things over. It's the future she has to look out for, Mitch. Five or ten years from now....
LINDA:	Five or ten years! Oh....
BABE:	Yeah, if things keep on like they're going now, you won't be so young no more in five or ten years. He'll get tired of you maybe. He'll look at you while you're bending over the wash-tub with your face all red and sweaty and your hair in your eyes and he'll say to himself, "There she is! My ball and chain! If I wasn't tied to her apron strings...."
LINDA:	(desperately) Stop it! Stop it, Babe! I can't stand anymore!
MITCH:	She's right, Duchess, the Babe is absolutely right!
	(There is a long silence. Linda slowly gets up from the couch. Mitch hands her his handkerchief.)
LINDA:	(brokenly) Maybe she is—I don't know.
MITCH:	(eagerly) There now! That's more like it.
BABE:	(throwing her arms around Linda) See! I knew she would come to her senses! It's just like Bergmann said, she's too smart....

MITCH: Won't old Bergmann throw a fit when he sees her down at the station? The old boy'll break down and cry. . . .
LINDA: (wringing the handkerchief) Wait! Not all at once! I can't decide right off like this!
BABE: You've got to, Honey! It's the only way!
LINDA: What time is it, Mitch?
MITCH: A quarter to six.
LINDA: He ought to be back by now.
MITCH: Don't wait for him. He'll talk you out of it!
BABE: Just do what you know is best for him, Duchess.
LINDA: What's best for him.
MITCH: Pack your things. Be ready in half an hour, Duchess.
BABE: Swell!
LINDA: How can I know—maybe you're wrong.
MITCH: What?
LINDA: If Wescott gives Jim a break?
BABE: You'd stick with him, kid. You'd be all right.
MITCH: Say, it's a cinch. We'll phone the station and reserve your berth. Yeah, a compartment.
BABE: We'll have a real celebration tonight. We'll have a time!
MITCH: Back on the road with the Duchess!
LINDA: You go too fast for me.
MITCH: Yeah! Back on the road.
BABE: Take it easy, Mitch.
LINDA: I don't know what you're talking about.
MITCH: Those pictures are no good. They ain't got anything!
BABE: Say, kid, how'll we know about this Wescott deal—if it goes through or not? Will you give us a ring?
MITCH: No time for that. Give us the old Bronx semaphore.
BABE: What's that?
MITCH: Honey, that's what got me out of many a tight spot before you and me started going steady! Look! It's like this. The dame goes to the window and if the coast is clear she hoists the shade like this—that means she's going, or I'm coming, as the case may be — — —
BABE: The Voice of Experience!
MITCH: Get it, Duchess? But if it's no go—if the old man's on the spot—pull the shade all the way down, like this; that means the game is called on account of rain—or something. Get the idea?
BABE: I getcha.
MITCH: Let's run through the routine. We don't want any slip-ups on this.

LINDA:	Up if I'm going—down if I'm not—is that it?
MITCH:	Smart girl! We'll be back in half an hour.
BABE:	Keep your chin up, Duchess. So long! (The stage is darkened for a moment to indicate the passing of about fifteen minutes. Linda is still standing by the window. Footsteps are heard slowly climbing the stairs)[10]
LINDA:	(turning from window, her eyes wide with emotion) JIM! (Door is pushed open and Jim comes in. He stands in the doorway without speaking, a dazed look on his face, the canvases sagging from under his arm) Oh, JIM—your pictures—they're all wet!
JIM:	(laughing bitterly) All wet? Yes! All wet! (Tosses them roughly to floor) That's what Wescott said about them—all wet! (Tosses soaked hat into corner of the room) Only he didn't put it quite so bluntly. Oh, he was very genteel about it. Used a lot of high-sounding language. Talked about planes of consciousness and esthetic values. All the usual tripe. Shook his head very sadly and said he feared the world wasn't ready quite yet for my kind of art. Go back to school, he said, and master your technique. You're still just a boy. You've got years and years, he said. Years and years of what? I asked him. Starvation? He laughed. He said I was taking it much too hard — — Oh, Linda! (He throws himself down on the couch) I'm so terribly disgusted with things! (As he cries her name Linda stretches her arms toward him and a look of tenderness comes over her face. She feels that he needs her now)
LINDA:	(lifting her hand slowly to the window shade) Jim, when I pull this window-shade down do you know what I'm really doing? I'm shutting out the whole world. Mr. Wescott was right, Jim. We have got years and years.
JIM:	(with choking bitterness) Of what?
LINDA:	(pulling the shade slowly down) Of each other!
JIM:	(tossing impatiently on the couch) Each other! Each other! Do you think we can EAT each other!
LINDA:	(astonished) Jim!
JIM:	Come down to earth, woman! You can't stay up in the clouds all your life....
LINDA:	It's not the clouds I'm up in, Jim—it's our magic tower!

JIM:	(brutally) Magic tower, boloney! It's Mrs. O'Fallon's attic that we're up in, Linda! Mrs. O'Fallon's lousey, leaking attic! And we're five weeks behind on the rent! Do you know what's going to happen to us, Linda? We're going to get kicked out on our ears, that's what!
LINDA:	I thought you said—in this state of enchantment—in which we lived—nothing ever happened—nothing ever mattered except our having each other!
JIM:	These were pretty words!
LINDA:	You didn't mean them? (Long silence) I see—just words! (She goes slowly back to the window, gives the cord a jerk, and the curtain flies up)
JIM:	What was that?
LINDA:	(dully) Just the shade flying up. (She turns toward him again. There is a faint, inscrutable smile on her lips) How old are you, Jim?
JIM:	(sleepily) Twenty-one. Why? (crossly) What's that got to do with the situation?
LINDA:	(softly) Twenty-one—how marvelously young that is! I'm twenty-six, Jim. You didn't know that?
JIM:	Gosh, Linda! You say such trivial things!
LINDA:	I know. I have a terribly trivial mind .... poor Jim. You're all tired out. And soaking wet. That long walk through the rain. All for nothing. Here. I'll put the screen in front of the bed. You can undress and have a nap. I still have some ironing to do. After a while you can go down and get a bite to eat from Mrs. O'Fallon! I'm sure she'll be glad to let you have something.
JIM:	(sleepily) She always used to be before I got....
LINDA:	Yes, I know. Before you got yourself tied up with a dame! Oh, well .... (she laughs softly) There's a price for everything! Nothing comes for nothing, Jim. You'll learn that some day. (With the screen drawn in front of Jim's couch, Linda hastily throws her things into the new traveling bag. She darts about the room with an almost frantic rapidity)
JIM:	My God, what a racket you're making! What are you doing?
LINDA:	Nothing much. Just straightening things up a little. I'm nearly through now.
JIM:	And that light's in my eyes. I can't sleep.

LINDA: Just a moment, darling. I'll turn it out.
(Goes over to window with traveling bag in her hand. Looks out, shading her eyes with one hand)
It's clearing up, Jim. The rain has stopped. It's going to be a wonderful night. Oh, my! There's a funny little slice of a moon coming out. Right over the Fixit Garage. It looks like a yellow dancing slipper—

Jim, tomorrow's going to be an awfully swell day! Almost like Spring, I imagine. Those awful wet spots on the floor will dry up—when the sun comes out—it will be very nice in here then—I'm sure it must be much healthier to live in a dry, bright attic—than a magic tower with a leaking roof!

JIM: (furiously) For God's sake, Linda, I'm trying to sleep!
LINDA: I'm sorry—poor Jim!
(Pulls a ring from her finger and lays it on the bureau)
I'll turn the light out now! Jim, are you asleep?
(She looks toward the screen. There is no answer)
Goodbye, Jim. Goodbye.[11]
(She switches off the light and goes quietly out the door and closes it behind her)

CURTAIN[12]

NOTES

We are grateful to Thomas Keith, Allean Hale, and Jackson Bryer for their help and advice—from material assistance in establishing the text, to elucidating its historical and biographical contexts, to the final labor of copyediting and proofing. Thanks are also due to staff at the Harry Ransom Humanities Research Center, especially Andi Gustavson and Richard Workman. In addition, we are indebted to Jeremy Lawrence, Mark Mallett, and the Stockton Theatre Club for their illuminating reading and discussion of *The Magic Tower* at The Richard Stockton College of New Jersey in November 2010.

Tennessee Williams's *The Magic Tower*, from the Tennessee Williams Collection at the Harry Ransom Humanities Research Center, The University of Texas at Austin, is published by generous permission of The University of the South, represented by Georges Borchardt, Inc., New York; copyright © 2011 by The University of the South.

The present scholarly edition of *The Magic Tower* appears simultaneously with a trade edition prepared by Thomas Keith—based on the same copy-text, but with slight differences in editing and formatting—that forms part of his new volume of previously unpublished or uncollected Williams one-acts, issued by New Directions in April 2011.

1. "State of Enchantment (A One-act Play)" is the title of a version of *The Magic Tower* filed at the Harry Ransom Humanities Research Center, in the same box (24) and folder (4) as our copy-text. It contains twenty pages that may or may not constitute a single draft (twelve pages are typed on paper that differs from that used for the other eight pages).

2. *Pelléas and Melisande* was published in French in 1892 and printed in English translation several times over the next few decades, including as part of a collection titled *Chief Contemporary Dramatists* (1915) that Williams the apprentice playwright might well have read. Indeed, the comparison of Linda's hair to Melisande's alludes to a particular scene (3.2) in Maeterlinck's *Pélléas et Melisande* (1892). Both texts frame the hair in a window, adding to

the irony (since Jim and Linda's apartment window will play a key role in the resolution of *The Magic Tower*).

3. "Macushla," with lyrics by Josephine V. Rowe, was published about 1910. It was recorded perhaps most successfully by the famed Irish tenor John McCormack (1884–1945). In it the lover appeals to his beloved to rise from the dead.

4. Allean Hale glosses the earliest version of *Moony's Kid Don't Cry*, the 1932 one-act play *Hot Milk at Three in the Morning*, as Williams's youthful "goodbye to the bonds of family" (14).

5. This point is suggested partly by a comment made in a personal communication from Allean Hale to Nick Moschovakis, July 2001.

6. The plain, awkward librarian Hertha Neilson tells the well-born local youth Arthur Shannon that she is the storybook lady "[e]very Tuesday, Thursday, and Saturday mornings, ten o'clock at the Carnegie Public Library. Have you ever heard what happened to the dark-haired princess in the magic tower when the handsome young prince went out to look for adventure?" (*Spring Storm* 24). Later in the play, a rather drunk Arthur kisses Hertha in the library. He recounts the incident as follows: "The Storybook Lady—the dark-haired princess in the Magic Tower. And I called her—The Carnegie Vestal—I called her that. And kissed her. And then she came alive in my arms and begged me to take her. Because she was like I was, lonely and hungry, and I—I lost my desire. I told her that she was disgusting" (*Spring Storm* 144–45).

7. In the copy-text, above the typewritten word "indifferent!" a hand resembling Williams's has written "incredibly casual." We have not given this reading authority because Linda's reply is not similarly annotated. To perform the alternate reading, it would be necessary to change the opening of Linda's next speech accordingly (from "Indifferent?" to something like "Casual?"). Note as well that the preceding two speeches could be placed slightly differently, as they constitute handwritten additions in the margin of the typescript.

8. On August 10, 1928, Williams, traveling with his grandfather in Europe, wrote his parents that he had taken a one-day trip on the Rhine: "There were many points of legendary & historical interest all along the way such as the Mouse tower of Bingen where the old Bishop of Bingen was supposed to have been devoured by rats" (*Selected Letters* 20). In the story, the Bishop hoarded grain while the population starved, eventually causing all the rodents in the area to come to his tower.

9. A handwritten alternative to the preceding stage direction—possibly added by Williams—reads

"Cut—music bridge."

10. A handwritten alternative to the preceding stage direction—possibly added by Williams—reads

"Music bridge."

11. This is likely one speech and assigned to Linda, as presented here. However, since it is a handwritten addition to the typescript margin and lacks speech headings, it might conceivably be two speeches: the first sentence spoken by Linda, the second (after her exit) by Jim. Having Jim reveal, by bidding goodbye to his departed wife, that he was not asleep but awake, and was presumably alert to her doings, would end the play with a surprise about his real character and would leave the audience curiously reconstructing his motives. So far as the typescript is concerned, either reading is possible.

12. A handwritten alternative to the preceding stage direction—possibly added by Williams—reads

"Music up."

WORKS CITED

Hale, Allean. "Early Williams: The Making of a Playwright." *The Cambridge Companion to Tennessee Williams*. Ed. Matthew C. Roudané. Cambridge, UK: Cambridge UP, 1997. 11–28. Print.

Leverich, Lyle. *Tom: The Unknown Tennessee Williams*. New York: Crown, 1995. Print.

Maeterlinck, Maurice. *Pélléas and Mélisande*. 1892. *Chief Contemporary Dramatists*. Ed. Thomas Dickerson. Boston: Houghton, 1915. 547–72. Print.

Mitchell, Tom. "Tennessee Williams and the Mummers of St. Louis: The Birth of a Playwright." *Tennessee Williams Annual Review* 10 (2009): 91–104. Print.

Rowe, Josephine V., and Dermot MacMurrough. "Macushla: Song. Sung by Mr. John McCormack and by Mr. Chauncey Olcott in His New Play 'Macushla.'" 1910. *Alexander's Ragtime Band and Other Favorite Song Hits, 1901–1911*. Ed. David A. Jasen. N.p.: Dover, 1987. 90–93. Print.

Spoto, Donald. *The Kindness of Strangers: The Life of Tennessee Williams*. Boston: Little, 1985. Print.

Williams, Edwina Dakin, as told to Lucy Freeman. *Remember Me to Tom*. New York: Putnam's, 1963. Print.

Williams, Tennessee. *Candles to the Sun*. Ed. Dan Isaac. New York: New Directions, 2004. Print.

———. *Collected Stories*. New York: New Directions, 1985. Print.

———. *The Fat Man's Wife*. T. Williams, *Mister Paradise and Other One-Act Plays* 119–42. Print.

———. *The Magic Tower*. Tennessee Williams Papers. Harry Ransom Humanities Research Center, U of Texas, Austin. Print.

———. *Memoirs*. Garden City: Doubleday, 1975. Print.

———. *Mister Paradise and Other One-Act Plays*. Ed. Nick Moschovakis and David Roessel. New York: New Directions, 2005. Print.

———. *Moony's Kid Don't Cry*. *American Blues: Five Short Plays*. New York: Dramatists Play Service, 1948. 5–14. Print.

———. *The Notebooks of Tennessee Williams*. Ed. Margaret Bradham Thornton. New Haven: Yale UP, 2006. Print.

———. *Selected Letters of Tennessee Williams, Volume I: 1920–1945*. Ed. Albert J. Devlin and Nancy M. Tischler. New York: New Directions, 2000. Print.

———. "Something Wild . . . " *New Selected Essays: Where I Live*. Ed. John S. Bak. New York: New Directions, 2009. 43–47. Print.

———. *Spring Storm*. Ed. Dan Isaac. New York: New Directions, 1999. Print.

———. *Stairs to the Roof*. Ed. Allean Hale. New York: New Directions, 2000. Print.

———. "State of Enchantment (A One-act Play)." Ts. Tennessee Williams Papers. Harry Ransom Humanities Research Center, U of Texas, Austin. Print.

———. *A Streetcar Named Desire*. New York: New Directions, 1947. Print.

———. *Thank You, Kind Spirit*. T. Williams, *Mister Paradise and Other One-Act Plays* 143–55. Print.

Breaking Fresh Ground:
New Releases from the Willa Cather Edition

JAMES A. JAAP
Pennsylvania State University, Greater Allegheny Campus

YOUTH AND THE BRIGHT MEDUSA. By Willa Cather. Historical Essay and Explanatory Notes, Mark Madigan; Textual Essay and Editing, Frederick M. Link, Charles W. Mignon, Judith Boss, and Kari Ronning. Lincoln: U of Nebraska P, 2009. xii + 613 pp. $80.

SAPPHIRA AND THE SLAVE GIRL. By Willa Cather. Historical Essay and Explanatory Notes, Ann Romines; Textual Essay and Editing, Charles W. Mignon, Kari Ronning, and Frederick M. Link. Lincoln: U of Nebraska P, 2009. xii + 719 pp. $80.

Between 1903 and 1940, Willa Cather (1873–1947) published a volume of poetry, three collections of short fiction, a collection of essays, and twelve novels. Since her death in 1947, Cather's works have continued to fascinate readers and critics, and her reputation continues to grow. The prestigious University of Nebraska Press, publisher of the journal *Cather Studies*, has, since 1992, published eleven highly praised scholarly editions of Willa Cather's works in the Willa Cather Scholarly Edition series. When the series began with *O Pioneers!* (1913) in 1992, Susan J. Rosowski, the late General Editor of the series, and Guy R. Reynolds had a vision (their preface to the first volume is included in all the subsequent books in the edition): "[T]o provide to readers—present and future—various kinds of information relevant to Willa Cather's writing, obtained and presented according to the highest scholarly standards" (preface vii). Under the direction of Rosowski, the series published six scholarly editions. After Rosowski's death in 2004, her vision has continued under the direction of General Editor Reynolds. After publishing editions of *Shadows on the Rock* (1931) and *One of Ours* (1922) in 2006, and *Alexander's Bridge* (1912) in 2007, in 2009 the series published *Youth and the Bright Medusa* (1920), Cather's second collection of short stories, and *Sapphira and the Slave Girl* (1940), her twelfth and final novel. *Youth and the Bright Medusa* consists of eight stories, four of which had previously been included in Cather's 1905 collection,

The Troll Garden, and four written between 1915 and 1920. All focus on art and the artist, and several of her most famous stories, including "Paul's Case" (1905) and "Coming, Aphrodite!" (1920), are included. *Sapphira and the Slave Girl* presents the story of a Southern family, its slaves, and a family divided by issues of race. Like the previous nine, the two most recent volumes of the Willa Cather Scholarly Edition are impeccably researched and thoroughly annotated, and they provide complete discussions of the critical and textual history of Cather's work. Moreover, like the previous volumes, each has been approved by the Committee on Scholarly Editions of the Modern Language Association. These accessible and wonderfully constituted editions are truly a welcome addition to Cather scholarship.

Central to each volume in the Willa Cather Scholarly Edition series is, of course, Cather's work. Using the first edition or first trade edition as the copy-text, the various versions of the specific work are collated, and, after documenting and comparing the substantive and accidental variants, the textual editors decide upon emendations to the text. This text is then examined in relation to other versions. Originally, scholars assumed that very few drafts or manuscripts of Cather's work existed, primarily because of her request to have all manuscripts destroyed. However, research shows this is not the case (Rosowski et al. 387). There are fourteen known prepublication versions of *Sapphira and the Slave Girl.* Examining the changes in these versions, the editors can see how the work developed and progressed. In addition, during Cather's life, her work went through multiple editions, and, in some cases, Cather revised her work after publication. *Youth and the Bright Medusa* includes four stories published in magazines between 1902 and 1905, republished in *The Troll Garden*, and revised again for the 1920 collection. This complex process is clearly discussed in a "Textual Apparatus" that includes a discussion of the work's background and printing history, as well as an exhaustive list of emendations and rejected substantives. The textual editors—the late Charles W. Mignon, Frederick M. Link, and Kari Ronning for *Sapphira and the Slave Girl* and Link, Mignon, Ronning, and Judith Boss for *Youth and the Bright Medusa*—deserve accolades for providing not only an authoritative critical text of each of these Cather works but also an exhaustive discussion of the progression of each text.

Also included in each volume is a "Historical Apparatus" that consists of a historical essay, explanatory notes, and a section of relevant images. According to Rosowski, "Because Cather in her writing draws so extensively upon personal experience and historical detail, explanatory notes . . . provide a starting place for scholarship and criticism on subjects long slighted or ignored" (preface xi). Written by Mark Madigan for *Youth and the Bright Medusa* and Ann Romines for *Sapphira and the Slave Girl*, each historical essay includes a discussion of personal, local, and national history, along with possible prototypes for many of the characters, biographical connections, and contemporary reviews. Each of these essays is supplemented by numerous photographs, illustrations, maps, facsimiles of manuscripts, and other items important to understanding Cather's work. All are outstanding, but the explanatory notes are particularly strong. These comprehensive notes identify Cather's references to such items as family history, popular music, literature, famous artists and painters, news events, and other biographical details. All are carefully documented, and all open many unexplored areas in the study of Cather. Importantly, these explanatory notes also detail many new discoveries that were made while preparing each volume—including the identification of the real-life models for Till and the other slaves in *Sapphira and the Slave Girl* and the robbery of the Denny Estate in Pittsburgh, which Cather drew upon for "Paul's Case."

One particularly interesting facet of these scholarly editions is the obvious care taken by the editors to ensure an enjoyable experience. In addition to the authoritative text and scholarly information, each book's design and layout are very reader-friendly. The font type and size are large and easy to read, and the pages are widely spaced. These choices, as the editors discuss, are directly linked to Cather, who brought her own editorial expertise to the publishing process: "Believing that a book's physical form influenced its relationship with a reader, she [Cather] selected type, paper, and format that invited the reader response she sought" (Rosowski ix). The editors thus "seek to represent Cather's general preferences in a design that encompasses many volumes" (xi). This includes the wide margins, the 6"×9" page layout, and the antique cream color of the paper. The result is a comfortable and enjoyable reading experience.

Cather was a prolific short story writer; she wrote dozens during her career, both beginning and ending her career writing short fiction. *Youth and the Bright Medusa* was her second collection of short stories. The four older stories revised from her first collection, *The Troll Garden*, appear last in the collection, and were written between 1896 and 1905, while Cather lived in Pittsburgh. During these formative years, Cather honed her writing skills as a journalist and editor for several periodicals, and she later taught high school. She also met Isabella McClung and was living in the McClung family home in Pittsburgh. All these stories have a strong connection to the Pittsburgh area. In "Paul's Case," Paul, like Cather, lives in the East Liberty area and attends musical events at the Carnegie Music Hall of Pittsburgh. In researching the edition, the editors discovered, as noted above, that Cather drew upon a real-life event, the robbery of the Denny Estate in 1902, by two young men, James J. Wilson, son of a local Methodist minister, and his cousin Harold Orr. After stealing about two thousand dollars, the two fled to Chicago, but the pair returned to Pittsburgh after they ran out of money. As the editors note, readers at the time would surely have known of the robbery (323–26).

"The Sculptor's Funeral" (1905) is based upon Pittsburgh painter and engraver Charles Stanley Reinhart (1844–96). Cather wrote about Reinhart's funeral for the *Lincoln Courier* in 1897 and was amazed at how few people attended (Cather, *The World* 510–12). According to Mark Madigan, Cather was "intrigued and disturbed" by "the discrepancy between his [Reinhart's] fame in the world and his reputation in Pittsburgh" (330). In "A Death in the Desert" (1903), Cather's friend, Pittsburgh composer Ethelbert Woodbridge Nevin (1862–1901), serves as the prototype for Adriance Hilgarde. Cather met Nevin in 1898, and he died three years later at the age of thirty-eight. "A Wagner Matinee" (1904) is a sentimental story about a woman from Nebraska who returns to Boston to hear a Wagner opera. Even though the story does not directly relate to Pittsburgh, Cather reviewed concerts and operas while working as a journalist, and as Madigan specifically details, Cather "saw Wagnerian opera for the first time in the spring of 1897, when Walter Damrosch brought his Metropolitan Opera company to Pittsburgh's Alvin Theatre" (327).

The first four stories in *Youth and the Bright Medusa*, "Coming, Aphrodite!," "The Diamond Mine," "A Gold Slipper," and "Scandal," were all written between 1915 and 1920, and all focus on the professional and personal lives of opera singers. "Coming, Aphrodite!" is one of Cather's most famous stories, and it centers on a painter, Don Hedger, and his brief affair with a young singer, Eden Bower. Originally titled "Coming, Eden Bower!" and published in *Smart Set* in August 1920, the story was praised by most reviewers of the collection. A critic from the *New York Times* wrote, "If Willa Cather had written nothing except 'Coming, Aphrodite!' . . . there could be no doubt of her to rank beside the greatest creative artists of the day" (qtd. 358). In this story, Don Hedger's idealistic and spiritual devotion to his impressionistic art is contrasted with the primarily material desires of the aspiring opera singer Eden Bower. Although no model for Don Hedger has been identified, the prototype for Eden Bower is Mary Garden (1874–1967), a Scottish-born opera singer who was well known for her acting and voice, as well as for her supposed sexual exploits. Garden may also have been the prototype for the main character, Kitty Ayrshire, in two other stories from *Youth and the Bright Medusa*, "Scandal" and "A Gold Slipper." Both stories, written in 1916, are centered on opera diva Kitty Ayrshire. "Scandal," originally published in *Century* in 1919 and called a "poor story" by James Woodress (283), focuses on the gossip and rumors surrounding the diva. "A Gold Slipper" tells of an industrialist who unhappily attends one of Ayrshire's performances in Pittsburgh, only later to share a compartment with her on the train to New York. Madigan argues that Ayrshire is a combination of three different singers, Mary Garden, Sibyl Sanderson (1864–1903), and Geraldine Farrar (1882–1967; see 339–40). "The Diamond Mine," written and first published in 1916, is based on the character of Lillian Nordica (1857–1914), the famous soprano, whom Cather had seen perform for the first time in 1893 (334).

The publication of *Youth and the Bright Medusa* was a turning point in Cather's career, for it was her first work with Alfred A. Knopf, the publishing house with whom she would spend the rest of her career. Houghton Mifflin had turned down the idea of doing a volume of Cather short stories on the grounds that short stories didn't sell. That was not the case. Published on October 3, 1920, the first printing of 3,500 copies sold quickly, and a second printing of 1,000 copies was issued in late 1920. In total, the first American edition went to seven printings for a total of 8,000 copies (355–56). Critics immediately recognized the quality of Cather's collection. According to Madigan, the "critical response to *Youth and the Bright Medusa* was almost universally positive, with 'Coming Aphrodite!' most often singled out for praise" (356). According to a review in the October 3, 1920, issue of the *New York Times Book Review, Youth and the Bright Medusa* was "decidedly a literary event which no lover of the best fiction will want to miss" (qtd. 358). H. L. Mencken, who had written two reviews of Cather's *My Ántonia* (1918), wrote that Cather was skilled at "the delicate and difficult art of evoking the feelings" (qtd. 360). Soon after the publication of *Youth and the Bright Medusa*, Sinclair Lewis called it "a golden book" (qtd. 365).

Despite being known today primarily for her novels, Cather was a prolific writer of short stories. Her first story, "Peter," was published in 1892, and her last, "The Best Years," was published in 1945, two years before her death. According to Madigan, the stories of *Youth and the Bright Medusa* "have introduced many readers to the author's work. Their lasting reputation suggests that they are created of the same whole as Cather's novels." Madigan asserts that many of Cather's novels, including *O Pioneers!*, which resulted from two short stories, and *My Ántonia*, which is filled with stories and tales, were shaped by the short story. Fortunately for us, Madigan writes, "Cather the novelist never really left the story behind" (365).

While several of the stories from *Youth and the Bright Medusa* were written at the beginning of Cather's career, *Sapphira and the Slave Girl*, as indicated earlier, was Cather's final novel. Begun in the spring of 1937, it took three and a half years to complete and was published seven years before Cather's death. This was a difficult time for her. She visited Virginia for the last time in April 1938, but soon after, her brother Douglass died at the age of fifty-eight, and in October, Isabelle McClung died of kidney failure. For a year, she did not work on the novel, but in the summer of 1939, she returned to writing it. It was published on her sixty-seventh birthday, December 7, 1940.

Set in her birthplace of Virginia in 1856, it is Cather's most personal work, for it draws upon her Southern family history to expose many of the conflicts that divided families and a nation in the years before the Civil War. *Sapphira and the Slave Girl* is also Cather's most developed engagement with Southern life. Critics have often tied her to a specific location, primarily Nebraska, and one often-neglected fact, writes Ann Romines, is that "Willa Cather was a child of the Reconstruction" (historical essay 315). Despite living the first nine years of her life in Virginia, Cather set only this one novel in the South, specifically Back Creek, Virginia, where Cather's family had a long history. One of the first settlers was Cather's great-great-grandfather, Jeremiah Smith (1711–87), a legendary figure in Virginia history, and at one time, one of the largest landholders in the region. Around 1742, Smith built a log house in the Back Creek Valley. This house was remodeled several times between 1800 and 1850, and it is here at the time of the novel, 1856, where Sapphira and Henry Colbert reside. Jacob Funk Seibert (1779–1858), Cather's great-grandfather, bought the house and the mill in 1836, and he and his wife Ruhamah (1791/92?–1873) serve as the prototypes for Henry and Sapphira (Romines, historical essay 304–5).

Romines also asserts that the novel was Cather's "most complex engagement with memory" (historical essay 297). By setting it in 1856 in the Shenandoah Valley, Cather revisits the place where she spent the first nine years of her life. She based many of the characters on people she knew or stories she heard, and through these stories, she delved into family history, social customs, her oldest memories, and "the intricacies of slaveholding culture" (297). Cather herself stated that little of the novel was fiction, and that is clear from this scholarly edition. Using census records (including slave censuses), local histories, and other archives, the editors explicate many characters and events in the novel and provide in-depth source material and invaluable information for anyone interested in learning more about the novel and its historical and biographical relation to Cather. Included are discussions of Cather's family's history; their relations to the Confederacy and the Union; and portraits of the relatives, ancestors, and homes connected to the novel. Especially interesting are the portraits of Ruhamah and Jacob Siebert done by an itinerant artist around 1850 and the discussion of the Siebert family and its heretofore-little-discussed slaves, who served as prototypes for many of the characters.

Cather's engagement with memory also includes an interesting epilogue to the novel, one that takes place twenty-five years after the action, in 1881. Cather often employed an epilogue in her novels, but this was the first time she spoke in her own voice. In this brief episode where Nancy the runaway slave returns, Cather herself appears as a young character who witnesses the event. Critics have frequently focused on the epilogue: Woodress calls it "problematic" (488); Romines calls it "fabulous" ("Willa Cather" 212). When Cather wrote of the epilogue to Alexander Woollcott in 1942, she stated, "In my end is my beginning" (qtd. 384). Through the re-creation of the past, Cather asserts her connection to Southern culture and explores the power of memory.

The publication history of *Sapphira and the Slave Girl* shows how much Cather's reputation had grown in the twenty years since the 1920 publication of *Youth and the Bright Medusa*. Published by Knopf, the first printing was for 50,000 copies. The Book-of-the-Month Club selected the novel in May 1941 and produced over 200,000 copies. Despite the brisk sales, initial reviews of the novel were mixed. While her friend Dorothy Canfield Fisher gave high praise to the work, others were not as positive. Alain Tairn wrote in the *Southern Literary Messenger* that *Sapphira* was "not a great book" (qtd. 372). An anonymous reviewer in the December 9, 1940, issue of *Time* contended that "Willa Cather could not possibly write a bad novel; but *Sapphira and the Slave Girl* bears witness that she can write a dull one" ("Books"). Interestingly, Romines points out that "Cather had been concerned that critics might fault her treatment of African American characters and their language" (historical essay 376). However, that was not the case. Clifton Fadiman wrote that her black characters are "allowed to be persons rather than shaped up to be object lessons" (qtd. 376). Although the novel was Cather's best-selling work, sales declined after her death. As African American writers and literature grew in popularity in the 1960s, "Cather's portrayal of slavery began to appear more conflicted and more problematic than it had to the book's initial reviewers." For many readers, Romines writes, "Sapphira seemed an anomaly and her [Cather's] least classifiable book" (historical essay 383). Today, however, thanks to the increasing sophistication of Cather scholarship, Romines writes, we "are learning to see *Sapphira and the Slave Girl* not as a curious late aberration but as one of Cather's most ambitious efforts—a triumphant moment in a great American career" (historical essay 383).

These two most recent volumes in the Willa Cather Scholarly Edition, *Youth and the Bright Medusa* and *Sapphira and the Slave Girl*, achieve the high standards set in 1992 when the series began. Both volumes are well researched and thorough, and each includes outstanding historical and textual essays that elucidate the composition and publication history of the work, along with detailed explanatory notes that explain Cather's references. This, I believe, was part of the vision of Susan Rosowski, a vision that continues today. These scholarly editions, as the late editor concludes in her preface, reflect "the individuality of each work while providing a standard of reference for critical study" (preface xii). Fans of Willa Cather certainly look forward to the remaining volumes of the Willa Cather Scholarly Edition.

WORKS CITED

"Books: Pre-War Tale." *Time* Dec. 9, 1940: 88. Print.
Cather, Willa. *The World and the Parish: Willa Cather's Articles and Reviews, 1893–1902.* Ed. William M. Curtin. Lincoln: U of Nebraska P, 1970. Print.
Madigan, Mark J. Historical essay. *Youth and the Bright Medusa.* By Willa Cather. Lincoln: U of Nebraska P, 2009. 313–75. Print.
Romines, Ann. Historical essay. *Sapphira and the Slave Girl.* By Willa Cather. Lincoln: U of Nebraska P, 2009. 297–404. Print.
———. "Willa Cather and 'the old story': *Sapphira and the Slave Girl.*" *The Cambridge Companion to Willa Cather.* Ed. Marilee Lindemann. Cambridge, UK: Cambridge UP, 2005. 205–21. Print.
Rosowski, Susan J. Preface. *O Pioneers!* By Willa Cather. Lincoln: U of Nebraska P, 1992. vii–xi. Print.
Rosowski, Susan J., Charles Mignon, Karl Ronning, and Frederick M. Link. "Editing Cather." *Studies in the Novel* 27.3 (1995): 387–400. Print.
Woodress, James. *Willa Cather: A Literary Life.* Lincoln: U of Nebraska P, 1987. Print.

Art as "An Everyday Affair": William Carlos Williams's Correspondence with His Brother

NATALIE GERBER
State University of New York Fredonia

THE LETTERS OF WILLIAM CARLOS WILLIAMS TO EDGAR IRVING WILLIAMS, 1902–1912. Ed. Andrew J. Krivak. Madison, NJ: Fairleigh Dickinson UP, 2009. 397 pp. $65.

Perhaps because William Carlos Williams (1883–1963) did not explicitly assign himself the task of writing essays to explicate, advance, and defend his poetics (as he writes in the preface to his *Selected Essay*, he composed "prose pieces ... from time to time, more or less at random, sometimes on the spur of the moment" [v]), his correspondence has continued to be of especially great interest to literary scholars. It is in individual letters found in *The Selected Letters of William Carlos Williams* that Williams most explicitly lays out some of his theories of versification, as it is in the letters of *The American Idiom* that Williams explores what he calls "the bedrock, the mother tongue of Brooklyn, USA" (William and Norse 47).

This new volume of letters to his younger brother, Edgar Irving Williams (1884–1974), not all of which were unknown before, as the thoughtful and careful editor, Andrew J. Krivak, reminds us, covers Williams's early years, from his studies at the University of Pennsylvania to the establishment of his medical practice in Rutherford, New Jersey, and promises significantly to enrich critical scholarship on early Williams in several respects. Most practically, the volume offers a robust complement to the earliest letters by Williams previously in print; the main period herein represented, 1902–12 (a final chapter presents key letters speaking to significant biographical and literary events transpiring from 1918 to 1959), occupies a slender twenty pages in John C. Thirlwall's *Selected Letters*. More substantially, since Edgar was, in Williams's own words, his "first intimate" (*I Wanted to Write a Poem* 3), these letters offer us a fascinating view of the young Bill Williams as a private man. Williams's letters to his dear brother "Bo," a budding and soon-to-be-successful architect, present what is likely a less-embellished portrait of the young medical student and would-be writer than that available even in the earliest Pound/Williams letters, which start in 1907. (As this volume confirms, Williams famously had mixed feelings about Ezra Pound from the start; here, a gem from 1909: "As to Pound he isn't at all affected he's just batty he really believes in the stuff he does and he's getting better and people like him which is saying a lot considering his style" [199].) That said, even these letters to Edgar—which frequently reveal a striking conflict between Williams's initially solicitous posture toward and his ultimate rejection of Edgar's opinions on topics ranging from changes to poems to proposed journeys that never materialize—give reason to examine Williams's candor and his equivocal role as the older but only briefly more successful brother openly soliciting and dispensing advice, pouring out his soul (with some increasing limits), and conveying in monthly—and at times weekly—installments reflections on his experiences and emerging art theories. That Williams late in life, and in the last letter included here, confesses to a "puzzled love" (318) for his brother only serves the more to foreground the relationship.

These letters date from the closest period of the brothers' relationship—a relationship perhaps captured best by Williams in a 1904 comment: "We are one, as it were, what I have is yours and what you have ought to be mine.... That is what I call brotherhood, it should not be even as two intimate friends but as part of the same being" (59). The letters themselves amply chronicle the brothers' friendly but competitive strain (see especially letter 144 on pp. 248–49); their reaching for excellence in their respective arts (writing and architecture); their struggles with "the blues"; and their complex relationship to their parents, especially to their father and his "17th century morality" (222; see 282 on their mother's "peculiar vigor"), to each other, to their Unitarian heritage, and to their hometown and its occupants. All of these topics emerge against what may now sound to us like an inflated rhetoric of closeness, as well as a frequently banal enumeration of sundry details—from train schedules, to health concerns, to their almost perpetual lack of cash, a recurrent concern for Williams.

The volume is beautifully presented, and the reader benefits from the extensive scholarly knowledge of its editor. Krivak's introduction of over twenty pages summarizes key facets of scholarly interest found in these letters and puts major biographical events and comments on aesthetics in dialogue with existing accounts in publications by and about Williams. Likewise, more than forty pages of notes supplement the letters with detailed glosses of foreign phrases and contemporary slang, as well as helpful identifications of persons, places, and events. These identifications also evaluate Williams's discussions—and omissions—of key biographical incidents in these letters in relation to their discussion in other works; to wit, the two brothers' contest for Charlotte Herman (who promised to wed Edgar but never did, and whom William also initially sought to marry although he eventually married her sister, Florence, a.k.a. "Flo" or

"Floss"), which goes almost untreated here compared to the significant discussion it receives in Paul Mariani's masterful biography, *William Carlos Williams: A New World Naked* (1981; 353n147).

Krivak's similar cross-referencing of anecdotes in the letters that reappear, often somewhat disguised, in Williams's fiction, plays, and verse usefully connects the biographical persons and events with the fictional characters and situations into which they are or may be transformed. His attention extends not only to well-known transformations (e.g., the brothers' romantic contest as transformed into the situation of William's novel *The Build-up* [1952]) but also to biographically slight but aesthetically important moments, such as the beggar Williams encounters in a Leipzig bar—a "wreck of the artistic spirit one might say the refuse of art"—"singing the old, old songs of the Italian operas with such feeling" (168). Krivak suggests that she may be echoed by "the bar scene in the poem 'The Desert Music' [1954], when WCW witnesses the stripper in Juarez, Mexico" (354n153), who is one of Williams's earliest portraits of the muse as beggar, akin to the "marvelous old queen" of "The Wanderer" (1914, 1917; *Collected Poems* 31).

What emerges most strongly through the two hundred letters from Williams and the surviving twenty-five letters from Edgar is an evolving debate over the nature and the role of art and the job of the artist and/or the man. That art and work (labor, effort, striving) are linked for the brothers is a clear theme, and one surely tied to their Unitarian upbringing, a striking and central value revealed by these letters, as Krivak clearly indicates in his introduction. The letters chronicle how the brothers' approaches to art mature and diverge as they develop in their respective fields. Edgar, a proponent of Beaux-Arts architecture, a moral compass of respectability, and eminently more famous in his lifetime, emerges as a perhaps-involuntary foil for Williams's vague theorizing about art, beauty, poetry, music, and, most of all in the earlier letters, drama.

Likewise, Edgar's technically dazzling but more conventional paintings, designs (including the 1909 bookplate for his brother's privately printed *Poems*), and architectural plans increasingly contrast with Williams's growing interest in irregularity in art and his tendency to find beauty not only in the ordinary, everyday ("Art is intrinsic it is not a plaything, it is an everyday affair and does not need a museum for its exposition it should breathe in the common places" [161]), but also in the imperfect, irregular, and impoverished figures and structures surrounding him. One might contrast Edgar's 1909 architectural drawings for "a summer resort in the mountains designed especially for those interested in aviation" (see plate 8, p. 160) with Williams's remark, from November 28, 1909: "I have often looked at the old peasant houses about Leipzig and wondered why they are beautiful in their ruin and filth and perhaps disease" (190).

Or consider the half of the exchange we have from 1912 over the achievement of Rodin: apparently responding to Edgar's "feeling against Rodin," Williams defends Rodin as an "innovator, a revolutionist," and characterizes his apparently "unfinished work" as a sign of the present revolutionary spirit, saying "at present art is breaking with all formality, all canons, all fixed standards and set forumulae" (291). Skip forward another thirty-four years and the lines are even more clearly drawn: now the brothers are in their sixties, and Williams declares that art "isn't an escape. No one can escape responsibility in the world" but that art is "a manner of attack . . . a subtly veiled attack on the evils of the world. That is my belief and my justification for writing" (315). Edgar replies, more in line with respectability, that a man's job is "to try to build a better world" (317) and that, "[a]s I grow older I care less about staggering the other guy with something odd, something he has to worry too hard to understand. But I recognize the force of the impact of the new and I when I am convinced of sincerity I search more deeply. Once in a while I am rewarded" (315–16).

Even as it charts the interrelated fluctuations in the two brothers' lives, relationships, and art beliefs, this volume of letters adds to our store of knowledge on several fronts. Most surprising, at least for this reviewer, is the seriousness of Williams's interest in drama as both an amateur actor and a dramatist. As the introduction stresses, Williams spends close to ten years imagining himself as a dramatist. His letters from Leipzig indicate his greater interest in coursework in English drama than in medicine (by 1910 medicine already comes last in Williams's "trinity" of occupations—"writing, Florence, medicine" [254]—and as early as March 1911 he is already declaring that he wishes he "were done with the profession of medicine . . . [so as] to go into the theater" [256]). His earliest artistic efforts as a young doctor also center upon writing and acting in plays, especially outdoor ones, the majority of which he never finished and/or later burned. Indeed, it was not until 1912 that Williams definitively turned to poetry, calling it "a higher reach to me and [one that] gives me greater satisfaction in the doing" (300); whether poetry is the higher calling or not, these letters suggest that Williams's turn is also motivated by the encouragement his fledgling efforts in verse received against the critical silence and lack of understanding his plays encountered (see 235, 244, and 249). At the same time, the letters provide clear evidence that Williams's efforts to create plays for a modern American theater, especially his drive to "master the English language" (187), come to fruition in the poems and the American style they embrace.

The letters also provide brief but important glimpses of Williams's early verse and nascent theories of poetic form. The enclosed poems are a mix of clearly bad imitative sonnets and rhymed poems, together with more compelling and energetic verses employing irregular lines, a lack of rhyme, and a smattering of what we have come to call the American idiom. In the latter poems we recognize the early budding of his mature style and the influence of his continuous discussions of technique throughout these letters. A particular find is his discussion of the importance of "rests or silent places caused by syllables that are dropped out" (245) to the modern verse line's cadence, which presages his later remark: "What else is verse made of but 'words, words, words?' Quite literally, *the spaces between the words*, in our modern understanding, which takes with them an equal part in the measure" (Williams, "Measure" 149). Here, the comment occurs in the context of meter, particularly trisyllabic meters, but the potential shift to free verse is already evident, and Williams's implicit shift in consciousness away from fixed meters to the energetic domain of free verse can be detected by his intentional replacement of the term "meter" in a letter to Edgar by the term "rhythm and counter rhythm" (253). Likewise, Williams's general discussions of the importance of "irregularity" against "conformity" in both art and poetry appear throughout the latter half of these letters and give a strong sense of the direction of his evolution away from established forms, or as he writes, in a different context, of his intention to "use the old as a check but not as a model" (179).

For those willing to read through the letters in their entirety, there are other hidden gems. Those interested in economies, both affective and monetary, will find a multitude of references to the correct investment of energies—sexual, intellectual, artistic, and commercial. Indeed, the wasting of energies, whether due to petty affairs, the influence of the rich, or the preoccupation with women, emerges as a strong theme with Unitarian undertones across these letters. Those interested in the theorizing of disappointment will find many examples of Williams's disappointments—in his early medical career, in the reception of his dramatic and early literary efforts, in his familial relationships—recounted from Williams's pen, with his characteristic mix of despair and ambition.

Those interested in lacunae will find strange ones: not only does Williams glide over the brothers' contest for the Herman sisters, but there are no letters regarding Williams's March 1910 visit with Pound in London; indeed, the late introduction of Pound in these letters is itself worth contemplating. And those fascinated by Williams's well-known proclivity for unfinished or abandoned efforts will find many examples both from life (a contemplated Army or Navy stint [142] is the most intriguing) and from writing (unfinished or burned plays are especially of note here), tempered by Williams's own sense that, "although I do miscarry and miscarry yet regularly, it seems, these miscarriages do ultimately lead to a deed" (257). Of course, his strained relationship with medicine (which always comes third in his trinity), his budding relationship with Florence (who emerges as a strong female), and his thoughtful reflections on Germany and the German sensibility on the brink of World War I are also rewarding.

Scholars with an interest in gender studies and/or sexuality will be particularly rewarded by a wealth of passages, too numerous to recount here, that counsel on the right use of masculine energy—which is always directed usably toward art, and at times, unavoidably but less profitably, toward sex (there are intriguing passages about smut fiction [237–38], as well as about masturbation and sexual promiscuity [267]). From the earliest letters, Williams lectures Edgar on the dangers that female involvement holds for the would-be artist and advises against entanglements: "Don't get mixed up seriously with any girl yet. . . . If you find yourself getting into trouble think of your ideal and then pick the girl apart. It is mean but it is *necessary*" (53). On the verge of marriage, Williams shows that his views about women have changed surprisingly little: "As a mother is the greatest woman so an artist is the greatest man but the man who thinks to share his love between art and a woman is gone" (277). His comment, in the same letter, that "[a] man's only hope is in regarding his wife as his enemy. He must not give when he will not give but must give only when he is able to give out of an abundance. . . . Man gives everything, woman nothing" (277). This will also hold ample interest for biographers, as will another, earlier passage, in which Williams, who has just contemplated a get-rich scheme of distributing a new cure for syphilis throughout South America, perhaps ill-advisedly, debates free love with his future wife, sister- and mother-in-law, and Flo declares "that she wouldn't trust the best man in Christendom to stick to a woman without a contract" (250).

Those attuned to Williams's involvement with the visual arts or to the particular complexities of his relationship with European art and artists will find compelling passages, such as this one about how his travels in Europe and his exposure to European art have helped shape his vision of local American scenes:

> Since returning from Europe I see color everywhere, this is the direct result of looking at the wonders of painting in Europe.... Really it's the greatest step toward happiness I have ever made to see things as I do now. I do not see them as an American any more but I see them from a universal standpoint with an American love at the bottom but not interfering with my eyes. I can now appreciate that which I never appreciated before. Now I see a sky, a patch of water, a background of trees and a spot of rare tender color in its place where formerly I saw a bunch of kids in swimming. (223)

This stirring depiction of a scene Williams encounters on a walk past "the old abandoned Morris and Essex Canal" (223) constitutes a realization of his pledge to "dignify" his local world (cf. "If I don't dignify America and home and even the Passaic River may I burn in everlasting fires. Nothing on earth is intrinsically low, ugly and insignificant; everything can and must be beautified at expense of human sweat, labor, love, suffering, perseverance, clear sightedness" [186]). At the same time, it is a useful reminder that Williams's methods are not, perhaps, unalloyedly American. Indeed, it is tempting to overread the importance of this passage, which dates from June 1910, the first month that Williams returns to the United States and to Rutherford from his nearly yearlong studies in Germany and extended European tour. Nonetheless, I will offer the notion that this passage—whose fragmented, Cezanne-like depiction of an everyday, local American scene throws us—foreshadows Williams's method (in works such as "Young Sycamore" [1927]) of connecting fragmented observations with quick energetic movements, and thereby suggests a more complicated view of Williams's admittedly mixed attitudes toward and debt to Europe.

Against the mature Williams's famous declarations of the virtues of the local, the American, and the common, these letters reveal the collegiate Williams engaging in aristocratic pastimes (e.g., taking fencing lessons and playing the violin), being transported by the greatness of high European drama and opera, and advising the precollegiate Edgar that "what you want is to get out of Rutherford. The sooner the better" (45). The twenty-something Williams likewise expresses an equivocal but genuine lust for Europe, one that coexists alongside a growing conviction of the importance of forging an American technique and style. And the genuine flagging of spirit that Williams conveys upon his return to Rutherford should give the reader pause, as he unfavorably compares his prospects of "sitting in one dull town" (218) to the opportunities he might find elsewhere and to the more cosmopolitan people he met upon his travels.

Thus, while the arc of the letters demonstrates Williams's evolution toward the belief that, circa *Paterson* (book 1 [1946]), "what I have learned in a lifetime seems to tell me that there's as much to be learned here about the world as elsewhere if one goes about it hard enough" (314), the mercurial changes, often in a matter of weeks, in his measure of his town, its people, and both the professional and the intellectual opportunities they hold for him (which, incidentally, are in keeping with the overall unpredictable reversals of opinion and plan characterizing these letters) provide an important corrective on a poet who has come to rival only Robert Frost as a defender of the local American homestead. And, just as recent works on Frost have reminded us of that poet's mixed relationship to New England, this volume strikingly displays how the home medical practice that defines two Dr. Williams, William Carlos and William Eric, emerges here as not inevitable, but rather as at least in part the result of failed explorations in establishing practice in the Bronx and in New York

City, and as a concession to economy. Indeed, Williams's conviction in his late twenties that his real existence lies "beyond life in this burg" (235) and that "there is here so little appreciation for the things I appreciate that I lack comradeship; the consequence is that I must repair to my letters or starve" (249) might reenliven our imagination as to Williams's apparent destiny (at the undergraduate level, at least) to be made into a chief proponent of the local strand of American modernism.

WORKS CITED

Mariani, Paul. *William Carlos Williams: A New World Naked*. New York: Norton, 1981. Print.
Williams, William Carlos. *The Build-up*. New York: Random, 1952. Print.
———. *The Collected Poems of William Carlos Williams. Vol. 1*. Ed. A. Walton Litz and Christopher MacGowan. New York: New Directions, 1986. Print.
———. *I Wanted to Write a Poem*. Ed. Edith Heal. New York: New Directions, 1977. Print.
———. "Measure." *Spectrum* 3.3 (1959): 130–57. Print.
———. *Paterson* [book 1]. New York: New Directions, 1946. Print.
———. *Poems*. Rutherford, NJ: Reid Howell, 1909. Print.
———. *Selected Essays of William Carlos Williams*. New York: New Directions, 1969. Print.
———. *The Selected Letters of William Carlos Williams*. Ed. John C. Thirlwall. New York: New Directions, 1957. Print.
Williams, William Carlos, and Harold Norse. *The American Idiom: A Correspondence*. Ed. John J. Wilson. San Francisco: Bright Tyger, 1990. Print.

Reconsidering Allen Ginsberg at the End of an Epistolary Era

TONY TRIGILIO
Columbia College Chicago

THE SELECTED LETTERS OF ALLEN GINSBERG AND GARY SNYDER. Ed. Bill Morgan. Berkeley: Counterpoint, 2009. viii + 321 pp. $28.

THE LETTERS OF ALLEN GINSBERG. Ed. Bill Morgan. Philadelphia: Da Capo, 2008. xxii + 468 pp. $30.

At every stage of his career, Allen Ginsberg (1926–97) was slowed by his correspondence. In letter after letter, he complains of the demands of writing letters—while, of course, he continues to make time to read and respond to correspondence. As the volumes under review demonstrate, the self-generated pressures of Ginsberg's responsibility to his letter-writing were as much a boon as a hindrance to his poetry. These collections trace Ginsberg's development as a poet and public figure, from his teen years through the final months of his life. They demythologize the self-generated hipster-hero image of Ginsberg that has been reified over the years by journalists and fans; in so doing, they suggest important paths for continued reconsiderations of the poet in the nascent field of Beat Studies. As one of the few poets in the United States with a major presence in popular culture, Ginsberg the media figure is rarely disentangled from Ginsberg the poet. Yet the extrication of the media personality from the poet is necessary to lessen the influence of hagiography on critical commentary. To be sure, the ground for sheer gossip in these books is fertile. Such is the case for any collection of a writer's correspondence, but especially with the Beats, for whom romanticized biographical detail too often overshadows the actual works of literature they produced.

These volumes chart the literary and cultural traditions that shaped Ginsberg's work, and they offer valuable contexts for studying the compositional strategies of his most well-known poems. These are important companion texts to the three major biographies of Ginsberg—by Barry Miles (1989), Michael Schumacher (1992), and Bill Morgan himself (2006)—all of which draw on his letters to some degree. Both of these volumes also complement, although at times with overlapping content, previously published collections of Ginsberg's correspondence: *As Ever: The Collected Correspondence of Allen Ginsberg and Neal Cassady* (Gifford; 1977), *Straight Hearts' Delight: Love Poems and Selected Letters, 1947–1980* (1980), *Family Business: Selected Letters Between a Father and Son* (Schumacher; 2001), and *Jack Kerouac and Allen Ginsberg: The Letters* (Morgan and Stanford; 2010). These collections deepen our understanding of how Beat Generation textual strategies emerged from the writers' vibrant participation in, as Morgan describes it, the great "era of letter-writing" that characterized postwar American culture (*Letters of Allen Ginsberg* xix).

Despite Ginsberg's prodigious correspondence, the letters collected in these volumes are by no means exhaustive. For *The Letters of Allen Ginsberg* alone, Morgan chose only 165 of the more than 3,700 letters by the poet that he had located. *The Selected Letters of Allen Ginsberg and Gary Snyder* collects 355 of the more than 850 letters the two poets exchanged. Perhaps Morgan's narrow principles of inclusion could be considered a flaw; still, most of the uncollected correspondence is available in university archival Beat holdings, and Morgan's selectivity as editor makes these volumes important for scholars and general readers alike. Indeed, one could not ask for a better editor in this context than Morgan, who worked as Ginsberg's archivist for two decades and whose biography of Ginsberg is the most comprehensive of the three biographies to date. Morgan also has edited several of the poet's publications over the years, including the only collection of Ginsberg's prose writing, *Deliberate Prose: Selected Essays, 1952–1995* (2001).

Taken together, the letters in these volumes chart a developing Beat Generation ethos and aesthetic as it was articulated, primarily, by the movement's most visible and popular poet. Ginsberg's peripatetic energy and media savvy made him the group's de facto literary agent and spokesperson. In the letters Morgan has compiled for both books, Ginsberg is working out a poetics and, he hopes, a legacy for himself and his fellow Beats. As seen in *The Selected Letters of Allen Ginsberg and Gary Snyder*, Ginsberg struggled to match the ideals of this legacy to the pragmatic pressures of everyday lived experience, as he and Gary Snyder (b. 1930) negotiated the administrative details of Kitkitdizee, the land they purchased in the Sierra foothills in 1967. Their Kitkitdizee letters span a quarter century, ranging from their initial discussions in 1966 about buying land together for a rural retreat through Ginsberg's decision, in 1992, to sell his share, Bedrock Mortar, to build a trust to support Peter Orlovsky. As the two exchange letters about the property over the years, the commitment to epic vision and vatic utterance in their poetry competes with the minute bureaucratic details involved in choosing, buying, and maintaining the land. For readers inclined only to accept at face value the Beat nomadic spirit, these letters offer an instructive alternative reading of Beat lives and letters. The two poets allowed fellow artists and writers to stay on the land for residency retreats for periods of weeks and sometimes months. At the same time, Snyder and Ginsberg labored to reconcile their increasingly privatizing visions—Snyder raising his family on the land, Ginsberg planning a future retirement refuge for himself—with the Beat Generation collectivist ethos that brought them together at Kitkitdizee in the first place.

Selected Letters also offers important new insight into the depth of Snyder's and Ginsberg's contributions to North American Buddhism, including their efforts to articulate a North American Buddhist poetics amid what Robert S. Ellwood has described elsewhere as an emergent "glossolalia" of religious practice in the United States in the 1960s (6). The letters trace the development of each poet's Buddhism, ranging from Snyder's early critiques of Ginsberg's desire to reach enlightenment through consciousness-altering drugs to the poets' sharing of mantras and new meditation practices that they hoped would loosen and transform what they saw as a moribund academic poetry establishment underwritten by Cold War principles of containment. Snyder more often than Ginsberg eschews the transcendental in favor of a sacred materiality as both seek a Buddhist middle way that resists a middling sensibility. This difference between the two should come as no surprise: while Snyder was studying formally in Zen monasteries, Ginsberg was building an autodidactic spiritual practice limited by, among other things, his frequent conflation of Hinduism and Buddhism. As early as 1956, just six months after the two poets met, Snyder and Ginsberg were debating their disagreements over questions of matter and spirit in Buddhist tradition. Much changed when Ginsberg formalized his Buddhist training with Tibetan lama Chögyam Trungpa Rinpoche, after taking Bodhisattva vows from Trungpa in 1972.

During the final quarter century of his life, as his commitment to Buddhism deepened in formal study with Trungpa, the differences between his vision and Snyder's began to blur. "Trungpa's teaching of nontheism seems to have penetrated my skull finally," he writes to Snyder in September 1976. "It does seem strange that for 20 years I've been yapping about God. Why didn't you tell me to shut up?" (182). Why, indeed, if not for Snyder's own pedagogical strategies with his close friend? In matters of Beat Generation spiritual poetics, *The Selected Letters of Allen Ginsberg and Gary Snyder* reads at times like a classroom conducted by Snyder, with Ginsberg adopting the role of dutiful pupil and Snyder the casual professor. The Beat suspicion of hierarchies always is in the offing, nevertheless, and this volume illustrates a developing mutual respect and eventual peer study between the two. Snyder does not tell Ginsberg to be quiet when he is "yapping about God" because, as we see in the letters, the dialectic produced by Ginsberg's "yapping" contributes usefully to Snyder's ongoing development of his own Buddhist-inspired aesthetic and conceptual strategies.

Despite the persistent belief within the critical community that the Beats were an antiacademic ragtag lot, most of the writers were at ease in—and actively desired—the pedagogical space of the classroom. Ginsberg often cited Jack Kerouac as his first Buddhist teacher; and despite the autodidactic imperatives of each writer, the teacher-student relationship between the two was never far removed from its classroom analogue. As Kerouac writes to Ginsberg in a 1954 letter included in Schumacher's biography, "For your beginning studies of Buddhism, you must listen to me carefully and implicitly as tho I was Einstein teaching you relativity or Eliot teaching the Formulas of Objective Correlation on a blackboard in Princeton" (194). Given their public resistance to what they perceived as a hostile academic establishment, it is easy to forget just how important the academy was for Beat writers. Many of them met while attending prestigious institutions such as Columbia University (Ginsberg) and Reed College (Snyder), and the readership they built over the years depended on readings and guest professorships at colleges and universities around the world.

The Selected Letters of Gary Snyder and Allen Ginsberg chronicles the Beat academic presence, which eventually led both Snyder and Ginsberg to accept academic positions: Snyder a long-term tenured position at the University of California at Davis, and Ginsberg—already a cofounder and steward of Naropa University's poetics program—a Distinguished Professorship at Brooklyn College. Nothing, perhaps, might demythologize these poets more than their correspondence over Ginsberg's progress on the tenure track (albeit an accelerated tenure clock) at Brooklyn College. Their mutual complaints about the academy in their letters of the late 1980s and 1990s suggest the dailiness of everyday kvetching that one would find in just about any English Department in the United States—nothing of the "cool eyes hallucinating Arkansas and Blake-light tragedy among the scholars of war" that is central to the vision of "Howl" (Ginsberg, *Collected Poems* 134). To be sure, these letters are not an indication that the academy severely domesticated the two poets. On the contrary, their correspondence suggests the extent to which the academy changed as new generations of readers constellated around the Beats and other postwar experimental traditions such as the New American and Black Mountain poets.

The earliest correspondence in *The Letters of Allen Ginsberg* reveals a Ginsberg deeply intent on impressing his former professors, Lionel Trilling and Mark Van Doren. In a 1948 letter to Trilling, commenting on a packet of poems Ginsberg had sent him, Ginsberg writes, "I feel guilty about not having developed my art any faster and finer than I have. As you see it still has the subjective elegiac voice, but essentially thickheaded, and I'm beginning to repent, to the point of thinking that I'm altogether on the wrong track" (22). Later that year, in a letter to Van Doren, Ginsberg describes himself as "a novitiate, of the lowest order," in a passage in which he confesses: "My verse *is* weak; there isn't anything I have written which will be anything like what I will write someday, I trust" (28). Early in his development as a poet, Ginsberg casts himself as the earnest, dutiful student, working diligently to shed an expressivist aesthetic in favor of his professors' depersonalized New Critical sensibilities.

This self-representation is, of course, far from the conventional image of Ginsberg we have come to know through, for instance, his famous defense of "Howl" (1956) in his 1956 letter to Richard Eberhart. The Eberhart letter, reproduced in excerpts in Ginsberg's *Howl: Original Draft Facsimile*, is available in Morgan's collection in its entirety (the full letter also was reproduced in the now out-of-print *To Eberhart from Ginsberg* [1976]). Morgan's inclusion of the entire letter is important because the excerpts published in *Howl: Original Draft Facsimile* tend to emphasize "Howl" at the expense of Ginsberg's other poems. The full letter to Eberhart, in contrast, integrates the compositional strategies of "Howl" into the wider scope of Ginsberg's work at the time—in the full letter, "Howl" is not an isolated event but part of a more ambitious, large-scale aesthetic project that Ginsberg is eager to discuss and defend. Seen in the entirety of the Eberhart letter, then, "Howl" is just one more facet—albeit a crucial one—of a broader commitment to which Ginsberg had pledged himself: "overturning any notion of propriety, moral 'value,' superficial 'maturity,' Trilling-esque sense of 'civilization' and exposing my true feelings—of sympathy and identification with the rejected, mystical, individual" (131). The prevailing conception of Ginsberg in the critical community resembles the poet who composed the Eberhart letter more than it does the writer of the Trilling and Van Doren correspondence. However, *The Letters of Allen Ginsberg* complicates the notion, propagated in large part, of course, by the Beats themselves, that this stance against literary and social propriety developed sui generis within wholly marginalized figures living on the edges of a compliant, decorous culture.

Indeed, the letters in this volume emphasize Ginsberg's studious absorption of Anglo-American poetry—not just his immediate inspirations from Romanticism onward but also his embrace of Renaissance and seventeenth-century traditions that were the foundations of his early imitative verse in the late 1940s. Thus, the letters remind us of the important literary-historical lineage to which Ginsberg's most well-known poems are indebted. They also heighten our understanding of Ginsberg's more familiar influences. The chain of events that produced "Howl" included, significantly, Ginsberg's 1949 meeting with Carl Solomon, when the two were patients at the New York State Psychiatric Institute. Herbert Huncke, later an icon among the Beats, and his fellow thieves had been storing stolen property in Ginsberg's apartment. A young, emotionally conflicted Ginsberg did not ask them to leave. When the apartment was raided, Ginsberg was charged with receiving stolen property; only through the intervention of Columbia University was he able to substitute a stint in the Psychiatric Institute for a jail term. In an April 1949 letter to Neal Cassady, Ginsberg confesses his ambivalence about the theft ring even as he admits that the police will likely catch them (indeed, the arrests occurred that same month): "The household setup which I both hate and desire, that I have, is an example of my uncertainty of path and dividedness" (32). As his July 1949 letter to Kerouac implies, this uncertainty was a vital catalyst for "Howl." Of the Psychiatric Institute, he writes, "There is a perfect opportunity here for existentialist absurdity" (53). He is speaking, of course, of the Institute itself, but the line lends itself to a pitch-perfect description of the poetics of "Howl." Indeed, this crucial letter to Kerouac emphasizes the archaeological roots of Ginsberg's most famous poem, both in its discussion of literary sources—his references to discovering Antonin Artaud's work, for instance—and in its language, which can be traced from the letter directly into the poem: from the treatment described in "Howl" as "hydrotherapy psychotherapy occupational therapy pingpong & amnesia" to his defense of those who "presented themselves on the granite steps of the madhouse with shaven heads and harlequin speech of suicide, demanding instantaneous lobotomy" (*Collected Poems* 138).

Some of the most important poems in Ginsberg's body of work took shape originally in the poet's correspondence. A November 1957 letter to Kerouac reveals that Ginsberg originally intended to open "Kaddish" (1961) with what would eventually become section 4 of the poem. In addition to this large-scale revision, which considerably alters the tenor and scope of the poem, crucial line-editing revisions to section 4 emerge when the finished poem is compared to the first drafts that Ginsberg discussed in his correspondence. For a poet known as an improvisatory writer—and who has been characterized, incorrectly, as a writer who did not revise—this exposure to Ginsberg's drafting and revising in the unvarnished space of his correspondence is crucial. As is the case with most literary figures, Ginsberg's letters often function as a writer's journal. Readers can see the extent to which Ginsberg reworked in "White Shroud" (1986; a poem in the "Kaddish" triptych that also includes "Black Shroud" [1986]) several photographs from Berenice Abbott's collection *Changing New York* (1973). Ginsberg reshapes her images to reflect the poem's dreamscape. In a January 1984 letter to Abbott, he explains his drafting and revision process for this poem, noting that he was determined to recast Abbott's images in language with "many details clear" but, significant to the poem's setting, with these same details deliberately rendered "dream-wrong" (*Letters of Allen Ginsberg* 414).

These volumes continue to revise our understanding of how Beat literary experimentation was shaped by community, memory, and desire. They remind readers that Beat Generation literature participated in a broad tradition that, in addition to the Romantic visionary line, included the experimental Anglo-American Modernists, European surrealists, the New Americans, the Black Mountain poets, the Eco-Poetics movement, and the hybrid spiritual poetics of North American Buddhism, among others. As these books humanize Ginsberg and his fellow Beats as writers rather than heroes, they illuminate matters of craft and textuality that too often get obscured in hagiography. The often-playful prose of these letters offers a glimpse of how less viable, perhaps, our language has become now that the great "era of letter-writing" has been supplanted, first by the telephone and now by e-mail. This loss is especially acute when applied to Beat Generation literature, insofar as their ethos of spontaneous composition was never more at home than in the improvisatory space of letter-writing.

WORKS CITED

Abbott, Berenice. *Changing New York.* 1973. New York: New P, 1997. Print.
Ellwood, Robert S. *The Sixties' Spiritual Awakening: American Religion Moving from Modern to Postmodern.* New Brunswick, NJ: Rutgers UP, 1994. Print.
Gifford, Barry, ed. *As Ever: The Collected Correspondence of Allen Ginsberg and Neal Cassady.* Berkeley: Creative Arts, 1977. Print.
Ginsberg, Allen. *Collected Poems, 1947–1997.* New York: Harper, 2006. Print.
———. *Deliberate Prose: Selected Essays, 1952–1995.* Ed. Bill Morgan. New York: Harper, 2001. Print.
———. *Howl and Other Poems.* San Francisco: City Lights, 1956. Print.
———. *Howl: Original Draft Facsimile.* Ed. Barry Miles. New York: Harper, 1986. Print.
———. *Kaddish and Other Poems: 1958–1960.* San Francisco: City Lights, 1961. Print.
Ginsberg, Allen, and Richard Eberhart. *To Eberhart from Ginsberg: a letter about Howl, 1956: an explanation by Allen Ginsberg of his publication "Howl" and Richard Eberhart's New York times article "West coast rhythms," together with comments by both poets and relief etchings by Jerome Kaplan.* Lincoln, MA: Penmaen, 1976.
Ginsberg, Allen, and Peter Orlovsky. *Straight Hearts' Delight: Love Poems and Selected Letters, 1947–1980.* Ed. Winston Leyland. San Francisco: Gay Sunshine, 1980. Print.
Miles, Barry. *Ginsberg: A Biography.* New York: Harper, 1989. Print.
Morgan, Bill. *I Celebrate Myself: The Somewhat Private Life of Allen Ginsberg.* New York: Viking, 2006. Print.
Morgan, Bill, and David Stanford, eds. *Jack Kerouac and Allen Ginsberg: The Letters.* New York: Viking, 2010. Print.
Schumacher, Michael. *Dharma Lion: A Critical Biography of Allen Ginsberg.* New York: St. Martin's, 1992. Print.
———, ed. *Family Business: Selected Letters Between a Father and a Son.* New York: Bloomsbury, 2001. Print.

Reviews

A NEW LITERARY HISTORY OF AMERICA. Ed. Greil Marcus and Werner Sollors. Cambridge, MA: Belknap P of Harvard UP, 2009. xvii + 1095 pp. $49.95.

In this volume, editors Greil Marcus and Werner Sollors have produced a polyvalent, polyvocal history that is truly new, truly literary, and truly American—in their own words, "a history of America in which literary means not only what is written but also what is voiced, what is expressed, what is invented, in whatever form," covering "the whole range of all those things that have been created in America, or for it, or because of it," revealing an overall story of "people taking up the two elemental American fables—the fable of discovery and the fable of founding" (xxiv). Given that ambition, to have brought their project to publication at all is a minor miracle; to have satisfied these claims is a major triumph. By the merits of its essays alone, all of which are intellectually rigorous, readable, thoughtful, and even sensitively done, inviting rather than foreclosing both reflection and further exploration, the volume avoids cacophony (the obvious peril of a work of such scope and diversity) while presenting a persuasive argument for the merits of dissonance.

Because such questions as "Who knows if it is John F. Kennedy delivering his Inaugural Address or Jay Gatsby throwing one more party who is more truly invoking John Winthrop's 'A Model of Christian Charity' from three centuries before?" (xxiv) have no ready answers, and certainly none on which any two scholars are likely to agree, the editors present a book that will promulgate questions (and quests) in which the journey becomes its own end. It is an ambitious undertaking for any single volume; the only thing more staggering than its scope is the extent to which it succeeds.

Presenting all new essays from scholars established and new in various disciplines and interdisciplines, from creative artists in various media, and from public intellectuals from diverse discourses, Marcus and Sollors deliver an astonishing symphony of sometimes harmonious and sometimes dissonant voices all speaking passionately and powerfully on their subjects—which are themselves equally diverse and sometimes delightfully surprising. Some essays are written by the "usual suspects," powerhouses of intellectual discourse—as, for example, Donald E. Pease (on C. L. R. James) or Camille Paglia (on Tennessee Williams). Other essayists' names are not as recognizable (some were, at the time of writing, doctoral students), yet the quality is consistently high and the engagement consistently exciting throughout the volume, no matter the essayist's preceding reputation.

As one might expect from a Harvard University Press Reference Library volume on history, the essays are presented within a chronological framework, beginning with 1507 (the first map appearance of the name "America") and ending on November 4, 2008 ("Barack Obama"), yet even a brief closer perusal reveals the instability of assumptions regarding the usual forms of chronology, rendering the volume's place as a "reference" work somewhat problematic in ways that, while not undermining the project's success or brilliance, do raise minor questions regarding its intended audience and, unfortunately, its usability (all of which could be easily addressed in a slightly reformatted second edition). The book offers four entries for the 1500s, ten for the 1600s, 44 for the 1700s, 66 for the 1800s, and 125 for 1900 to the present; some years have multiple entries whereas others have none. (The introduction explicitly states that the years post-1865 are given proportionately greater emphasis in accordance with the growing complexity of discourses emerging from an increasingly diverse population and with heightened attention afforded "American literature, voices, and expression" by the rest of the world [xxvi].) The lacunae themselves are neither regular nor particularly troubling; overall, dates assigned to trends and movements such as Literary Imperialism or "The Birth of Cool" are appointed with erudition and elegance (Amy Kaplan's Imperialism essay highlights June 22, 1898, the publication date of Stephen Crane's dispatch from Guantanamo; Ted Gioia's "Birth of the Cool" essay, subtitled "Miles Davis goes into the studio with Gil Evans," focuses on 1949–50). In other cases, specific dates are obvious (the editors locate their discussion of Hurricane Katrina as the entry for "2005—August 29"). Notable by its absence is any entry for September 11, 2001.

Even within the somewhat-flexible parameters that govern assigning a date to an ongoing social or cultural phenomenon or discursive trend, not all dates or years will make obvious sense even to experts in specific fields. The volume's single essay for 1943 discusses Ernest Hemingway. This is a doubly strange choice; even dismissing other topics that could have been considered for that year, selecting 1943 from Hemingway's life makes little sense in terms of his writing or his biography. The year is neither representative nor remarkable; the editors' (or essayist's) choice is thus confusing, especially given the lack of editorial restriction upon the number of essays included for any given year evidenced by the rest of the volume. Equally problematic for the non-expert user is the other major entry concerning Hemingway, which is listed in the table of contents only as "1961, July 2—The Author as Advertisement." A Hemingway scholar or aficionado will immediately recognize the date of Hemingway's suicide and will instantly appreciate the richly subtle approach to Hemingway studies implied by the title, which encapsulates the central problem of both life and works. One need not locate one's expertise very far outside the very narrow field of Hemingway biography, however, to miss the significance of that date and thus have no idea that the entry pertains to Ernest Hemingway without turning to the essay itself, where the editorial headline explains the date as the one on which "Ernest Hemingway Stops Listening." Unfortunate, on many levels.

That both essays are excellent, representing the absolute best of current discourse while beckoning further inquiry and musing, almost renders the various questions of date and form irrelevant.

Almost.

Those seeking fixed referents in this volume rather than the intellectual jeremiads the editors invite readers to experience are in for a slightly greater challenge than the book's form seems to promise, especially if one does not read the six-page introduction—which many users of a reference book will skip on their way to The Massachusetts Bay Colony (27, 40), or Tin Pan Alley (508, 510, etc.), or whatever their intended destination may be. Toward the end of the introduction, the editors acknowledge that the book "can be read in many other ways than its chronological order: the reader might select entries from the table of contents or from the headlines that appear in front of each essay, or read all those entries together first that the index tells us mention, say, Lincoln or Whitman" (xxvi). As a "reference" volume, the book functions very much like an almost Utopian wiki—a wiki in which every page presents and every link leads to some of the best thinkers and thinking on the topic at hand; all but the most hide-bound Luddites will instantly recognize the difficulties and wonders of presenting such a form in a single-bound print volume and find themselves feeling obscurely but appropriately like a humble supplicant before the editors' and essayists' individual and collective achievements.

Yet even as I use the wiki model to illustrate the work's greatest strength (it is a treasure trove of riches, a symphony worth submersion; each grace note profound; each chord worthy of reflection), I have to extend the conceit to end with a wish for a slightly reformatted second edition. The book has put the wiki before the Google; *pace* the editors, but there is simply no way to use the work as the ready reference its organizational structure and bibliographic form imply it actually *is*. Its sheer size and heft render chronological perusal lamentably unlikely (a "world enough and time" factor that is admittedly beyond editorial control; a paperback edition, please?), its table of contents provides as much ambiguity as clarity, and its index—the most potentially useful tool for those seeking to *use* this work as well as to *read* it—suffers from the lingering "Great Man" (or at least Great Person) hierarchy, according to which one will find *Adventures of Huckleberry Finn* (1884) under only the entry for "Twain, Mark," and find "Clemens, Samuel" not at all (films, magazines, legal cases, and other collectively or institutionally produced works are listed by title). As a reference work for serious thinkers, the book is of inestimable value; would that its form rendered it more usable for an even broader audience. Donning again the supplicant's undyed linen, one would suggest to the editors and the press that providing a more-detailed index at the beginning of the work (in addition to one of the usual form at the end) would, even at the risk of raising the price, close the gap between brilliance and perfection.

Hilary K. Justice
Illinois State University

FIRST LADY OF LETTERS: JUDITH SARGENT MURRAY AND THE STRUGGLE FOR FEMALE INDEPENDENCE. By Sheila L. Skemp. Philadelphia: U of Pennsylvania P, 2009. xvi + 484 pp. $39.95.

The clever title of Sheila L. Skemp's biography of Judith Sargent Murray (1751–1820), *First Lady of Letters*, hails the vital work of her project in several ways. While "First Lady" seems to imply the office of a U.S. President's wife, Skemp means to place Murray at the head of the office of American national letters. The term *lady* is no accident, as Skemp discloses Murray's lifelong obsession with gentility and class hierarchies. Skemp's biography illuminates the life of one of our most important literary foremothers, warts and all, a life masked in mystery until 1984, when Murray's letter books were discovered in Natchez, Mississippi. Skemp has been at the forefront of recovering Murray's life and work through the repository of these letter books, which Murray compiled vigilantly throughout her life.

Skemp's focus on "letters" in her title and account places this work among the recent revival of letters as a literary genre worthy of our consideration. The publication of several books about letters in the past decade shows that scholars are now determined to give letters their due: Rebecca Earle's *Epistolary Selves: Letters and Letter-writers, 1600–1945* (1999), Elizabeth Hewitt's *Correspondence and American Literature, 1770–1865* (2004), Eve Tavor Bannet's *Empire of Letters: Letter Manuals and Transatlantic Correspondence, 1680–1820* (2005), Sarah Pearsall's *Atlantic Families: Lives and Letters in the Later Eighteenth Century* (2008), Konstantin Dierks's *Letter Writing and Communication in Early America* (2009), and Theresa Strouth Gaul and Sharon M. Harris's *Letters and Cultural Transformations in the United States, 1760–1860* (2009). Skemp's *First Lady of Letters*, which views the letter as a forum for the expression of personal agency and development, the transmission of cultural values, and the maintenance of personal and financial relationships, must also be situated in the project of recovering letters.

Rather than affording Murray's letters independent literary status as does Skemp's slim, classroom-ready *Judith Sargent Murray: A Brief Biography with Documents* (1998), *First Lady of Letters* treats Murray's letter books as a source of information about Murray. Certainly, Skemp values letters as literature, considering them as both private and semipublic documents; however, her purpose and focus are on what these documents can tell us about Murray's life and work and how they position her in American literary history.

Unlike the smaller volume, which approaches its subject thematically, this capacious literary biography recounts Murray's life chronologically. Skemp, a social historian, consistently focuses on those economic, social, political, and religious contexts that shaped her subject's experience, thought, and work. Throughout this wonderfully thick and readable biography, Skemp addresses how sociohistorical conditions shaped Murray's life and thought and, moreover, how that life and thought intersect with larger issues that concern scholars of early American literary history.

Part 1, "Rebellions: 1769–1784," treats the foundations of Murray's thought. Skemp attributes Murray's attitudes toward gender to her patrician roots in the Sargent family of Gloucester, Massachusetts; her introduction to Universalism; the American Revolution; and the context of Republican civility. Part 2, "Republic of Letters: 1783–1798," considers Murray's relationship with and marriage to Universalist minister John Murray; the birth of their daughter; and her pursuit of literary fame (driven both by ambition and by financial need) through periodical publication under the pseudonyms "The Gleaner" and "Constantia," forays into writing for the Boston stage, and the printing of her collected "Gleaner" works in three volumes titled *The Gleaner: A Miscellaneous Production* (1798). Finally, part 3, "Retreat: 1798–1820," examines Murray's withdrawal from the literary world; her assiduous yet often unrewarding oversight of the education of her daughter, her nephews, and family friends sent to her for this purpose; the death of her beloved husband; her own declining health; and her decision to move with her daughter and granddaughter to Natchez, Mississippi.

Skemp adeptly portrays the role that "[t]own, congregation, [and] family" (14) played in shaping Murray's life and thought and considers the ways in which Murray's early religious rebellion galvanized her views on gender. Her Sargent family name led Judith to expect a life of ease and privilege even as she was denied access to formal education and the opportunities her younger brother Winthrop enjoyed as a result, an omission that pained her throughout her life. Deftly linking Murray's early efforts to her privileged youth, Skemp maintains that Murray used the letter to develop her distinct voice. Skemp's analysis of Murray's attraction to Universalism is especially convincing and astute. Universalists maintained, Skemp explains, that "humans were originally spiritual entities . . . before they took on a material form" and "were one with each other, and one with Christ" (51–52). Therefore, "[i]f spirit was the defining human characteristic, then women and men were not only equal, they were in every area that mattered identical" (56). Murray used Universalism to "transcend traditional definitions of feminine and masculine qualities"; of course, as Skemp admits, this "genderless ideal" did not match the distinctly gendered reality that she lived (56).

Another important influence is the experience of the American Revolution, which, as historians such as Linda Kerber and Rosemarie Zagarri have written, enabled women's increased politicization, even if the end of the war, as Zagarri and Skemp note, saw women's roles even further circumscribed. The war disrupted whole economies, especially in seaport towns such as Gloucester. According to Skemp, Murray emerged, as did many women, believing that "a love of freedom was not distinctively male or female": "Her religious faith, the egalitarian ideals that animated the War for Independence, her growing alienation from the ethos of military life, and her abiding belief in the value of education for women all coalesced with breathtaking rapidity in these years, allowing her to begin her career as a public advocate for the rights of 'the Sex' " (94).

Yet Murray was no republican. Skemp demonstrates consistently her subject's belief in genteel hierarchies; Judith's privileged youth, education, and freedom of religious thought arose from her position as a Sargent while her limitations were tied to her gender. Even as modern readers may lament her failure to extend to class her thinking on gender, her need to retain the former and question the latter makes human sense. Murray pursued this dissolution of gender hierarchies in her philosophy of education, which Skemp unfolds adroitly. In letter after letter to her adoptive niece, her nephew, and, eventually, her only daughter, Murray hammers home advice about the value of learning and civility. While she presents a time-management system that rivals Benjamin Franklin's, her theories of education reveal a belief in separate spheres and a conviction that even an educated woman's happiness lay in the private, domestic world. Still, as Skemp notes, "[s]imply writing about domestic affairs was an assertion of the importance of women's activities" (128).

Skemp's account of Murray's life relies on close and careful documentation and analysis of her letters. Mary Ann Caws contends that "[i]n the best biographies, even if we were not there, we feel we were" ("On the Horizontal: Women Writing on Writing Women," *PMLA* 122.2 [2007]: 552). Furthermore, as Paula Backscheider notes in *Reflections on Biography* (New York: Oxford UP, 1999), women's life stories may require more domestic detail and attention to ordinary living (153). To some extent, Skemp provides us with what Caws terms "high gossip" (549), such as Murray's insistent need to control her work and its reception; her relentlessly admonitory letters to various relatives, charges, critics, and friends to behave according to her own expectations (her micromanagement of the subscription list for her *Gleaner* collection is particularly telling); and her persistently unattractive classism and self-victimization. Skemp describes Murray's pain at failing to become a mother with her first husband, John Stevens, and her joy upon the birth of her daughter with John Murray. Through Skemp's honest and humane treatment, I grew to understand Murray as a woman both enabled and limited by her time and circumstance. Yet Skemp does not let her subject off the hook for her sense of entitlement or lack of self-awareness; rather, she judiciously balances between presenting Judith as a creature of her time and a unique and talented individual who used what was at hand to create a self.

Because Skemp rarely presents individual letters at any length, however, Murray remains at a distance. As a literary scholar, I would have appreciated more extensive citation of Murray's own voice as a way to feel her distinct presence and personality. To some extent, as Skemp notes, this distance results from Murray's careful self-construction in her letters and her methods of preserving her correspondence in letter books. Even as a girl, Skemp observes, Murray rewrote her letters before including them in her letter books, and she "carefully excluded from her permanent collection any number of letters that—for whatever reason—she did not wish to share with anyone" (31). Furthermore, the letter books contain no letters from others, since Murray wished to preserve her correspondents' privacy. Skemp skillfully manages her subject's self-construction by means of meticulous historical research in church and town meeting records, as well as the personal papers of family (including brother Winthrop Sargent and husband Rev. John Murray) and acquaintances (including Benjamin Rush and novelist Sally Wood).

In addition, the chronological approach tends to diffuse discussions of Judith Sargent Murray's individual works. Skemp considers, for example, the origins and operations of Murray's Universalist *Catechism* (1782) and especially "On the Equality of the Sexes" (1790) and "Desultory thoughts" (1784) in several chapters, and readers bent on plumbing Murray's life for insight into her works will need to jump around with the help of Skemp's excellent index.

Skemp's work stands as an important moment in the recovery of women's texts and lives. I look forward to using it in a course on Murray and her age. I can only admire Skemp's nimble selection of the details, no doubt from a complex file system of cards and paper, that reveal in stunning, sad, and human detail the mind and life of a brilliant woman who advocated for women's equality well before Mary Wollstonecraft.

Lisa M. Logan
University of Central Florida

NED MYERS; OR, A LIFE BEFORE THE MAST. By James Fenimore Cooper. The Writings of James Fenimore Cooper. Editor-in-Chief, Lance C. Schachterle; Textual Editors, Karen Lentz Madison and R. D. Madison; Historical Introduction, William S. Dudley and Hugh Egan. New York: AMS Press, 2009. liii + 252 pp. $125.

Ned Myers, a nineteenth-century common sailor and onetime shipmate of James Fenimore Cooper (1789–1851), has his voice aired once more thanks to a welcome new edition of Cooper's *Ned Myers; or, a Life before the Mast* (1843). This "profligate, alcoholic, and disabled lifetime seaman" (Hester Blum, *The View from the Masthead: Maritime Imagination and Antebellum American Sea Narratives* [Chapel Hill: U of North Carolina P, 2008]: 92] contacted Cooper by letter in January 1843, asking if the novelist was the same person who had worked with him on the merchant ship *Stirling* in 1806. Cooper, by then famous for maritime romances such as *The Pilot* (1824) and *Red Rover* (1827), as well as the more recent *The Wing and Wing* (1842) and *Two Admirals* (1842), quickly penned the intimate response: "I am your old ship-mate, Ned" (xxiii). As scholars have pointed out, this reunion was mutually beneficial. Their collaboration on the book during Myers's five-month stay at Cooperstown yielded, for Myers and his family, financial support and, for Cooper, though not a best seller by any stretch, a book to rival Richard Henry Dana Jr.'s celebrated *Two Years Before the Mast* (1941), along with, perhaps, a newly invigorated stylistic focus on first-person narration.

The irony is that the very element of the book that may have plagued it during its time—its rather ambiguous status as autobiography, biography, first-person fiction, and, more likely, a hybrid mix of the three—may constitute the greatest aspect of its historical value for students and scholars today. As Hugh Egan aptly suggests in his portion of the historical introduction, it is a text "that raises compelling questions about authorship, autobiography, and personal memory" (xxii–xxiii).

This edition provides an authoritative version of the novel, painstakingly melding Cooper's original handwritten manuscript with his subsequent emendations within the first American printer's copy, produced by Lea and Blanchard. Consequently, it provides an "unmodernized critical text, without silent emendations at any point" (224). The edition's apparatus includes useful closing commentary on textual concerns and manuscript development and an exhaustive record of textual notes and emendations; in addition, the "Historical Introduction" offers insight on Cooper and Myers's composition process. Egan's third section on "*Ned Myers*: The Book" is especially illuminating. Establishing the landscape of competing views about the book's authorial status—from nineteenth-century accounts by George Pomeroy Keese and Benjamin B. Griswald to modern reevaluations—Egan's analysis affords a productive foundation for examining the text. Egan notes that Myers's claim of veracity at the close of the tale (Myers states: "[T]his is literally my own story, logged by my old ship-mate" [216]) is actually Cooper's interlinear addition to the manuscript, inserted after he and Myers had stopped collaborating (xxx). Egan goes on to note several infelicitous editorial interjections (listing all of the thirty-two additions that were in Cooper's hand [xlix n40]) and conspicuous moments when Cooper apparently draws on his previous publications and puts them in Myers's voice.

As I have argued elsewhere ("Antebellum Fantasies of the Common Sailor; or, Enjoying the Knowing Jack Tar," *Criticism* 51.1 [2009]: 29–61), the authorial ambiguity in *Ned Myers* can be a useful and interesting symptom, one that scholars and students might use to explore issues of class and labor experience, authenticity and the literary marketplace, and discourses of knowledge in antebellum America. That is to say, we might conceive of Cooper's rendition of his shipmate's life as a means to explore much more than narrow historical interest in naval events on Lake Ontario, a topic that catalyzed a 1983 *National Geographic* article and the 1989 Naval Institute Press edition of the book.

As William S. Dudley suggests in his section of the introduction, "We need to know why men went to sea, how they looked at their captains, . . . what they thought about their treatment, . . . and what happened to them in their old age" (xxi). In other words, *Ned Myers* offers not only a lens for exploring the narrative and ideological construction of the common sailor but also a means to begin conceiving of the actual experiences of maritime laborers in this age. Citing Gary Nash, Marcus Rediker points out that such information is not easily come by, for American seamen "are perhaps the most elusive social group in early American history because they moved from port to port . . . , shifted occupations, died young, and, as the poorest members of the free white community, least often left behind traces of their lives" (*Between the Devil and the Deep Blue Sea: Merchant Seamen, Pirates and the Anglo-American Maritime World, 1700–1750* [Cambridge, UK: Cambridge UP, 1987]: 5). *Ned Myers* offers a narrative of one seaman's life. Like other destitute antebellum common sailors, such as John Hoxse and Reuben Delano, Myers helps produce an account of a schizophrenic-like circulation across ships, space, and national registers, as well as a portrayal of the "alcoholic haze," to use Wayne Franklin's phrase, that accompanied and, at times, precipitated such experience (*James Fenimore Cooper: The Early Year* [New Haven: Yale UP, 2007]: 72; see Hoxse's *The Yankee Tar* [1840] and Delano's *Wanderings and Adventures of Reuben Delano* [1846]). Indeed, Myers's years as a sailor comprise a bewildering chain of events, bringing him into contact with sailors and citizens of various races, nations, and classes: from his childhood in Nova Scotia to a brush with the doomed Miranda expedition to Venezuela, from naval battles on New York lakes and imprisonment on Melville Island to opium smuggling, near suicide, and religious conversion. In fact, as Dudley points out, Myers touched foot on nearly one hundred vessels during his time as a sailor (xv). In Myers's words, he was, quite often, "adrift in the Imperial Empire" (119).

This edition of *Ned Myers* should also be seen as an important text for studies of both the genre of sea narratives and Cooper's rich corpus. As others have noted, in terms of the former, *Ned Myers* appears at an anxious moment in the development of nineteenth-century sea narratives, when romance was giving way to shades of realism with hits such as Dana's aforementioned memoir and national fervor over events such as the USS *Somers* mutiny and the U.S. Exploring Expedition. In regard to the latter, besides Thomas Philbrick's seminal *James Fenimore Cooper and the Development of American Sea Fiction* (1961), few book-length studies have explored Cooper's influential maritime texts. Consequently, *Ned Myers* may provide students and scholars with new perspectives on Cooper's thought and work.

In light of recent theoretical reevaluations of the nineteenth-century maritime world, Cooper's book should be seen as a timely narrative. As mentioned, this edition's historical introduction helpfully lays the groundwork for directions of scholarly inquiry. Yet, scholars of American literature and American Studies may question some of the ideological parameters of this introduction. At times, Dudley's analysis slips into romantic conjectures, such as his claim, within his account of the development of the American shipping industry, that "sailors' unbridled, nomadic instincts were channeled and used for profit" (xv). This can also be seen in his description of Myers as "a reclaimed soul" and in his notion that it is "very unlikely that this memoir could have been written had Ned not had a conscience" (xvi). A similarly troubling construction is found in Egan's argument that, in *Ned Myers*, "the sea and America are thus intimately connected—*tabulae rasae* on which one can write one's own life" (xxiv). Of course, Egan is loosely referencing Myers's claim that, despite being born in the domains of England to German parents, America was the "the country of... [his] choice" (84). Yet, Egan's uncritical adoption of Myers's rhetoric clearly elides the historical forces and violence that shape Myers's identifications and choices.

This is not at all to disparage the usefulness of the introduction. I point out these moments because of the way they may limit implicitly our conception of the text and its content—both the questions we might ask and the ideological position from which we might ask them. It should be noted that such conditioning occurs also in seemingly neutral descriptions, such as the opening statement that *Ned Myers* is an "autobiography" (viii), or Dudley's claim that Cooper's early maritime romances "demonstrate his mastery of the seafaring world and its strange colloquial language" (viii). Although the latter comment is superficially valid, it glosses over the interesting class and experiential anxieties that shape Cooper's relation to maritime labor. For example, Franklin has pointed out that in crafting *The Pilot*, a text Dudley references to make his point, Cooper not only likely used Cmdre. Richard Dale for historical maritime details relating to John Paul Jones but also relied on his distant cousin Benjamin Cooper (a navy sailor) to correct his nautical terminology (Franklin, *James Fenimore Cooper* 409).

In 1844, the *Ladies' Companion* joined a growing list of journals that viewed *Ned Myers* as a flawed text, calling the book "a commonplace affair, sold for three shillings, York currency, and scarcely worth the attention bestowed upon it by its distinguished *editor*" (qtd. xli–xlii). Perhaps readers today will disagree. And not merely on the merits of the narrative alone, but because of the very complications and limitations it faced in the antebellum marketplace. In short, *Ned Myers* is a rich narrative that cuts across a myriad of historical, sociopolitical, and literary contexts and is undoubtedly worthy of renewed attention.

Jason Berger
University of South Dakota

WIELDING THE PEN: WRITINGS ON AUTHORSHIP BY AMERICAN WOMEN OF THE NINETEENTH CENTURY. Ed. Anne E. Boyd. Baltimore: Johns Hopkins UP, 2009. xxx + 452 pp. $77, hardback; $36, paperback.

In the introduction to her edited collection of women's writings on authorship, Anne E. Boyd makes a compelling argument for revising our understanding of women's attitudes toward and practices of authorship in the nineteenth-century United States. As she astutely points out, a first wave of feminist literary historians tackling "the absence of women writers from the canon . . . focused on how they were constrained and discouraged from picking up the pen" (xv). In a sort of circular fashion, such inquiries displaced the culpability of twentieth-century literary historians onto the nineteenth-century culture. After all (the implicit assumption was), the twentieth century must certainly have a more enlightened attitude toward women as cultural producers than the nineteenth century did. Quickly discovering that women were far from silent, the next move was to locate the "shame, fear, ambivalence, and self-deprecation" (xv) women authors certainly must have felt—this is, of course, the argument of Mary Kelley's highly influential *Private Woman, Public Stage: Literary Domesticity in Nineteenth-Century America* (1984). Reflecting on the wide variety of attitudes toward authorship evident in the 153 items (some complete, some excerpted) by 81 authors collected in her anthology, Boyd rightly observes that no one narrative or set of attitudes can account for all these texts, or even a majority. Most notably, however, only a minority evidence shame or fear, and the ambivalence and self-deprecation they do evidence is often more cultural than personal—that is, unashamed and self-confident women confronted a cultural ambivalence about women's authorship and may have used self-deprecation as a strategy for reaching an audience.

The diversity of texts Boyd collects in the anthology is both a virtue and a weakness, however. The texts are presented in a roughly chronological order (a chronology sometimes broken by the inclusion of more than one text for a given author), and Boyd provides at the back of the volume an alphabetical author list, a list by genre (i.e., autobiography; essays, editorials, and criticism; fiction and sketches; letters and journals; poetry; and prefaces and conclusions), and a list by theme. Certainly, regional, racial, class, and chronological diversity are a virtue, but the generic diversity makes it difficult to read the pieces together in any interpretive frame. Nearly half of the texts are poems, including more than a dozen by Emily Dickinson. Some of these poems, in the fashion of Anne Bradstreet's "Prologue" (1650), take an argumentative posture toward male condescension about women as creators, and these poems clearly fit into the category of "writings on authorship," as do, to a slightly lesser degree, poems about the function of poetry or invocations to the muse. The many poems on spinning and weaving, however, seem more tangential—certainly these activities have long been metaphors for women's writing, but few of these ostensibly metaphorical poems point explicitly to women's authorship.

Likewise, the many prefaces to women's books—frequently quite short—often only tangentially touch on authorship, and many in formulaic ways. Many of these prefaces are widely available in teaching editions of the books they introduce (such as Lydia Maria Child's *Hobomok* [1824], Harriet Beecher Stowe's *Uncle Tom's Cabin* [1852], Harriet Wilson's *Our Nig* [1859], Harriet Jacobs's *Incidents in the Life of a Slave Girl* [1861], and Pauline Hopkins's *Contending Forces* [1900]). Just what is a reader to *do* with a paragraph-long preface detached from the book that it introduces? Similarly, the inclusion of both public and private writing poses challenges. Letters and journals were not strictly private forms in the nineteenth century, but Grace Greenwood's "letter" "To an Unrecognized Poetess" (1846), which was written specifically for publication, is certainly very different from Augusta Jane Evans's 1860 letters to her friend Rachel Lyons encouraging her to take up novel-writing.

For me, the most satisfying works included and the easiest to read productively together, across, and against one another are the published essays and short stories in which women's authorship is central. Short stories and sketches such as Fanny Fern's "A Practical Blue-Stocking" (1853), Rose Terry Cooke's "The Memorial of A. B., or Matilda Muffin" (1860), Elizabeth Stoddard's "Collected by a Valetudinarian" (1870), Rebecca Harding Davis's "Marcia" (1876), Constance Fenimore Woolson's "Miss Grief" (1880), and Mary Wilkins Freeman's "A Poetess" (1890) are highly teachable. Some of them have been anthologized elsewhere, but having them together is useful and provocative, especially in an anthology that collects many examples in the durable genre of "advice to aspiring writers" from established writers. In my view, the most unfamiliar and revelatory were published pieces from relatively obscure—and sometimes entirely anonymous—writers about their motivations for writing and the conflict between domestic duties and authorship.

I could easily imagine teaching many of them alongside Fanny Fern's *Ruth Hall* (1855), for example (thankfully, Boyd has not anthologized excerpts from novels, although she recommends novels that might be read with the anthology). Also fascinating is Helen Gray Cone's long essay from the *Century Magazine* in 1890 that surveys the literary history of women in America up to her own time. On the one hand, Cone—joining in an emerging consensus that would soon banish most nineteenth-century women authors from American literary history—laments "sentimentalism" as a sort of disease that "infected" America and England in the early nineteenth century (346) and regrets the "quantity, dilution, [and] diffusiveness" of women's writing (347). On the other hand, she treats many of the writers she writes about at some length (including Stowe and Catharine Maria Sedgwick) with respect and from a position of authority—unlike many early twentieth-century literary historians, she has clearly actually *read* them.

Having cut across such a wide swath of literary history, Boyd necessarily ranges widely beyond her developed scholarly expertise (her first book, *Writing for Immortality: Women and the Emergence of High Literary Culture in America* [2004], focuses on the second half of the nineteenth century and four women who primarily wrote fiction: Louisa May Alcott, Elizabeth Stuart Phelps, Elizabeth Stoddard, and Constance Fenimore Woolson). Each author in the anthology gets a bare, undocumented paragraph of introduction, and reading from within my own developed expertise, I spotted many errors. Sedgwick is an example and is crucial in Boyd's general introduction. Why, she asks, have so many anthologies included Sedgwick's "negative" portrayal of authorship in "Cacoethes Scribendi" and ignored her "more positive" portrayal in "A Sketch of a Blue Stocking," a story "reprinted here for the first time"? (xvi). I have been reading, teaching, and thinking about "Cacoethes Scribendi" for fifteen years and am still not entirely sure I know what Sedgwick is doing, but framing it as purely negative and a "denunciation of public authorship" (xiv) does not do the story justice.

That is a question of interpretation, but there are also important questions of fact to consider. Later in the general introduction, citing no authority (but probably relying on Kelley), Boyd claims that "Sedgwick published nearly all of her work without her name on them" (xxii), a claim that is, as I have argued elsewhere, only true in a very limited and partial sense ("Behind the Veil?: Catharine Sedgwick and Anonymous Publication," in *Catharine Maria Sedgwick: Critical Perspectives*, ed. Lucinda Damon-Bach and Victoria Clements [Boston: Northeastern UP, 2003]: 19–35). Boyd furthermore misdates both stories based on a common misunderstanding about how to read gift book title pages—"Cacoethes" appeared in the *Atlantic Souvenir* "for 1830," published in late 1829, and "Sketch" appeared in the *Token and Atlantic Souvenir* "for 1832," published in late 1831 (with a byline "by Miss Sedgwick"—not anonymous). Boyd, however, dates the stories 1830 and 1832, respectively (see my bibliography of Sedgwick's shorter works in *Catharine Maria Sedgwick: Critical Perspectives*, which establishes the correct publication dates). In her biographical headnote for Sedgwick, Boyd has both of Sedgwick's parents die "when she was young" (17); actually, she was an older teenager when her mother died, and her father remarried—to a woman his adult children despised. Her father did not die until Catharine Sedgwick was in her mid-twenties, fully an adult. Boyd also classes together Sedgwick's second and third novels, *Redwood* (1824) and *Hope Leslie* (1827), as "[h]er historical novels . . . [that] helped to construct the nation's view of its origins" (17). *Redwood*, however, unlike *Hope Leslie* (set in seventeenth-century Puritan Massachusetts) is a contemporary novel of manners, not a historical novel.

These errors do not invalidate the anthology's potential usefulness for research and teaching—and, indeed, just about every headnote for Sedgwick in an American literature survey anthology makes similar errors. The errors do, however, point to the need to use this book with caution and to do your own homework. If Boyd's anthology sends many of us back into the archive to find more writings such as these, and in particular the published prose writings most specifically grappling with women's authorship, it will do valuable work.

Melissa J. Homestead
University of Nebraska-Lincoln

COLLECTED WORKS OF RALPH WALDO EMERSON, VOLUME VIII: LETTERS AND SOCIAL AIMS. By Ralph Waldo Emerson. Textual Editors, Glen M. Johnson and Joel Myerson; Historical Introduction, Ronald A. Bosco. Cambridge: Harvard UP, 2010. cclxxiv + 397 pp. $95.

The past half century in studies of Ralph Waldo Emerson (1803–82) might be called the Age of Editions. The monumental sixteen-volume *Journals and Miscellaneous Notebooks of Ralph Waldo Emerson*, the first volume of which appeared in 1960, concluded in 1982, the year Emersonians observed the centennial of Emerson's death. Two years later, Lawrence Buell surveyed the state of the "Emerson Industry" and predicted that the annual outpouring of Emerson scholarship, which had doubled since 1965, would only increase ("The Emerson Industry in the 1980's: A Survey of Trends and Achievements," *ESQ: A Journal of the American Renaissance* 30.2 [1984]: 117–36). In the quarter century since Buell's forecast, the volume of books and articles about Emerson has redoubled, fueled in large part by the publication of several more editions of Emerson's writings that have made available not only works newly edited according to the best modern critical standards but also massive amounts of previously unpublished (even unknown) Emerson material.

Already available when Buell surveyed the state of Emerson scholarship were the *Letters* (6 vols., 1939) and the *Early Lectures: 1833–1842* (3 vols., 1959–72). Then in rapid order appeared the *Poetry Notebooks* (1986), *Complete Sermons* (4 vols., 1989–92), *Topical Notebooks* (3 vols., 1990–94), four more volumes of *Letters* (1990–95), *Antislavery Writings* (1995), *Later Lectures: 1843–1871* (2 vols., 2001), and *The Emerson Brothers: A Fraternal Biography in Letters* (2006). Conspicuously absent has been a complete flagship edition of writings published during Emerson's lifetime. The *Collected Works of Ralph Waldo Emerson*, conceived in 1961 to supersede Edward Waldo Emerson's Centenary Edition of the *Complete Works* (12 vols., 1903–4) and put under contract with Harvard University Press in 1968, published its first volume—*Nature, Addresses, and Lectures*—in 1971. But the rate at which subsequent volumes have appeared has been fitful, even glacial (*Essays: First Series* [1979], *Essays: Second Series* [1983], *Representative Men* [1987], *English Traits* [1994], and *The Conduct of Life* [2003]), requiring responsible scholars for decades awkwardly to cite the volumes-to-date in the *Collected Works*, and the 1903–4 *Complete Works* for what had yet to appear in the ongoing edition.

After Ronald A. Bosco assumed the General Editorship in 2005 and Joel Myerson was named Textual Editor in 2007, the pace of *Collected Works* quickened dramatically. Bosco is a seasoned Emerson editor, having done volumes in the *Journals and Miscellaneous Notebooks, Sermons,* and *Topical Notebooks,* and Myerson, the dean of Transcendentalist studies and the premier Emerson bibliographer, coedited *Antislavery Writings* (with Len Gougeon). The two collaborated, moreover, on the *Later Lectures* and the *Emerson Brothers.* Volume 7 of *Collected Works, Society and Solitude,* promptly appeared in 2007. Publication of the present volume, *Letters and Social Aims,* in 2010 and the anticipated publication of the two remaining volumes—*Poems* in 2011 and *Uncollected Prose Writings* in 2011 or 2012—finally will bring *Collected Works* to completion half a century after its conception. The first six volumes having taken thirty-five years since the initial contract with Harvard University Press to appear, the final four, barring a catastrophe, will have taken only six or seven.

This accelerated progress is all the more impressive given the complicated biographical issues and the tangled textual history that faced the editors of volume 8 in the *Collected Works*—*Letters and Social Aims.* Initially published by James R. Osgood in December 1875, this was the first book bearing Emerson's name that he did not prepare himself. In a historical introduction of nearly two hundred pages—tantamount to a full biography of Emerson's final decade—general editor Bosco shows how Emerson's mental "descent" (xxix) made it necessary for his daughter Ellen and literary executor James Elliot Cabot to compile a new book from four essays previously published in magazines and seven that had to be constructed from lecture manuscript leaves—with Emerson taking a mainly passive role in the process. Work on what became *Letters and Social Aims* felt forced upon him when in July 1870 Emerson learned that, without consulting him, Moncure Conway had promised a new collection of his essays to the London publisher John Camden Hotten. Preoccupied with his University Lectures at Harvard (1870–71), still working on *Society and Solitude* (1870) and his cherished anthology of his favorite world poetry (which would become *Parnassus* [1874]), and pondering an introduction to W. W. Goodwin's five-volume edition of *Plutarch's Morals* (1870), Emerson was annoyed and overwhelmed by this unexpected obligation.

Aggravating Emerson's distress was his diminishing intellectual power, which Bosco describes in surprising and often moving detail. The story that Bosco tells was made possible by his access to papers of the Forbes family at the Massachusetts Historical Society and to an extraordinary cache of Emerson family papers deposited by Roger L. Gregg shortly before his death in 2004. Gregg's mother, Edith E. W. Gregg, it turns out, had been highly selective when she published her great-aunt's correspondence nearly three decades ago (*The Letters of Ellen Tucker Emerson* [2 vols., 1982]). Bosco's discoveries about Emerson family matters are always illuminating and sometimes shocking. Among the revelations: when fire broke out at Emerson's house, "Bush," on July 24, 1872, he " 'deliberately' " tossed "mementoes" of his first wife, Ellen Tucker Emerson, and his late son, Waldo, into the flames (xxxii). The fire did not cause his aphasia, as is widely believed; though the trauma undoubtedly accelerated his intellectual troubles, signs of his decline were apparent in the late 1860s (xxxix). The collaboration of daughter Ellen and James Elliot

Cabot as Emerson's literary executors has long been known. Obscured until now is the role of daughter Edith and her husband, Will Forbes, in shaping his late works and his reputation. It was Edith who championed and oversaw the publication of *Parnassus* and who, recognizing the importance of the Emerson-Carlyle correspondence, arranged to gather and preserve it (xxxiv–xxxv). Son Edward, moreover, was more closely involved in the 1876 and 1884 editions of *Poems* than has been known (xxxvi).

Bosco's observation that the critical reception of *Letters and Social Aims* was generally positive—several reviewers praising the essays as evidence of Emerson's continuing relevance and vitality—is ironic in light, not only of his passive role in the volume's construction, but also of the enormous span of time and circumstances in which the essays had emerged. Seven were "previously unpublished but drawn from Emerson's lectures with extensive genealogies" ("Poetry and Imagination," "Social Aims," "Eloquence," "Resources," "Inspiration," "Greatness," and "Immortality") while "versions" of the other four had already appeared in serials—"The Comic" as early as the October 1843 issue of *The Dial*, as well as "Quotation and Originality" (*North American Review* Apr. 1868), "Progress of Culture" (*Atlantic Monthly* Jan. 1868), and "Persian Poetry" (*Atlantic Monthly* Apr. 1858) (xx). This volume simply cannot be read as the embodiment of Emerson's creative vision and vitality in 1875.

In the "Statement of Editorial Principles," Joel Myerson explains how the "tortured textual history" (ccxx) of *Letters and Social Aims* affected the unique editorial decisions for volume 8. The "central editorial principles of this edition," writes Myerson, "are that the copy-text is the text closest to the author's initial coherent intention and that determining his subsequent intention depends on the use of evidence from other relevant forms of the text according to conservative editorial principles" (ccxv). The classic Greg-Bowers-Tanselle "line of textual editing presumes authorial control throughout the writing and publication process," which simply does not work in this case. Emerson's passive role in producing *Letters and Social Aims* makes "identifying Emerson's initial coherent intention . . . difficult if not impossible for the volume as a whole" (ccxvi). (Compounding the problem for his editors then and now, Emerson on the lecture platform often " 'shuffled his sheets several times to see what will turn up,' " as Bronson Alcott witnessed [qtd. ccxlvi], and after the mid-1840s, Myerson notes, Emerson "viewed units of prose as completely fluid" [ccxlvii].) Thus copy-texts for the essays in this edition are previous magazine publications (and manuscript printer's copy where available) or, in the case of lectures compiled by Cabot and Ellen, the versions they published in 1875, "lightly emended" because "Emerson had no active intentionality in the final form that these texts took" (ccxvii). The clear text presented is "critical and unmodernized," Myerson writes in the textual introduction, as was the case with volumes 1–7 of *Collected Works* (ccxliii). The appendixes include a textual apparatus comprising emendations in copy-text and rejected substantives and spellings for each essay, along with a description and discussion of the manuscripts. More than one hundred pages of notes on sources and historical context by Glen M. Johnson continue the high standard of the earlier volumes of *Collected Works*, and his valuable compilation of parallel passages is perhaps even more essential, given the complex textual history of the eleven essays.

As Myerson deftly puts it, "[F]or *Letters and Social Aims,* Emerson's creative powers were in decline and the impetus for the book itself came from efforts in England by others, initially without his permission; he received significant assistance in the selection, composition, and revision process from others; and his participation in the proofing process was minimal" (ccxx). Particularly ironic, then, is Myerson's disclosure that many critics admired the book as being less aphoristic and more carefully structured than Emerson's previous books (ccxxxvi). Not privy to the textual history of this latest "Emerson" book, most conferred praise on the aging icon now revered as the Sage of Concord.

Tangled issues of its genesis, intentionality, chronology, and coherence notwithstanding, this book is packed with wit and wisdom, with variety, and even with milestones in literary history. "Quotation and Originality" has one of the quirkiest openings to be found in any Emerson essay. Puckishly, he declares the parasitic "suction" found in the "insect world" to be the prototype of human "quotation": "If we go into a library or news-room, we see the same function on a higher plane, performed with like ardor, with equal impatience of interruption, indicating the sweetness of the act" (93). The aging champion of self-reliance further disorients the reader, stating that "in a large sense, one would say, there is no pure originality" (94)—a point he drives home with his familiar aphoristic punch ("A great man quotes bravely" [96]; "Next to the originator of a good sentence, is the first quoter of it" [100]). Yet toward the end, the old idealism reappears: "Every mind is different"; genuine "Originality" "is being; being oneself; and reporting accurately what we see and are" (105). Stubbornly asserting that "the moment has the supreme claim," Emerson concludes this engaging essay by conceding that the individual is absorbed into cosmic wholeness and continual natural, organic process (which romanticism and the scientific spirit of the 1860s asserted rather differently)—a vision that celebrates the creative "instant life" of the present even as it acknowledges that this moment is inevitably absorbed "in the omnipotency with which Nature decomposes all her harvest for recomposition" (107).

A very different essay, "Persian Poetry," has new significance in our time as Emerson, once admired as a prophet of American exceptionalism, is increasingly appreciated in global context and as a champion of world literatures. Emerson's attempt to distinguish the "violent contrast" between the "[a]ll or nothing . . . genius" of "Oriental life and society" and "the multitudinous detail, the secular stability, and the vast average of comfort of the Western nations" (124) may seem primitive by modern standards. But he embraces the Persian poets—especially the fourteenth-century Hafiz, whom he read in the nineteenth-century German translation of Joseph von Hammer-Purgstall—for their "Gnomic verses," ethical intensity, and "inconsecutiveness" (127). Hafiz, who has "the insight of a mystic" (129) and embodies "intellectual liberty" that disdains "Hypocrisy" (132), wrote frankly "erotic and bacchanalian songs," but these are "not to be confounded with vulgar debauch" (133). The sensuousness of Hafiz might seem incompatible with the Yankee sensibility until we remember that, as a critic of materialism and deadening social convention and hypocrisy, Emerson, too, was deeply passionate (see Len Gougeon, *Emerson and Eros: The Making of a Cultural Hero* [2007]). Indeed, the plentiful poems and excerpts with which Emerson fills the essay are a virtual bacchanalian celebration of the Persians.

The publication of *Letters and Social Aims* and the two remaining volumes in the *Collected Works* will only stimulate further the already-robust Emerson Industry.

Wesley T. Mott
Worcester Polytechnic Institute

THE ARBITERS OF REALITY: HAWTHORNE, MELVILLE, AND THE RISE OF MASS INFORMATION CULTURE. By Peter West. Columbus: Ohio State UP, 2008. xiv + 229 pp. $44.95.

In "The Story Teller," one of the lost collections he assembled only to dismantle and publish piecemeal, Nathaniel Hawthorne (1804–64) devised an elaborate narrative frame in which an itinerant raconteur regales his listeners with stories produced in response to audience demand. In *The Arbiters of Reality: Hawthorne, Melville, and the Rise of Mass Information Culture,* Peter West begins his discussion of antebellum romance by peering inside the box-within-a-box structure of "The Story Teller" to disclose the author's mode of self-definition within a culture of commercial display and Barnumesque hype. The chapter offers a compelling reading of the remnants of "The Story Teller"; it also allows West to create a framing device of his own in which romance itself comes sharply into focus.

The six chapters of *The Arbiters of Reality* are divided equally between Hawthorne and Herman Melville (1819–91) and arranged in symmetrical concentric frames. In each half of the monograph, West presents a sequence of chapters that begins with a lesser-known text and gradually expands to encompass a broader historical context, increasingly substantial texts, and more sweeping implications about the literary artist's self-fashioning and ontological claims with respect to an unstable "reality" freshly marketed to the masses as the real deal. The effect of this double tripartite structure—comparable to "the layered narrative approach" (53) of "The Story Teller"—is to profile each author's engagement with changing notions of authenticity, reality, truth-telling, and the self within increasingly intricate frames of signification. Focusing by turns on the background, middle ground, and foreground (a relevant swath of cultural history, a well-selected swatch of contemporaneous print culture, and the primary texts), *The Arbiters of Reality* offers an interpretation of antebellum romance that is at once detailed, nuanced, and expansive. Not only does it present insightful, well-informed readings of individual texts; *The Arbiters of Reality* achieves the far more ambitious goal of "recast[ing] the persistent American belief in a reality uncorrupted by commercialization as the powerful legacy of romanticism" (xi).

Exploiting what he identifies as "the shared logic of new historicism and romance" (94; see also 17), West performs a kind of literary archaeology in his reconstruction of "The Story Teller" that informs the study as a whole. West excavates the broken shards of Hawthorne's lost collection and then pieces together the fragments on the basis of evidence culled from letters, journals, and the surviving stories themselves. Elsewhere in his book, West extends this practice of textual archaeology by reconstructing around texts that are, in themselves, intact, an elaborate peritext of cultural relics: newspaper articles, advertisements, popular books, letters, daguerreotypes, moving panoramas, telegraphic dispatches, and political propaganda. With a nimble handling of archival sources, West provides a rich, often unexpected, and always illuminating context to reveal how Hawthorne and Melville conceived of the art of romance as a mode of truth-telling grounded in an unmediated or "foundational" reality in contradistinction to a range of emerging popular forms that asserted their own claims to authenticity in an increasingly commercialized marketplace.

West's project is to examine "how Hawthorne and Melville defined themselves and their art against the informational practices of an emergent mass culture" and "imagined themselves . . . as 'arbiters of reality'—privileged seers who portrayed the antebellum commercial revolution as a threat to the very stability of truth" (x). West is to be commended for his refusal to take the comfortable, well-traveled path in this meticulous study. While acknowledging the contributions of new historicists who have positioned Hawthorne and Melville as astute cultural critics who managed to step outside their own historical frames, West argues that "Hawthorne's and Melville's shared sense of 'reality' as a word to be placed in scare quotes seems less a vehicle of social critique than a language for imagining and communicating a self beyond the threat of collective identity-making" (18). As West states in his introduction, his chapters "[approach] the deconstructive worldview of romance as both historical (shaped by particular discursive and material contexts) and rhetorical (employed by its practitioners as a means of negotiating such contexts)." In pursuing this double-edged strategy, he suggests, his work "offer[s] . . . an account of the romantic flight from contingency that has been informed by the insights and priorities of new historicism, a reading of antebellum literature and culture that sees the romancer's desire for a different kind of reality as a dream that was firmly grounded in place and time" (22). In its effort to accomplish this critical goal, *The Arbiters of Reality* does not disappoint.

West's section on Hawthorne begins by examining the journalistic treatment of a sensational 1830 Salem murder case and then contrasts the coverage of the crime in the press with Hawthorne's response, as reflected in his private correspondence. West then analyzes a little-known tale based on the incident to show how Hawthorne positioned his own mode of storytelling against the narrative logic of the emerging penny press. "Mr. Higginbotham's Catastrophe" (1834) is, as West points out, the only tale in "The Story Teller" cycle that was published in its original narrative frame. The fact that the frame remains intact allows West to analyze closely Hawthorne's positioning of the story's teller as "both the producer and the peddlar of his tales" (45) vis-à-vis the narrator-author, who remains safely outside the jostle and fray of the marketplace. West's larger analysis extends to such familiar tales as "Wakefield" (1835), "The Ambitious Guest" (1835), and "The Devil in Manuscript" (1835), and the section concludes with a careful reading of tropes of representation in *The House of the Seven Gables* (1851).

In the second half of the book, West complicates recent readings of Melville by demonstrating how his critique of popular culture functioned simultaneously as a form of self-invention. The section opens with a compelling reading of Melville's "Old Zack" articles (1847), a series of satirical sketches published anonymously during the administration of Zachary Taylor and the ramp-up to the Mexican War. "At a time when American journalism was churning out broad and consequential myths about American expansion, Mexican inferiority, and racial heterogeneity as a threat to national cohesiveness, all under the aegis of a technology-based claim to infallible and instantaneous communication," West argues, "Melville's parodic sketches exposed journalism as a carefully manufactured product that empowered such mythmaking" (96). In the subsequent two chapters—on *Typee* (1846) and "Benito Cereno" (1856)—West "reveal[s] that, as in the 'Old Zack' sketches, these works reflect Melville's particular subject position as a white male American author continually evading the authorial and communal identities foisted upon him by the mass marketplace" (128).

West's readings are substantial, original, surprising, and deep. Occasionally, the journey itself is more interesting than the destination. In the chapter on *Typee*, the conclusion seems visible from the outset, a limitation largely mitigated by the acumen of the twenty intervening pages. And in a few places, West's extrapolations recall Julian Hawthorne's reference to the great romancer's "power of making bricks without straw, and even without clay upon occasion" ("The Salem of Hawthorne," *Century Illustrated Monthly Magazine* 28.1 [1884]: 4). From Hawthorne's statement in his notebook that "[t]here is no such thing as a true portrait.... They are all delusions," West overreaches when he concludes that "to reject all portraits as 'delusions' is to redefine the human subject as that which no representation could ever contain" (71). Yet each chapter is replete with brilliantly historicized textual analysis so that what might otherwise seem a significant flaw in the argumentative fabric appears merely a distracting slub.

One of the satisfactions of *The Arbiters of Reality* is its tendency to give readers more than they bargained for. What the title, table of contents, and cover copy do not reveal is the impressive range and imaginativeness of West's textual juxtapositions: Hawthorne's "Story Teller" mingles with Edgar Allan Poe's Dupin; Clifford Pyncheon rubs shoulders with Ned Buntline; "Benito Cereno" stands alongside Harriet Beecher Stowe, Frederick Douglass, and William Wells Brown (to say nothing of *Moby-Dick* [1851] and *The Confidence Man* [1857]). Topping it all off, West's "Coda" presents an engaging discussion in which Rebecca Harding Davis's *Life in the Iron Mills* (1861) is cleverly enlisted to reveal the unexpected continuity between romance and realism: a much-needed corrective for the abrupt and artificial rupture that has become nearly axiomatic in the conventional two-semester anthology-driven delineation of American literary history. In the end, what appears on the outside to be a modest two-author study telescopes out to encompass much more. *The Arbiters of Reality* illuminates not only how Hawthorne and Melville engaged with the rapidly changing technologies and economies of representation in antebellum America but also the complex ways in which romance negotiates an unreal world where "authenticity" circulates as currency, information is manufactured for mass consumption, and reality itself is neatly packaged for a ready sale.

Sarah Wadsworth
Marquette University

CULTURE CLUB: THE CURIOUS HISTORY OF THE BOSTON ATHENAEUM. By Katherine Wolff. Amherst: U of Massachusetts P, 2009. xviii + 204 pp. $80, hardback; $26.95, paperback.

Those of us who are fortunate to have worked at the Boston Athenaeum will remember its sense of quiet in the midst of a bustling city, with views from the windows over the Granary Burying Ground, the superb collection of nineteenth-century books (bought, for the most part, as they were published), and its many early newspapers (whose fragility often left the tables filled with paper shards akin to bread crumbs left by a sloppy eater). But, as Katherine Wolff argues in her fascinating book, the Athenaeum was more than a place of refuge; it played a vital part in the culture wars fought in Boston during the nineteenth century (the book follows its subject through roughly the Civil War).

Wolff, unlike other book-length chroniclers of the Athenaeum's history, shies away from a full-scale chronological study; instead, she uses case studies based on individuals and artifacts to pursue a cultural history of the Boston Athenaeum that, in her words, probes "the origins of 'high culture' in America." (Biographies of the major players are in an appendix.) In her reading, the "Athenaeum's founders purposely built a center for culture, a place where they could control chaos and celebrate civility" (xi). She argues that the institution "stood at the intersection of three themes in American life: the tension between inherited European and emerging American aesthetic models; the relationship between a city and its artificial cultural center; and the persistence of narrative as a means of establishing personal and institutional identity" (xiv).

Libraries usually mean repositories of books, but the Athenaeum members saw the role of the institution to be much more, a type of cultural and aesthetic leadership in which "establishing standards of taste to combat chaos and vulgarity was considered tantamount to moral action." This attitude followed naturally from earlier New England and British attitudes that the "true gentleman was always a reader" (9). As a result, there was a sense of civic responsibility inherent in being a member of the Athenaeum, and much of Wolff's book deals with how individual members carried out what they considered to be their responsibilities.

The first two chapters diverge from the usual narrative that the founding of the Athenaeum was merely a logical progression from the meetings of the Anthology Society by focusing on two individuals, William Smith Shaw of Boston and William Roscoe of Liverpool, England. Shaw, John Adams's nephew, was the Athenaeum's first librarian, and his comprehensive accumulating habits informed the encyclopedic collecting policies of the library's early years. Just as creating a venue for culture acted as an antidote to the unease the Athenaeum's members felt because of the changes in society, so too did assembling and classifying books fill a void in Shaw's life after an unsatisfying career and the death of a dear friend. In Roscoe, a successful merchant, philanthropist, collector, and bibliophile, the businessmen of the Athenaeum (and they comprised some 70 percent of the officers and trustees between 1816 and 1830) could see a validation of their own aspirations and a stabilizing of "the competing demands of public service, bookishness, and commerce" (43). And just as Roscoe had made his own home a center of culture, the Athenaeum gained permanent clubrooms in 1822 when it moved into a mansion on Pearl Street donated by the merchant James Perkins.

If the Athenaeum members found in Roscoe a model for their own actions, then their treatment of the historian Hannah Adams shows how they used the actions of others to further their own image. The subject of the third chapter, Adams is portrayed as a representative of true republican womanhood who, even though childless, is, through her writings, able to advise and encourage the young to be good citizens. The Athenaeum served as her patron, allowing her to use one of the best libraries in Boston, and, in return, basked in the reflection of her own high standing. (Here, as with the subjects of other paintings, Wolff includes an interesting reading of the painting of Adams that hangs at the Athenaeum to show how the visual image was construed to support the cultural image of her that the members wished to employ.) Still, she was not given "formal access" to the library until two years before her death (80).

The second set of three chapters focuses on events rather than on people. The fourth chapter, which shows the importance of the visual arts at the Athenaeum, follows the debates over whether European art should be championed or, rather, as Chester Harding argued, the works of living American artists should be supported. (European art won out for painting, but in sculpture, Americans were enthusiastically encouraged.) The Athenaeum was probably one of the premier places for Bostonians to see artistic exhibitions prior to the opening of the Museum of Fine Arts (to which the Athenaeum eventually donated many of its best works) in 1876; and between 1827 and 1873, it offered forty-six annual exhibitions that were open to the (paying) public. When the new library building on Beacon Street, based on the architecture of an Italian Renaissance palace, was completed in 1850, the holdings were divided between two-thirds art and one-third books. The Athenaeum's focus on cultural influence was now firmly on the side of the visual arts.

The cultural contributions of the Athenaeum as depicted in the fifth chapter, "The Color of Gentility," are less favorable. Beginning in the 1830s, the citizens of Boston, often led by the cultural elite, pushed for the abolition of slavery. While the Athenaeum itself was not involved in the antislavery crusade, its very absence in the main reform event of nineteenth-century America was telling. Because so many of the members were businessmen, and a number of them involved in textiles and thus economically connected to Southern interests, the idea of a "gentlemanly" thing to do took second place to economic interests. Also, the supporters of abolition, especially William Lloyd Garrison, did not forward their cause by means that were considered "civil" by the Athenaeum's members. The supremacy of commercialism to gentility, on the one hand, and the concerns that the reforms themselves were uncivil, on the other, show how strained the original standards of the institution were becoming. Also, during this time, there had been a complete turnaround from the pro-American, anti-English attitudes inherited from the Anthology Society that reflected the first years of America's own striving for cultural independence to an affirmation of British-made abolitionist wares sold at antislavery fairs and praise for Britain's freeing slaves in the West Indies in the late 1830s.

Two case studies inform this chapter: Lydia Maria Child, whose visitation rights to the library were revoked after she published antislavery works, and Charles Sumner, one of their own who led the way for change.

The final chapter examines the pamphlet war in the mid-1850s over whether the Athenaeum and its collections should be folded into those of the nascent public library. On one side, Josiah Quincy argued for maintaining the Athenaeum as a separate entity, based in part on the wishes of the founders, while George Ticknor argued for what he saw as the greater good of a library decidedly for the people. This discussion, played out in public, forced Athenaeum members to recognize that their attachment was not necessarily, as the founders had thought, to a *public* place for reading and viewing art, but, rather, to the Athenaeum as an institution, being a combination of library, art gallery, social club, and building, a physical and intellectual space in which they felt secure.

Wolff has given us a well-written study of a Boston institution, a work that firmly situates it within the artistic, bibliophilic, social, and cultural attitudes and struggles of its time. Because of her work, we have a better understanding of what she calls "a resilient institution that continued to attract substantial funding in spite of its limited reach and discreet image" (147).

Joel Myerson
University of South Carolina

JOURNAL. VOLUME 7: 1853–1854. By Henry D. Thoreau. Ed. Nancy Craig Simmons and Ron Thomas. Princeton: Princeton UP, 2009. 552 pp. $65.

Recently published by Princeton University Press, the latest volume of the definitive edition of Henry David Thoreau's (1817–62) massive *Journal* covers a span of roughly six months: from August 1853 to February 1854. Volume 7 of the *Journal*, edited by Nancy Craig Simmons and Ron Thomas under the direction of *The Writings of Henry D. Thoreau* Editor-in-Chief Elizabeth Hall Witherall, is, like its predecessors, a gift to serious readers of Thoreau. Printed in clear text, with extensive annotations, textual and historical introductions, tables of alterations and revisions, and a complete cross-reference to Thoreau's published works, this edition of the *Journal* provides not only the definitive text of what Philip P. Gura has called "Thoreau's *magnum opus*" ("Review: A Riddle Worth the Reading: Thoreau's Works and Days," *New England Quarterly* 55.3 [1982]: 448) but also a number of indispensible tools for tracking his extraordinary and evolving process as writer and observer of the natural world.

The volume spans three seasons: late summer, fall, and winter. Thoreau's custom during this period was to write in the morning and walk in the afternoon; he often composed entries for several days at a time, aided by field notes made while walking. As is the case with other volumes of the *Journal* from 1851 on, much of the text of volume 7 is devoted to precise observation of the natural world. Though Thoreau often expressed ambivalence about science, his interests and activities during this period are increasingly scientific. In Maine he records the measurements of a dead moose ("I did not wish to be obliged to say merely that the moose was large—but wished to be able to say exactly how large she was . . . " [65]). At home in Concord he devises a painstaking method—involving sixty-five discrete measurements—for the accurate measurement of the depth of snow. In a passage marked by an enthusiasm for science that he did not consistently feel, he writes,

> The skeleton which at first sight excites only a shudder in all mortals—becomes at last—not only a pure, but suggestive and pleasing object to science. The more we know of it, the less we associate it with any goblin of our imaginations. . . . We discover that the only spirit which haunts it is a Universal Intelligence which has created it in harmony with all nature. Science never saw a ghost—nor does it look for any—but sees everywhere the traces—and is itself the agent—of a Universal Intelligence. (186)

Tracking this "Universal Intelligence" through the unfolding of the seasons is Thoreau's major preoccupation during these months. He records the first leaf fall, the first frost, the freezing and thawing of Walden Pond, among hundreds of other seasonal phenomena (38). As the editors note, many of the observations recorded in this portion of the *Journal* would ultimately be transcribed into the series of lists and charts, drawn up beginning in 1860, that comprise his unfinished Kalendar project: "Long before he created the lists and charts, however, Thoreau began selecting phenomena to observe based on his understanding that the patterns he sought would be revealed by evidence collected with patience and care over many years" (408). Thoreau's intentions for these observations are the point at which he parts company from the increasingly professionalized science of the mid-nineteenth century. Years later he would express the difference this way:

> I think that the man of science makes this mistake, and the mass of mankind along with him: that you should coolly give your chief attention to the phenomenon which excites you as something independent on you, and not as it is related to you. . . . With regard to such objects, I find that it is not they themselves (with which the men of science deal) that concern me; the point of interest is somewhere between me and them (i.e. the objects). . . . (Nov. 5, 1857, MS vol. 24, 12: 267–68, The Writings of Henry D. Thoreau, Davidson Lib., U of California, Santa Barbara)

One of Thoreau's primary ambitions in collecting seasonal data seems to have been to determine, "though at the risk of endless iteration," the essence of each month, as revealed over time (140). On October 31, he asks, "Is not this already November when the yellow and scarlet tints are gone from the forest?" In November he observes, "October is the month of painted leaves—of ripe leaves—when all the earth—not merely flowers but fruits & leaves are ripe—with respect to its colors and seasons it is the sunset months of the year" (160). Related to Thoreau's desire to capture the essence of the months is his habit of assigning human life its place within the seasons, or, as in this entry, ascribing seasonal qualities to phases of human life: "October answers to that period in the life of man—when he is no longer dependent on his transient moods—when all his experience ripens into wisdom—but every root branch leaf of him glows with maturity— What he has been & done in his spring and summer appears— He bears his fruit" (160). Here we see the way Thoreau's characteristic desire to recontextualize the human as part of nature directs his process of observation. He records not only the inches of snowfall and the depth of ice but also the day (Dec. 11) he is first "without greatcoat" (196). He is concerned throughout the volume with views, landscapes, and perception—not merely the object observed but its relation to the observing eye. In November, he notes "that intimate mingling of wood & water which excites an expectation which the near & open view rarely realizes. We prefer that some part may be concealed—which our imaginations may navigate" (143).

A particular advantage of this volume over the corresponding portion of the 1906 edition of the *Journal* is its inclusion of an account of Thoreau's September 1853 trip to Maine, which would eventually become the "Chensuncook" section of *The Maine Woods* (1864). Excised from the *Journal* by the editors of the 1906 edition because of its similarity to the published account, this section of the *Journal*, along with the scholarly apparatus, illuminates both Thoreau's unique method of documenting experience—a multistage process in which observations originally collected in field notes were first expanded into journal entries and then sometimes revised and incorporated into essays and lectures—as well as the centrality of the *Journal* to all of Thoreau's written work. The editors note that Thoreau did not take his journal with him to Maine, but rather "followed his standard practice and recorded daily events in field notes that he kept separately" and began expanding the notes into full entries upon his return on September 27, "labeling the entries with the dates on which events had occurred rather that with the dates on which he was writing them" and composing only cursory "new" entries for the dates between September 28 and October 19 (423–24). The temporal disjunction here highlights Thoreau's interest—evident in the structure of both *A Week on the Concord and Merrimack Rivers* (1849) and *Walden* (1854)—in the problem of how best to document the passage of time.

The present volume spans a period in which Thoreau was immersed in composing the fifth, sixth, and seventh drafts of *Walden*, and readers will recognize here early versions of key passages from the published text. In addition, passages from this volume would later appear in "Walking" (1861), *Cape Cod* (1865), and "Autumnal Tints" (1862), as well as *The Maine Woods* (394). For readers familiar with those works, to read this volume is to realize the status of the *Journal* as a central node in a dense network of textual relations and to perceive the inextricability of Thoreau's writings—the field notes, the *Journal*, the published essays and books, and finally the charts and graphs—from one another.

One of the gossamer threads connecting these texts, and running most vividly throughout this volume of the *Journal*, is memory. Through the multistage process of observation and documentation that was his daily practice, Thoreau continually locates himself not only in place but also in time, drawing together past, present, and future in his records of the cyclical movement of the seasons: "It is surprising how any reminiscence of a different season of the year affects us—When I meet with any such in my journal it affects me as poetry and I appreciate that other season and that particular phenomenon more than at the time.— The world so seen is all one spring and full of beauty" (115). Indeed, it often seems that Thoreau's central ambition in these pages is simply to *realize* the seasons, and through this realization to integrate his own life, and that of his community, into the life of the natural world. "Let us sing winter," he writes at the end of January, "What else can we sing—and our voices be in-harmony with the season[?]" (256).

Kristen Case
University of Maine at Farmington

WALT WHITMAN AND THE CIVIL WAR: AMERICA'S POET DURING THE LOST YEARS OF 1860–1862. By Ted Genoways. Berkeley: U of California P, 2009. viii + 210 pp. $24.95.

Walt Whitman (1819–92) loved boats. He loved spending time with the men who piloted them, and "the great tides of humanity" who crowded onto ferries fascinated him (*Specimen Days* [1882], in *"Leaves of Grass" and Selected Prose* [New York: Modern Lib., 1981]: 563). The water also mesmerized him. Throughout his writings, Whitman associates rivers and oceans, as well as ferry rides and boats, with multitudes, movement, transformations, and activity, but also with the afterlife, the merge, and death. So, it seems appropriate that Ted Genoways begins and ends his biography of Whitman during the Civil War with images of a boat carrying a dead body. Genoways opens his narrative with the body of John Brown being unloaded from a boat in December 1859; the story closes in December 1862 with a steamer moving up the Potomac with Whitman and a crush of wounded soldiers, including the body of one who died on the journey. Without overt commentary or labored explanation (like Whitman, Genoways is also a poet), these images capture his narrative precision and his interest in seeing Whitman in motion, surrounded by a whirlwind of events and throngs of people, living and dead.

Previous biographies have shed surprisingly little light on these three years. Before Genoways began his research, only about a half-dozen letters written by Whitman during these years seemed to have survived, and his autobiographical *Specimen Days* (1892) says relatively little about his life in this period. Thus, in the words of Jerome Loving, "The first two years of the Civil War are among the most obscure in the record of Whitman's life" (*Walt Whitman: The Song of Himself* [Berkeley: U of California P, 1999]: 3). Moreover, a few critics and biographers have used this perceived gap in the record, this lack of evidence, to suggest that Whitman deliberately evaded at first any sort of engagement with the war. Genoways's beautifully written book provides a detailed, eye-opening account of Whitman's life from the arrival of John Brown's body in New York in December 1859 to the death of the unnamed soldier on the steamboat in the Potomac in December 1862. In the process, this three-year microbiography "debunk[s] the myth that Whitman was uninvolved in and unaffected by the country's march to war" (11).

The picture that emerges instead is of a deeply engaged Whitman. We find him in Boston in early 1860 in the company of radical abolitionists who wanted to plot jailbreaks and John Brown–like revolutions. When he returned to New York, he continued to spend many a night at Pfaff's Restaurant and Lager Beer Saloon with a dynamic group of the city's literary and artistic bohemians. As positive and negative critical responses to the third edition of *Leaves of Grass* (1860) appeared, inciting occasional media controversies and more frequent parodies, and as the nation headed into recession, political crisis, and war, Whitman supported himself by writing numerous newspaper articles on a range of subjects—some appeared with his real name in the byline while others were published anonymously or pseudonymously. He also continued to draft new poems. Some of them were not published during these years because of the bankruptcy of his publisher, Thayer and Eldridge; the demise of the *Saturday Press* (a weekly that had actively promoted Whitman's work); and the rejection of his verse by mainstream literary magazines such as *The Atlantic*. Other poems were published, however. The stirringly pro-Union and pro-war "Beat! Beat! Drums!" (1861) ignited a barroom clash at Pfaff's when Whitman read it there, and the poem later turned into a literary sensation, becoming "the most widely reprinted and circulated poem of Whitman's career" (117). The Whitman of these so-called "lost years" had not retreated into silence. Instead, he appeared in the thick of things, surrounded by activity and people and occupied with writing and the unfolding events of the era.

Previous biographers have overlooked these years in part because Whitman's own letters, notebooks, and autobiographical writings say so little. Genoways makes exhaustive use of clues left in these texts and carefully analyzes the poems Whitman composed in this period. His research also adds to the Whitman archive four recently discovered letters and moves out to a range of other documents about these years—correspondence to Whitman, stories and poems in the popular press, forgotten publications of the period, and more. His attention to the era's periodicals, including their editors and writers and audiences, and the wealth of historical and biographical information submerged within them is particularly revealing. Genoways uses a pair of June 1862 newspaper articles—one from the New York *Sunday Mercury* and the other from the *New York Herald*—to identify the previously mysterious Ellen Eyre. In March of 1862, Eyre wrote Whitman a flirtatious, provocative letter asking him "to renew the pleasures you afforded me last P.M." (qtd. 155). The discovery of the letter itself is not new. In 1955, Gay Wilson Allen had assumed that it could be evidence that Whitman was having an affair with a woman during the spring of 1862. Later, Justin Kaplan suggested that Eyre was really the actress Ellen Grey from Brooklyn, and Loving has speculated more recently that Eyre was really Ada Clare, one of Whitman's literary friends from Pfaff's. What is new in Genoways's account is the revelation that Ellen Eyre was in fact a young man, the cross-dressing William Kinney, who used a combination of romantic charm, sex, and "threats of exposure of improper intimacy" (*New York Herald*; qtd. 158) to extort his lovers out of thousands of dollars. Although this newly uncovered information "presents as many new questions as it answers" (156), Genoways's connection of Whitman's correspondence and notebook entries to these previously overlooked newspaper stories expands our picture of Whitman, his daily life, and his cultural context in a year that biographers have tended to fill in with speculations because of the seeming absence of concrete information.

In multiple ways, *Walt Whitman and the Civil War: America's Poet during the Lost Years of 1860–1862* is an impressive achievement and one of the most valuable and surprisingly original contributions to Whitman studies in recent memory. With new discoveries, penetrating close readings, and engaging prose, Genoways has patiently pieced together a coherent and exciting narrative of Whitman's life in the three years prior to his relocation to Washington, DC. Literary scholars and historians will find a few imperfections, however. Some are minor—the misspelling of Adah Isaacs Menken's name, for example, and missing footnotes. The story of Whitman on the boat with the dead and wounded soldiers, which is quoted and used to end the biographical narrative, is not cited. The original source for the story, Whitman's own *Memoranda during the War* (1875–76), places this journey in early January 1863, not late December 1862, which might leave some scholars wondering how Genoways arrived at his dating. And the index seems a little too thin for a complex story with a large cast of fascinating but relatively unknown characters, such as Charles Graham Halpine, John Clancy, and Andrew Demarest.

The subtitle might also raise concerns for a few. Although there is a dearth of evidence about Whitman's activities and daily existence in 1862, the Civil War more generally is one of the most discussed periods in Whitman's life. In fact, some parts of Genoways's narrative—Whitman's trip to Boston in 1860, for example, or his reactions to the First Battle of Bull Run—are fairly well known to Whitman scholars. In other words, these years might not really seem "lost" to those who study Whitman, perhaps just vague in places. Relatively speaking, an 1853 or an 1857 seems much more lost to the documentary record of Whitman's life than these early years of the Civil War. Such criticisms are nitpicking. Still, Genoways's scrupulous scholarship and meticulous reconstruction of Whitman's life invites readers to pay careful attention to names and identities, sources and documentation, and the difference between speculation and evidence. His work shows us that what we might see as a historical void is actually a historical question that can, with solid research and nifty detective work, generate quite interesting and surprising answers.

This story of "America's Poet during the Lost Years of 1860–1862" is just the beginning of Genoways's study of Whitman during the Civil War. The recent recipient of a 2010 Guggenheim Fellowship, Genoways is currently working on three new Whitman projects: the second volume of *Walt Whitman during the Civil War*, a one-volume paperback version of the five-year biography for general readers, and an online critical edition of Whitman's Civil War–era writings (Anne Bromley, "English Professor, VQR Editor Receive Guggenheim Fellowships," *UVaToday* Apr. 15, 2010; Web, May 28, 2010). The more fully documented period from 1863 to 1865 in Whitman's life will be a different kind of challenge for Genoways. Still, his cleverly connective research methods and masterful close-reading skills should yield not only a richer understanding of the poet and his era but also, one hopes, a few more surprises.

Gregory Eiselein
Kansas State University

MARK TWAIN: UNSANCTIFIED NEWSPAPER REPORTER. By James E. Caron. Columbia: U of Missouri P, 2009. xiv + 448 pp. $49.95.

As he begins his comprehensive study of how Samuel L. Clemens (1835–1910) adopted and then adapted and developed his literary persona Mark Twain, James E. Caron sets a clear direction for the discussion. In his "Prologue," Caron writes:

> Readers today remain bedazzled by Sam Clemens' fictions and artful performances; they remain confused, too, because talking about the narrator and comic character Mark Twain easily becomes talking about Sam Clemens the man—and vice versa. Most people, even biographers, say "Mark Twain" at times when they mean "Sam Clemens." Clemens so obviously poured his own personality into the character of Mark Twain that is seems natural to conflate the one with the other. *Sam Clemens was not Mark Twain*, but in order to puzzle out the significance of 'Mark Twain,' one must sometimes proceed as though he were. (11; emphasis added)

That we most often and simplistically mix the man with the literary creation serves as the backdrop for Caron's discussion; the book as a whole is a carefully constructed argument for untangling Clemens/Twain and a celebration of the complexity of Sam Clemens's attempts to fashion a persona that, in time, moves from a distinctively western roar to a sophisticated urban, even cosmopolitan, provocateur. Caron charts Clemens's creative journey, but the strength of the volume is not its touting of Clemens as an isolated and self-contained artist, which is often the way we like to think of our artists in a post-Romantic age, but its presentation of him as a navigator of a complex set of literary approaches and influences that he combines to create a character who stands both within and apart from his home culture and who uses his familiarity and distance to lob complaints to demonstrate and criticize human foolishness.

Every student of American humor and Mark Twain is familiar with the scholarly work that names Twain as an inheritor (and often as the pinnacle) of western and southwestern literary humor (consider the foundational work of Constance Rourke, Walter Blair, and Kenneth Lynn, as well as the extension of that work by David E. E. Sloane). Caron offers a broad examination of the numerous writers and literary comedians who paved the way for Mark Twain. Those voices, interestingly, are most often male, though Caron does break this emphasis when he describes expectations and assumptions that underlie the development of an eastern audience and the creation of the magazine market for humor, one that expands beginning in the early nineteenth century; the brief discussion of writers such as Fanny Fern (Sara Willis Parton) is especially welcome. Caron reaches deeper into the cultural context and offers a comprehensive cast of writers as he demonstrates the attachments that voice and personality have to place and to the experiences of humor that are tied to place.

This is particularly effective in Caron's discussion of Sam Clemens's experiences as a reporter in Virginia City. He moves well beyond the basic description of Clemens's ties to contemporaries to show how Clemens created a complex weave of reporting, commentary, jokes, and hoaxes to break the boundaries of acceptable humor. Caron's discussion of Clemens's embrace of the carnival in Virginia City (in social, cultural, and distinctly literary terms) demonstrates an appreciation for the subversive character of Mark Twain. There is also a good balance in the idea that Clemens's Mark Twain was not always embraced by the community but at times tested its patience and wore out his welcome. The discussion of Mark Twain's fun at the expense of the community's women who worked on behalf of the Western Sanitary Commission is especially revealing (148–55). Placing this within the context of the roughhousing and personal-attack humor of the Washoe newspaper community helps to explain Clemens's lapse of propriety and reminds us that not everyone was fascinated by or forgiving of carnival breaches of decorum (it is good to remind readers that Mark Twain was not universally loved or even appreciated).

Most useful is Caron's discussion of Sam Clemens's experiences in San Francisco and, ultimately, in the Sandwich Islands. The discussion of his shift away from daily newspapers to regional literary magazines reframes our understanding of the value and history of the literary persona Mark Twain. In San Francisco, Sam Clemens shifted his attention and deliberately set about courting a broader regional and, ultimately, national audience. As Caron comments at the beginning of his discussion, "Concentrating his best efforts on writing sketches for the world of literary weeklies committed Clemens not just to a professional writing career much more ambitious than newspaper reporting. Writing for the literary weeklies also committed Clemens to a readership different from that of newspapers, one whose aesthetic taste differed because its gender and economic status were typically different" (167). As well, Clemens's attempts (not always successful) to navigate and meet the demands of a mixed gender and more extensively literate audience pushed him toward a more complex Mark Twain. In Caron's words, "The story of Sam Clemens in San Francisco . . . is the story of how he reworked Washoe Mark Twain to fit this more literary ambition" (167). The result of that ambition was to introduce Mark Twain as *feuilletoniste* and, eventually, as a mix of bohemian and *flâneur*. Much more than a reporter charged with gathering facts or instigating newspaper brawls, Clemens, in the guise of this evolved Mark Twain, saw an opportunity to change both his status as a literary worker and his reputation for humor. He would opt now for a deeper, socially conscious satire.

Clemens worked hard to capitalize on his changed narrator, and Caron sees the east's 1865 embrace of "The Notorious Jumping Frog of Calaveras County" as out of phase with Clemens's own ambitions and intentions for his career. By this time Mark Twain was a known quantity, especially in *The Californian*. Caron suggests that "[t]he attention of Mark Twain created by 'Jim Smiley and His Jumping Frog' in the periodical world . . . represents a high-water mark early in the literary career of Sam Clemens only because it crested above an entire year of previous success" (261). Ultimately, writes Caron, "Clemens called [the story] 'a villainous backwoods sketch' because he had worked hard to make his comic writing acceptable to the standard literary papers in San Francisco and New York City. Written mainly in dialect, 'Jim Smiley and His Jumping Frog' was not an obvious candidate for periodicals with high-culture taste" (261).

Ironically, then, the story that is used most often to introduce Clemens and Mark Twain to readers, a story that supposedly presents Sam Clemens at the start of a notable career, is seen by Clemens as a step back from the more sophisticated readers that he craved. Caron concludes, "Trimmed to fit an interpretation by twentieth-century scholars about regional influence and misunderstood within the context of the contemporary periodical world, 'Jim Smiley and His Jumping Frog' has assumed a significance out of proportion to the facts. Moreover, these misapprehensions have obscured the Mark Twain Clemens created in San Francisco, one representing neither the vernacular West nor the genteel East but rather the Bohemia of a literary avant-garde" (261–62). The correction is a splendid exclamation point for Caron's full treatment of Sam Clemens.

As the discussion moves toward Clemens's preparations for the Quaker City Tour, Caron spends a final section on Clemens's experience in the Sandwich Islands and the impact that experience had on his literary persona. Here we once again find a more complex reading of Clemens's Mark Twain, especially in the persona's response to the conflicting cultures and political agendas of indigenous peoples and a mix of British and American commercial and political interests. Clemens uses his persona to move beyond the role of correspondent, and his letters offer a voice that is perhaps not as critical of imperial ways as we like to think. This continues through Mark Twain's correspondence that covers the travel from San Francisco to New York. These letters shape his approach to the correspondence during the Quaker City Tour. There are shifts and changes here as Clemens continues to experiment and as he reenters a voice that offers multiple perspectives and that does not allow for an easy identification with either "civilization" or "savagery."

Caron's extended discussion of Sam Clemens's literary evolution enhances our understanding of the values of and uses for the literary character Mark Twain, from newspaper to literary magazine to lecture platform. All these reinforce the potential that Mark Twain contained for a humor based ultimately on the recognition of human failing and a voice that challenges, pokes at, and risks alienating the reader. Close to the end of his discussion, Caron suggests, "Mark Twain by late 1866 had become . . . the means by which Sam Clemens could perform whatever comic role he might imagine, strike whatever comic pose he might fancy—as though he were a one-man tableau vivant" (371). It is no wonder, perhaps, that we find it so difficult to separate these twins; it is no wonder that Sam Clemens at times disappears behind the electric charge of his own creation.

Michael J. Kiskis
Elmira College

BRICKS WITHOUT STRAW: A NOVEL. By Albion Tourgée. Ed. Carolyn L. Karcher. Durham: Duke UP, 2009. 464 pp. $84.95.

It is Albion Tourgée's (1838–1905) time in U.S. studies—again. A best-selling novelist and activist, Tourgée fought against Jim Crow but was eclipsed by its dark shadows. Returning to prominence in the 1960s, following the Civil Rights movement and historians' revisionist readings of the Reconstruction era, this important American author from the post–Civil War era was primarily defined then as an activist lawyer and crusader for black civil rights. Tourgée's second afterlife began in the last decade or so, as American cultural studies has been transformed by poststructuralism, critical race studies, and the new historicism, with the result that we now can understand more profoundly than before why Tourgée's innovations as a *novelist* were central, not peripheral, to his critique of U.S. fictions of white supremacy. Charles Chesnutt's fiction and Mark Twain's late, darker writings became integrated into the U.S. literary canon, thereby opening up a new context for Tourgée, for his mixed-mode novels also blend satire and melodrama, dialogue and oratory, to construct counternarratives undoing America's racial masquerade and historical amnesia. The second phase of Tourgée's revival does not negate the emphases of the first; rather, it expands the methods of inquiry.

Unlucky in life, Tourgée has proved fortunate in his biographers and critical commentators, beginning with Edmund Wilson (in *Patriotic Gore* [1962]), Theodore Gross, and Otto Olsen in the 1960s and continuing, most recently, with Mark Elliott (in *Color-Blind Justice: Albion Tourgée and the Quest for Racial Equality* [2006]). My own *Sitting in Darkness: New South Fiction, Education, and the Rise of Jim Crow Colonialism* (2008) placed Tourgée's quest for equal educational opportunities for blacks and whites and his first two novels (*A Fool's Errand* [1879] and *Bricks Without Straw* [1880]) in the context of many other fictional representations of black schools in the Reconstruction and post-Reconstruction eras, including those by Lydia Maria Child, Frances Harper, W. E. B. Du Bois, Walter Hines Page, and George Washington Cable. In that study I made the case that *Bricks Without Straw* was Tourgée's best novel and should be back in print and widely taught. Now Carolyn L. Karcher has accomplished the first of these goals and made probable the second, offering footnotes, a chronological overview, and a sixty-four-page essay that should become *the* source for a critically sophisticated introduction to Tourgée's life and work in historical context.

As Karcher says, Tourgée should be taught alongside Chesnutt and Twain in any in-depth literary-historical study of the period; he will also pair well with other figures, such as Ida B. Wells and Du Bois. In addition, Tourgée proves indispensable to any history of Reconstruction—both its reformist promise and its limitations and tragic demise. Elliott showed in more depth than ever before how profound was the twenty-nine-year-old Tourgée's influence on North Carolina's Reconstruction constitution of 1868, arguing that "nearly every article" of the document bore Tourgée's influence (qtd. in Karcher 17). Karcher has done her own extensive research in the Tourgée archives and puts it this way:

> Among the innovations he introduced were the division of counties into self-governing townships that elected their own commissioners, school boards, justices of the peace, and constables; the abolition of property qualifications for holding political office; the popular election of superior court judges, hitherto appointed by the state legislature; . . . the banning of stocks, whipping posts, branding irons, and other methods of corporeal punishment; . . . the elimination of court costs for defendants found innocent in criminal proceedings; and the incorporation of a "Homestead Clause" that protected debtors from having their land seized by creditors. (17–18)

These and other changes connected to Reconstruction caused Tourgée and his wife to be ostracized by some of his white neighbors in Greensboro while blacks endured revenge killings throughout the state.

Tourgée had an equally profound effect on U.S. history. His defense of the plaintiff Homer Plessy before the U.S. Supreme Court in 1896 is fairly well known, but what other novelist, except perhaps Harriet Beecher Stowe, may legitimately claim to have influenced a major political party's platform and the outcome of a presidential election? In Tourgée's case, the party was the Republican Party and the elected president was James Garfield—who was assassinated after just a few months in office and replaced by Chester A. Arthur, who showed much interest in cultivating his prodigious sideburns but little enthusiasm for Garfield's reformist agenda involving racial and educational equality. The newly egalitarian North Carolina constitution also proved short-lived, brought down in the 1870s by resurgent white supremacists.

Building on Elliott's research but going beyond it, Karcher has a profound grasp of Tourgée's innovations as a novelist, including how they are constitutive of, not just adjunctive to, his activist work and his historical analysis of America's postwar crisis. Here is Karcher's adept summary of some of *Bricks Without Straw*'s innovations:

> an array of complex, full rounded characters; a plot that successfully integrates the political action centered on African Americans with the love story centered on whites; a sophisticated narrative technique that relies on flashbacks rather than linear progression; a self-conscious use of dialogue and dialect to give voice to the voiceless; and an experimental open ending that calls attention to the problems history has left unresolved. (1)

The novel's portraits of blacks defending their rights, building their communities, and creating coalitions with whites were particularly daring. As Karcher shrewdly states, this narrative was Tourgée's clever revision of the "romance of reunion" theme involving southern and northern whites that was fast becoming a best-selling formula in postwar fiction (44–48). (Think of John De Forest or Joel Chandler Harris.) Newly powerful interracial coalitions during Reconstruction, Tourgée makes clear, provoked the white terrorist atrocities that followed.

Tourgée also sought in his novels to counter slanders against the Freedmen's Bureau; black students, teachers, and legislators; and the aims of Reconstruction itself. Instead, he offered alternative narratives, testimony, facts, and an appeal to the nation's founding ideals. Tourgée's defense of Reconstruction recognized its internal flaws but saw it in sum as a potential second American Revolution tragically betrayed. He demonstrates that, had it been defended and implemented by the full force of federal power, it could have assuaged class as well as racial divisions throughout the South. Such a reading of Reconstruction, of course, soon lost out to white supremacist narratives that treated it as a blot on American history worse than slavery. But Tourgée's "fool's errand" eventually had the last laugh. As Karcher says, Tourgée not only influenced Du Bois's *Black Reconstruction* (1935) but also has had many of his claims validated by contemporary historians of the postwar period (4, 50–52).

Karcher is equally astute when assessing some of the limitations of Tourgée's fiction. Despite the egalitarianism at the core of *Bricks Without Straw*, its creator was drawn to romanticizing crusading whites, most notably during a scene in which his heroine, "a white set face, mounted on her black horse" (186), miraculously reduces black demonstrators and white counterprotesters to equanimity and then cheers. Karcher observes, "The episode foreshadows the disempowerment Tourgée's African American characters undergo after the overthrow of Reconstruction, a development reflected in the plot's shift away from them and toward their white benefactors" (40).

Other intriguing anomalies in *Bricks Without Straw* are not much discussed by Karcher, although they should be evaluated when the book is newly taught. Literacy was well understood by both blacks and Tourgée to be a prerequisite for empowerment, but there is curious slippage in Tourgée's novel as it juxtaposes the life stories of its paired black heroes, one apparently illiterate and the other well educated. Nimbus needs others to help him purchase property and register his marriage, yet in one key scene Nimbus confronts a white man defrauding a black female employee by citing her "papers" to show she is owed wages, not just rations (153). Tourgée's narrator suggests that "army life" taught this black hero to "stand his ground" (153), but Karcher misses a chance here to ask whether Nimbus is indeed as illiterate as Tourgée elsewhere portrays him. Could he have received instruction in the Union Army's experimental literacy programs, especially those initiated by General Benjamin Franklin Butler in North Carolina? It is a moment where one element of Tourgée's fiction, his fondness for fixed binaries, conflicts with another, his intent to depict the complex causes of historical change.

Karcher correctly emphasizes how Tourgée deploys a convention from popular romances, a stolen inheritance plot, to revolutionary new effect when he links it to the betrayal of Reconstruction. But for Karcher's point to be truly effective, we must understand how this key narrative motif evolved in varied historical contexts: it was used differently by Scottish, Irish, and British authors, and by white and black writers depicting the U.S. South (E. D. E. N. Southworth's *The Hidden Hand* [1859] and Pauline Hopkins's *Hagar* [1901–2] are two examples). Further, given the current state of scholarship on *Huckleberry Finn* (1884), it was not propitious for Karcher to elevate Tourgée's blacks by putting down Twain's Jim as simply "one-dimensional" (33). Elsewhere, when she gives us reasons for teaching Twain and Tourgée contrapuntally, she's on firmer ground (see 46–48).

At least two future approaches to *Bricks Without Straw* will prove fruitful. One should both test the novel's factual claims still more rigorously and confront the paradox that in 1880 the most veracious and powerful historical account of postwar events in the South was written in fiction, not other modes. The ending of *Bricks Without Straw* that Karcher rightly celebrates includes an eloquent peroration by Tourgée's primary white hero on not only federal support for education as the solution to racism but also township-hall meetings and local elections as the cure for statewide political corruption. But how demonstrably true is Tourgée's broad claim in *Bricks Without Straw* that the South's lack of township-based elections weakened its democratic traditions compared to New England? A second, complementary approach to *Bricks Without Straw* should focus on the variety of literary forms used by Tourgée, including how they interact in both successful and unsuccessful ways. Sentimental romance, legal disquisition, and Socratic dialogue are just three of many. Tourgée was hardly a ventriloquist virtuoso of rhetorical forms like Twain, but the structure of *Bricks Without Straw* is deeply dialogic, both on the level of individual scenes and as a whole, through its audacious mix of genres, styles, and voices. We need to investigate more thoroughly the ways in which a hybrid narrative such as *Bricks Without Straw* enacts change *textually*; it does not just argue for it. We have done that recently with Harriet Beecher Stowe and Frederick Douglass; now it is the turn for a writer who is one of their most honorable heirs. It is Tourgée's time again, and Carolyn L. Karcher has helped make it so.

Peter Schmidt
Swarthmore College

THE COMPLETE LETTERS OF HENRY JAMES, 1872–1876. VOL. 1. Ed. Pierre A. Walker and Greg W. Zacharias. Lincoln: U of Nebraska P, 2008. lxxi + 410 pp. $125.

The goal of publishing every one of Henry James's (1843–1916) more than 10,000 extant letters represents an inspired undertaking—an enormous commitment by the Center for Henry James Studies, General Editors Greg W. Zacharias and Pierre A. Walker, and the University of Nebraska Press. The 410 pages of the present volume include eighty letters. At this rate, it will take 125 volumes to publish them all. The present volume is the third volume of *The Complete Letters* to be published. Two earlier volumes include letters from 1855 to 1872. Readers may be confused by the decision not to number the volumes consecutively. The present volume is actually the first of three covering 1872–76 and includes letters written over just a fourteen-month period (May 20, 1872–July 8, 1873) even though the title page indicates otherwise. Volume 2 (letters written July 15, 1873–October 15, 1875) was also published in 2009 while the third volume is advertised for 2011. Unfortunately, you have to go to each table of contents to see the dates of letters included in each volume. An additional problem: Millicent Bell's introduction appears in this volume but is intended to cover all three volumes.

These labeling and marketing problems, of course, say nothing about the remarkable contribution to James studies that this volume and the others will make. The early 1870s represented a crucial stage in Henry James's career—an incubation period in which he tested his ability to observe and write. Could he really be a professional writer? Could he really be an expatriate American writer in Europe? Most of the letters are to his family: father (12), mother (7), both (17), William (11), Alice (5)—52 of 80. He addressed multiple letters to Grace Norton (8), Lizzie Boott (8), Charles Eliot Norton (6), and Thomas Sergeant Perry (3), and single letters to Jane Norton, Mary Lucinda Holton James, Sarah Butler Wister, William Dean Howells, and Wendell Phillips Garrison. Considering the correspondents James eventually had, this is a small circle of acquaintances. It is a sympathetic group, however, and the Jamesian voice in these letters seems frank and confident, as if aware of the security that such a support group afforded.

The first thirty-two letters derive from the five-month European tour on which James escorted his sister, Alice, and their aunt, Catherine Walsh ("Aunt Kate"). They spent May and June in England, stopped briefly in Paris en route to Switzerland, where they spent July and August. They traveled in September, with stops in Italy, Austria, Germany, and Paris, before James returned his companions to England for their return voyage to America. Because the tour with Alice was intended to improve her mental and physical health, James dutifully reports on her progress. Mostly, he reassures his parents that she is having a wonderful time: "The thing you most feared, naturally enough, Viz: that excitement should carry her too far & be followed by a reaction—has never come to pass in any degree" (43). Alice does so well that James feels comfortable acknowledging that she did suffer one severe nervous attack (84).

Being responsible for Alice did not prevent Henry from keeping and publishing a written record of their tour. Several letters from the British leg contributed to essays that appeared serially in *The Nation* under the title "A Summer in Europe," and some of his Roman letters provided material for essays in *The Atlantic*. Most interestingly, the letters reveal James's evolving reunion with Europe, confirming his tastes and preferences for scenery and society and his steadily advancing confidence in his ability to translate experience into salable prose.

"Land is just in sight—divine vision!" James exclaims in the middle of the volume's first letter (3), as if he cannot wait to tell his parents that he is finally—nearly—back in Europe. Three days later, now on English soil (in Chester), he confirms the particular pleasure of his return and the angle of vision that would serve him for years afterward: "I find England just as I left it—still, to American eyes, full of the old world" (5). He could hardly have realized at this moment that he would capitalize for a career on his ability to represent the "old world" through new "American eyes." Like many of his later characters, moreover, he self-consciously watches himself watching, assessing the type and quality of his responses—the beginning of his later self-conscious style. From the Peacock Inn in

Derbyshire, he writes to Charles Eliot Norton, "I find I am taking England in the calmest & most prosaic manner—without heart-beats or raptures or literary inspiration of any kind. After a certain hour, one can't live on the picturesque & extract essential nutriment from it. Here we are in a show region—rather too utterly one—yet I think if it wasn't for my sister, I should take the train straight for London, mankind & the newspapers" (14–15). He expands upon this idea in a letter to his brother William: "I find my feelings, this time, as to Europe considerably less elastic than before, & am conscious mentally, of the wholesome hand of time. Switzerland I enjoy about as I expected to—not so much but that I would be willing at any moment to leave it for a more humanly interesting land" (56).

Ever the entrepreneur, James often resorts to financial metaphors to describe the benefit of his sightseeing. The Cathedral at Wells surprised him. Nothing "beats this wondrous little ecclesiastical city," he observes. "It had for us, too, the added charm of a surprise—one of the discoveries of travel; for I simply knew that the Cathedral, in a general way, was fine, & we were not prepared for the very perfect & rounded phenomenon we chanced upon. So that Wells is a valuable acquisition" (25). Aesthetic and materialistic values compete with one another as James converts aesthetic surprise into property. The turning point of this entrepreneurial adventure comes in a well-known letter to his parents on September 9, 1872. In successive epiphanies, he announces his decision to remain in Europe and expresses confidence that writing can be his profession. "My own desire to remain abroad has by this time taken very definite shape," he tells them. "In fact, I feel as if my salvation, intellectually & literarilly [*sic*], depended upon it. I have had too little time to write, to lay up any great treasure to commence with; but I shall need but little to start with & shall be able to add to it fast enough for comfort" (100–101). James is the literary capitalist in the bull market of European experience: "My improvement is going on now at so very rapid a ratio that I feel an almost unbounded confidence in my powers to do & dare. In short, I am really well—am confident of being able to work quite enough to support myself in affluence" (101). This is James as the overly enthusiastic Roderick Hudson rather than the reflective, more typically Jamesian Rowland Mallet.

As he refines his sense of purpose in subsequent letters, James comes to terms with questions of material, style, audience, and publication venues. Both William James and William Dean Howells had cautioned him to avoid "over-refinement" in his writing, and he feels some confidence that he can do so even as he resists any temptation to be a common writer. He will not work off all his stylistic refinement, he tells William. He "must give up the ambition of ever being a free-going & light-paced enough writer to please the multitude. The multitude, I am more & more convinced, has absolutely no taste—none at least that a thinking man is bound to defer to. To write for the few who have is doubtless to lose money—but I am not afraid of starving" (114–15). Such a characterization of his writing and his audience reinforces one popular view of James as a snobbish, elitist writer. As it turns out, of course, he is right about both the level of refinement he would practice for his career and the level of success he would enjoy. He would lose money, but he would not starve.

In addition to confirming a career choice, James was deciding where he wanted to live and, as it would turn out, where he would set his first major novel. As we observe him trying out his judgments of Europe, refining his tastes, fine-tuning his responses, we see him sampling locations and finally trying to make a decision between Paris and Rome. In effect, as an expatriate American writer, he triangulates America and these two European cities: "Every thing Italian & especially everything Roman, that is not a ruin, a landscape or a museum has such a deadly provinciality & more than American dreariness, that in coming here with a mindful [*sic*] of Parisian memories, one seems to have turned one's back on modern civilization" (178). James kept returning to Rome, of course, even as he struggled to define its appeal: "What I find Rome and am likely to find it, it is hard to say in few words. Much less simply & sensuously & satisfyingly picturesque than before, but on the whole immensely interesting" (179). He distinguishes between Paris and Rome as he distinguishes between Europe and America. Rome represents the ancient world and appears primitive, even barbaric. Paris is more modern, but in a refined, European way.

James also defined himself against the American colony in Rome. He seems determined to feel superior to his provincial compatriots. He will be the professional tourist with the authority and taste to contribute written reports of European sights to American periodicals. His judgments of American artists in Rome seem especially snobbish. Nastily, he compares Harriet Hosmer to a "remarkably ugly little grey-haired boy, adorned with a diamond necklace" (210). He calls William Wetmore Story a "case of prosperous pretention" (251). He tells Jane Norton that Sarah Butler Wister's "beautiful hair is the thing most to be praised about her" (223). Although he claims that "Rome has come to seem a sort of home to me & I have adopted it into my innermost heart" (222), he reverts to form when he observes, "I turned out to know a good many people here of whom I have inevitably seen a good deal—more at times than I want to. It doesn't make very 'middling' American society any better to be disporting itself against a Roman background" (222–23).

This early phase of James's career would culminate in the publication of *Roderick Hudson* (1875). In a May 3, 1874, letter to Howells, James outlines the novel that, he says, he has "had in my head a long time," so it is surprising that he gives no hint of having such a work in mind in the letters comprising the present volume (*The Complete Letters of Henry James, 1872–1876, Vol. 2*, ed. Pierre A. Walker and Greg W. Zacharias [Lincoln: U of Nebraska P, 2008]: 156). His experience with the American art colony in Rome obviously provides raw material for the Roman scenes in *Roderick Hudson*. There is also the intriguing admission, in a letter to his brother William, that an "intelligent male brain to communicate with occasionally would be a practical blessing. I have encountered none for so long that I don't even know how to address your's [*sic*] & find it impossible to express a hundred ideas which at various times I have laid aside, to be propounded to you" (294). James's feeling of bursting with ideas and longing for an intelligent man to whom he might express them anticipates Roderick Hudson's situation and the role Rowland Mallet plays in his life. For details of James's negotiations with *The Atlantic* and his commentary on the yearlong serialization of the novel, readers will have to refer to relevant letters collected in volume 2 of the 1872–76 letters. Those letters end just as James describes reading final proofs for the novel that would confirm him as not just a travel and story writer but a novelist.

Leland S. Person
University of Cincinnati

THE SELECTED LETTERS OF CHARLOTTE PERKINS GILMAN. Ed. Denise D. Knight and Jennifer S. Tuttle. Tuscaloosa: U of Alabama P, 2009. xiii + 367 pp. $60.

Writing to her daughter, Katherine, after the death of her second husband, Houghton Gilman, Charlotte Perkins Gilman (1860–1935) described her grief: "All my Human life is untouched; only the personal life is injured; and I live mostly outside personality" (201). Gilman's voluminous oeuvre of fiction, poetry, essays, and books has made what she saw as her "Human life" visible to audiences while her autobiography (of which, it turns out, she thought little) reveals some aspects of her "personal life," but in a self-conscious and partial way. The most provocative events of Gilman's personal life—particularly her postpartum illness, divorce, and unconventional parenting arrangements—captured public interest during her life and after, but they have not been well understood. Denise D. Knight and Jennifer S. Tuttle have mined Gilman's correspondence to reveal these events—and many more—in complex detail. In doing so, they have made a major contribution to the study of Gilman and the era during which she lived.

Perhaps the most striking feature of this collection is the scope and depth of Gilman's lifetime correspondence, which is judiciously managed by Knight and Tuttle through clearly defined editing choices. They focus some chapters on a particular period in Gilman's life (e.g., "The Twilight Years: 'my writing . . . simply doesn't come' ") while others chart decades-long, intimate relationships (e.g., "A Mother's Love: 'to the best of daughters' "). Thus, Gilman's letters reveal her evolving relationships and self-presentation—from an ambitious but lonely young girl raging against Victorian morays (a girl, she insists repeatedly, who "died" during her years of postpartum illness) to a happily married, mature woman who contentedly tends her garden in Connecticut while also contending with an aging body and waning popularity. Her middle years are characterized by frenzied work, constant travel, financial anxiety, and a growing national reputation as one of the first woman thinkers in America. It is good to be reminded of the length of Gilman's life in this collection: though best remembered for "The Yellow Wall-paper" (1892) and its critique of the Cult of True Womanhood, she lived long enough to enjoy Katharine Hepburn films, take a transcontinental flight from New York to Los Angeles, and ride the financial storm of the Great Depression. Given the variability of Gilman's epistolary voice, altered not only by time but also by the different expectations of her correspondents, one discovers that, though these letters reveal her "personal life," they do not reveal a coherent, "private" self. The sometimes self-effacing Gilman of letters to mentors William Dean Howells and Lester Ward is quite different from the concerned mother of her epistles to her daughter, Katherine, or the frank cultural critic of her youthful correspondence.

Because of the popularity of "The Yellow Wall-paper" and *Women and Economics* (1898), readers have tended to see Gilman's life and work through the lenses of heterosexual wifehood and motherhood; even as she interrogates those roles, Gilman remains enmeshed in the discourse. In this way, the intense emotional attachments that Gilman forged with a series of important women throughout the course of her life can be overlooked. This collection of letters demonstrates that, although her first husband, Walter Stetson, and rest cure doctor, Dr. S. Weir Mitchell, were important to Gilman, they figure much less prominently in her inner life than do Martha Luther Lane and Grace Ellery Channing Stetson. Most instructive is her passionate, youthful love affair with Martha, documented through letters in which Charlotte seems to be courting Martha, her "Little Pet," at the same time that Martha's future husband is wooing her. As Gilman feels a marriage proposal to Martha looming, she urges her to "tell him you are spoken for by a female in Providence, and can't marry just yet" (23). Knight and Tuttle wisely refrain from labeling Gilman's sexual and gender identity in modern terms, letting Gilman's own descriptions stand on their own. As an example, Gilman confesses in one letter, "It is awful to be a man inside and not able to marry the women you love!" (87). Predictably, Martha married, and the narrative created by the arrangement of Gilman's letters here subtly suggests that Gilman married Walter on the rebound; their life together, she hoped, would "have enough of joy to keep me sane" (37). Of course, we know that the misgivings about the marriage with which Gilman peppers the letters from this era were well founded. But she later confessed to Martha, "[T]hrough the first year or two of my marriage, in every depth of pain and loss and loneliness, yours was the name my heart cried—not his. I loved you better than any one . . ." (55). Gilman later expressed similar feelings for Grace Ellery Channing, who apparently rebuffed them more definitively than Martha had. However, Knight and Tuttle reveal a pattern, for when Grace marries Gilman's ex-husband and moves east with him, Gilman again laments, "I suffer more in giving you up than in Walter—for you were all joy to me" (87).

Gilman's letters to Grace and her daughter, Katherine (born in 1885), are the most poignant in the collection, as they express the pain and ambivalence caused by Gilman's separation from nine-year-old Katherine when she sent her from California to live with Walter and Grace in the east. Indeed, as Knight and Tuttle also note, more than anyone else, Grace made Gilman's career possible. When Grace married Walter, she eased Gilman's guilty conscience and also became an "other mother" (77) to Katherine, caring for her for several years while Gilman wrote, lectured, and "k[ept] moving" to safeguard her health (98). Gilman insisted on the felicity of this arrangement in her letters: "[Grace's] influence will be lovely for Kate; and we all four love each other dearly. Is that clear? I suppose it does look rather queer from the outside" (67). And, indeed, it did look "queer," for the California press publicized her private arrangements and drove her from the state. As late as 1929, we learn here, Gilman still hated Ambrose Bierce, the "Public Executioner and Tormentor" who had broadcast her affairs (273). And the unconventional family was not without its troubles. Gilman's letters to both Grace and Katherine tend to juxtapose outpourings of love, gratitude, and longing with bragging accounts of her great professional successes. And as Knight and Tuttle emphasize in their introduction to "A Mother's Love," Gilman tried rather awkwardly to inculcate a social conscience in her daughter from afar. In both cases, perhaps Gilman was justifying her decision to divorce and then share the care of Katherine with others. Was her contribution to the world worth it? she implicitly asks in these letters. Much of the correspondence between mother and daughter in later life revolves around the financial assistance Gilman provided to Katherine's family: "There has been so much, so very much that I I [sic] failed in giving you, dear child," she writes to thirty-six-year-old Katherine in 1921. "It is a joy to my heart to be of some use now" (141).

The second half of the book tends to focus on Gilman's varied career. Asked by one correspondent what she "does," she responds, "I am that perpetual motion engine a Reformer" (74). We learn here that she made her living primarily as a lecturer, sending letters to procure engagements, arrange travel, and negotiate fees. As she crisscrossed the country on her speaking tours, she became involved with all of the important suffragettes and reformers of the era: Jane Addams (with whom she lived at Hull House for a period of time), Susan B. Anthony ("Aunt Susan," as she calls her), Carrie Chapman Catt, and Anna Howard Shaw. These letters also reveal Gilman as a hustler, dickering with editors, trying to find publishers, even proposing new projects, such as turning "The Yellow Wall-paper" into a monologue. One of the most intriguing features of Gilman's work is the coexistence of her progressive tendencies with her trenchant racism, which is in full evidence here from her abhorrence of "promiscuous interbreeding" (268) to her removal from New York to Connecticut in 1922 to escape the "jostling aliens" (228). Increasingly, Gilman found work hard to come by, her views out of step with those of the 1920s and 1930s.

Knight and Tuttle have provided meticulous, detailed notes to all of these letters, which are extraordinarily helpful to readers as we navigate the dense network of lovers, family members, friends, and professional contacts that emerge through the correspondence. Their fine index is also a boon to scholars of the period. Gilman's networks are emphasized in thematic chapters such as "Work, Reform, and Activism: 'I love to preach better than anything.' " However, most compelling is the clarity—indeed, the purity—of the chapters that focus on Gilman's epistolary relationships with her closest friends and family. Even though this volume makes no claims to comprehensiveness, one does feel the absence of Gilman's letters to Houghton, and a taste of her personal relationship with the man with whom she had hoped "with all of her [heart]" to have a baby would be handy (188). Mary A. Hill's *A Journey From Within: The Love Letters of Charlotte Perkins Gilman, 1897–1900* (1995) supplements this text on that account. That said, Knight and Tuttle consistently provide helpful interpretive frames for navigating Gilman's correspondence, suggesting in their introduction that Gilman's letters can be read simultaneously as missives of the heart, as revelations of the more unsavory aspects of her life, and as evidence of Gilman's work ethic. They have gracefully provided the appropriate setting for Gilman's voice, which allows the energy and force of her personality to shine.

Finally, this collection gives us valuable, extended insight into the last years of Gilman's life, which are often overshadowed by the dramas of her youth. In 1932, Gilman was diagnosed with inoperable breast cancer and in 1934 Houghton died suddenly of a cerebral hemorrhage. She faced both crises with good cheer, writing to friends of the mercy of Houghton's quick death and describing her disease as "the best-behaved cancer you ever saw" while also sharing plans to take her own life when she was of no more use (304). Fascinatingly, the "talk of . . . chloroform"

(40) and suicide that swirled during her debilitating postpartum illness is echoed in her last letters, where she determines to "go peaceably to sleep with my beloved chloroform" (305). She is almost exuberant about her impending death and writes proudly to Grace that her cousin Lyman Stowe thinks "it is fine that my last act should be to help establish a principle for the good of humanity" (123). Perhaps what Gilman never accepted fully, but these letters clearly reveal, is that the personal life she devalued was always inextricable from her human life.

Lisa Long
North Central College

MARY AUSTIN AND THE AMERICAN WEST. By Susan Goodman and Carl Dawson. Berkeley: U of California P, 2008. xviii + 323 pp. $29.95.

In *Mary Austin and the American West*, Susan Goodman and Carl Dawson offer a compelling portrait of Mary Austin's (1868–1934) complex and unconventional personality in relation to a mythic and actual early twentieth-century American West. Organized chronologically, the twelve chapters outline the parameters of Austin's "western" sojourns from 1868 to 1934 and navigate her artistic detours from 1907 to 1920 through Italy, England, and New York before her final return to the American West, or, more specifically, the American Southwest. What emerges is an intriguing and well-documented discussion of Austin's life, one that contextualizes her authorial accomplishments and personal eccentricities in relation to what the authors describe as Austin's "West," which "becomes the West through its particular interchanges, elemental and human," since "she believes the land itself to be inspirited and inspiring, a perspective that reflects her faith in a benign higher power" (272).

The first chapter describes Austin's movement from Carlinville, Illinois, where she was born, to her "West" at the age of twenty, to help her family homestead in the Tejon district near Bakersfield, California, in 1888. The authors briefly discuss Austin's struggles with her Midwestern family (most notably her mother) and her fundamentalist religious heritage. Before the move to California, they write, "Mary had given little thought to where she might live. In years to come she argued the regional nature of art, which grows from the artist's association with a specific landscape and its past, but as a young woman she intended to write or, if necessary, to teach, either of which she could do as well in one place as another. The first sight of the thirty-thousand acre Rancho El Tejon changed her horizons and marked the beginning of her understanding, not only about who she was, but where she needed to be" (6–7). I cite this passage at length because it reveals the strengths, as well as, for me, a minor weakness, of the book. That is, while Austin's cultural experience of the "West" undeniably influenced her artistry, so, I think, did her Midwestern roots. In the first chapter, the authors write that Austin "rebelled against the strictures of her sex as well as the middle-class, Midwestern life she and writers such as Sherwood Anderson and Sinclair Lewis would pillory" (14). However, Austin, like both Anderson and Lewis, displays not only a severe but also, at times, strangely sentimental attitude toward Midwestern cultures or characters in later fiction such as *A Woman of Genius* (1912) or *No. 26 Jayne Street* (1920).

Arguably, Austin's "western" resistance to mainstream American culture may be significantly traced to her rebellion, like that of Anderson and Lewis, against her Midwestern heritage. The authors cite her twenty-five-year friendship with Lewis and her 1931 letter to him "about the possibility of their collaborating on a great American novel" since she believes his "genius" could help her address the mystical aspects of a projected novel about the turbulent history and hypocrisies of the California-based cultural wars in Owens Valley (216). However, they do not speculate about why Austin thought Lewis's Midwestern sensibility might help her, seeming to treat it instead as another of her eccentric gestures (which, in part, it may have been). In my view, Austin's often-troubled Midwestern childhood and young adulthood is significant not only to her imaginative experience of the "West" but also to her attempts to negotiate other cultures, whether Western, Native American, Spanish American, or European.

The remainder of the book impressively traces and documents Austin's literary and literal wanderings as a kind of metaphoric walking (or returning) Western woman. All of the chapters offer concise interpretive summaries of Austin's fictional and nonfictional writings (particularly those that lend insight into her authorial development). They include thorough, substantial, and illuminating discussions of her personal and professional relationships, ranging from her husband Wallace Stafford Austin (and their daughter Ruth), John Muir, Charles Lummis, Sinclair Lewis, Jack London, and Ansel Adams to Herbert and Lou Hoover, William James, D. H. Lawrence, H. G. Wells, Lincoln Steffens, Willa Cather, Daniel MacDougal, Frank Cushing, and Mabel Dodge. Chapters 2 and 3 detail Austin's impressions and experiences in various parts of the Owens Valley from 1892 to 1905. They offer not only useful historical insight into the water rights issue that still plagues the region but also Austin's personal and authorial struggles with it. In these chapters, the authors examine the differences between her developing artistry in relation to other Western writers, such as Owen Wister and Bret Harte, even as she experiences an increasingly distressing domestic situation that leads to a major marital rupture. Chapter 4 traces her subsequent three-year association with a loosely organized art colony and its denizens at Carmel. The next three chapters examine Austin's relationships with such figures as Herbert and Lou Hoover, Ansel Adams, H. G. Wells, and Lincoln Steffens, as well as her thirteen-year journey through Italy, England, and, more notably, New York. Along with interpretive summations of Austin's literary wanderings and milieu, these chapters afford new insight into Austin's efforts to integrate her "West" into national, if not international, culture. The remaining three chapters trace her return to the Southwest, partially through the prompting of Daniel MacDougal and partially through Austin's persistent identification and commitment to Western, Native, and Spanish American cultural arts.

One particularly difficult question that Goodman and Dawson address is Austin's enthused but problematic role as a self-declared advocate, if not authority, on Native cultures. When Austin first began writing about Native peoples in *The Land of Little Rain* (1903) or in her children's book, *The Basket Woman* (1904), she was not, as the authors observe, "in competition with Native writers" since there were "few examples beyond Sarah Winnemucca's *Life among the Paiutes: Their Wrongs and Claims* (1883)" (65). Austin's general rejection of then-emerging anthropological studies of Native cultures, as well as her sympathies for Native cultures and art in the Owens Valley, reveals as much about the limitations of then-contemporary anthropology as about Austin's culturally essentialist misreadings. The authors document Austin's marketplace awareness, not only of a "growing audience for things 'Indian' " at the turn of the twentieth century, but also of the "American public's fascination with 'primitive' peoples, especially American Indians" (66). They offer a sympathetic but balanced perspective on the relationship between Austin's marketing of Native cultures and her seemingly sincere efforts to redress historical wrongs against them.

After discussing possible influences on Austin's method of addressing the "American Indian" question, most notably Sir James Frazer's *The Golden Bough* (1880–1922), the authors conclude that her "main contribution to the recognition of Indian poems, songs, and dance rests on her bridging seemingly antagonistic traditions, oral and literary, or Anglo-European and American Indian. In this she carried on the great traditions of Henry Schoolcraft and Lewis H. Morgan, the early nineteenth-century pioneers who saw in the culture and imagination of American Indians what Austin, without their guidance, discovered for herself" (68). Later chapters both reinforce and modify this view. In chapter 10, "Indian Detours and Spanish Arts," Goodman and Dawson note that, despite Austin's cultural battles for Native cultures, such as the Pueblo, she "and other supporters of the Pueblo walked a fine moral line. Naïve, quixotic, at times self-serving, they offered themselves as the initiated, if not the chosen guardians" (226). In offering additional details about Austin's written reactions to other ethnic groups (notably, African Americans and Hispanic Americans), the authors provide a useful context for understanding Austin and the Indian question in relation to her own and other cultural perceptions or misperceptions about race in early twentieth-century America.

Finally, in offering their "accounting" or "sorting out of legacies" (264) in the last chapter, the authors assert that Austin, despite her inconsistencies and eccentricities (or perhaps because of them), maintained "an independent and original voice" and that hers was "a representative Western, or maybe American story of self-transformation and grit" (272). Their candid and well-documented research makes a compelling case for regarding her as such a voice. Although a brief review cannot do justice to the intricacies either of Austin's life or of a book that deals so comprehensively, as does this one, with Austin's "wrestl[ing] with the world and with herself" (272), *Mary Austin and the American West* is an impressively written and researched text, one that provides valuable insights for both general readers and scholars of Austin and the literary settling of the American West.

Beverly A. Hume
Indiana University-Purdue University

LETTERS TO WOMEN. NEW LETTERS, VOLUME II. By Theodore Dreiser. Ed. Thomas P. Riggio. Urbana: U of Illinois P, 2009. xxxvi + 376 pp. $60.

Thomas P. Riggio's *Letters to Women*, the second of two new volumes of Theodore Dreiser's (1871–1945) letters (the other is *A Picture and Criticism of Life* [2008], edited by Donald Pizer), captures Dreiser in various moods. We see him sentimental, confident, dejected, philosophical, playful, morose, self-pitying, wise, foolish—and, of course, amorous. Dreiser addresses topics from the Quaker faith to the New York Armory Show, from a party at W. C. Fields's summer home to the Great Depression. As the latest volume in the Dreiser Edition, a series that brings to print previously unpublished works, these letters show the private side of a very public figure.

This window into Dreiser's private life is especially illuminating for its focus on women with whom he had personal relationships—usually, but not always, sexual relationships. *Letters to Women* thus provides considerable data on a much-discussed topic: Dreiser's attitudes toward women. W. A. Swanberg's 1965 biography established the image of Dreiser as a Don Juan, and like most such legends, that one blends insight with oversimplification. There is no question that Dreiser slept with many women, but debate persists on two fronts. First, does Dreiser's "varietism" (his signature term for promiscuity) indicate a tendency to treat real-life women as sexual objects? Second, what light might his sexual practice shed on his literary portrayals of women, many of whom rebel against conventions and sometimes also against men? While no group of letters can conclusively settle those debates, this collection allows readers to reach informed decisions based on primary documents rather than hearsay and assumption.

The chronological arrangement of *Letters to Women* allows the reader to follow the development of Dreiser's attitudes—and his relationships. Those with his first and second wives, Sara Osborne White and Helen Patges Richardson, receive ample coverage. His letters to these women document how domesticity both enticed and threatened him. Courtship letters to Sara show him fantasizing about the day their shoes would be cozily tucked together under a bed, even as he frets over the cost of establishing a home. With the benefit of hindsight, another letter forecasts subsequent marital problems: "I cannot help noticing," Dreiser writes of a recent letter from his fiancée, "how the miserable matter-of-fact details exclude rapturous expression of love" (31). He strikes a different note with the woman who would become his second wife and with whom he felt a "mystical and magical . . . union" (154). Helen manifested what Dreiser calls an "untutored and uncontaminated emotional response to beauty" that deeply moved him (263). In one of the more interesting letters to Helen, Dreiser blends the roles of tutor and lover to advise her on poetry she has been writing (266).

Letters to Women establishes that another relationship rivaled Dreiser's two marriages in importance. For three years beginning in 1913, he lived intermittently with Kirah Markham, an actress, painter, writer, set designer—and the model for

Stephanie Platow in *The Titan* (1914) and Sidonie in *A Gallery of Women* (1929). Dreiser displays contradictory attitudes when he writes to the woman he calls "my mate intellectually, emotionally & artistically" (71). An early letter chides Kirah for "the exaggerated Bohemianism and the rapid intimacy" of her relationship with Dreiser's recent rival, novelist and Greenwich Village denizen Floyd Dell (64). Echoing his courtship letters to Sara, Dreiser rhapsodizes about domestic bliss with Kirah: a monogamous home "and maybe a baby or two" (87). In another, he characterizes himself as "pathetically faithful" and not cut out for promiscuity (98). But Dreiser soon changes his mind. Like many sexual progressives and bohemians of his day (and since), Dreiser maintains, "Love is a question of mood—not of rules or conditions" (110). He insists on freedom to see others while refusing to share Kirah with another man, and this double standard proved intolerable to her. It is regrettable that the edition's focus on letters *by* Dreiser, but not *to* him, precludes back-and-forth interchanges, although Riggio uses headnotes to provide some quotations from the correspondents. Many letters to Dreiser, particularly by women, have vanished, but a substantial cache of Kirah's letters survives, and they also merit publication.

In addition to documenting Dreiser's relationships, the intimacy of these letters fosters self-analyses that illuminate his emotional makeup. He admits, "No individual, not even Jennie Gerhardt [the title character of one of his novels], craved affection as much as do I" (75). Another time Dreiser confesses, "I crave affection of a high order so desperately that unless I can have it, only complete resignation & withdrawal from the sight of the universe & the world will help me. It is, with my temperament, all or nothing" (59).

This edition demonstrates that mutual respect was for Dreiser a precondition for sexual intimacy, and that he maintained friendships with many women well after their sexual relations had concluded. As he explains to Provincetown Players actress Margaret Johnson, "Mere cuties & flappers never interested me. I like to talk too much—and that intelligently—so I seek circles wherein people are emancipated" (136). These letters also provide glimpses of the commonly overlooked fact that Dreiser's lovers had sexual passions of their own. He marvels at Sara's "Sapphic" erotic intensity; relishes Helen's "lust"; and frets that Harriett Bissell, a Smith College graduate with whom he had a particularly stormy relationship, had "pick[ed] me as a fairly agreeable means to an ultimate varietistic end" (12, 165, 288). A late letter to Hazel Godwin pays tribute to the sexually emancipated woman: "You come to me frankly with your love and desire" (326). *Letters to Women* reveals a man conflicted yet honest about his feelings, one whose passion for intelligent, emancipated women included but cannot be reduced to sexual intimacy.

These letters also illuminate Dreiser's views of artistic currents in his day and of what he thought of his own books. He considered his autobiography, *A Book about Myself* (1922; later retitled *Newspaper Days* [1931]), to have "the quality of a novel" (145); felt "[t]he psychology of Hurstwood's decline [in *Sister Carrie* (1900)] was his own social conviction that he had sinned—(morally, socially, anyway you please)" (205); and found *The Titan* "a godless thing,—cold, calculating" (84). A 1924 letter documents his struggle to compose his masterpiece, *An American Tragedy* (1925): "I will never be able to write this book fast: It is too intricate in its thought & somehow my method if not my style has changed. I work with more care and hence more difficulty" (160). Another letter during the same period elaborates on his working methods: "The trouble with me when I set out to write a novel is that I worry so over the sure even progress of it. I start & start & change & change. Have done so with nearly every one. What I really ought to have is someone who could decide for me— . . . or one who would take all the phrases I pen down & piece them together into the true story as I see it" (152).

Dreiser turned to women for just such editorial help. His signature overlapping of romantic and professional relationships could produce tangles of conflicts. He admits to Sallie Kussell, who helped him with *An American Tragedy* and *A Gallery of Women*, that her "gripping sex appeal" entices him to "fag myself daily & then lie about" (148), and so writing goes more smoothly without the distraction of her editorial assistance. Yet that tangle was necessary for Dreiser, for whom creativity and sexuality were fused: "A creative atmosphere is one in which the emotions thrive" (358). *Letters to Women* demonstrates the inextricability of Dreiser's writing and his loving.

The extensive work of editing a volume such as this is largely invisible. Unlike the author of a scholarly monograph, the editor of primary documents effaces himself to let the documents speak for themselves while also providing necessary background information for readers. It is a difficult balance, but Riggio's editing is impeccable, beginning with headnotes and endnotes that are ample yet restrained. He provides all necessary factual information (all the more essential here than for correspondence with better-known figures). Gems include a mini-biography of Kirah Markham (58) and a lengthy headnote quoting Dreiser's account of his first meeting with Helen Richardson (154). Meticulous cross-references within endnotes allow even the casual reader to follow individual letters with ease. Riggio has personally interviewed some of the women to whom Dreiser wrote, adding another dimension to his unsurpassed expertise. The substantial introduction outlines Riggio's conclusions: the letters document changes in women's status during the first half of the twentieth century; Dreiser's "erotic preoccupations were entangled with his social, political, and philosophical ideas" (xv); the correspondence challenges the reductive portrait of a lecherous Dreiser; and the novelist saw many parallels between his own life and those of women.

Some may question Riggio's and Pizer's decision to divide the two volumes as they did—with Pizer's containing only a handful of letters to women, defined as those with whom Dreiser had no personal relationship. The division by gender provides a more creative focus than the standard "early" and "late" chronology, but may prove awkward for researchers tracing a particular topic or interested in a certain period. This edition jumps from September 1898 to March 1907, a crucial period including publication of Dreiser's first novel, *Sister Carrie*. Yet the best justification of Riggio's editorial decisions is that *Letters to Women* makes for a lively and informative read, whether for the expert or the general reader. The letters provide, as Dreiser remarks in one of them, "A primary confession" (185) of the first order.

Clare Eby
University of Connecticut

FITZGERALD AND HEMINGWAY: WORKS AND DAYS. By Scott Donaldson. New York: Columbia UP, 2009. 511 pp. $32.50.

Works and Days is a collection of twenty-four essays on Scott Donaldson's two premier subjects, F. Scott Fitzgerald (1896–1940) and Ernest Hemingway (1899–1961). All but one of the essays have been previously published. Donaldson, as is well known, is also the author of biographies of these two figures—*By Force of Will: The Life and Art of Ernest Hemingway* (1977) and *Fool for Love: F. Scott Fitzgerald* (1983)—as well as a book on their famous rivalry: *Hemingway versus Fitzgerald: The Rise and Fall of a Literary Friendship* (1999). The present volume is not a dual biography in the strictest sense of the term, but it does trace a long list of convergences and divagations on the timeline of their relationship that reveals interesting overlaps in how each author wrote and what they wrote about. The book is probably not, as the publisher's grandiose jacket claims, "a reorientation of how we read twentieth-century American literature," but the scholarship is solid and the results are valuable. Donaldson begins with an introduction that is an auto-bibliography of sorts—an account of his forty-year academic life researching and writing on Fitzgerald and Hemingway. The rest of the book is then given over to eleven essays on Fitzgerald and thirteen on Hemingway.

The topic is, to be sure, a great one. As we comb through the pages of the many biographical volumes that have been written about the two figures, we may naturally see them as alter egos: both were products of the Midwest and of families comprised of an overbearing mother and an ineffectual father, but there the similarities end. Fitzgerald was the recipient, initially, of both bountiful royalties and critical respect; Hemingway at the start of his career was much admired but netted very little in the way of income. So too, Fitzgerald, in writing for the magazines, reached the masses whereas Hemingway had to settle for an avant-garde readership of the literary journals and small-press followers of Paris. One could hold his liquor better than the other; and that same one seemed to dominate his wives whereas his counterpart was—in a phrase from the title of one of Donaldson's other books—a "fool for love." The Minnesotan had the delicate features and light skin of someone who spent most of his time indoors; the Oak Parker was big and rough, with a weathered complexion chiseled in the sunlight of exotic locales—Africa, Montreux, Havana. Both were noncombatants in the Great War, but the former saw no action; the latter, as a Red Cross ambulance driver, became the first American wounded in Italy by going after the action, even when he did not have to. Each man eventually won the fame he sought, but each also paid a heavy price for securing it.

Donaldson brings out these elements in a prose style that is enviable—it is clear-eyed, accessible, and mercifully devoid of the academic jargon that often cripples good literary criticism. Originally a journalist like Hemingway, Donaldson punctuates his writing with the fresh insights of the educated observer—something else sometimes missing from academic prose. What a pleasure to read a book about literature that is itself actually literary! Donaldson writes with clarity, elegance, and wit.

The Fitzgerald section is organized topically—"The Search for Home," "Love, Money, and Class," "Fitzgerald and His Times," and "Requiem." Two astute biographical pieces begin this Fitzgerald section, one of them about his attitudes toward the American south as they were shaped by his father and by his wife, Zelda. There is also one essay on Fitzgerald's first novel, *This Side of Paradise* (1920). Two other essays are critical analyses of *The Great Gatsby* (1925): one elucidates the twin principles of acquisition and consumption in the title character's life; the other is an extended meditation on class, money, and materialism. Each, however, is subtitled "Reading Gatsby Closely," which makes for a somewhat awkward reading experience: one reads with the expectation of seeing critical commonplaces challenged or assumptions overturned, but because both pieces, like so many in the book, were published so long ago, the interpretations seem more nostalgic than cutting-edge. It is for this reason that one wishes that, in revising the pieces for publication (as Donaldson says in the introduction) as "a new book," he had taken into account some of the more recent critical approaches that have come about since his work first saw print.

Donaldson says he gave the individual pieces a thorough working-over before publishing them in the present volume. But in comparing the chapters to their original appearances in academic journals and other books, the extent of his revisions seems to have been mostly stylistic, much of it aimed at eliminating repeated quotations from chapter to chapter. Moreover, the documentation is minimal, and the bibliography at the rear of the volume is very selective.

In some cases the absence of specific documentation gives one pause, for in discussing some topics, such as the composition of *Tender Is the Night* (1934), or the censorship of *A Farewell to Arms* (1929), the definitive treatments of the subject are nowhere mentioned. I am thinking of Matthew J. Bruccoli's 1963 book on the first topic and James B. Meriwether's seminal 1964 essay on the second one, as well as later scholarship updating their theses with new information that has come to light in the authors' papers at the Princeton and Kennedy libraries.

Fitzgerald's novels get the usual expected treatments, but Donaldson may actually be strongest in his discussions of the nonfiction: there is a lengthy chapter on "The Crack-Up" essays (1936), the analytical counterpart to another extended essay on the author's political development, and a shorter but no less penetrating study of the other nonfiction—specifically, the early magazine articles. This strand in Donaldson's critical interpretation of Fitzgerald is so strong, in fact, that one wishes more had been said about Hemingway's nonfiction too.

The Hemingway section is divided into "Getting Started," "The Craftsman at Work," "The Two Great Novels," "Censorship," "Literature and Politics," and "Last Things." These essays furnish a frank, unvarnished assessment of the writer as a person: We see him in Paris manipulating his editors back at the Toronto newspaper syndicate into granting him choice assignments and then selling the same story twice to competing news agencies. We look over his shoulder as he chooses a course of self-enforced poverty, taking advantage of the good exchange rate of francs for dollars and letting the café du jour pay his light and heat bill, so to speak, while he writes at one of their window-side tables. We take note of the archly satiric bent of not just his early adolescent writings but much of his entire output over the course of his career—a writer who seemed almost to smirk behind the dialogue of his wise-guy characters. In terms of critical analysis, we are treated to two somewhat interesting readings of the character of Frederic Henry (as self-determining rather than passive and as self-implicated in the corruption that surrounds him), but those too, like the essays on *Gatsby*, have a bit of a sense of datedness about them, as critically sound as they are.

The Hemingway section has a measure of the cohesiveness that the Fitzgerald section somewhat lacks. Parts of the Hemingway chapters dovetail neatly with each other. In "Humor as a Measure of Character," Donaldson discusses Mike Campbell's iconic line about going broke, "first gradually, then suddenly"; that comment hearkens back to a discussion in the previous essay, "Hemingway's Morality of Compensation," in which the author analyzes Jake Barnes's meticulous auditing of his own accounts, both financial and personal. Donaldson rounds out the Hemingway segment with two complementary pieces, on death and on fame, the two issues most consistently relevant to just about everything Hemingway wrote or said or did.

The book presents the narrative elements of biography without belaboring famous episodes or overanalyzing famous figures: Donaldson walks us through such events as Hemingway's drunken encounter with the skylight chain in his Paris bathroom or his speech before a packed house of 3,500 at Carnegie Hall during the Second Congress of the League of American Writers, but at just the right length. And all the secondary characters in the Fitzgerald and Hemingway dramas make their memorable appearances without outstaying their welcomes: Maxwell Perkins, Ginevra King, Morley Callaghan, Gerald and Sara Murphy, Buck Lanham, Budd Schulberg, and others.

Lastly, Donaldson's book shows the results of probably his greatest contribution—his several decades' work in manuscript archives. Donaldson is not just thoroughly conversant with these papers; his analyses of the authors' revisions are invaluable. This is especially illuminating for Hemingway, given the long-standing interest in his "craft of omission," but it is even more so for Fitzgerald. One of the best stand-alone histories of the composition of *Tender Is the Night*—a novel with a labyrinthine and tortuous textual history—is given here with clarity and ease.

Works and Days is a testament to Donaldson's literary labors over the course of a long and fruitful career. It is safe to say that all scholars have a more varied, more nuanced, and more informed understanding of these two titans of modern American literature in part because of Donaldson's intelligent, conscientious, and persistent investigations into who they were and why they wrote what they did.

James M. Hutchisson
The Citadel

ALL MAN!: HEMINGWAY, 1950s MEN'S MAGAZINES, AND THE MASCULINE PERSONA. By David M. Earle. Kent, OH: Kent State UP, 2009. xii + 177 pp. $35.

There cannot be too many academic books more entertaining than this snappily written study of the intersection between the world of pulp magazines and the charismatic Ernest Hemingway (1899–1961). On the cover, a brooding, taut-mouthed image of the author taken from a 1959 *Man's Magazine* glares out from under the blaring, pulpish title *All Man!*, shunting aside the scholarly subtitle into something of a parenthesis. But it works. It captures the pulp atmosphere of truculent masculinity David M. Earle analyzes so well in this book and anticipates his success at breaching that practically undiscovered territory lying between academic readers and a nonscholarly audience. Provocatively illustrated with dozens of photos from pulps, *All Man!* looks as if it belongs on a coffee table. Kudos to Earle for writing the kind of informed and erudite study that could actually make its home there as well as in a research library.

Tracing a history of the pulps from the 1920s through the 1960s, Earle argues convincingly that Hemingway retained a long-term interest in the genre—an interest amply repaid in the 1950s when the pulps turned obsessively to celebrating "Hemingway himself as a fiction, as a popular representation" (4) of manhood. A primary goal of *All Man!* is to explore how the pulps exploited the tough, straight-talking, "all man" persona of Hemingway as part of a larger cultural project to reconstruct a traumatized American masculinity in the wake of World War II. It was not, Earle notes, a symbiosis that was wholly beneficial to Hemingway. The author himself seemed conflicted, wavering between a desire for privacy—in fact, he was "tortured by his own fame" (23)—and a relentless urge toward self-promotion. More unsettling is the way his brand of iconic masculinity accompanied the kind of pervasive misogyny that had one 1958 manifesto (from *Jem: The Magazine for Masterful Men*) proclaiming, "From now on, we men are going to sit high in the saddle, apply the spurs deep and, when necessary, use the whip!" (qtd. 8). A few years after his death in 1961, second-wave feminists turned the pulps-inspired image of Hemingway against his fiction and thence into a more general condemnation of a male-dominated canon.

Earle's account of the author's reciprocal relationship with the pulps in the 1950s is an intriguing study of masculine mythmaking, but he notes still more interestingly that few biographers and scholars have paid any attention to the earlier "shadow history of Hemingway" (19): the fact that the author's first writing efforts were not only heavily influenced by magazines such as *Physical Culture*, *Short Stories*, and *All-Story Magazine* (27–33) but also directed toward publishing in pulp magazines. Fragmentary manuscripts and rejection slips from pulps such as *Adventure* and *Popular Magazine* (41) archived in the Kennedy Library make a convincing case that, in style and choice of topic, Hemingway's apprenticeship to writing owed as much to the hard-boiled conventions of pulp writing as to his journalism. This leads Earle into some provocative readings of Hemingway's published fiction, notably *To Have and Have Not* (1937), which he insightfully reads as a stylistic and cultural appropriation of the pulp milieu. He argues that Hemingway modeled Harry Morgan on the ambiguous characters of the "gangster and detective pulps" where "heroes inhabited a space somewhere beyond pure good and evil" (48) while structuring the story itself around a contrast between the elite writer Richard Gordon and the tough, working-class characters who like to read *Western Stories* and *War Aces*. *To Have and Have Not*, in short, deliberately evokes the world of pulp fiction as a sign of working-class solidarity and in the process perfects what Earle sees as a "sparse, workmanlike modernist culmination of his own pulp tutelage" (50).

Though brief, Earle's extrapolation from Hemingway's interest in pulps to the fashioning of modernism in general is potentially weighty. Noting that originally the "demarcation between popular and early modernist fiction was not so easy to see" (43), Earle broadly sketches in a relationship between modernism and the pulps that develops over several decades. The little-known fact that 1950s pulps frequently published and wrote about elite writers such as Hemingway, D. H. Lawrence, William Faulkner, and James Joyce is, Earle argues, no quirk of history: it suggests a "genealogy, an evolution of modernism from little magazines through *Esquire* to fifties men's magazines" (113) attributable to a shared celebration of male privilege. Male "High" modernists marketed themselves like the popular men's magazines, "misogynistically defin[ing] themselves against the female reader and consumer" (111) and, as Hemingway's work seems to demonstrate so well, borrowing from the pulp repertoire of "all man" subjects. It is hard to know which is more provocative here: the claim that male modernists incorporated pulp styles and themes or the implication that by midcentury the much-denigrated genre of pulp fiction evolves out of and is even the "culmination of a masculine, misogynistic modernism started in the teens" (113).

Like many areas of this study—and this is the downside of Earle's determination to write for a cultural middle ground—his account of misogynistic modernism and its relationship to the pulps is merely sketched. It is certainly true that Hemingway's interest in hunting, fishing, travel, and war overlaps the concerns of popular men's magazines. But how to understand or theorize that overlap? Hemingway's "most literary work," *The Sun Also Rises* (1926), may be "akin to [the] contemporary and sensational risqué pulp magazines" (44) beginning to swamp the mid-1920s popular fiction market, but does "akin" signify influence, or sameness, or difference? His elevation to "virtuoso modernist minimalist" (41) on the basis of his hard-boiled style "parallels the movement in pulp writing from melodramatic romantic adventure to cynical hard-boiled themes and stylistics" (41), but does "parallels" mean parallel and the same, or parallel but separate? In one sense it is pointless to quibble: Earle expressly states that his focus is public fictions about Hemingway, not Hemingway's writing. But the lack of a sophisticated consideration of how "akin" the author really is to pulp fiction means that there is little to dispel the pulps-inspired fiction of an "all man" misogynist. Despite mentioning the fact that Hemingway's reputation as a misogynist is "finally under revision" (19) in numerous recent studies, and despite a footnote that admits that the "concept of a single, male . . . modernism has been exploded over the past few decades" (165), Earle's focus on Hemingway's debt to the pulps and his genealogy leading from the misogynist origins of male modernism to midcentury men's magazines leaves the reader with the inevitable impression that a one-dimensional narrative is in fact the correct one. It is one of the few aspects of *All Man!* that demands a more complex engagement with the scholarship, with literary history, and with Hemingway's fiction.

Still, if *All Man!* leaves open the question of how Hemingway's fiction engages a pulp milieu, it makes the exciting case *that* it does, and Earle should be commended for launching what could prove to be a rich area of Hemingway studies. The thought that this might send scholars to eBay rather than to the nearest research library is a sign of the additional challenge Earle makes to business-as-usual in academic study. The pulps turn out to be important cultural texts—troubling in their persistent misogyny, to be sure, but a rich vein of material about changing ideologies of masculinity as well as an index to celebrity culture and a culture of visuality. And in Earle's hands the relationship between Hemingway and the pulps encourages an interestingly heady mix of Cultural Studies, American Studies, literary and popular culture studies, scholarly insight, and general interest. All man he may be, but, as ever, Hemingway proves his worth as a generous and generative writer. And the inquiry into Hemingway and the pulps is not yet over.

Thomas Strychacz
Mills College

THE FOUR LOST MEN: THE PREVIOUSLY UNPUBLISHED LONG VERSION. By Thomas Wolfe. Ed. Arlyn Bruccoli and Matthew J. Bruccoli. Columbia: U of South Carolina P, 2008. xxi + 92 pp. $22.

In February 1934, *Scribner's Magazine* published Thomas Wolfe's (1900–1938) short story "The Four Lost Men." As with the author's short fiction that preceded its appearance in the periodical since August 1929, the story suffered from the editorial practices of Maxwell Perkins and Alfred Dashiell, which supposedly created an untrustworthy text of the story that has been "perpetuated in uncorrected reprints and inaccurate resettings" ever since (ix). With *The Four Lost Men: The Previously Unpublished Long Version*, the late Matthew J. Bruccoli, the foremost expert on the House of Scribner, and his wife Arlyn, a notable Wolfe scholar, seek not only to "recover Wolfe's intentions" with the story but also to establish a template by which critical editions of all of Wolfe's works may follow (ix). While both of these aims are admirable in intent, the Bruccolis' edition of "The Four Lost Men" actually creates more problems than it corrects. As their introduction to the volume illustrates, establishing reliable editions of Wolfe's work is more difficult than first appears. It also raises questions concerning the best way to resurrect the author's declining reputation.

One of Wolfe's weakest stories, "The Four Lost Men" is a nostalgic piece with a first-person narrator who remembers returning home from college at the start of World War I as its frame. Due to the excitement, patriotism, and anxiousness of the period, the narrator's ailing father "seemed to live again in his full prime" to tell stories of his youth (74), especially the Republican era of Reconstruction and post-Reconstruction at the close of the nineteenth century. Repeating the refrain of "Garfield, Arthur, Harrison, and Hayes" (the four Republicans who succeeded Grant in the office of president), Wolfe presents not only an old man's remembrance of his own youthful vigor, paralleling it with the nation's growth, but also his knowledge of his forthcoming death, a fate that these American presidents could not escape.

Because of the complicated manuscript evidence surrounding "The Four Lost Men," it is unfortunate that the Bruccolis chose this story to begin establishing critical editions of Thomas Wolfe's short fiction. Although their purpose is to use "the surviving story manuscripts and typescripts" to establish Wolfe's intentions (x), as Matthew J. Bruccoli reveals late in his introduction, Wolfe actually wrote two versions of the story: a short version that was used for *Scribner's Magazine* and a long version that enlarged the short one by 21,000 words, including two additional characters and a story line that never appeared in print (xvi). From this evidence alone it is impossible to know which Wolfe intended as the final "approved" form of the story. This becomes apparent when Bruccoli also notes that "there is no evidence that Wolfe wrote any of the manuscript material more than once: no rewriting, copying, or cutting on the manuscript pages" occurred (xvi). The fact that no revision happened after initial composition is especially problematic in establishing Wolfe's intention. Indeed, from the evidence the Bruccolis provide, it is impossible to know which version Wolfe favored or labored over more intently, especially since "Wolfe was more concerned with getting it all down than with publication" (xx). More than likely Wolfe privileged each version of the story at different times in his career depending on the narrative on which he was working at a particular moment. Perhaps this is why the editors included both versions of "The Four Lost Men" in their small volume.

The main problem with this book arises, however, when Arlyn Bruccoli states in her "Editorial Plan/Emendations Policy" that "there is no coherent manuscript draft for any version, short or long. The segments of manuscript demonstrate that Wolfe wrote a short version of the story first; he did not cut a finished long story to make it conform to acceptable magazine length" (xxiii). From the additional evidence provided by Matthew J. Bruccoli's introduction then, it appears that he and his wife are as guilty as the editors they condemn for perpetrating a fiction of "authorship" on the reading public. In discussing Alfred Dashiell, the managing editor of *Scribner's Magazine*, and Maxwell Perkins, Wolfe's book editor at the House of Scribner, Bruccoli charges that "blame attaches to the editors and publishers who did not serve [Wolfe] well.... [M]ost of his published work—lifetime and posthumous—exists in unreliable or suspicious editions" (xx). If indeed "literary crimes are collaborations" in creating multiple authors of Wolfe's texts (xx), as the Bruccolis argue, then they are as guilty of collaboration as Dashiell and Perkins since their edition of "The Four Lost Men" promotes a fictional representation of Wolfe's intent, a troubling basis for editing that they encourage future scholars to employ. Unfortunately, the author's complicated composing practices, constantly changing publishing plans, and early death muddy the waters to such an extent that there is no way of knowing his definitive plans for this piece or most of his work. They changed from day to day.

As Matthew J. Bruccoli discusses at length in his introduction, Wolfe originally composed "The Four Lost Men" from research he was conducting about the year 1881 for a proposed novel titled "The Good Child's River," based on the life and ancestry of his mistress Aline Bernstein (xii). After composition of the short version, which appeared in *Scribner's* "much as Wolfe originally wrote it" (xvi), the author apparently drafted the long version as a section of "The Hills Beyond Pentland," a "fictionalized history of Wolfe's mother's people he worked on from 1932–33" (xvi). Adding to the confusion is the fact that one of the cover pages of "The Four Lost Men" typescript identifies the piece "as part of 'The Hound of Darkness,' Wolfe's unfinished saga of nighttime America," which he later thought of using as the prologue for "The Hills Beyond Pentland" (xvi). Such evolving plans were typical of Wolfe during the 1930s, especially since he rarely discarded a piece of writing and found places to use it in later narratives. If ever there was a situation where the error of intentional fallacy should have been evoked for the editors, this is it.

While many literary critics have used biographical criticism to discuss the ways in which Wolfe's life influenced his work, almost as many textual scholars have mined the author's manuscripts in an attempt to raise his canonical stock, combating decades-old arguments against Wolfe's verbosity and formlessness that their newly edited pieces actually confirm. As Matthew J. Bruccoli writes in his introduction,

> The familiar criticism of Thomas Wolfe is that he was deficient in sense of form: that his novels and stories are loosely organized or even unstructured and include unnecessary material. The terms "self-indulgent" and "undisciplined" have been freely applied to his published work. This influential charge interferes with the proper evaluation and understanding of his work. At its most pernicious, it provides an alibi for the failure to publish trustworthy Wolfe texts. (ix)

Although it is commendable of Bruccoli not to use "The Four Lost Men" in an attempt to raise Wolfe's literary reputation, a common move employed by Wolfe scholars, what he means exactly by "the proper evaluation and understanding of [Wolfe's] work" is never sufficiently explained (xi). While it is an important undertaking to publish "trustworthy Wolfe texts" (xi), editors who use authorial intention as the basis for their textual decisions are troublesome, especially when many edit raw, unrevised sections of manuscript to establish reliability.

Not only is it impossible to get inside of Wolfe's head at any time during the creative process, but this approach also ignores countless cultural pressures that influenced the composition, revision, and publication of his work. In Wolfe's case, the focus on intention discounts conditions that influenced the publication of "The Four Lost Men." Denying the conventional publishing practices of the 1930s, a process that Wolfe struggled to comprehend throughout his career, is not realistic when attempting to establish trustworthy texts. The mere existence of a manuscript or typescript alone does not establish "trust" or "intent." Unfortunately, the Bruccolis lost their chance to change the critical discourse concerning Wolfe's work. They could have refocused their discussion by turning to new ways of assessing his composing practices and eventual appearance in print. For these reasons, I believe that the short version of "The Four Lost Men" that originally appeared in *Scribner's* IS the reliable and trustworthy version.

As stated previously, it is important to encourage current Wolfe scholars to focus on more complex discussions of the author's work before undertaking the project of establishing reliable editions of his texts. Because Wolfe is unnecessarily maligned and misunderstood in the literary community, his reputation can benefit from refocusing discussions of his novels and stories to issues much different from the usual biographical and textual criticism. Placing his work within the appropriate historical and cultural discourses of his era as well as employing new strategies through which to read his work should do much to realign his reputation to its rightful place in the literary canon. Only then should scholars focus on establishing reliable editions of his texts by employing paradigms more complex than intent. Until this occurs, editors such as the Bruccolis will keep relying on an outdated methodology by which to make editorial decisions, a mistake that has plagued Wolfe's career ad nauseam. We should always keep in mind, as the Bruccolis themselves insist, that "blame attaches to the editors and publishers who did not serve [Wolfe] well" (xx). Even though their book includes some unpublished material, *The Four Lost Men: The Previously Unpublished Long Version* does little to change our knowledge of Thomas Wolfe and his work.

Shawn Holliday
Northwestern Oklahoma State University

ARTHUR MILLER 1915–1962. By Christopher Bigsby. Cambridge, MA: Harvard UP, 2009. x + 739 pp. $35.

Over nearly ninety years, Arthur Miller (1915–2005) lived a long and complicated life. It is fortunate that within five years of his death, Christopher Bigsby, a decades-long friend of the playwright and one of his most prominent interpreters, has already offered up a biography on the heels of his *Arthur Miller: A Critical Study* (2004). Bigsby, who directs the Arthur Miller Centre for American Studies at the University of East Anglia, has long been recognized for his scholarship on American drama, receiving the American Society for Theatre Research's Barnard Hewitt Award for outstanding research in theater history, among many other honors. Bigsby's *Arthur Miller 1915–1962* is not the first Miller biography—Martin Gottfried's *Arthur Miller: His Life and Work* appeared in 2004—but it will quickly become the standard by which to judge the others. It is both sympathetic and comprehensive, and it brings together Bigsby's roles as literary critic and biographer. For two years, Bigsby had exclusive access to Miller's papers, now at the Harry Ransom Center of the University of Texas at Austin. As Bigsby states in his preface, "This is the story of a writer, but this is also the story of America" (ix). *Arthur Miller 1915–1962* succeeds, not only because of Bigsby's reading of Miller's life and works, but also because it benefits from an outside observer's keen portrait of Miller's American century.

One of the most interesting contrasts, however, is not between this volume and other biographical studies, but between Bigsby's well-researched account and Miller's voluminous writing about his own life, particularly his 1987 memoir, *Timebends*. Arthur Miller always insisted on telling his story his way, and while he lived, he largely succeeded. In a 2004 profile that coincided with the opening of Miller's final play, *Finishing the Picture*, Deborah Solomon reported his continued determination to frame his own retelling of the making of *The Misfits* (1961) in 1960: "There is no correct version," Miller claimed. "It's purely the way I see it." When Solomon asked Miler, "But what if the rest of us see it differently?" he replied, "It doesn't matter. It's my truth. It's not your truth" (*New York Times Magazine* Sept. 19, 2004: 64).

Miller used his drama as well as his personal fame to put "his truth" out into the public sphere, and this is a quality his admirers and interpreters value. *Timebends* will always have value as Miller's own version of his life story, but Bigsby's biography gives a more complete, and more integrated, picture of Miller's life and legacy: scholarship and stage, biography and theory, the private world and the public one. In an appreciation published just after Miller's death, ABC News quoted Dean Richards as saying, "A bit of his legacy gets amplified by the pizzazz with which he lived his life, but it's his warts-and-all study of who we are that will be remembered best years from now" ("Playwright Arthur Miller Dies," ABC News, Feb. 15, 2005: http://abcnews.go.com/Entertainment/Health/story?id=491164&page=1). Those who care most about Miller's legacy should value him as he saw us, "warts-and-all." To do less is to do less than he deserves, and Bigsby succeeds in this difficult task.

Arthur Miller 1915–1962 begins not with Miller's own childhood but with those of his parents. This move contextualizes Miller's childhood in many important ways and illuminates many of the themes Miller's plays develop. Both his mother's and his father's families emigrated from the Polish town of Radomizl, headed for an America teeming, they hoped, with both prosperity and freedom from anti-Semitism. Like others of their place and time, both Isidore and Augusta Miller saw themselves as Americans, meaning they largely severed their relationships with their parents' culture. Bigsby usefully quotes Miller explaining the costs and benefits of this rapid change: "The original impulse of the immigrant," Miller explained, "was to become an American, not, as is the fashion now, to emphasize the ethnicity of everybody, to show how different people are. There is something to be said for both, because my parents' generation was deformed by having, in effect, to conceal themselves" (24). Bigsby does an admirable job of offering Miller's own commentary where he deems it useful, but he does not allow the playwright's words to dominate the story, or to drown out voices whose perspectives differ. Bigsby also draws a detailed portrait of Isidore and Augusta Miller's marriage and its effects on all three of their children, both before and after the crash of 1929 forced the family out of Harlem, where the Millers enjoyed a much more prosperous life than Isidore and Augusta experienced on the Lower East Side, into the relatively poor and bucolic Brooklyn.

Thanks in large part to *Death of a Salesman* (1949), Brooklyn looms large for Miller's admirers, and Bigsby puts forth substantial effort to recreate the borough as Miller lived in it and to show the many ways in which the Miller family's view of America changed there. Bigsby weaves together the well-known events from Miller's youth—the football injury, his indifferent high school grades, the job in an auto parts warehouse where he was the only Jew—with careful portraits of a tension-filled home life that Miller was often eager to escape. Here again, Bigsby uses ample material from Miller's siblings and other relatives to show us the young Art as others saw him, even when that picture is rather less than heroic. Miller's decision, after two years of low-wage work, to pursue an education at the University of Michigan is often characterized as a Horatio Algerish moment of self-invention. Bigsby, telling this story, foregrounds the effects of this choice on Miller's father, who was counting on his help to reestablish the business, and on his brother, Kermit, who was left to bear that load alone.

As the scene shifts to Michigan, Bigsby again balances many competing elements of Miller's story, from shaky finances and his reliance on Hopwood Award prize money to pay his tuition and board—a scheme that would strike fear in the heart of any financial aid counselor today—to the crash course in union politics he received while covering the automotive industry for the campus newspaper. Bigsby also spends considerable time and attention on Miller's developing romance with Mary Slattery, who would become his first wife. Bigsby portrays a relationship in Michigan and back in New York that might not have survived less momentous challenges than Marilyn Monroe, and he makes no effort to protect Miller from the reader's censure. He also complicates the common narrative of Miller's early dramatic success, giving a good overview of Miller's time in the trenches of radio drama and other commercial endeavors, along with the obstacles that lay in the path of his first commercial and critical success, *All My Sons* (1947).

Once Miller establishes himself on the New York stage with *Death of a Salesman* (a play that, Bigsby notes, forever removed Miller himself from the working class), Bigsby turns much of his attention toward Miller's political life, and he shows again how much Miller's story is the story of his time and place. Bigsby is careful to note how events in Miller's political life will later resonate during the blacklist era, but he does not allow this foreshadowing to obscure or distort the narrative. One of the strongest sections of the book examines Miller's participation alongside Clifford Odets and Aaron Copland in the Cultural and Scientific Conference for World Peace, held at New York's Waldorf-Astoria Hotel in March 1949, and allows Bigsby to draw a nuanced view of Miller's leftist politics, as well as his political blind spots. The Waldorf Conference, Bigsby explains, "was seen as disastrous for the communists.... Far from breeding peace and harmony, [it] had, in fact, played its part in prompting a cultural cold war which would effect a generation of writers and intellectuals" (363). When, shortly afterward, Miller's older brother, Kermit, joins the shooting war in Europe, Bigsby keeps the family dynamic firmly in focus.

Through the years for which Miller still remains best known in the United States and abroad, the 1950s, Bigsby balances the personal and the political, Miller's confrontation with Senator McCarthy and the House Un-American Activities Committee, as well as his relationship with Marilyn Monroe. For many of Miller's fans, particularly in the United States, this is the climax of Miller's story, and *The Misfits* and Monroe's death mark the end of what interests them. In lieu of the promise of a second volume, Bigsby adds a final chapter, "Inge" (named for Inge Morath, Miller's third wife, creative partner, and the stable center of his later life), in which he sketches out Miller's last four decades. Miller scholars, as well as anyone with an interest in contemporary American drama, will wish for that second volume, but Bigsby's in-depth focus on the first half of Miller's life and career is well worth any later omission. A sequel would be welcome, but if Bigsby does not undertake that project, *Arthur Miller 1915–1962* will stand on its own, providing a daunting model for anyone who undertakes the rest of Miller's story.

Katherine Egerton
Berea College

LETTERS TO MY FATHER. By William Styron. Ed. James L. W. West III. Baton Rouge: Louisiana State UP, 2009. xxix + 238 pp. $28.

William Styron's (1925–2006) letters to his father contribute significantly to the body of his earlier work. James L. W. West III, Styron's authorized biographer, has done a superior job of annotating the letters, as well as including and organizing other material in this small but intriguing book, material that helps enhance appreciation of Styron. A foreword from Rose Styron elaborates the relationship between father and son and gives considerable insight into the personality and interests of the older Styron. Next come the 102 letters Styron wrote to his father in the years between 1943 and 1953.

West includes a previously unpublished photograph of Styron aged five with his father, asserting that it is the only known photograph of the two together. Facsimile photographs of several of Styron's letters; a "new" photograph of Rose Burgunder, who married Styron in 1953, in Rome; and photographs of original covers of *Lie Down in Darkness* (1951) also add interest. At the end, West includes three letters from William C. Styron to his son, a brief biography of his son that he (Styron's father) wrote for the Duke Alumni Association in 1951, and five stories that Styron produced during his years at Duke, all of which show the promise fulfilled in his later novels.

The apprenticeship work seems remarkable in two ways: Styron's power with language has already emerged, and he writes about what he knows rather than—with one exception—pursuing the exotic. The exception is his story "The Long Dark Road," first published in 1944 in *Archive*, the Duke literary magazine. The story, set in Mississippi, owes a considerable debt to William Faulkner's "Dry

September" (1931); yet Styron adds originality by filtering the experience of a lynching through the perspective of a sensitive fourteen-year-old boy.

Letters to My Father, most tellingly, reveals the poignant relationship between Styron and his father; in the process, the letters also help to humanize a writer who was often reserved about giving insights into his private life. With evident affection and respect, Styron begins his letters with "Dear Pop" and signs off with "your son, Bill." The letters pay tribute to William C. Styron Sr., a man whose great generosity provides an antidote to the many parents who, not understanding the dreams of their children, try to force them to choose paths antithetical to their talents and desires.

Styron's most appreciative words about his father's influence on his life come in a letter he wrote in June 1951 from Camp Lejeune, NC, after he was recalled by the Marine Reserve:

> Of course you must know what you've done for me. If it hadn't been for your faith in me, and your gentle and constant encouragement, it [*Lie Down in Darkness*] would never have been written.... [Y]ou have been faithful to the very end of my first endeavor and I appreciate it from the bottom of my heart. (115)

Styron's father's constant support shows both how much he loved his talented son and how sure he was that William Styron would succeed as a writer. In her foreword, Rose Styron comments further on the father's influence on his son: "Pop's idealism, his empathy for the less fortunate, and his hatred of racial prejudice and meanness and hypocrisy became Bill's" (xiii).

The letters, covering the years between January 1943 and October 1953, present, in the style of a *bildungsroman*, Styron's growth as a young man and a writer. He was a sixteen-year-old freshman at Davidson College in North Carolina when he first began to write letters home. The content of the early letters is what one would expect from a young Southerner of his generation. He was more interested in joining a fraternity than in doing well in classes, and beyond that, his first concern was becoming a member of the U.S. military. Like many others of his generation, he was eager to join the war effort. He also talks about his college friends—both male and female—and the fun of being at Davidson; he was also already writing. In the biographical sketch, Styron's father writes: "He was a 'feature' writer on the newspaper The Davidsonian, and was on the editorial board and contributed articles to the monthly magazine Scripts 'n Pranks" (169). Nearly every early letter also contains a request for money, to cover fraternity and other expenses. His father was unfailingly accommodating and the son properly grateful.

Once Styron transferred to Duke (because of the Marine ROTC program there), he fell under the influence of English professor William Blackburn, who discovered Styron's talent as a writer of fiction and encouraged the young student to perfect it. In the biographical sketch, the elder Styron shows appreciation for Blackburn's early encouragement of his son's writing: "It was through this teacher-pupil relationship that was formed one of the great friendships of his life" (169). Styron's letters to his father contain many references to his early stories and his pleasure in having them published in the *Archive*; he also talks of the great "debt of gratitude" (46) that he owes to Professor Blackburn.

Aside from an interest in reading and writing and his dedication to both, Styron was a self-proclaimed poor student whose failing grades in a required physics course kept him from earning a Rhodes Scholarship after his graduation from Duke. He wrote to his father about this failure, relating that one of the judges later told him that "[i]t was a toss-up between myself and a fellow from Florida, and they finally decided to give it to him instead of to me because of the three very black 'F's' which I received in Physics" (46). Regardless of that outcome, Styron's father gloried in his son's talent and never wavered in his belief that he would become a well-known writer.

Particularly heartening was his father's financial generosity after Styron moved to New York City and was writing the work that would become *Lie Down in Darkness*. When Styron lost his job at McGraw-Hill publishers, his father agreed to send him $100 a month while he finished the novel. As West points out, the $100 then approximates $900 today (76). Styron accepted the money with the "counterproposition, that it be in the nature of an informal sort of loan to be repaid when I've made some money at this writing game" (76). In later years, Styron did help his father financially. In *William Styron, a Life* (New York: Random House, 1998), West writes:

> In the fall of 1957, W. C. Styron had a minor surgery that, with some other bills, put a strain on his resources. His son was able to ease the pinch and continued to do so throughout the next ten or fifteen years. Eventually W. C. Styron came to depend on his son for considerable financial support, especially during the last years of his life. (284)

West recalls as well that Styron bought his father an Oldsmobile in the late 1960s after the success of *The Confessions of Nat Turner* (1967; e-mail to the author, Apr. 12, 2010).

Styron's letters to his father also show, as he asserted fictionally in *Sophie's Choice* (1979), that he was interested in writing a novel about Nat Turner early in the 1950s. From Paris, in May 1951, he wrote to his father:

> I've finally pretty much decided what to write next—a novel based on Nat Turner's rebellion. The subject fascinates me, and I think I could make a real character out of old Nat. It'll probably take a bit of research, though, and I've written to people in the U.S.—among them Prof. Saunders Redding . . . of Hampton Institute—asking him to pass on any reference material they might have. . . . If you can get your hands on something on that order without too much trouble I'd appreciate your letting me know. I don't know but whether I'm ploughing into something over my depth, but I'm fascinated anyway. (*Letters* 130)

Saunders Redding did send Styron information about Nat Turner that became pivotal to the novel that he wrote about the early African American hero fifteen years later. Styron's comments unequivocally prove that he planned to write a study of the heroic black figure long before the Civil Rights movement. Of particular interest to *Sophie's Choice* are Styron's descriptions of the rooming house and its environs in the Flatbush section of Brooklyn where he lived in 1949. He does not, however, mention the woman who became the model for Sophie Zawistowski.

By the time of the last letter in October 1953, Styron, recently married to Rose Burgunder, was living in Ravello, Italy, but planning to return soon to the United States; he had achieved considerable success with *Lie Down in Darkness* and had recently published his novella *The Long March* in *Discovery* magazine. His career as a writer was firmly launched.

In publishing these letters, Rose Styron and James L. W. West III have made a major contribution to enthusiasts of Styron and his work. The collection gives new insights into Styron as a young man working to join the ranks of the best twentieth-century novelists.

Jean W. Cash
James Madison University

RAYMOND CARVER: A WRITER'S LIFE. By Carol Sklenicka. New York: Scribner, 2009. xi + 578 pp. $35.

Raymond Carver's (1938–88) life was a cautionary tale. Growing up poor in working-class logging and sawmill towns in the Pacific Northwest, he dreamed of the writer's life, his version of the American pop culture dream, until alcoholism turned the dream into a nightmare and sobriety returned the dream to him for the eleven years he had before cancer claimed his life when he had barely turned fifty. Called the American Chekhov at the time of his death, Carver is arguably the most influential American fiction writer since Ernest Hemingway. He is certainly a popular writer, both in English-speaking countries and in the nearly thirty countries where his work has been translated, as well as a source for films including *Short Cuts* (1993), Robert Altman's jazzy collage of short stories, and Australian Ray Lawrence's *Jindabyne* (2006), based on Carver's disturbing story "So Much Water So Close to Home" (1977).

Carol Sklenicka's book, named one of the top ten books of 2009 by the *New York Times*, locates itself in the long tradition of the literary biography that suffers diminishment by a barrage of literary biopics in which all too often writers are simply names tacked on to the celebrity faces pasted into slots of Hollywood costume dramas and predictable romances. Sklenicka is not, however, the first to attempt to present the life of this important writer. Bob Adelman's *Carver Country* (1990), Marshall Bruce Gentry and William L. Stull's *Conversations with Raymond Carver* (1990), Sam Halpert's *Raymond Carver, an Oral Biography* (1995), his widow Tess Gallagher's *Soul Barnacles: Ten More Years with Ray* (2000), and first wife

Maryann Burk Carver's *What It Used to Be Like: A Portrait of My Marriage to Raymond Carver* (2006) have offered biographical collage, collected interviews, oral biographies, and memoirs, respectively. There is also Philippe Romon's *Parlez-moi de Carver: Une biographie littéraire de Raymond Carver*, published in Paris by Agnès Viérnot Editions in 2003, but it remains untranslated.

Carver was born in Clatskanie, Oregon; his family moved to Yakima, Washington, when he was four. His father worked as a saw filer at a lumber mill and his mother as a waitress, giving Carver a blue-collar and working-class background. His childhood was not distinguished academically and his major interests seem to have been fishing and hunting in the Pacific Northwest. At eighteen he married his sixteen-year-old girlfriend, Maryann Burk, and within the next two years the couple had two children. Rather than being limited by their circumstances, they participated in the important social shift of the 1950s by enrolling in college in order to acquire degrees that would help them rise into middle-class, white-collar jobs, and it worked after college when Maryann taught high school and Ray worked for SRA, an educational publishing company.

But some things happened along the way. Ray took a creative writing class at Chico State with then-unpublished novelist John Gardner and he founded and edited the Chico State literary magazine: for him, this was the beginning of his writing career. While he was working for SRA, he met Gordon Lish, who would become his editor at *Esquire* and later Knopf. His drinking, which had been social, became a habit and then a problem as he descended into alcoholism, the "Bad Raymond" days. These threads shape the early life researched by Sklenicka, who presents Carver as a man driven by his desire to be a successful writer. She details his early publications with Noel Young's Capra Press, his Stegner Fellowship and the Iowa Writers' Workshop years, his growing presence in ever-more-impressive magazines, and his first major press book, *Will You Please be Quiet, Please?* (1976). Yet she also explores how, by the time Carver was thirty-eight, alcohol had ravaged his marriage, his family, and ultimately his career, leading to bankruptcies, blackouts, and hospitalization for acute alcoholism.

What saved him from destruction is the subject of the second half of the book, the period Carver himself called his "second life" or "Good Raymond" period when a second set of things happened: he quit drinking and began a relationship with Tess Gallagher, a poet from Port Angeles, Washington, whom he had met at a writers' conference. What follows is the period he later called the "gravy" on his life, filled with friendships with writers Tobias Wolfe and Richard Ford, among others; awards, including the Strauss Living Award, which provided him a five-year stipend to write; tenure at Syracuse University; and three critically praised collections of short stories—*What We Talk About When We Talk About Love* (1981), *Cathedral* (1983), and *Where I'm Calling From: Selected Stories* (1988)—and three collections of poetry—*Where Water Comes Together with Other Water* (1985), *Ultramarine* (1986), and *New Path to the Waterfall* (1989). Carver's literary output was prodigious during his sobriety, but equally remarkable is that he accomplished all this in just eleven years. By all counts, Carver had achieved and was living his version of the American Dream.

What Carol Sklenicka has taken on so effectively in her biography is the relationship between Carver and his friend and editor, Gordon Lish, the powerful and dynamic editor who was known as Captain Fiction for his success in finding and marketing writers while concurrently advancing his own career. Stories of the editor-writer relationships between literary celebrities are part of the lore of writers, with Maxwell Perkins and Thomas Wolfe, or Ezra Pound and T. S. Eliot often cited as examples of the logical editorial mind reigning in the effusive creative impulse of the writer. Lish's relationship, Sklenicka demonstrates, was quite different; she shows Lish as domineering, manipulative, and exploitative, particularly as he cut 40 percent of Carver's manuscript of *Beginners* into his minimalist set piece *What We Talk About When We Talk About Love* as he purged what he considered sentimentality, changed endings and titles, and altered the writing style and sentence rhythms by replacing sentences with fragments, story with scene, and textured language with intentional cliché. She shows how Carver was both overly trusting of his friend and simultaneously desperate to move his career forward in his sobriety. *What We Talk About When We Talk About Love* was a success and career maker, but it cost Carver his friendship with Lish. Based on the strength of his literary reputation, however, Carver was able to assert editorial control over his next two books, *Cathedral* and *Where I'm Calling From*. At the very point in his life when he had achieved his literary aspirations and had freed himself from the ravages of alcoholism and the exploitation of his ruthless editor, he was sadly diagnosed with lung cancer, then brain cancer, and died in 1988 at home in Port Angeles with Tess Gallagher, his partner whom he had married just two months earlier.

Carver's story of a recurring pattern of loss and recovery, of dreams and disappointments, is the raw material for the stories of the working-class people and the working poor who inhabit what has been called Carver Country, a place where all the good luck goes south and where insolvency, infidelity, and inexplicable dissociation provide his characters with experiences that take them beyond their abilities of articulation, leaving them often in silence or in unclosed parentheses. There are, though, moments of transcendence, or momentary triumph, particularly in the late stories, as evidenced by the widely anthologized "Cathedral" (1983), in which a biased man helps his wife's blind friend understand what a cathedral is by having the blind man move his hand as he traces its shape.

Carol Sklenicka has exhaustively researched Carver's career to write a nearly 600-page biography, interviewing family, friends, writers, and publishers to piece together the tight chronology necessary to understand the brief and complicated events of Carver's life. While some of these voices have been available in fragments scattered across various previous publications, Sklenicka has effectively stitched them cohesively together. Moreover, she has brought his children, Christine and Vance, alive with memories both of their difficult childhoods and their adult memories, including Vance's years at Syracuse when Carver was a professor there. His first wife, Maryann Burk Carver, is shown as his early soul mate and eventual codependent, and as his consistent source of material. Additionally, Sklenicka is the first to conduct extensive interviews with Carver's only sibling, his younger brother James, who dispels a number of stereotypes about their childhood that have been perpetuated as part of the celebrity mythmaking machine. She manages to get almost all the important voices into her biography. She especially and effectively incorporates Carver's voice since he was frequently interviewed and wrote several essays about his work and life. As a result of her ten years of research, the chronology of Carver's life is sequenced and corroborated, presenting readers and scholars for the first time with the full arc of his short life and of his significant literary career.

What is the message of this cautionary tale? Not, I think, clichéd didactic morals such as "Stay true to your dreams" or "Love conquers all," but rather that we can salvage our lives of addiction no matter how wrecked they may seem, that we can recover the loss of control that limits the damage of which we are capable, and that it is possible to construct another life upon the foundations of the first. As a literary biography, this too: that when we are in control of our lives, focused on our craft, we are capable of producing a body of the best work of which we are capable, both completing our lives and making it possible to share our stories with those who read our work. Carol Sklenicka has given readers the story of one of America's greatest storytellers in *Raymond Carver: A Writer's Life*.

Robert Miltner
Kent State University at Stark

Index to Volume 34 of *Resources for American Literary Study*

Index of Authors

Berger, Jason, review: Karen Lentz Madison, R. D. Madison, and Lance C. Schachterle, eds., *Ned Myers; or, A Life before the Mast*, by James Fenimore Cooper, historical introductions by William S. Dudley and Hugh Egan, 245–48

Bristol, Mark Lambert. *See* Roessel, David

Bucker, Park, " 'To Weave the Whole Thing Together': Thomas Wolfe's Revisions of *From Death to Morning*," 129–83

Campbell, Donna, "W. D. Howells's Unpublished Letters to J. Harvey Greene," 73–94

Case, Kristen, review: Nancy Craig Simmons and Ron Thomas, eds., *Journal. Volume 7: 1853–1854*, by Henry D. Thoreau, 260–63

Cash, Jean W., review: James L. W. West III, ed., *Letters to My Father*, by William Styron, 296–99

Dooley, Patrick K., "Prospects for the Study of Stephen Crane," 1–32

Eby, Clare, review: Thomas P. Riggio, ed., *Letters to Women. New Letters, Volume II*, by Theodore Dreiser, 282–84

Egerton, Katherine, review: Christopher Bigsby, *Arthur Miller 1915–1962*, 293–96

Eiselein, Gregory, review: Ted Genoways, *Walt Whitman and the Civil War: America's Poet during the Lost Years of 1860–1862*, 263–65

Gerber, Natalie, "Art as 'An Everyday Affair': William Carlos Williams's Correspondence with His Brother," 223–30

Goldman-Price, Irene C., "Young Edith Jones: Sources and Texts of Early Poems by Edith Wharton," 95–106

Hammond, Alexander, "Poe, Scott's Fiction, and the Holt Source Collection: The Example of *Ivanhoe* and 'The Fall of the House of Usher,' " 47–71

Harris, Jennifer, "Aprons and Pearls: Images of Phillis Wheatley," 33–45

Holliday, Shawn, review: Arlyn Bruccoli and Matthew J. Bruccoli, eds., *The Four Lost Men: The Previously Unpublished Long Version*, by Thomas Wolfe, 290–93

Homestead, Melissa J., review: Anne E. Boyd, ed., *Wielding the Pen: Writings on Authorship by American Women of the Nineteenth Century*, 248–51

Howells, William Dean. *See* Campbell, Donna

Hume, Beverly A., review: Susan Goodman and Carl Dawson, *Mary Austin and the American West*, 279–81

Hutchisson, James M., review: Scott Donaldson, *Fitzgerald and Hemingway: Works and Days*, 285–87

Jaap, James A., "Breaking Fresh Ground: New Releases from the Willa Cather Edition," 215–22

Jones, Edith. *See* Goldman-Price, Irene C.

RESOURCES FOR AMERICAN LITERARY STUDY, Vol. 34, 2009.
Copyright © 2011 AMS Press, Inc.

Justice, Hilary K., review: Greil Marcus and Werner Sollors, eds., *A New Literary History of America*, 239–41

Kiskis, Michael J., review: James E. Caron, *Mark Twain: Unsanctified Newspaper Reporter*, 266–68

Logan, Lisa M., review: Sheila L. Skemp, *First Lady of Letters: Judith Sargent Murray and the Struggle for Female Independence*, 242–45

Long, Lisa, review: Denise D. Knight and Jennifer S. Tuttle, eds., *The Selected Letters of Charlotte Perkins Gilman*, 276–79

Miltner, Robert, review: Carol Sklenicka, *Raymond Carver: A Writer's Life*, 299–302

Moschovakis, Nicholas, and David Roessel, "*The Magic Tower*: An Unpublished One-Act Play by Tennessee Williams," 185–213

Mott, Wesley T., review: Glen M. Johnson and Joel Myerson, eds., *Collected Works of Ralph Waldo Emerson, Volume VIII: Letters and Social Aims*, by Ralph Waldo Emerson, historical introduction by Ronald A. Bosco 251–55

Myerson, Joel, review: Katherine Wolff, *Culture Club: The Curious History of the Boston Athenaeum*, 258–60

Person, Leland S., review: Pierre A. Walker and Greg W. Zacharias, eds., *The Complete Letters of Henry James, 1872–1876. Vol. 1*, 272–75

Roessel, David, "New Information on Hemingway's '3 very fine weeks' in Constantinople in 1922," 107–28; *see also* Moschovakis, Nicholas, and David Roessel

Schmidt, Peter, review: Carolyn L. Karcher, ed., *Bricks Without Straw: A Novel*, by Albion Tourgée, 269–72

Strychacz, Thomas, review: David M. Earle, *All Man! Hemingway, 1950s Men's Magazines, and the Masculine Persona*, 288–90

Trigilio, Tony, "Reconsidering Allen Ginsberg at the End of an Epistolary Era," 231–37

Wadsworth, Sarah, review: Peter West, *The Arbiters of Reality: Hawthorne, Melville, and the Rise of Mass Information Culture*, 255–57

Wharton, Edith. *See* Goldman-Price, Irene C.

Williams, Tennessee. *See* Moschovakis, Nicholas, and David Roessel

Wolfe, Thomas. *See* Bucker, Park

Index of Subjects

African American literature: Jennifer Harris, "Aprons and Pearls: Images of Phillis Wheatley," 33–45; review: Greil Marcus and Werner Sollors, eds., *A New Literary History of America* (Hilary K. Justice), 239–41; review: Anne E. Boyd, ed., *Wielding the Pen: Writings on Authorship by American Women of the Nineteenth Century* (Melissa J. Homestead), 248–51; review: Katherine Wolff,

Culture Club: The Curious History of the Boston Athenaeum (Joel Myerson), 258–60; review: Karcher, Carolyn L., ed., *Bricks Without Straw: A Novel*, by Albion Tourgée (Peter Schmidt), 269–72

Austin, Mary: review: Susan Goodman and Carl Dawson, *Mary Austin and the American West* (Beverly A. Hume), 279–81

INDEX

bibliography: Patrick K. Dooley, "Prospects for the Study of Stephen Crane," 1–32; Alexander Hammond, "Poe, Scott's Fiction, and the Holt Source Collection: The Example of *Ivanhoe* and 'The Fall of the House of Usher,' " 47–71; Park Bucker, " 'To Weave the Whole Thing Together': Thomas Wolfe's Revisions of *From Death to Morning*," 129–83; James A. Jaap, "Breaking Fresh Ground: New Releases from the Willa Cather Edition," 215–22; review: Karen Lentz Madison, R. D. Madison, and Lance C. Schachterle, eds., *Ned Myers; or, A Life before the Mast*, by James Fenimore Cooper, historical introductions by William S. Dudley and Hugh Egan (Jason Berger), 245–48; review: Glen M. Johnson and Joel Myerson, eds., *Collected Works of Ralph Waldo Emerson, Volume VIII: Letters and Social Aims*, historical introduction by Ronald A. Bosco (Wesley T. Mott), 251–55; review: Katherine Wolff, *Culture Club: The Curious History of the Boston Athenaeum* (Joel Myerson), 258–60; review: Nancy Craig Simmons and Ron Thomas, eds., *Journal. Volume 7: 1853–1854*, by Henry D. Thoreau (Kristen Case), 260–63

biography: Patrick K. Dooley, "Prospects for the Study of Stephen Crane," 1–32; Donna Campbell, "W. D. Howells's Unpublished Letters to J. Harvey Greene," 73–94; Irene C. Goldman-Price, "Young Edith Jones: Sources and Texts of Early Poems by Edith Wharton," 95–106; David Roessel, "New Information on Hemingway's '3 very fine weeks' in Constantinople in 1922," 107–28; Natalie Gerber, "Art as 'An Everyday Affair': William Carlos Williams's Correspondence with His Brother," 223–30; Tony Trigilio, "Reconsidering Allen Ginsberg at the End of an Epistolary Era," 231–37; review: Sheila L. Skemp, *First Lady of Letters: Judith Sargent Murray and the Struggle for Female Independence* (Lisa M. Logan), 242–45; review: Karen Lentz Madison, R. D. Madison, and Lance C. Schachterle, eds., *Ned Myers; or, A Life before the Mast*, by James Fenimore Cooper, historical introductions by William S. Dudley and Hugh Egan (Jason Berger), 245–48; review: Glen M. Johnson and Joel Myerson, eds., *Collected Works of Ralph Waldo Emerson, Volume VIII: Letters and Social Aims*, historical introduction by Ronald A. Bosco (Wesley T. Mott), 251–55; review: Nancy Craig Simmons and Ron Thomas, eds., *Journal. Volume 7: 1853–1854*, by Henry D. Thoreau (Kristen Case), 260–63; review: Ted Genoways, *Walt Whitman and the Civil War: America's Poet during the Lost Years of 1860–1862* (Gregory Eiselein), 263–65; review: James E. Caron, *Mark Twain: Unsanctified Newspaper Reporter* (Michael J. Kiskis), 266–68; review: Pierre A. Walker and Greg W. Zacharias, eds., *The Complete Letters of Henry James, 1872–1876. Vol. 1* (Leland S. Person), 272–75; review: Denise D. Knight and Jennifer S. Tuttle, eds., *The Selected Letters of Charlotte Perkins Gilman* (Lisa Long), 276–79; review: Susan Goodman and Carl Dawson, *Mary Austin and the American West* (Beverly A. Hume), 279–81; review: Thomas P. Riggio, ed., *Letters to Women. New Letters, Volume II*, by Theodore Dreiser (Clare Eby), 282–84; review: Scott Donaldson, *Fitzgerald and Hemingway: Works and Days* (James M. Hutchisson), 285–87; review: David M. Earle, *All Man!: Hemingway, 1950s Men's Magazines, and the Masculine Persona* (Thomas Strychacz), 288–90; review: Christopher Bigsby, *Arthur Miller 1915–1962* (Katherine Egerton), 293–96; review: James L. W. West III, ed., *Letters to My Father*, by William Styron (Jean W. Cash), 296–99; Carol Sklenicka, *Raymond Carver: A Writer's Life* (Robert Miltner), 299–302

Bristol, Mark Lambert: David Roessel, "New Information on Hemingway's '3 very fine weeks' in Constantinople in 1922," 107–28

Carver, Raymond: review: Carol Sklenicka, *Raymond Carver: A Writer's Life* (Robert Miltner), 299–302

Cather, Willa: James A. Jaap, "Breaking Fresh Ground: New Releases from the Willa Cather Edition," 215–22

Clemens, Samuel. *See* Twain, Mark

Cooper, James Fenimore: review: Karen Lentz Madison, R. D. Madison, and Lance C. Schachterle, eds., *Ned Myers; or, A Life before the Mast*, by James Fenimore Cooper, historical introductions by William S. Dudley and Hugh Egan (Jason Berger), 245–48

Crane, Stephen: Patrick K. Dooley, "Prospects for the Study of Stephen Crane," 1–32

drama: Nicholas Moschovakis and David Roessel, "*The Magic Tower*: An Unpublished One-Act Play by Tennessee Williams," 185–213; Natalie Gerber, "Art as 'An Everyday Affair': William Carlos Williams's Correspondence with His Brother," 223–30; review: Sheila L. Skemp, *First Lady of Letters: Judith Sargent Murray and the Struggle for Female Independence* (Lisa M. Logan), 242–45; review: Christopher Bigsby, *Arthur Miller 1915–1962* (Katherine Egerton), 293–96

Dreiser, Theodore: review: Thomas P. Riggio, ed., *Letters to Women. New Letters, Volume II*, by Theodore Dreiser (Clare Eby), 282–84

Emerson, Ralph Waldo: review: Glen M. Johnson and Joel Myerson, eds., *Collected Works of Ralph Waldo Emerson, Volume VIII: Letters and Social Aims*, historical introduction by Ronald A. Bosco (Wesley T. Mott), 251–55

Fitzgerald, F. Scott: review: Scott Donaldson, *Fitzgerald and Hemingway: Works and Days* (James M. Hutchisson), 285–87

Gilman, Charlotte Perkins: review: Denise D. Knight and Jennifer S. Tuttle, eds., *The Selected Letters of Charlotte Perkins Gilman* (Lisa Long), 276–79

Ginsberg, Allen: Tony Trigilio, "Reconsidering Allen Ginsberg at the End of an Epistolary Era," 231–37

Greene, J. Harvey: Donna Campbell, "W. D. Howells's Unpublished Letters to J. Harvey Greene," 73–94

Hawthorne, Nathaniel: review: Peter West, *The Arbiters of Reality: Hawthorne, Melville, and the Rise of Mass Information Culture* (Sarah Wadsworth), 255–57

Hemingway, Ernest: David Roessel, "New Information on Hemingway's '3 very fine weeks' in Constantinople in 1922," 107–28; review: Greil Marcus and Werner Sollors, eds., *A New Literary History of America* (Hilary K. Justice), 239–41; review: Scott Donaldson, *Fitzgerald and Hemingway: Works and Days* (James M. Hutchisson), 285–87; review: David M. Earle, *All Man!: Hemingway, 1950s Men's Magazines, and the Masculine Persona* (Thomas Strychacz), 288–90

Howells, William Dean: Donna Campbell, "W. D. Howells's Unpublished Letters to J. Harvey Greene," 73–94

James, Henry: review: Pierre A. Walker and Greg W. Zacharias, eds., *The Complete Letters of Henry James, 1872–1876. Vol. 1* (Leland S. Person), 272–75

Jones, Edith. *See* Wharton, Edith

journalism: Patrick K. Dooley, "Prospects for the Study of Stephen Crane," 1–32; Donna Campbell, "W. D. Howells's Unpublished Letters to J. Harvey Greene," 73–94; David Roessel, "New Information on Hemingway's '3 very fine weeks' in Constantinople in 1922," 107–28; review: Greil Marcus and Werner Sollors, eds., *A New Literary History of America* (Hilary K. Justice), 239–41; review: Sheila L. Skemp, *First Lady of Letters: Judith Sargent Murray and the Struggle for Female Independence* (Lisa M. Logan), 242–45; review: Anne E. Boyd, ed., *Wielding the Pen: Writings on Authorship by American Women of the Nineteenth Century* (Melissa J. Homestead), 248–51; review: Glen M.

Johnson and Joel Myerson, eds., *Collected Works of Ralph Waldo Emerson, Volume VIII: Letters and Social Aims*, historical introduction by Ronald A. Bosco (Wesley T. Mott), 251–55; review: Peter West, *The Arbiters of Reality: Hawthorne, Melville, and the Rise of Mass Information Culture* (Sarah Wadsworth), 255–57; review: Ted Genoways, *Walt Whitman and the Civil War: America's Poet during the Lost Years of 1860–1862* (Gregory Eiselein), 263–65; review: James E. Caron, *Mark Twain: Unsanctified Newspaper Reporter* (Michael J. Kiskis), 266–68; review: Scott Donaldson, *Fitzgerald and Hemingway: Works and Days* (James M. Hutchisson), 285–87; review: David M. Earle, *All Man!: Hemingway, 1950s Men's Magazines, and the Masculine Persona* (Thomas Strychacz), 288–90

letters: Donna Campbell, "W. D. Howells's Unpublished Letters to J. Harvey Greene," 73–94; Irene C. Goldman-Price, "Young Edith Jones: Sources and Texts of Early Poems by Edith Wharton," 95–106; David Roessel, "New Information on Hemingway's '3 very fine weeks' in Constantinople in 1922," 107–28; Park Bucker, " 'To Weave the Whole Thing Together': Thomas Wolfe's Revisions of *From Death to Morning*," 129–83; Natalie Gerber, "Art as 'An Everyday Affair': William Carlos Williams's Correspondence with His Brother," 223–30; Tony Trigilio, "Reconsidering Allen Ginsberg at the End of an Epistolary Era," 231–37; review: Sheila L. Skemp, *First Lady of Letters: Judith Sargent Murray and the Struggle for Female Independence* (Lisa M. Logan), 242–45; review: Anne E. Boyd, ed., *Wielding the Pen: Writings on Authorship by American Women of the Nineteenth Century* (Melissa J. Homestead), 248–51; review: Glen M. Johnson and Joel Myerson, eds., *Collected Works of Ralph Waldo Emerson, Volume VIII: Letters and Social Aims*, historical introduction by Ronald A. Bosco (Wesley T. Mott), 251–55; review: Ted Genoways, *Walt Whitman and the Civil War: America's Poet during the Lost Years of 1860–1862* (Gregory Eiselein), 263–65; review: Pierre A. Walker and Greg W. Zacharias, eds., *The Complete Letters of Henry James, 1872–1876. Vol. 1* (Leland S. Person), 272–75; review: Denise D. Knight and Jennifer S. Tuttle, eds., *The Selected Letters of Charlotte Perkins Gilman* (Lisa Long), 276–79; review: Thomas P. Riggio, ed., *Letters to Women. New Letters, Volume II*, by Theodore Dreiser (Clare Eby), 282–84; review: James L. W. West III, ed., *Letters to My Father*, by William Styron (Jean W. Cash), 296–99

literary history (general): review: Greil Marcus and Werner Sollors, eds., *A New Literary History of America* (Hilary K. Justice), 239–41; review: Anne E. Boyd, ed., *Wielding the Pen: Writings on Authorship by American Women of the Nineteenth Century* (Melissa J. Homestead), 248–51

Melville, Herman: review: Peter West, *The Arbiters of Reality: Hawthorne, Melville, and the Rise of Mass Information Culture* (Sarah Wadsworth), 255–57

Miller, Arthur: review: Christopher Bigsby, *Arthur Miller 1915–1962* (Katherine Egerton), 293–96

Murray, Judith Sargent: review: Sheila L. Skemp, *First Lady of Letters: Judith Sargent Murray and the Struggle for Female Independence* (Lisa M. Logan), 242–45

Myers, Ned: review: Karen Lentz Madison, R. D. Madison, and Lance C. Schachterle, eds., *Ned Myers; or, A Life before the Mast*, by James Fenimore Cooper, historical introductions by William S. Dudley and Hugh Egan (Jason Berger), 245–48

Poe, Edgar Allan: Alexander Hammond, "Poe, Scott's Fiction, and the Holt Source Collection: The Example of *Ivanhoe* and 'The Fall of the House of Usher,' " 47–71 poetry: Patrick K. Dooley, "Prospects for the Study of Stephen Crane," 1–32; Jennifer Harris, "Aprons and Pearls: Images of Phillis Wheatley," 33–45; Irene C. Goldman-Price, "Young Edith Jones: Sources and Texts of Early Poems by Edith Wharton," 95–106; Natalie Gerber, "Art as 'An Everyday Affair': William Carlos Williams's Correspondence with His Brother," 223–30; Tony Trigilio, "Reconsidering Allen Ginsberg at the End of an Epistolary Era," 231–37; review: Greil Marcus and Werner Sollors, eds., *A New Literary History of America* (Hilary K. Justice), 239–41; review: Anne E. Boyd, ed., *Wielding the Pen: Writings on Authorship by American Women of the Nineteenth Century* (Melissa J. Homestead), 248–51; review: Ted Genoways, *Walt Whitman and the Civil War: America's Poet during the Lost Years of 1860–1862* (Gregory Eiselein), 263–65; review: Carol Sklenicka, *Raymond Carver: A Writer's Life* (Robert Miltner), 299–302

Scott, Sir Walter: Alexander Hammond, "Poe, Scott's Fiction, and the Holt Source Collection: The Example of *Ivanhoe* and 'The Fall of the House of Usher,'" 47–71

Snyder, Gary: Tony Trigilio, "Reconsidering Allen Ginsberg at the End of an Epistolary Era," 231–37

Styron, William: review: James L. W. West III, ed., *Letters to My Father*, by William Styron (Jean W. Cash), 296–99

textual studies: Patrick K. Dooley, "Prospects for the Study of Stephen Crane," 1–32; Alexander Hammond, "Poe, Scott's Fiction, and the Holt Source Collection: The Example of *Ivanhoe* and 'The Fall of the House of Usher,'" 47–71; Irene C. Goldman-Price, "Young Edith Jones: Sources and Texts of Early Poems by Edith Wharton," 95–106; Park Bucker, "'To Weave the Whole Thing Together': Thomas Wolfe's Revisions of *From Death to Morning*," 129–83; Nicholas Moschovakis and David Roessel, "*The Magic Tower*: An Unpublished One-Act Play by Tennessee Williams," 185–213; James A. Jaap, "Breaking Fresh Ground: New Releases from the Willa Cather Edition," 215–22; review: Karen Lentz Madison, R. D. Madison, and Lance C. Schachterle, eds., *Ned Myers; or, A Life before the Mast*, by James Fenimore Cooper, historical introductions by William S. Dudley and Hugh Egan (Jason Berger), 245–48; review: Glen M. Johnson, and Joel Myerson, eds., *Collected Works of Ralph Waldo Emerson, Volume VIII: Letters and Social Aims*, historical introduction by Ronald A. Bosco (Wesley T. Mott), 251–55; review: Nancy Craig Simmons and Ron Thomas, eds., *Journal. Volume 7: 1853–1854*, by Henry D. Thoreau (Kristen Case), 260–63; review: Karcher, Carolyn L., ed., *Bricks Without Straw: A Novel*, by Albion Tourgée (Peter Schmidt), 269–72; review: Scott Donaldson, *Fitzgerald and Hemingway: Works and Days* (James M. Hutchisson), 285–87; review: Arlyn Bruccoli and Matthew J. Bruccoli, eds., *The Four Lost Men: The Previously Unpublished Long Version*, by Thomas Wolfe (Shawn Holliday), 290–93; review: Carol Sklenicka, *Raymond Carver: A Writer's Life* (Robert Miltner), 299–302

Thoreau, Henry David: review: Nancy Craig Simmons and Ron Thomas, eds., *Journal. Volume 7: 1853–1854*, by Henry D. Thoreau (Kristen Case), 260–63

Tourgée, Albion: review: Carolyn L. Karcher, ed., *Bricks Without Straw: A Novel*, by Albion Tourgée (Peter Schmidt), 269–72

travel: David Roessel, "New Information on Hemingway's '3 very fine weeks' in Constantinople in 1922," 107–28; review: Karen Lentz Madison, R. D. Madison, and Lance C. Schachterle, eds., *Ned Myers; or, A Life before the Mast*, by James Fenimore Cooper, historical introductions by William S. Dudley and Hugh Egan (Jason Berger), 245–48;

review: Nancy Craig Simmons and Ron Thomas, eds., *Journal. Volume 7: 1853–1854*, by Henry D. Thoreau (Kristen Case), 260–63; review: James E. Caron, *Mark Twain: Unsanctified Newspaper Reporter* (Michael J. Kiskis), 266–68; review: Pierre A. Walker and Greg W. Zacharias, eds., *The Complete Letters of Henry James, 1872–1876. Vol. 1* (Leland S. Person), 272–75; review: Denise D. Knight and Jennifer S. Tuttle, eds., *The Selected Letters of Charlotte Perkins Gilman* (Lisa Long), 276–79; review: Susan Goodman and Carl Dawson, *Mary Austin and the American West* (Beverly A. Hume), 279–81

Twain, Mark: review: James E. Caron, *Mark Twain: Unsanctified Newspaper Reporter* (Michael J. Kiskis), 266–68

Wharton, Edith: Irene C. Goldman-Price, "Young Edith Jones: Sources and Texts of Early Poems by Edith Wharton," 95–106
Wheatley, Phillis: Jennifer Harris, "Aprons and Pearls: Images of Phillis Wheatley," 33–45
Whitman, Walt: review: Ted Genoways, *Walt Whitman and the Civil War: America's Poet during the Lost Years of 1860–1862* (Gregory Eiselein), 263–65
Williams, Edgar Irving: Natalie Gerber, "Art as 'An Everyday Affair': William Carlos Williams's Correspondence with His Brother," 223–30
Williams, Tennessee: Nicholas Moschovakis and David Roessel, "*The Magic Tower*: An Unpublished One-Act Play by Tennessee Williams," 185–213
Williams, William Carlos: Natalie Gerber, "Art as 'An Everyday Affair': William Carlos Williams's Correspondence with His Brother," 223–30
Wolfe, Thomas: Park Bucker, " 'To Weave the Whole Thing Together': Thomas Wolfe's Revisions of *From Death to Morning*," 129–83; review: Arlyn Bruccoli and Matthew J. Bruccoli, eds., *The Four Lost Men: The Previously Unpublished Long Version*, by Thomas Wolfe (Shawn Holliday), 290–93
women's studies: Jennifer Harris, "Aprons and Pearls: Images of Phillis Wheatley," 33–45; Irene C. Goldman-Price, "Young Edith Jones: Sources and Texts of Early Poems by Edith Wharton," 95–106; James A. Jaap, "Breaking Fresh Ground: New Releases from the Willa Cather Edition," 215–22; review: Greil Marcus and Werner Sollors, eds., *A New Literary History of America* (Hilary K. Justice), 239–41; review: Sheila L. Skemp, *First Lady of Letters: Judith Sargent Murray and the Struggle for Female Independence* (Lisa M. Logan), 242–45; review: Anne E. Boyd, ed., *Wielding the Pen: Writings on Authorship by American Women of the Nineteenth Century* (Melissa J. Homestead), 248–51; review: Katherine Wolff, *Culture Club: The Curious History of the Boston Athenaeum* (Joel Myerson), 258–60; review: Denise D. Knight and Jennifer S. Tuttle, eds., *The Selected Letters of Charlotte Perkins Gilman* (Lisa Long), 276–79; review: Susan Goodman and Carl Dawson, *Mary Austin and the American West* (Beverly A. Hume), 279–81; review: Thomas P. Riggio, ed., *Letters to Women. New Letters, Volume II*, by Theodore Dreiser (Clare Eby), 282–84

Index of Books Reviewed

Bigsby, Christopher. *Arthur Miller 1915–1962* (Katherine Egerton), 293–96

Bosco, Ronald A. *See* Johnson, Glen M., and Joel Myerson

Boss, Judith. *See* Link, Frederick M., et al.

Boyd, Anne E., ed. *Wielding the Pen: Writings on Authorship by American Women of the Nineteenth Century* (Melissa J. Homestead), 248–51

Bruccoli, Arlyn, and Matthew J. Bruccoli, eds. *The Four Lost Men: The Previously Unpublished Long Version*, by Thomas Wolfe (Shawn Holliday), 290–93

Bruccoli, Matthew J. *See* Bruccoli, Arlyn, and Matthew J. Bruccoli

Caron, James E. *Mark Twain: Unsanctified Newspaper Reporter* (Michael J. Kiskis), 266–68

Cather, Willa. *See* Link, Frederick M., et al.; Mignon, Charles W., et al.

Cooper, James Fenimore. *See* Madison, Karen Lentz, et al.

Dawson, Carl. *See* Goodman, Susan, and Carl Dawson

Donaldson, Scott. *Fitzgerald and Hemingway: Works and Days* (James M. Hutchisson), 285–87

Dreiser, Theodore. *See* Riggio, Thomas P.

Dudley, William S. *See* Madison, Karen Lentz, et al.

Earle, David M. *All Man!: Hemingway, 1950s Men's Magazines, and the Masculine Persona* (Thomas Strychacz), 288–90

Egan, Hugh. *See* Madison, Karen Lentz, et al.

Emerson, Ralph Waldo. *See* Johnson, Glen M., and Joel Myerson

Genoways, Ted. *Walt Whitman and the Civil War: America's Poet during the Lost Years of 1860–1862* (Gregory Eiselein), 263–65

Gilman, Charlotte Perkins. *See* Knight, Denise D., and Jennifer S. Tuttle

Ginsberg, Allen. *See* Morgan, Bill

Goodman, Susan, and Carl Dawson. *Mary Austin and the American West* (Beverly A. Hume), 279–81

James, Henry. *See* Walker, Pierre A., and Greg W. Zacharias

Johnson, Glen M., and Joel Myerson, eds. *Collected Works of Ralph Waldo Emerson, Volume VIII: Letters and Social Aims*, historical introduction by Ronald A. Bosco (Wesley T. Mott), 251–55

Karcher, Carolyn L., ed. *Bricks Without Straw: A Novel*, by Albion Tourgée (Peter Schmidt), 269–72

Knight, Denise D., and Jennifer S. Tuttle, eds. *The Selected Letters of Charlotte Perkins Gilman* (Lisa Long), 276–79

Krivak, Andrew J., ed. *The Letters of William Carlos Williams to Edgar Irving Williams, 1902–1912* (Natalie Gerber), 223–30

Link, Frederick M. *See* Link, Frederick M., et al.; Mignon, Charles W., et al.

Link, Frederick M., Charles W. Mignon, Judith Boss, and Kari Ronning, eds. *Youth and the Bright Medusa*, by Willa Cather, historical essay by Mark Madigan (James A. Jaap), 215–22

Madigan, Mark. *See* Link, Frederick M., et al.

Madison, Karen Lentz, R. D. Madison, and Lance C. Schachterle, eds. *Ned Myers; or, A Life before the Mast*, by James Fenimore Cooper, historical introductions by William S. Dudley and Hugh Egan (Jason Berger), 245–48

Madison, R. D. *See* Madison, Karen Lentz, et al.

Marcus, Greil, and Werner Sollors, eds. *A New Literary History of America* (Hilary K. Justice), 239–41

Mignon, Charles W. *See* Link, Frederick M., et al.; Mignon, Charles W., et al.

Mignon, Charles W., Kari Ronning, and Frederick M. Link, eds. *Sapphira and the Slave Girl*, by Willa Cather, historical essay by Ann Romines (James A. Jaap), 215–22

Morgan, Bill, ed. *The Letters of Allen Ginsberg* (Tony Trigilio), 231–37; *The Selected Letters of Allen Ginsberg and Gary Snyder* (Tony Trigilio), 231–37

INDEX

Myerson, Joel. *See* Johnson, Glen M., and Joel Myerson

Riggio, Thomas P., ed. *Letters to Women. New Letters, Volume II*, by Theodore Dreiser (Clare Eby), 282–84
Romines, Ann. *See* Mignon, Charles W., et al.
Ronning, Kari. *See* Link, Frederick M., et al.; Mignon, Charles W., et al.

Schachterle, Lance C. *See* Madison, Karen Lentz, et al.
Simmons, Nancy Craig, and Ron Thomas, eds. *Journal. Volume 7: 1853–1854*, by Henry D. Thoreau (Kristen Case), 260–63
Skemp, Sheila L. *First Lady of Letters: Judith Sargent Murray and the Struggle for Female Independence* (Lisa M. Logan), 242–45
Sklenicka, Carol. *Raymond Carver: A Writer's Life* (Robert Miltner), 299–302
Snyder, Gary. *See* Morgan, Bill
Sollors, Werner. *See* Marcus, Greil, and Werner Sollors
Styron, William. *See* West, James L. W., III

Thomas, Ron. *See* Simmons, Nancy Craig, and Ron Thomas

Thoreau, Henry David. *See* Simmons, Nancy Craig, and Ron Thomas
Tourgée, Albion. *See* Karcher, Carolyn L.
Tuttle, Jennifer S. *See* Knight, Denise D., and Jennifer S. Tuttle

Walker, Pierre A., and Greg W. Zacharias, eds. *The Complete Letters of Henry James, 1872–1876. Vol. 1* (Leland S. Person), 272–75
West, James L. W., III, ed. *Letters to My Father*, by William Styron (Jean W. Cash), 296–99
West, Peter. *The Arbiters of Reality: Hawthorne, Melville, and the Rise of Mass Information Culture* (Sarah Wadsworth), 255–57
Williams, Edgar Irving. *See* Krivak, Andrew J.
Williams, William Carlos. *See* Krivak, Andrew J.
Wolfe, Thomas. *See* Bruccoli, Arlyn, and Matthew J. Bruccoli
Wolff, Katherine. *Culture Club: The Curious History of the Boston Athenaeum* (Joel Myerson), 258–60

Zacharias, Greg W. *See* Walker, Pierre A., and Greg W. Zacharias

GUIDELINES FOR CONTRIBUTORS TO
Resources for American Literary Study

Preparation of Copy

All manuscripts should be in the English language. All articles deemed appropriate for *RALS* are sent for anonymous peer review. A separate title page should include the title of the article and the author's name, affiliation (if appropriate), address, phone number, and e-mail address. An author should not include his or her name on the manuscript; all internal identifying references and notes should be masked for the review process. Manuscripts should be typed double-spaced, with notes and a list of works cited (also double-spaced) following the text. Manuscripts should be prepared according to the new MLA style, with internal citation wherever possible. Necessary notes should be numbered consecutively throughout the article, and note numbers in endnotes must correspond to the note numbers in the text. A "Works Cited" list must accompany all manuscripts. Please number the manuscript pages consecutively.

Submission of Manuscripts

Please send three copies of the manuscript to Jackson R. Bryer, *Resources for American Literary Study*, Department of English, University of Maryland, College Park, MD 20742. If you wish to have your manuscript returned, please include a large, self-addressed, stamped envelope (USA only). Electronic submissions may be sent as e-mail attachments to jbryer@umd.edu. The following formats, listed in order of preference, will be accepted: Microsoft Word 6.0 or higher, rich text format (rtf), or simple text. Please check for and eliminate all viruses before sending. (*Note: All accepted articles must be available in electronic format.*) The editors cannot review or accept articles that have been previously published or are under consideration at any other journal or publisher.

Books for Review

Please send review copies of scholarly books based on archival research in American literature and invitations to review digital American resources to MaryEllen Higgins, Penn State Greater Allegheny, 4000 University Drive, McKeesport, PA 15132. Persons interested in reviewing books or digital resources should also contact MaryEllen Higgins (e-mail: mxh68@psu.edu).